ART DECO

Identification
and Price Guide

5/94

To Milt —

with best wishes —

Tony Fusco

Avon Books are available at special quantity discounts for bulk purchases for sales promotions, premiums, fund raising or educational use. Special books, or book excerpts, can also be created to fit specific needs.

For details write or telephone the office of the Director of Special Markets, Avon Books, Dept. FP, 1350 Avenue of the Americas, New York, New York 10019, 1-800-238-0658.

ART DECO

Identification and Price Guide

2nd Edition

TONY FUSCO

The CONFIDENT COLLECTOR™

AVON BOOKS ◆ NEW YORK

Important Notice: All of the information, including valuations, in this book has been compiled from the most reliable sources, and every effort has been made to eliminate errors and questionable data. Nevertheless, the possibility of error always exists in a work of such scope. The publisher and the author will not be held responsible for losses which may occur in the purchase, sale, or other transaction of property because of information contained herein. Readers who feel they have discovered errors are invited to *write* the author in care of Avon Books so that the errors may be corrected in subsequent editions.

THE CONFIDENT COLLECTOR: ART DECO (2nd edition) is an original publication of Avon Books. This edition has never before appeared in book form.

AVON BOOKS
A division of
The Hearst Corporation
1350 Avenue of the Americas
New York, New York 10019

Copyright © 1993 by Tony Fusco
Cover photo courtesy of Carole A. Berk, Ltd., Bethesda, MD. Photo by Lisa Masson.
The Confident Collector and its logo are trademarked properties of Avon Books.
Interior design by Robin Arzt
Published by arrangement with the author
Library of Congress Catalog Card Number: 93-213
ISBN: 0-380-77012-1

Library of Congress Cataloging in Publication Data:

Fusco, Tony.
Art deco identification and price guide/ Tony Fusco.
  p.cm.
Includes bibliographical references.
1. Decoration and ornament—Art deco—Catalogs. 2. Decorative arts—History—20th century—Catalogs. 3. Art Deco—Catalogs.
I. Title.
NK 1986.A78F87 1993   93-213
709'.04'012075—dc20   CIP

First Avon Books Trade Printing: July 1993

ACKNOWLEDGMENTS

A volume such as this one is just not possible without the support and participation of hundreds of individuals, many of whom deserve special recognition.

First, we would like to thank those individuals who agreed to contribute or be interviewed for our numerous "Special Focus" sections, which provide an in-depth look at specific collecting areas: Ric Emmett, Modernism Gallery, Coral Gables, Florida; Linda Cheverton, Linda Cheverton Art & Antiques, Colebrook, Connecticut; Mike and Sherry Miller of Tuscola, Illinois; Carole Berk and Penny Morrill, Carole A. Berk, Ltd., Bethesda, Maryland; Thomas G. Boss, Thomas G. Boss Fine Books, Boston; Dan Golden, Golden Telecom, Carlsbad, California; Steve Starr, Steve Starr Studios, Chicago; and Stephen Visakay, West Caldwell, New Jersey; and Arlene Lederman, Arlene Lederman Antiques, Nyack, New York. We know that you will benefit by their expertise and insights.

On a subject-by-subject basis, we would also like to thank the following individuals who generously contributed their time, advice, collecting information, and photographs:

Furnishings: Robert Aibel, Moderne, Philadelphia; Sam Bass, Sambeau's Ltd., St. Louis; Jack Beeler, Decorum, San Francisco; Gary and Janet Calderwood, Calderwood Gallery, Philadelphia; Paul Fuhrman, The Warehouse, Allentown, Pennsylvania; Thomas Lennon, Vintage Modern, San Francisco; Bill Meisch, Of Rare Vintage, Asbury Park, New Jersey; Anne McGahan, Salvage One, Chicago; and Michael Turbeville, The Florida Picker, Webster, Florida.

Glass: Robert Aibel, Moderne, Philadelphia; Nicholas M. Dawes, New York; Mark Feldman and Corey Warn, Antiquers III, Brookline, Massachusetts; Madeleine France, Madeleine France Antiques, Plantation, Florida; and author and collector Jack Wilson, Chicago.

Ceramics: Morton Abromson, Morton Abromson Decorative Arts, Brookline, Massachusetts; Robert Aibel, Moderne, Philadelphia; Richard Fishman, As Time Goes By, San Francisco; and Diane Petipas, Mood Indigo, New York.

Fashion and Jewelry: Luisa DiPietro, Shadowfax Studio, Maryland; Marsha Evaskus, Zig Zag, Chicago; Ed Forcum, Rosebud Gallery, Berkeley, California; and Ruth Smiler, Glad Rags Fine Vintage Clothing and Antiques, Montpelier, Vermont.

Art Deco on Paper: Bernice Jackson, Bernice Jackson Fine Arts, Concord, Massachusetts; and Nancy Steinbock, Nancy Steinbock Fine Posters and Prints, Albany, New York.

Ocean Liner Memorabilia: Ken Schultz, Hoboken, New Jersey.

World's Fair Memorabilia: Herb Rolfes, Yesterday's World, White House Station, New Jersey.

Industrial Design: Ken Berkowitz, The Discerning Eye, Port Chester, New York; Jacques-Pierre Caussin, First 1/2, Detroit; Bill Meisch, Of Rare Vintage, Asbury Park, New Jersey; and Stephen Visakay, West Caldwell, New Jersey.

Catalin Radios: Jim Meehan, Radioart, Centerbrook, Connecticut; and John Sideli, John Sideli Art & Antiques, Malden Bridge, New York.

Chase Chrome: Ken Berkowitz, The Discerning Eye, Port Chester, New York; and special thanks in memoriam to Richard Kilbride, Jo-D Books, Stamford, Connecticut.

We are sure that you will note the wide-ranging participation of numerous auction houses throughout this volume. We want to extend our special gratitude to the numerous individuals who worked with us to provide background information, photographs, and prices realized on the full range of collecting areas you find represented here.

Our special thanks to Jon King, Cynthia Stern, and Pamela Tapp at Butterfield & Butterfield; Nancy McClelland, Peggy Gilges, Roberta Maneker, and Abby O'Neill at Christie's; Kathleen Guzman and Hélène Petrović at Christie's East; Jane Haye and Mark Wilkinson at Christie's South Kensington; Eric Silver and Susan Roediger at William Doyle Galleries; Maron Matz at Leslie Hindman Auctioneers; Michael Myers at Myers Antiques Auction Gallery; Mary Brady at Savoia's Auction; Lousie Luther, Alicia Gordon and Sarah Hammill at Skinner, Inc.; Don Treadway, Jerri Durham, and Holland Berhrens at Treadway Gallery; and Kathleen Isenhart and Thomas Eville at Wolf's Fine Arts Auctioneers.

We would also like to thank the following museums and collections: Cowan Pottery Museum; Cranbrook Academy of Art Museum; Museum of the City of New York; Norwest Corporation; Society for the Preservation of New England Antiquities; Virginia Museum of Fine Arts; and numerous others you will find listed in the "Resource Guide."

Also, a special thanks to the following individuals in Art Deco societies and preservation organizations: Chuck Kaplan, president, Chicago Art Deco Society; Helene Linne, board member, Art Deco Society of Boston, for the "shopping tips" concept; photographer Gene Ritvo, Art Deco Society of Boston; Dennis Wilhelm, board member, Miami Design Preservation League; and Craig Holcomb, executive director, Friends of Fair Park, Dallas.

Last but not least, we wish to express our thanks to our editor and friend, Dorothy Harris, for her great support and for believing the idea that "Confident Collectors" need substantive guides and not just price lists, and we also wish to thank her assistant editor, Karen Shapiro, for always being there to help.

When we started out to create this volume, we told those who might be interested that our real goal was not just to create a price guide, but to foster a network of Art Deco collectors, dealers, auction houses, Art Deco societies and other preservation organizations, museums, and resources. In this, our second edition, we hope that we have strengthened that network even further. Now we invite you to join the network by taking advantage of the hundreds of resources we have assembled here.

CONTENTS

ART DECO

Identification
and Price Guide

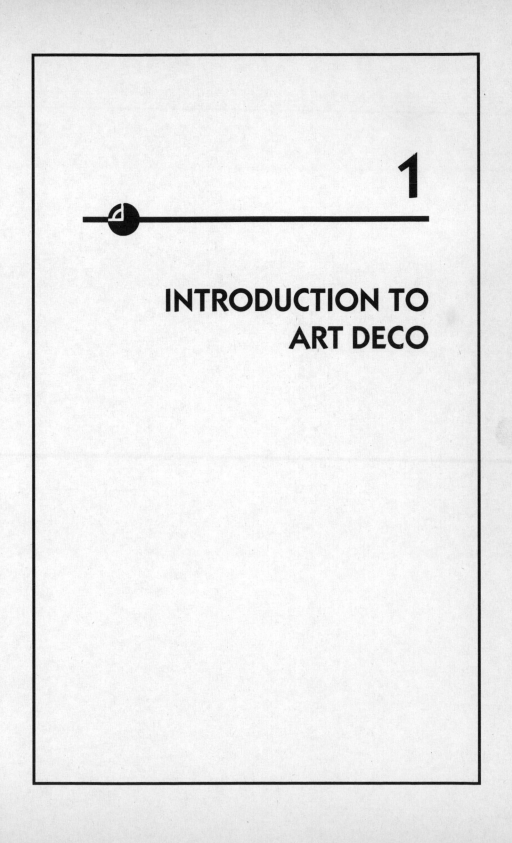

1

INTRODUCTION TO ART DECO

WHAT IS ART DECO?

The term "Art Deco," which came into popular usage only during the late-1960s revival of interest in the style, is derived from the title of the 1925 Parisian Exposition Internationale des Arts Décoratifs et Industriels Modernes, which emphasized the "Arts Décoratifs," or the decorative arts.

Wrongly thought by many to be the starting point of Art Deco, the 1925 Exposition actually marked the culmination of a luxurious French Art Deco style and the emergence of a more geometric, Germanic "Modern" style. Scholars have traced many of the influences on Art Deco to turn of the century and pre–World War I European design movements: Arts and Crafts, the Vienna Secession, the Glasgow School in Scotland, Czechoslovakian Cubism, the De Stijl movement in Holland, and Italian Futurism. In addition, Art Deco was highly influenced by the design of numerous traditional and ancient cultures around the world: Egyptian, Japanese, sub-Saharan Africa, Mayan and Aztec cultures, and others.

Today, accurately or not, the term "Art Deco" is applied to a whole complex of trends in the decorative and applied arts and architecture in the period roughly between 1909 and 1939. We say "roughly" because the influence of Art Deco lingered into some of the designs of the 1940s and 1950s and can even be seen in today's Post-Modernist styles.

The early French designers were influenced by the opulent sets and costumes of Les Ballets Russes, which arrived in Paris in 1909 and set off an explosion in the design and fashion world. However, the full emergence of the style was delayed by the advent of World War I. A few years thereafter, interior designers, fine furniture makers, and boutique workshops of the great French department stores took the spotlight at the 1925 Exposition.

For the most part, the early French designers worked with expensive woods and exotic materials for a wealthy clientele who commissioned them to produce handmade, often unique items. Even the designers who headed department store boutiques commissioned household furnishings in relatively small series. These designers would be horrified to learn today that their work is identified by the same name as that of the "Moderns" who, in Le Corbusier's terms, thought of furniture as "household equipment," introducing such items as chairs made with tubular steel. Even further removed from early French Art Deco are the broadly mass-produced furniture, appliances, chrome, and ceramics of the Depression-era 1930s in America.

The emergence of the Bauhaus as an important school of design in Germany, itself influenced by earlier Germanic and Austrian schools of design, strongly affected French and American designers after 1925.

In the 1920s and 1930s, it was this more Modern style that became popular in America, due in part to the ease with which objects could be fashioned for industrial mass production. No doubt this popularity was also due to the large number of talented designers from Austria, Germany, and Scandinavian countries who emigrated to this country.

What could be called the last phase of the Art Deco style fully reflected the impact of the "industrial designer" on household appliances in the 1930s, and is referred to by many as "Streamline."

Perhaps this complex evolution explains why there is such confusion when someone uses the term "Art Deco." Adding to the difficulty is the fact that as Art Deco spread to become the first truly international design style, it was confronted and changed dramatically by national preferences, cultural differences, and social and economic forces. In addition, in today's marketplace, you'll still hear people wrongly refer to a 1940s Biomorphic chair or a 1950s Bohemian coffee table as "Art Deco."

Dozens of other names have been coined in an attempt to come up with something better, or to name a specific style within the style: Twenties Decorative, Jazz Modern, Style Moderne, Depression Modern, International Style, Zigzag Moderne, and others have all been used. New designations are frequently used to imply a regional style, such as Florida's "Tropical Deco" and the Native American–influenced "Pueblo Deco" of the Southwest. In a spirit of fun, the restrained Art Deco public buildings, post offices, and courthouses that sprang up under the Works Progress Administration (WPA) are sometimes called "Greco Deco."

In America, Art Deco was also to become highly associated with Hollywood. The costumes, set designs, furnishings for movies, posters, and other Hollywood design from the 1920s through the 1940s helped to popularize the style to the widest possible audience. In the end, perhaps, it was Hollywood's "Screen Deco"—a continual exaggeration of the style—that caused Art Deco to fall out of favor with designers. No leading-edge designer wants to be thought of as merely repeating popular styles.

Many think a final, great explosion of Art Deco design came with the New York World's Fair of 1939. This was soon followed by the real explosion of World War II, the final blow to a style thought of as just "too chic" for wartime.

How far Art Deco had changed from the extremely delicate eggshell lacquer of Jean Dunand, the exceptional glass sculptures of René Lalique, and the sharkskin-covered exotic wood furniture of Emile-Jacques Ruhlmann to the mass-produced household furnishings of the Depression and the razzmatazz of Hollywood!

FROM ARTISTE DÉCORATEUR TO INDUSTRIAL DESIGNER: DESIGN IN A WORLD OF CHANGE

Before World War I, urbanites "with taste" in the United States and France were reading by the light of their Tiffany lamps, which epitomized the Art Nouveau style, and modeling their clothes styles on Alphonse Mucha's curvaceous females with tendril-like hair.

Art Nouveau was dominant for a relatively short period of time, and was not as widespread as one might believe, given its popularity today. Most urban Americans, for example, were still living in modest post-Victorian or neo-Colonial settings, still immune to the lures of the advertising poster, and still shocked by the seductive goddesses of Art Nouveau.

In England and America, the moralistic Arts and Crafts movement looked down on the extravagance of Art Nouveau. In addition, in several other European countries, emerging Modernist design movements reacted against the flowery decoration and overornamentation of the Art Nouveau style.

Just after the turn of the century, early pioneers of new Modern styles included architects Joseph Maria Olbrich and Josef Hoffmann in Vienna, who created angular silver tea sets and restrained bentwood furniture; the Scottish architect and designer Charles Rennie Mackintosh; and German architects Otto Wagner and Adolf Loos, who influenced the De Stijl group of Holland and later the German Bauhaus.

These designers would initially not have as much impact on design in France as did the arrival in Paris in 1909 of Diaghilev's Les Ballets Russes. Many talented young fashion designers and artists were captivated by the colorful costumes and Oriental influence of its set and costume designs.

Among those most influenced by Les Ballets Russes were such notable fashion designers, interior designers, and illustrators as Paul Poiret, Paul Iribe, Paul Follot, Erté, Georges Lepape, and André Marty.

Many fashion designers moved into the field of interior design, becoming interior designers or *ensembliers* for wealthy Parisian clients. Poiret's firm Martine sought to entirely integrate the "look" of a room, and therefore commissioned or created its own textiles, pottery, porcelain, and wallpaper, as well as furniture. A room became the vision of one designer, rather than a collection of the works of many. Poiret made no bones about the fact that he wanted to control every aspect of design in a client's home, right down to the throw pillows on the low-slung divan.

Jacques Doucet, an important fashion designer, was very influential and was considered avant-garde, a military term that roughly translates as "leading edge." He collected Cubist paintings, early Surrealist works, and exotic African and Chinese art.

5

He commissioned and bought from talented designers to furnish his own home: Pierre Legrain, Clement Rousseau, Eileen Gray, Gustav Miklos, and René Lalique. It is said that André Breton, the fiery author of Surrealism, helped Doucet select his contemporary art.

Doucet had great influence with the younger generation of designers as well. Paul Poiret was a former employee of Doucet's when his career was at its highest. Poiret, in turn, later hired notable designers such as Paul Iribe and George Barbier to execute or render illustrations of his designs. Poiret traveled to Vienna and Moscow where he met a young man named Romain de Tirtoff, who simplified his name to Erté, based on the French pronunciation of his initials "R. T."

Many of the best furniture designers were working to combine exotic or new materials, traditional methods, and simpler design. These *ébénistes*, or "cabinetmakers," also worked for wealthy, knowledgeable, and status-conscious clients.

After World War I, architect Louis Süe and painter-decorator André Mare founded the Compagnie des Artistes Français. They were among the first to bring together artists from many disciplines in their search for "total design." Their company designed and commissioned ceramics, glassware, bookbindings, textiles, and furniture, as well as architecture.

Süe et Mare were among those designers who considered themselves "tastefully modern," as did many of their talented contemporaries such as Emile-Jacques Ruhlmann, who had his first major exhibition at the Salon d'Automne in 1913. Other designers of this period include Maurice Dufrène, Jean Dunand, Léon Jallot, Edgar Brandt, Raoul Dufy, and Jules Leleu. The production of designers such as these really dominated French decorative arts until 1925. In fact, it was their overwhelming strength and influence in the right circles that kept more Modernist designs from appearing in the 1925 Exposition.

A Süe et Mare cabinet, 1927.
*Courtesy of the Virginia
Museum of Fine Arts.*

Many people wrongly believe that Art Deco was a revolt against Art Nouveau as the dominant style. French Art Deco was not a "movement"—it had no name at the time, no books had been written to establish the "rules" of the new design style, and no angry theorists argued for the adoption of Art Deco over Art Nouveau. While the artists mentioned did seek to find new, more simplified lines, forms, and stylized decorations, they were really part of a continuum of French traditional design and often looked to French 18th-century furniture for their inspiration. Even when the more Modern style became prevalent, the grand style of the early Art Deco designers would prevail in official commissions for ocean liners and public buildings into the 1930s.

If a center for the new design is to be identified, it would perhaps be the Société des Artistes Décorateurs, to which many of the designers named above belonged, and which had been founded in 1900.

An "Artiste Décorateur," as the name implies, considered himself or herself an "artist" who produced furnishings and objects, or "decorative arts." The new design ideas of these decorative artists were spread by the society's annual "salons" or exhibitions featuring their latest creations, and by magazines such as *Art et Décoration* and *L'Art Décoratif*.

The new style was popularized through the French department stores, which carried high-quality furniture and decorative objects such as Lalique glass and Longwy pottery. Each major French department store had its own atelier, or workshop, to create exclusive designs. These specialized boutiques within the department stores were headed by some of the best designers of the day, and gave commissions to others. Their contributions to early French Art Deco design were apparent at their pavilions for the 1925 Paris Exposition.

However, even as this luxurious Art Deco style evolved and gained a wider acceptance in the Parisian upper-middle class, it faced pressure from the Modern design movements in other countries, and from the changes that were taking place in society.

Early Modernist designers in France maintained a handcrafted aesthetic, but were less resistant to the use of machines, new techniques, and modern, less-expensive materials. One notable event that impacted early French Modern designers was the 1910 exhibition of the Deutscher Werkbund in Paris. German workshop and machine-made design influenced such French designers as Francis Jourdain, René Herbst, René Joubert, Robert Mallet-Stevens, and Le Corbusier.

Décoration Interieur Moderne, or DIM, founded in 1919 under the direction of René Joubert, was the first French firm to create tubular steel furniture a few years later. The ideals and designs of these Modern artists would not gain wide acceptance until after 1925, when the deluxe phase of Art Deco was no longer a reality in economic and social terms, and when influences from other countries were clamoring too loudly to be ignored.

After 1925, the Modern movement gained strongholds across Europe. The centers of the movement were the German Bauhaus school and the Parisian Union des Artistes Modernes, founded by those who did not gain acceptance into the Salon des Artistes Décorateurs, which had now become the "design establishment."

By 1928, the company Thonet was producing tubular bent steel furniture designed by Le Corbusier. In 1931, Practical Equipment Limited, or PEL, was creating modern furniture for a wealthy clientele in England. And by the mid-1930s, even Süe et Mare were making furniture in aluminum with a Modern style.

The "Machine Age" was coming into maturity, and international travel and exchange of ideas were facilitated by the "wireless," telephones, passenger trains, steamships, and, of course, airplanes. The stock market crash of 1929 and the ensuing world-wide Depression became the social and economic imperative for mass-produced furnishings made from less expensive materials.

The Modern movement clearly broke with the past, dedicated itself to the use of new materials, and adopted a socialistic view of the artist's role in society. Unlike the early French Art Deco style, Modernism did have its doctrines and manifestos, which overtly proclaimed it to be an attempt to bring together art and industry. Its primary goal was to create less expensive, yet still well-designed, furnishings and other objects. Its optimistic political goal was to put the machine to the service of the masses.

In America, groundbreaking Modern designers had been at work since the turn of the century. Frank Lloyd Wright, influenced by Louis Sullivan and by the Arts and Crafts movement, had been creating Modern architectural designs since around 1900. Joseph Urban, a member of the Vienna Secession, emigrated to America and founded the Wiener Werkstätte, or "Vienna Workshops," gallery in New York in 1922. Paul Theodore Frankl was building his "skyscraper" bookcases as early as 1925.

Although Art Deco and Modern were set in opposition to each other, both emphasized quality styling, even though handcrafting slowly gave way to mass production. One way of describing the transition that took place is that Art Deco design first reflected the handcrafted French luxury of the artiste décorateur, and later the German and American economically influenced functionalism of a machine aesthetic.

In the United States, French Art Deco did not gain wide acceptance. In fact, a number of manufacturers from the United States had visited the 1925 Paris Exposition, but came away unimpressed. In 1926, a collection of objects from the 1925 Paris Exposition traveled to New York, Boston, Philadelphia, Detroit, and other cities. Department stores such as Macy's and Lord & Taylor in New York, Barker Brothers in Los Angeles, and Gimbel's in Pittsburgh, among others, hosted special showings of Parisian design.

However, the French style of Art Deco continued to be seen essentially as a "foreign" style, although it did greatly influence Hollywood through designers such as Erté, who came to America in 1925 and began designing sets and costumes for the screen almost immediately.

Designers from Scandinavia, Germany, and Austria would have a wider impact than the French in the United States. Finnish architect/designer Eliel Saarinen became the first director of the Cranbrook Academy of Art near Detroit in 1922. American ceramic artists from Ohio exchanged visits with artists from Vienna. Architects such as Walter Gropius and Marcel Breuer eventually established themselves in the United States to avoid the rise of fascism in Germany.

The Modern style fit America's rapid industrialization and quickly captured the entire market. It created a staggering variety of both functional and decorative high- and low-cost objects during the 1920s and 1930s, which are sought-after by Art Deco collectors today.

It was clear that the new Modernism was the major design style of the day as early as the 1929 exhibition entitled "The Architect and the Industrial Arts" at the Metropolitan Museum of Art in New York, which highlighted rooms of furnishings designed by architects. The rise of design for the machine to the status of art was confirmed in 1934 by both the "Contemporary American Industrial Art" exhibition at the Metropolitan and the "Machine Art" exhibition at New York's Museum of Modern Art.

As production increased, manufacturers began to rely increasingly on industrial designers to style products both to public taste and to mass production. In many cases, the leading industrial designers came from the world of advertising or the theater, such as Norman Bel Geddes.

Bel Geddes was a New York City theater set designer and worked for one of America's first major advertising agencies, J. Walter Thompson. Bel Geddes coined the term "industrial designer" in 1927, at the age of thirty-three, when he opened the first industrial design studio. By the 1930s, the term had become widely accepted, although other terms such as "design engineer," "consumer engineer," and "product designer" were also used.

In 1929, Bel Geddes was hired as design consultant for the upcoming 1933 Chicago "Century of Progress" Exposition. His book *Horizons*, published in 1932, promoted his theories of industrial art. He felt that the same emotional reaction one has when viewing great works of art like the Parthenon or paintings of Michelangelo should be felt in response to everyday objects. He designed everything from gas stoves to the interior of Pan American Airways clipper airplanes. He went on to design the General Motors Pavilion City of Tomorrow for the 1939 World's Fair.

An economic revolution that haunts many of us to this day—personal credit—came into being. The advent of credit had the advantage of opening up huge new markets for manufacturers. Another new animal—the annual model change—began to appear. Model changes were, and still are, meant to increase consumption by casting older models as "out of style." Wider varieties of sizes and colors were introduced, as well as broader lines of consumer items.

To spur consumption, manufacturers turned to talented graphic designers and advertising illustrators to render products on paper, and, as mentioned, in many cases to design the products themselves. This was especially imperative after the stock market crash of 1929 and during the Depression which followed.

An ad from a 1932 magazine for the New York industrial design firm of George Switzer stated:

> A few alert manufacturers have given the public a taste of designed merchandise. This has started a strong and increasing desire for good-looking products. People are tired of the old and worn-out things they have been using for the last 3 years, and are going to buy new things shortly. Manufacturers who retain the best design council and talent available now, will capture a leader's share in the forthcoming surge of replacement buying.

Switzer went on to define design as "control of appearance so as to give style and please the eye; plus the invention and engineering of utility and convenience; plus the specification of materials best suited to minimum cost in machine production."

In an article entitled "American Advertising Arts," published in the annual *Modern Publicity* for 1931, Harry N. Batten, a vice president for N. W. Ayer & Son advertising agency, wrote:

> It is undoubtedly a fact that during the spring and summer of 1929 a sort of gambling fever spread into every level of society. So sudden was the crash when it came, that retail outlets everywhere were caught with shelves overstocked to serve the orgy of spending produced by the bull market. When, almost overnight, people stopped buying, it was necessary to reduce these stocks. Prices were cut right and left, and

thousands of retailers took big losses on their inventories. The retail buying public is 85 percent women. To reach and influence a public of this sort calls for authentic skill. It means that advertising must combine force with taste, blend fact with imagination.

The result of the crash and Depression was a redesign and advertising frenzy. From the late 1920s through the 1930s, leading American architects and industrial designers such as Walter Dorwin Teague, Raymond Loewy, Donald Deskey, Kem Weber, Gilbert Rohde, Walter von Nessen, Russel Wright, and others too numerous to mention were commissioned to design and redesign furniture and other articles for mass production: glass, chrome, appliances, radios, lamps, and office equipment.

The 1934 Industrial Arts Exposition held at Rockefeller Center in New York displayed such industrial designs as a Todd "protectograph" designed by Henry Dreyfuss, a Coca-Cola dispenser designed by John Vassos, a Quiet May Oil Burner designed by Donald Deskey, and a refrigerator designed by Lurelle Guild for the Norge Corporation.

Walter Dorwin Teague designed glassware for Steuben Glass, tabletop and floor-model radios, the Kodak Bantam Special and other cameras, and desk lamps for Polaroid Corporation. He conceived Con Edison's "City of Light" and the giant National Cash Register at the 1939 New York World's Fair.

Teague was another leading theorist for industrial design. He wrote in an article entitled "Designing for Machines" in the April 2, 1930 issue of *Advertising Arts* magazine:

> Like it or not, we find ourselves living in a Machine Age, an Age of Power, an Age of Mass Production. You may hate it and maintain that the turmoil grows ever more unbearable, the confusion more hopeless. You may curse the machines and turn your back on them. But unless you become a hermit you cannot escape them. They are inextricably involved in living at all in this age, and every one of us is a machinist of one sort or another.... Here is the greatest problem of design: to adapt itself to machine and mass production. Our job is to make the machines bring forth beauty. We shall have to recast all the things we make in forms natural and right for the machines to make, and stirring to the sensibilities of mechanized age. We shall have to end the flood of futility and pretence poured out of the machines when they are set to rival the ancient handicrafts; and set them to create the geometrical precisions, the rhythmic harmonies of which they are so admirably capable.... And don't tell anybody that this is Modern Art: keep that as a secret among ourselves. The word Art has so long been drearily associated with mummies and masterpieces, and the self-confidence of this modern age is still so fragile, that the term thus applied would be alarming. By the time this age realizes what Modern Art really means, we shall be living in a frame of beauty, heartily and gustily enjoying it, rich in the possession of authentic style, happy once more in a harmonious, co-ordinated environment where we feel luxuriously at home.

The complete fulfillment of this vision was not to be. A friend of mine says he was totally disillusioned as a child when the fabulous things he saw at the New York World's

Fair of 1939 never came to pass, and World War II seemed to erase the 1930s vision of "Progress via the Machine."

Some industrial designers' concepts for how the future would look read today like science fiction. Take, for example, the following excerpts from a 1934 article by Raymond Loewy, "Evolution of the Motor Car," in which he wrote:

> Automobile designers pretty generally agree on the car of the future . . . The next really important step will be to place the engine in the rear instead of the front . . . It will be capable of a speed of 150 to 200 miles per hour. It will probably seat eight people comfortably. There will be nothing to disturb the smoothness of its tear-drop silhouette as it cuts through the air. There will be ample baggage compartments. Since the car will be capable of such great speed, there will probably be a vertical fin at the rear to keep it on an even keel. The front end will be weighted down with units like the radiator, water tank, large battery, spare wheels, etc., and designed so that air pressure will keep it in close contact with the road . . . Specially built highways with steeply banked turns, overhead crossings and automatic illumination will permit, in safety, speeds of 150 miles an hour or more. The highways will be equipped with photo-electric cells built on the side of the road and spaced at intervals of approximately 150 feet. As the car intercepts the rays of the first photo-electric cell, it will light an area in front of the car. As the car passes the second cell it will light a still further area. Thus the car will always be preceded by an area of brightly illuminated highway, the lights behind the car being automatically switched off as the car progresses. The aim of this device is to reduce accidents due to glaring headlights and also to reduce the consumption of current which would be prohibitive should extremely powerful light equipment be constantly in operation . . .

Though the outstanding industrial designs of the period do capture and embody the spirit in which they were produced, in many mass-produced items, cheaper materials only underscored poor design. This production has made a lasting bad impression on what Art Deco really means. Poor chromium plating, base metals painted to appear as bronze, dime store ceramic statues, and the like are evidence that the style was in decline. Although some of these have become "design icons" in the collecting world today and fetch high prices, they were for many years dismissed as "kitsch," a German word meaning "trash."

Earlier in the Art Deco movement, even when the objective was quantity, production was still controlled. At that time the French term *article de séries* indicated simply that an object was not unique. Today, the term is used derisively, for even French-made goods have succumbed to the need to produce cheap manufactured household items for the millions of people who inhabit urban centers.

High style adapted to industrial production meant that the masses could enjoy at least the illusion of grandeur that had been the standard of Art Deco design. However, the trend toward poorly manufactured goods increased as the Depression wore on. Hollywood movies were the best escape from troubled times, and "having style" was a way of pretending times weren't so bad. Hollywood producers engaged the talents of designers such as Kem Weber, Joseph Urban, Coco Chanel, and Hermes, and the

A glimpse of the future:
Elektro the Moto-Man at the
New York World's Fair
Westinghouse exhibit.
*Courtesy of the Museum of the
City of New York.*

masses yearned for the styles on the screen. Hollywood borrowed and glamorized the Art Deco style, and in the process "standardized" it for mass consumption.

The proliferation of Modern and Streamline memorabilia that accompanied the New York World's Fair of 1939, on the brink of World War II, was the style's last hurrah. Over fifty million people streamed through "the future." When that future did not come to pass, and a terrible war took place instead, no wonder Americans turned their back on the style.

One of the secrets of having "style" and "taste," however, is belonging to an "in" crowd. It seems that the moment a design trend or style becomes truly popular, it begins to decline—even if Art Deco had survived the war, it would not have survived popularization. Designers and artists, always looking for new ground, had begun to turn away from the style long before the public did.

Today, the Art Deco collecting field runs the entire gamut from luxurious pieces designed by the French *artistes décorateurs* to the mass-produced output of American industrial designers in the 1930s.

The transition of style is evident in every area: from a fine macassar ebony desk by Ruhlmann to the inventive tubular chrome "Z" stool by Gilbert Rohde; from a rare eggshell lacquer bookbinding to 1930s geometric paper dust jackets; from a silver coffee set with quartz handles by Jean Puiforcat to Walter von Nessen's streamlined cocktail shaker designs for Chase Chrome; from the exquisite jewelry of Cartier to jazzy Bakelite plastic bracelets; from hand-painted studio ceramics to bold-colored "Refrigerator Ware" from Hall China; and from a rare sapphire-blue vase by Lalique to Anchor Hocking's stylish "Manhattan" Depression glass.

One of the joys of being a collector of Art Deco is that no matter where you stand along this continuum, no matter what you collect, you can see into the past and catch a glimpse of the once-possible future. Through the evolution of Art Deco design, you can witness how the world was changing.

RECOGNIZING ART DECO

MOTIFS

Knowing the different motifs can help you recognize and distinguish between various styles.

Art Nouveau

The Art Nouveau style was characterized by curving, swaying lines, often in asymmetrical patterns. Plant imagery was used frequently: tendril-like vines such as morning glories, entwined leaves, and flowers such as calla lilies. You'll see this kind of imagery in glass designs by Tiffany and Galle, in marquetry in furniture by Louis Majorelle, and in the posters of Alphonse Mucha—the works of some of the leading designers of the Art Nouveau period.

Figures were usually women with flowing hair who were more full-bodied than the later, sleeker Art Deco figures of women. The mermaid was a popular Art Nouveau motif, and animal motifs often included snakes, dragonflies, peacocks, and lizards. Toward the end of the style, many designers felt that Art Nouveau ornamentation had become excessive.

Early Art Deco

Although emphasizing simplicity of line and form, early French Art Deco designers used still somewhat romantic, albeit more highly stylized, motifs: bubbles, rainbows, and flowing water. The fountain was a particularly popular motif and was used frequently in both furnishings and architecture. Flowers and ferns were still used, but their lines were simplified, and the overall effect was that of a symmetrical pattern. One frequently sees stylized baskets and cornucopias of fruits and flowers on everything from clocks to compacts.

Lithe women without the flowing robes and hairstyles of the Nouveau period became popular, clothed or nude, influenced by changes in fashion brought about after World War I by designers such as Coco Chanel.

The impact of Oriental design, especially Japanese design, can be seen in the simplicity of line and the use of bright color combinations. The rediscovery of the tomb of King Tut in Egypt in 1922 sent shock waves of Egyptian motifs through all areas of Art Deco design.

Pottery vases by Boch Frères, Belgium, reflect early flower motifs. *Author's collection. Photo by Robert Four.*

The impact of Egyptian design is reflected in this exquisite French brooch. *Courtesy of Skinner, Inc., Massachusetts.*

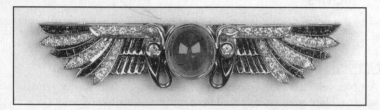

Jazz musicians, designed by Hagenauer, Vienna. *Courtesy of William Doyle Galleries, New York.*

Modern

The Modern phase of Art Deco design, and its desire to make a break with the past, brought motifs that were more rectilinear, geometric, or Cubist in inspiration.

Motifs suggesting movement, speed, or the machine were popular decorative devices. The fountain motif became repetitive line patterning, more and more abstracted and geometric, almost to the point of nonrecognition.

Jazz itself was a favorite subject for decorative artists, and its syncopated rhythms were reflected in urban, offbeat and angular motifs that appeared in sculptural forms, posters, glassware such as "Ruba Rhombic," ceramic decoration, and more.

For the collector, recognizing some Art Deco motifs in the decorative arts becomes easier if one studies the architecture of the period. For example, the skyscraper, whose basic form was borrowed from the "ziggurat" tower and Mayan and Aztec temples, became perhaps the most American Art Deco motif in decorative arts as well. The stepped-back form was reflected in everything from the "Skyscraper Furniture" of Paul Frankl to finials on forks. (*See one of Frankl's designs in the color section.*) By the end of the era, the skyscraper style had been used so often that many architects and designers were bored with it.

Other architectural influences that had an impact in the decorative arts were drawn from ancient cultures such as the Mesopotamian, Assyrian, and Egyptian, and, closer to home, Native American. Decorative arts can also reflect the architectural devices that emphasized the soaring verticality of the building.

The stepped look was sometimes curved into repeating arcs. The Deco "arc ziggurat" looks like scoops of ice cream topping one another, or a stylized cloud formation. Repeating sunburst patterns were also popular. Half-circles radiating out were used to represent sound, telegraph or radio signals, and other invisible forces of modernity such as "progress."

In some instances, the repeating half-circle motif was replaced with repeating mechanical gears or other industrial images, adding to the design's visual connection to industry. The imagery on the Chrysler Building in New York, for example, is composed of hubcaps and other automobile design components.

The zigzag, lightning bolt, and chevron became popular Art Deco motifs in America, in everything from neon signs to designs on the faces of countertop radios and handles of hairbrushes. A lightning bolt turned on its side could represent electricity, and was often used on modern kitchen appliances.

Streamline

As household appliances began to be produced in a Streamline style, Modernism lost some of its right angles to curved corners and teardrop shapes. Geometric design became aerodynamic design, greatly influenced by the new design for trains, ocean liners, and cars. One of the first styles of roadside diners manufactured during the period was called the "Sterling Streamliner."

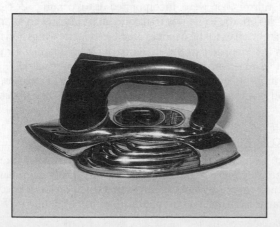

Streamlined "Petipoint" iron by Waverly Tool Company, Ohio.
Photo by Robert Four.

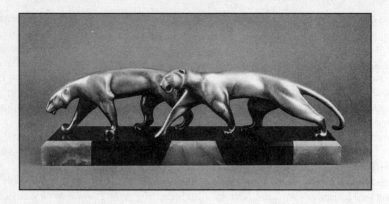

Sleek panthers by Decour. *Courtesy of Christie's, New York.*

This phase of Art Deco was the most devoid of ornamentation. Little if any applied ornamentation was used, and the form of the object itself had to carry the visual impact. Only simple motifs, such as three parallel "speed lines" are seen on Streamline objects. Often, the most decorative element on appliances is the applied company logo.

Art Deco Animals

Art Deco animals typically were exotic, sleek, and fast: antelopes, gazelles, deer, horses, and greyhounds (and not only in American bus terminals). Antelopes and gazelles were everywhere—leaping across metalwork by Edgar Brandt, grazing around a bowl of Steuben crystal, and animating department store pottery.

A favorite family of animals were the big cats: tigers, panthers, jaguars, and leopards, which were more exotic than endangered at the time. Their sleek, graceful forms lent themselves to sculpture in bronze or ceramic. They were so popular that they continued to be made as inexpensive ceramics that lurked behind low-slung couches and under cocktail tables for decades.

Parakeets, parrots, doves, and other small birds were used for decorating vases, perched on the frames of mirrors, or were incorporated into ceramic design. In American architecture and design, the eagle was transformed; its already angular beak and flat head naturally lent themselves to the Modern angular style. Its wings and feathers were straight back, again in a stepped pattern. In Tropical Deco, flamingos, herons, and pelicans standing or in flight became part of the popular design menagerie.

Some animals appeared more urbane and sophisticated than ever. Penguins, with their natural "tuxedos," and sometimes complete with top hat and cane, became a favorite cocktail hour motif.

The Decline of Art Deco Motifs

The popularity of some Art Deco symbols and motifs, and of bold angular lines and graphics, waned rapidly when they began to be used more and more in Nazi propaganda art. The Modern style in some eyes was a Germanic style, and therefore associated with the Third Reich. In fact, American design had been influenced by the Bauhaus, Wiener

Werkstätte, and dozens of immigrants who had come to this country before the war. Just as cans of sauerkraut were taken down from the shelves and replaced by "Liberty cabbage," the German influence in American design was ignored or denied well into the 1950s.

In the 1940s, when Biomorphism and other postwar design styles replaced Art Deco, form, ornamentation, and motifs changed again. Chairs and other objects took on the shapes of amoebas—or, some say, "potato chips"—and one of the most enduring images of the new "Atomic Era" was the kitchen wall clock in the shape of a molecule.

MATERIALS AND TECHNIQUES

Early Art Deco artists continued to work in traditional woods and other materials, but, like the Art Nouveau artists before them, they displayed a love of exotic materials as well. Materials such as inlaid mother of pearl, semiprecious stones, lacquer, enamel, and unusual woods were used.

Both Art Deco and Art Nouveau were influenced by contact with the cultures of Africa, the Orient, and the Americas, and imported quantities of macassar ebony and ivory. The rarity of these materials today makes the cost of objects produced much higher, but many were available in abundance at the time. In fact, the Belgian government at one time held contests to encourage artists to use the tons of ivory being brought back from the Congo. These contests helped increase popularity of chryselephantine, or bronze and ivory, sculptures. Today, if you purchase a bronze and ivory statue, you may encounter problems if you plan to ship it to one of the many countries now banning ivory importation.

Distinctive woods, such as African ebony, visually transform Art Deco furniture.
Courtesy of Savoia's Auction, Inc., New York.

Furniture

In France, furniture makers used native sycamore, oak, and walnut, as well as more exotic burled woods, zebrawood, amboyna, amaranthe, olivewood, rosewood, violet wood, Rio palissandre, palmwood, and a host of others. These gave artists a wide choice for the color, texture, and grain of furniture. On some of these woods, the graining is so bold that it can be seen across a room, and actually changes the visual impact of the piece.

Another favorite, if somewhat bizarre, material was galuchat, actually the skin of a dogfish, which was treated and used like leather. Today, you'll hear people call it shark-skin, which sometimes substituted for it, or "shagreen." It became a favorite for desk tops, bleached to pale green, gray, or beige. It could be tooled with geometric, sunburst, or other Deco designs, and had its own repetitive design of scales.

In 1925, Bauhaus designer Marcel Breuer pioneered the use of steel tubing for furniture, "updating" the bentwood designs of the Vienna Secession and leading to the later use of tubular chrome. As the use of metal and industrial materials in furniture spread, it was at first met with shock or laughter.

But there was no turning back the clock. The world was rapidly changing, and today we recognize that these industrial materials were used with great genius by the "Moderns." Their work was art suited to industrial production, and for designers like Le Corbusier and Robert Mallet-Stevens, these easily mass-produced materials supported their social philosophy and politics, as well as their design goals.

Lacquer and Enamel

The use of lacquer began in earnest with the arrival in Paris in 1918 of the Japanese artist Sugawara. Paris had a rage for things Oriental, and Sugawara's influence on two noted designers to whom he taught the ancient art, Eileen Gray and Jean Dunand, would make lacquer an overwhelmingly popular technique. Although both artists are renowned for their lacquer, Dunand is more recognized as the master.

White was the only color that could not be produced by lacquer, and Dunand discovered the art of using crushed eggshells to create his patterns. Lacquered pieces were often rendered in geometric red, black, and silver designs, a favorite Deco color combination. Other artists began working in lacquer on everything: little boxes and big boxes, panels, and furniture. Later, fast-drying industrial lacquer would replace the painstaking layering process, meaning that more items could be produced in "lacquer" finishes.

Enameling was also a popular technique for enriching vases and other decorative objects. In the 1930s, industrial baked enamel finishes on household appliances became popular.

Jewelry and Fashion

The designs of Raymond Templier and George and Jean Fouquet created new markets for boldly colored enameled jewelry.

More semiprecious stones and materials came to be used. Often, these materials were selected for the color value they gave to the new geometric design, such as coral and jade. Rhinestones and marcasite made it possible for every woman to afford jewelry that sparkled like diamonds. Bakelite and Catalin costume jewelry was colorful and inexpensive and could be mass-produced by machines.

At the beginning of the Art Deco period, the "lamés" that were so popular for evening dresses were interwoven with real gold and silver thread. Little fabric was man-made, except for artificial silk. Embroidery was often used to enrich the look of a piece, and pure silk crêpe de chine was a favorite for women's lingerie. By the 1930s, synthetic textile production and ready-to-wear styles had proliferated.

Metal

Traditional metals, like bronze and wrought iron, continued to be used. As before, wrought iron was used extensively in architectural detail, and bronze as a medium for sculpture. However, perhaps due to the genius of designers such as Edgar Brandt, wrought iron became popular in tables, lamps, and other furnishings. Glass and metal artists, such as Brandt and Daum, collaborated to create stunning lighting fixtures, showing off each other's talents even more.

Precious metals such as copper, silver, and gold maintained their value, but were used in different ways. New metal-crafting techniques also came along, such as autogenous welding, which allowed two different metals—bronze and silver, for example—to be welded together.

New Materials and Techniques

In the 1930s, mass-production brought with it the advent of kitchenware made from machine-produced, highly polished chrome. Ceramics were able to be fired and glazed in one step. Wood veneers replaced inlaid wood, and cheap woods were hidden under industrial enamels. Whole walls of houses were constructed with glass block, and toward the end of the period, aluminum became increasingly popular.

Radios, kitchen utensils, household decorations, ashtrays, and production furniture were made using materials such as chrome or nickel-plated steel, painted base metal, a wide range of trademarked plastics, and mirrored glass. Materials such as these were often decorated through a variety of methods in bright, jazzy colors or Floridian pastels.

By 1939, the use of industrial materials had come so far that Pittsburgh Plate Glass Company designed a chair for the New York World's Fair using a single sheet of plate glass, with an upholstered snakeskin seat!

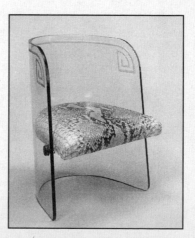

Chair by Pittsburgh Plate Glass
exhibited at the 1939
New York World's Fair.
Courtesy of Christie's, New York.

You'll read a lot more about materials and techniques in the pages of this book. Understanding the materials used in Art Deco design can help a collector evaluate a piece. The intrinsic value of some materials can greatly enhance the price. Also, it is important for the collector to know and recognize the materials used in order to avoid deception.

For example, onyx bases on clocks and statues can be passed off to the unwary as marble. Early decorative statues used bronze and ivory, and the later ones and imitations used "ivorine," a composition plastic. No shiny brass telephones existed before 1950.

Today, when numerous fakes and reproductions of Art Deco designs are on the market, knowing the materials can help you avoid both well-made replicas and poorly made imitations of the real thing. In each chapter, we've included as much information as we had available on fakes and reproductions to help you spot them.

DECORATIVE INFLUENCES

In the world of design, sometimes a direct connection between one designer and another can be seen, especially if one was the teacher of another, if they were working partners, or if they belonged to the same "school." The exchange between styles that causes a new style to emerge, however, is a more complex interaction.

This is certainly true of the emergence of art deco and of its evolution. In some ways, Art Deco emerged from the headlong impact of a number of national styles to become an international style.

At the turn of the century, the exchange of design ideas was facilitated by a shrinking world, improved communications and magazine publishing, and international design expositions. In looking a bit more closely at this history, the collector of Art Deco begins to see the connections, to understand what Art Deco refused, borrowed, and reinterpreted from other styles.

Art Nouveau Poster, 1897, by Alphonse Mucha.
Courtesy of William Doyle Galleries, New York.

ART NOUVEAU

Art Nouveau was the predominant European design style for only about twenty years, between about 1890 and 1910, reaching its peak in about 1900. Art Nouveau was a conscious attempt to create a new style. Essentially a French style, it flourished in France more than in any other European country, and in Europe very much more than in America.

Art Nouveau was a sculptural style that tried to diminish the importance of the Industrial Revolution and totally ignored machine-produced materials. Some say it was a style "in denial"—that Nouveau could do little more than postpone the emergence of a more modern style.

The term originated in France when Seigfried Bing opened a shop called Maison de l'Art Nouveau, selling furnishings and objets d'art in Paris in 1895. Bing exhibited some of the most outstanding artists of the day in his gallery, including Bonnard, Vuillard, and Aubrey Beardsley.

When he visited the United States, Bing was impressed by the work of glassmaker Louis Comfort Tiffany, the son of the owner of the famous Fifth Avenue jewelry store. Tiffany was a master artist who achieved magnificent colors, breathtaking iridescence, intricate designs, and new textures in glass. Tiffany's output was tremendous, and his name remains at the top of the list of American Art Nouveau designers.

René Lalique also worked with Bing and designed exquisite Art Nouveau jewelry. By 1914, he was considered the most outstanding jeweler in Europe, and created abstract designs of plants and insects using semiprecious stones and glass paste. Ultimately, he devoted himself to glassmaking in earnest. Lalique was a truly original designer and was able to survive the transition in French decorative arts from Art Nouveau to Art Deco.

Art Nouveau was the first French design movement to stress the connections between decorative and fine arts, helping boost the recognition of individual decorative artists. In England, the Arts and Crafts movement attempted the same reconciliation of roles, but for more moralistic than aesthetic reasons.

Bing helped along this synthesis of the arts in French Art Nouveau. For example, he had painters such as Bonnard and Toulouse-Lautrec make designs for stained glass windows, and then had Tiffany execute them.

Many European countries produced some variation of the Art Nouveau style, and by the 1900 Exposition, it was obvious that Art Nouveau dominated the design field.

In Germany, the Art Nouveau style was called Jugendstil, or the "new" or "youthful" style, and was promoted through a journal entitled *Jugend*. Germany, however, was faced with very different social and economic conditions than France, and would soon reject the Art Nouveau style.

In Italy, Art Nouveau was called "Stile Liberty" because of the popularity of goods from the London shop of A. L. Liberty. In England, where Art Nouveau was not popular, the best known Art Nouveau artist is perhaps Aubrey Beardsley. In the United States, besides Tiffany, the best-known name is perhaps that of graphic artist Will Bradley.

Other outstanding French Art Nouveau decorative artists include the glassmaker Emile Gallé, who was a botanist before entering the design trade; furniture designer Louis Majorelle, whose wood marquetry designs are masterpieces of Art Nouveau; and Alphonse Mucha, who was one of the first to recognize the power of poster advertising and helped set the tastes of his era through his graphic work. Looking at the work of artists such as these, one will quickly learn to identify Art Nouveau and distinguish it from Art Deco.

Art Nouveau's ornamentation, which was largely organic, never lent itself to architecture, except perhaps that of Spaniard Antoni Gaudi and Frenchman Hector Guimard as exemplified in his Parisian town houses and his famous Metro entrances created in 1900.

Few architects could achieve the fusion of natural forms with architectural forms the way Guimard did, and he became Art Nouveau's leading architect, as well as a furniture designer. Gaudi's work, especially for the well-known church of the Sagrada Familia in Barcelona, is clearly a new vision in architecture, but one that was costly and would not endure.

THE TURIN EXPOSITION OF 1902

Art Nouveau carried on its excesses of ornamentation until it seemed that the basis of the style was for the sake of ornamentation itself. The strongest criticism was that Art Nouveau failed to integrate art and life because it got stuck on decoration for its own sake. It seemed to reach its most elaborate phase at the Turin Exposition of 1902.

Italian artists represented at Turin are today seen as precursors of the Modern style, such as Carlo Buggati, who showed a pair of egg-shaped chairs connected by one continuous curved support to circular seats, with highly stylized, geometric carvings. Carlo's son, the engineer Ettore Buggati, later gave the family name to an automobile that became synonymous with streamlined luxury and speed.

Other significantly Modern designs at the exhibition came from Scotland's Glasgow School and its leading artist, Charles Rennie Mackintosh. Mackintosh had developed his own style, with influences from the Arts and Crafts movement as well as Art Nouveau. He was attracted to functional furniture, geometric forms, and clean lines. He and his colleagues, such as Margaret Macdonald and Herbert and Francis McNair, had already exhibited in the Vienna Secession Exhibition of 1900 and had had a profound influence on Austrian artists. In fact, Josef Hoffmann eventually married Mackintosh's sister.

The Wiener Werkstätte was represented at Turin as well. It was evident that the works of the Vienna Secessionists were even more Modern than those of Mackintosh, who had inspired them. The Secession was a proclaimed and highly promoted clean break from the overly flowery Art Nouveau style and traditional Austrian styles.

THE OPPOSITION MOVEMENTS

The opposition to Art Nouveau did not come from within France as strongly as it did from other countries. In England, the Arts and Crafts movement voiced its opposition to Art Nouveau, more for moral reasons than for a desire for modernity.

Vienna was more forward-looking. There, architect Otto Wagner developed an architecture of straight lines and geometric forms. He consciously chose to use modern materials such as concrete, plate glass, and aluminum in his buildings. In 1908, architect Adolf Loos attacked what he called the "ornamental delirium" of Art Nouveau. Two years later, he designed the Steiner house, a concrete cube that would inspire the De Stijl designers in Holland, the Bauhaus in Germany, and designers such as Le Corbusier in France.

Viennese designer Josef Hoffmann is now recognized as a major individual precursor of Modern design in decorative arts. He was known especially for his furniture and silver designs, many of which were produced by the Wiener Werkstätte or "Vienna Workshops," which he founded in 1903, and which opened a gallery in New York in 1922.

In Germany, the architect Muthesius proclaimed that art could no longer disassociate itself from the machine, leading to the creation in 1907 of the Deutscher Werkbund, a society of industrialists and artists that was an ancestor of the Bauhaus. A Werkbund exhibition of decorative arts in Paris in 1910 exploded like a bombshell—or a bomb. Many designers were influenced by the Germanic style.

In France and in America, again it was architects who broke with the Art Nouveau style. The Chicago School led by Louis Sullivan used metal frameworks for buildings that were first and foremost functional. In 1910, Europe discovered the work of Frank Lloyd Wright and was influenced by his Prairie School. Above all, Art Nouveau came to be seen as "out of date." In the modern, faster world, its fluid, subtle, and often languorous aspect was considered too slow, and its asymmetrical lines and ornamentation made machine production impossible.

Between 1909 and the outbreak of World War I, the Cubists, Stravinsky, Les Ballets Russes, and many other artistic influences were adding to the excitement of an era that could be called the Golden Age of Art Deco. Even in Czechoslovakia, a small, groundbreaking group of designers and architects had discovered Cubism and were applying it to buildings with highly exaggerated angles, interiors with slanting walls, and furniture and accessory design.

As early as 1907, there were demands for an exposition of contemporary arts in Paris. However, because of the war, the Exposition des Arts Décoratifs et Industriels Modernes, which had been scheduled for 1916, did not happen until 1925.

The early style of Art Deco, as we have mentioned, relied on a wealthy clientele which commissioned designers to create deluxe furnishings and objects. The opposition to early Art Deco in France would come through the work of Le Corbusier, designer René Herbst, and other artists who founded the Union des Artistes Modernes in 1930.

Le Corbusier, a Swiss-born Frenchman whose real name was Charles-Edouard Jeanneret, was the theoretical and design leader of the movement in France, and his influence had been gradually building for many years. His Pavillon de l'Esprit Nouveau at the Parisian 1925 Exposition was sneered at by the more established Art Deco artists, but it was really the only French pavilion that promoted the Modern style.

Bentwood settee, c. 1908, designed by Vienna Secessionist Josef Hoffmann. *Courtesy of Gallery Vienna, Illinois.*

The Vienna Secession

Josef Hoffmann, the leading Viennese designer from the turn of the century until about 1930, was influenced by his teacher, architect Otto Wagner. Wagner's book *Moderne Architektur* is generally considered the inspiration for the Wiener Sezession, or Vienna Secession, which Hoffmann and some of his fellow students founded in 1897. The Secessionists promoted their ideas through a journal called *Ver Sacrum*, or *Sacred Spring*, which was started in 1898.

This movement openly "seceded" from the Viennese design establishment, rejected or severely modified Art Nouveau motifs, and borrowed from leading Modern concepts such as the somewhat stark, geometric work of Glasgow's Charles Rennie Mackintosh. Reflective also of Cubism and the German Expressionism in the fine arts, and committed to functionality, the Wiener Werkstätte's production was highly Modern in style long before World War I.

In 1903, Hoffmann established the Wiener Werkstätte, which brought together artists and craftsmen working in a variety of media to produce a range of furnishings and decorative arts. Most of its work is based on geometry, and often used black and white as dominant colors.

The range of articles produced by the Wiener Werkstätte was considerable, including not only the finest in home furnishings, but also ice cream molds, lorgnettes, stuffed toy animals, enamel matchboxes, cactus pots, pearl bags, and hat and coat racks.

Under the trade law at the time, the early production of the Wiener Werkstätte was classified as handicrafts, but in 1914, the handicrafts trades were reclassified as factories. There is evidence of industrial production along with crafts production right from the start. In 1913, the name "Wiener Werkstätte" was registered as a trademark for the first time.

Today, Wiener Werkstätte pieces are rare and highly valued. It must be remembered that the output was small by comparison to later industrial mass production. Even Hoffmann's designs for bentwood furniture for the manufacturer Thonet were not produced in huge quantities. Since the 1986 Museum of Modern Art exhibition, entitled "Vienna 1900," Secessionist furniture and decorative arts have continued to increase in price beyond the reach of most collectors.

Motifs used by Secessionists became the outstanding symbols of the Modern movement: the zigzag and lightning bolts. "Borrowed" as well by Art Deco designers would be the geometric forms, stylized flower motifs, gazelle fabric patterns, and other imagery.

Wiener Werkstätte coffee sets, tableware, and other household furnishings were an inspiration to American designers after the opening of its New York gallery in 1922, headed by Joseph Urban. Several American ceramic artists and other designers traveled to study in Vienna. In addition, when the Wiener Werkstätte was forced to declare bankruptcy in 1932, many of its artists came to America, including ceramic artist Vally Wieselthier, whose lower-cost designs for General Ceramics in New Jersey are collectible today. Josef Hoffmann's son, Wolfgang, later became known for his furniture designs in chrome-plated steel and black lacquered wood for American manufacturers such as Howell Manufacturing.

The English Arts and Crafts Movement

William Morris set the tone for the Arts and Crafts movement in England. He rejected past styles and traditional ornamentation as well as the extravagances of Art Nouveau, and looked to the simplicity of a cottage-industry lifestyle and to nature for inspiration.

Although refined, his work expressed itself in strong, pure colors in paint or dye, red brick, and solid work in native woods.

The movement was encouraged and nurtured by theorists like John Ruskin, who promoted a moralistic view of design. People like Ruskin were as concerned with social reform as with art, and championed a craft-based, rather than machine-based, ethic.

Arts and Crafts designers condemned the Art Nouveau style as decadent and bizarre. One of the leaders of the movement, C. F. A. Voysey, an architect who derived his inspiration from Gothic medieval architecture, claimed that the Art Nouveau style was "out of harmony" with the British national character and climate.

Several "guilds" were created for the production of crafts for discerning clients. The first of these, the Century Guild, was founded in 1884. It was the first time artists had banded together to produce decorative arts.

The British art establishment rejected the work of the guilds and denied them access to official shows. As happened in other countries, these craftsmen organized their own exhibitions, creating the Arts and Crafts Exhibition Society in 1888. They held their first show and sale the same year in London and sponsored numerous other events in the years to follow.

The most popular publication to chronicle Arts and Crafts design in England was *The Studio*, started in 1893 and later financed by Charles Holme, a wealthy manufacturer who lived in a house designed by Morris. While *The Studio* did much to publicize the work of designers who would become known as the beacons of the Arts and Crafts movement, it also published the drawings of Aubrey Beardsley, which embodied the "bizarre decadence" that Arts and Crafts designers disdained. Many years later, *The Studio* published the work of leading Art Deco and Modern designers as well.

The strength and appeal of the Arts and Crafts movement declined in the face of many pressures. It could not recapture a past idyllic age as the world went spinning onward, and it failed to recognize the strength and potential of the Machine Age. Although its influence is felt until this day, like Art Nouveau, it was a style that could not stand against the economic, social, and political complexity that was to become modern life.

Though it was not a forward-thinking style, its straight lines and angular furniture captured the imagination of early Modernists such as Mackintosh in Scotland and Josef Hoffmann in Vienna.

The American Arts and Crafts Movement

American architect Will Price coined the expression "The Art That Is Life" in 1903 as the subtitle of his periodical *The Artsman*. The Arts and Crafts designers in America were also reformers who tried to lead a movement against an increasingly industrialized and urban society.

Like their English counterparts, they condemned routine industrial labor as unfulfilling and dismissed the whole range of ornate styles popular in the United States, such as Louis XIV, the Rococo Revival, and Art Nouveau. The evangelistic energy of Ruskin and Morris reached across the ocean and had a profound impact in this country on any artists who considered themselves part of the English tradition, especially in New England. Solid native woods took the place of imported veneers. Unnecessary ornamentation was abandoned. Hundreds of Arts and Crafts societies sprang up around the country, and the very first, Boston's Society of Arts and Crafts, is still operating today as a gallery for contemporary decorative arts.

Periodicals such as *The Craftsman*, *Ladies Home Journal*, and *House Beautiful* were founded as part of this movement. Women discovered a new role, and were active in teaching skills and handcrafting. They actively applied the ethical principles of the movement to social reform and created or helped create and sell crafts for philanthropic purposes.

The ideal was to teach people to be self-supporting through crafts rather than having to work at a factory. For example, Paul Revere Pottery in Boston, which produced breakfast sets, vases, and other utilitarian objects from 1907 to 1942, grew out of a Girls Club where young Italian immigrant women in Boston's North End were taught the potter's skills.

The emphasis on the individual craftsmanship of the artist led to the creation of thousands of small studios, shops, and printing presses, and even affected factory production at the time. Bookcases and chairs by Gustav Stickley, with their clean straight lines, were produced by the thousands for middle-class purchasers for the first two decades of this century.

This furniture production, along with anything in the notable California "Mission" styles, is in vogue with collectors today. Mission-style decorative arts were derived in the 1890s from a style of architecture used in the missions built by the Franciscans in the late 18th century and early 19th centuries, and swept California.

Irving Gill, an architect who arrived in San Diego from Chicago in 1893, took up this Mission style in earnest. In 1914 and 1915, as his style evolved, he designed buildings that ten years later might have been taken as examples of the Modern style in architecture.

While the Arts and Crafts movement offered some inspiration for early Modernists looking for a truly American design style, the movement itself can hardly be called "Modern." In fact, it was its purposeful intention to look "un-Modern" in the face of Art Nouveau that makes it appear to be a Modern style. Arts and Crafts looked backward, the Modernists looked forward.

Frank Lloyd Wright and the Prairie School

In 1900, Frank Lloyd Wright was a young man of thirty living in Chicago, a city that was very much alive to the influence of the Arts and Crafts movement. However, the young architect took his teacher Louis Sullivan's stance and believed the machine was the "normal tool of our civilization" and could be controlled to fulfill a humanistic, almost utopian, vision.

Wright initially saw his work, and that of talented designers working with him—Burley Griffen, Marion Mahoney, William Drummond, and Barry Byrne—as a "New School of the Middle West," which became known as the "Prairie School."

The buildings of the Prairie School of architecture, exemplified by the Ward W. Willits home in Highland Park, Illinois, built in 1902–1903, are characterized by horizontal lines that hug the flat plains of the prairie—thus the name. However, Wright designed homes in Illinois, New York, California, and elsewhere as well.

Everything he created for the interiors of his architecture—furnishings, stained glass windows, textiles, and statuary—is extremely expensive on the collecting market today. Even his architectural renderings and drawings can command tens of thousands of dollars.

Many design movements lay claim to Frank Lloyd Wright. Modernists point to his

Chair, c. 1903,
by Frank Lloyd Wright.
Photo by Robert Four.

design for the Guggenheim Museum. Art Deco enthusiasts pay top dollar for his furnishings from the Imperial Hotel in Japan. Dutch De Stijl designers were influenced by his early exhibitions in Europe. The fact is that Frank Lloyd Wright was a towering genius, and belonged to none of these movements.

The Bauhaus

In Germany, toward the end of the century, numerous werkstätte, or "workshops," for the production of furniture and other objects were created, and from as early as 1904, several were experimenting with serial production. Germany was determined to establish its reputation for design and architecture based on practical as well as aesthetic principles. In Germany, the economic and social imperatives behind such manufacture was stronger than in other countries.

International cultural exchange aided the Germans in their efforts. Hermann Muthesius, often noted as the father of the German Modern movement, spent several

Bauhaus architect
Walter Gropius's home in
Lincoln, Massachusetts.
*Courtesy of the Society
for the Preservation of
New England Antiquities.*

years in England before World War I, studying architecture and design. He and Henri van de Velde were members of the Deutscher Werkbund, and in 1906, van de Velde founded the design school that would later become the Bauhaus. Van de Velde also received commissions in Holland and played a leading role in the development of the Dutch De Stijl design movement.

The creation of the Werkbund marked the end of the Art Nouveau, or Jugendstil, in Germany, and its followers launched a campaign of reform directed toward the improvement of industrial rather than handcrafted design. As previously mentioned, the Werkbund held an exhibition in Paris in 1910, which had an impact on French Art Deco's change from the early to the Modern style.

The Bauhaus was founded as an art institute in Weimar in 1919. Much more concerned with practice than with theory, it was from the start fairly anti-academic. It became one of the world's great centers for the development of a particular design philosophy. Integration of the arts with the machine and industrial culture was its motivating philosophy. The Bauhaus had a mission that affected all aspects of design. It changed homes several times, moving around Germany to Dessau in 1925 and to Berlin in 1932.

When its founder, Walter Gropius, fled the Third Reich, he became a professor at Harvard University and was joined on the faculty there by Marcel Breuer. The Bauhaus relocated to Chicago in 1937. Gropius and Breuer affected an entire generation of American designers and architects. Much of American Art Deco architectural design, such as the small Art Deco hotels of Miami Beach, owes more to the Bauhaus than to any French school of design.

Other leading Bauhaus artists and designers include Mies van der Rohe, Wassily Kandinsky, Marianne Brandt, Marcel Breuer, Lazlo and Lucia Moholy-Nagy, Paul Klee, and Josef and Anni Albers. These artists transformed architecture, art, furniture, metalwork, typography, and even color theory. Many of them also fled Germany for America.

Marcel Breuer, who pioneered the use of tubular steel in furnishings, spent time in England before emigrating to the United States. There he designed furniture for Isokon Furniture Company and influenced English architectural design of the 1930s by such architects as Wells Coates.

Rather than trying to hide from the Machine Age as the Arts and Crafts movement had, the Bauhaus tried to create a world of industrially produced high-quality crafts without sacrificing human qualities.

ARTISTIC INFLUENCES

Before the turn of the century, generally speaking, the worlds of fine and applied arts had traditionally remained far apart, each drawing on its own traditions, materials, and philosophies. Design movements such as Art Nouveau, Arts and Crafts, the Vienna Secession, and Art Deco made a conscious attempt to realign the fine arts and the applied arts. In essence, their goal was to gain the title of "artist" for the craftsman. Artistic influences, both from Europe and from cultures around the world, affected the development of the Art Deco style. This was true not only of the fine arts, but of the performing arts as well.

FAUVISM

The work of such artists as Derain, Matisse, Vlaminck, Marquet, Friesz, Jean and Raoul Dufy, and Braque greatly affected design. Many of these artists were also commissioned to execute designs for decorative arts.

These artists were called "Fauves," or "wild beasts," by critics and the more conservative art community after their Salon D'Automne exhibition in 1905, due mostly to the shocking, bright-color combinations and two-dimensional representation they used in their paintings. The Fauvist movement in art lasted only a few years, but it broke new ground and opened a window through which Modern design could emerge.

FUTURISM

Chronologically, Futurism was happening in Italy around the same time Cubism was happening in France. The same year that Les Ballets Russes arrived in Paris, a Futurist poem published in a Parisian newspaper proclaimed, "Speed is our god, the new canon of beauty."

One year later, in 1910, the Futurists published *Manifesto of Futurist Painters* to help disseminate their work. Parisians were shocked by the violent nature of many of the paintings, and acceptance was slow in coming.

Among the leading Futurist painters and sculptors were Umberto Boccioni, Giacomo Balla, Gine Severini, and Martinetti. They succeeded at depicting speed and movement in their work through the use of multiple imaging, oblique angles, and shading.

The favorite overall themes besides speed were power and energy—both industrial and natural. Paintings depicted cars and railroad trains at full throttle, and industrial motifs were juxtaposed with natural ones. Nature itself made the canvas quiver in the form of storms, lightning bolts, volcanoes, tidal waves, and rearing horses. By the beginning of World War I, the influence of Futurism was apparent in many applied arts.

CUBISM

It was the 1907 exhibition of Picasso's famous painting *Demoiselles d'Avignon* that effectively began the Cubist revolt. Picasso and Braque broke with the Fauves and tried to represent volume on flat planes without perspective or light.

Cubism was itself influenced by the introduction of African folk art and masks to Europe, and the elongated outlined faces of primitive masks were soon apparent in Modern sculpture by Gustav Miklos and Alexander Archipenko. Their sculptures were among the first objects to transform into three dimensions what the Cubist painters had been expressing in two.

Even when portraying everyday scenes drawn from traditional genre painting, such as portraiture and still life, it was the nature of Cubism to reveal new dimensions in the volumes of seemingly everyday objects, and new psychological dimensions in humanity. Overall form was achieved through a layering and juxtaposing of geometric forms.

Cubism also uncovered new dimensions in art, and in the process gave the decorative artist new freedom in the form and decoration of objects. Coffee pots and teapots need not be round—they could indeed be angular if they held and poured hot liquids correctly. Form and function did not necessarily have to match, and whimsy was allowed. Painted design could be purposely abstract, and not even pretend to hang on to "stylized" natural forms. Tables and cabinets and doors need not be squared but could be oddly angled. Carpets could imitate the bold abstract designs of the African Berbers. In addition, like the new design movement that was to emerge, Cubism rejected decoration for its own sake.

Unlike the world of decorative arts, which came to a screeching halt for social and economic reasons during World War I, the Cubists as individual artists and as a school of thought continued to pursue their geometric vision of the world. Their effect would be felt even more strongly much later in the Modern movement in applied arts.

LES BALLETS RUSSES

The colorful, opulent sets and costumes by Leon Bakst for Sergei Diaghilev's Les Ballets Russes, or "Russian Ballet," gained popularity immediately on their arrival in Paris in 1909. They greatly influenced fashion, design, and illustration of such artists as Erté, André Marty, and Paul Poiret. Many decorators such as Paul Iribe were also influenced by the great theatrical artists who designed for Les Ballets Russes.

From the first performance through a total of about forty productions over the years, Les Ballets Russes was a new kind of spectacle in which dancing, music, art, and design were integrated. The painter or illustrator was no longer confined to the two-dimensional canvas, but actually created decors, accessories, and costumes. Les Ballets Russes and its most famous principal dancer, Nijinski, were the rage of Paris for years after the First World War.

The great Russian musicians who composed for the ballets in the early days, such as Stravinsky and Prokofiev, were joined by the likes of Satie, Poulenc, Milhaud, and others considered avant-garde. The public discovered Fauvism, Cubism, and the other avant-garde movements through ballet designs. Painters such as Picasso, Matisse,

Braque, Max Ernst, Miro, and Utrillo, and sculptors Laurens, Gabo, and Pevsner were commissioned.

With talent like that, it is no surprise that the production's colorful splendor, extravagant costumes, and stage settings would be immediately seized upon by the designers for their very discerning (and ballet-going) clientele. Strong colors were in favor, lighting was dimmed and diffused, cushions were everywhere, and strong use had been made of Bakst's "pattern on pattern" design techniques. Furniture was redesigned to fit the new slinky dresses. Chaises longues, or "long chairs," appeared frequently as salon furniture, and the now-popular cocktail or coffee table as an accessory to the low-slung design made its emergence.

Soon, every French stage was employing contemporary artists to take part in theatrical productions.

MONDRIAN AND THE DE STIJL GROUP

Dutch painter Piet Mondrian had been influenced by Cubism when he visited Paris in 1911. He struggled to achieve a pure plastic art through the exclusive use of right angles in horizontal-vertical positions, and the use of three primary colors with white, black, and gray.

The De Stijl group would defend and imitate Mondrian in the creation of its sparse household products. This design movement would have a profound impact on the later, more geometric phases of the Art Deco style.

The De Stijl group was founded in Holland during World War I. The same year, one of its most noted artists, Rietveld, designed his now well-known angular all-wooden chair—one of the first examples of all-out "Modernism" in furniture.

The De Stijl group would also give tremendous expression to their ideas through Dutch graphic expression in poster art. For many reasons, this poster art also remained relatively unknown until an exhibition traveled through the United States to seven museums, closing at the Cooper-Hewitt in New York in 1989.

Wendingen, **the
publication of the
De Stijl movement.**
*Courtesy of Bernice Jackson
Fine Arts, Massachusetts.
Photo by Robert Four.*

JAZZ

The Jazz Age, like the world around it, was full of new syncopated rhythms and dynamism. Popular dances made their way to Paris: the Black Bottom, the fox trot, the shimmy, and the Charleston. The style of dancing and of dresses was slyly innocent or coyly seductive. You could miss the ballet and the opera and still find style in a nightclub.

Parisian audiences in 1925 thrilled to the Revue Nègre of the famed Josephine Baker. In the same year, a visitor to Paris might view Les Ballets Russes or Corbusier's Pavillon de l'Esprit Nouveau at the International Exposition.

Josephine Baker was worshipped in Paris, as were many things "Negro" at the time. Black Americans were exotic talents and became the French nightclub set's prized performers. The poster for Revue Nègre by Paul Colin was in a whole new idiom for advertising art. Baker, with her feather fans, was also often depicted in bronze or bronze and ivory statues.

In America, George Gershwin's "Rhapsody in Blue" sent jazz on a dizzying climb of popularity. Jazzy, zigzag designs echoing urban themes proliferated in ceramic design, fashion accessories, and glass such as "Ruba Rhombic," introduced in 1928 by Consolidated Lamp and Glass Company.

DADAISM AND SURREALISM

Dadaism and Surrealism did have some effect on the decorative arts, but many would say that the influence of these styles was not felt until much later. Only a few Parisians knew of the Dada movement, born in Switzerland in World War I. The work of such artists as Arp, Picabia, Marcel Duchamp, Max Ernst, and later Salvador Dalí would more strongly affect later design styles, such as Biomorphism, in the late 1930s and 1940s.

OTHER INFLUENCES

A host of other influences also affected Art Deco design, and an appreciation of them helps an Art Deco collector understand the style in its full historical context.

ORIENTALISM

As previously mentioned, Orientalism as expressed through the work of Bakst for Les Ballets Russes had a profound effect on early French Art Deco fashion and interiors. However, the rage for things Oriental did not stop there. Parisians had toyed with Oriental influence in the arts since the beginning of the century.

Ancient Japanese lacquering techniques became highly popular. For twenty years after the end of World War I, lacquer reigned supreme, and its finest artist, Jean Dunand, was treated as something of a national treasure.

In addition, the angles and patterns of Japanese ukiyo-e, or "floating world," prints influenced advertising and fashion illustration art of the Art Deco period. These Japanese prints were highly accomplished in their use of oblique and odd angles, subtle color combinations, plain or screened backgrounds that allowed the figures to be more prominent, and the simplicity of their lives.

EGYPTIAN DESIGN

The masks and tribal artifacts that so affected the Cubists are not the only African influence that was strongly felt in design in this period. The uncovering of the Tomb of

Mayan pyramids—some of the first skyscrapers.

34

King Tutankhamun by Howard Carter and Lord Carnavon in 1922 brought Egyptian symbols such as sphinxes, hieroglyphics, bright colors, and famous faces such as that of Cleopatra to the consciousness of Europeans.

The influence of Egyptian design was most strongly felt in fashion and jewelry, but other areas of design, including architecture, also borrowed Egyptian themes. Necklaces, chokers, and bracelets were fashioned using Egyptian symbols or directly copied from Egyptian jewelry. Lapis lazuli and other gemstones came into popularity. English 1930s potter Clarice Cliff's "Archaic" vases are direct steals from the capitals of Egyptian columns.

ANCIENT ARCHITECTURE

The ziggurat or stepped temple, as mentioned in the section on "Motifs," had a strong influence on architecture. Its lines were also abstracted to create many of the patterning motifs commonly associated with Art Deco.

The ziggurat had parallels in the New World: Native American, Mayan, and Aztec pueblo and temple designs and architecture can be said to have influenced the stepped-back look of everything from skyscrapers and other buildings to mantel clocks, radios, and American Paul Frankl's famous bookcases.

In addition, this native American architecture greatly influenced the architecture of the Southwest, in both the line and color of its decoration, friezes, moldings and more, to a point where some have called this style "Pueblo Deco."

SCIENCE FICTION

Science fiction, too, played an important "modernistic" and "mechanistic" role. H. G. Wells' books were tremendously popular in the early 1930s. In popular culture and graphics, no influence was greater than Buck Rogers and Flash Gordon.

Urban utopian worlds were envisioned, where the machine was put to the service of humanity. Frank Lloyd Wright's 1934 proposals for "Broadacre City" were utopian in concept. Le Corbusier's projects for the "Radiant City," 1930–1936, and the earlier 1925 "Plan Voisin" for Paris, were idealistic and socialistic. His idea was to level certain arrondissements, or "districts," of Paris and create a model city of high-rise structures that would house three million inhabitants.

The 1926 German movie *Metropolis* by Fritz Lang showed the utopian city to be mechanistic, populated by human robots as envisioned by Lang's pre-Expressionist designers. In Germany, Lang's film had had a profound effect on graphic design and advertising art.

THE MACHINE

The machine would be perhaps the greatest influence of all, and the one that was most internationally felt. The goal of the Machine Age was to mass-produce, mass-distribute, and a-mass the profits. Design changed to fit the mode of production, and the results were far removed from the early French Art Deco creations of designers in the Société des Artistes Décorateurs.

Modes of transport—the airplane, train, ocean liner, and automobile—came to symbolize a new generation in which people traveled everywhere and speed reigned. But speed could only reign if the designs were streamlined and aerodynamically sleek.

All other design would be swept along in Machine Age style: advertising art, fashion, tableware, salt and pepper shakers, compact cases, earrings, dressing tables—the list is endless. Even public monuments became simpler and more streamlined. Ultimately, it was the machines themselves—refrigerators, stoves, irons, phonographs, radios, and toasters—that became the main objects of design for the machine.

THE PARIS EXPOSITION OF 1925

The 1925 Paris Exposition Internationale des Arts Décoratifs et Industriels Modernes was underwritten by the French government. It was the Ministry of Finance which called for the exposition to be held. The French government controlled important industries for the manufacture of household goods and furnishings, such as the National Manufacture for porcelain and pottery at Sèvres. The goal of the Exposition was blatantly to promote French production and to establish the French as the arbiters of "good taste" for the entire civilized world.

Well, it worked to a certain degree!

A long time had passed since the last major international exhibition in Paris in 1900. At that time, Art Nouveau still dominated the avant-garde. The 1925 Exposition had been planned as early as 1909. At that time, concerns about the quality of decorative arts had promoted the department stores to organize competitions. The government agreed that an exposition was needed and started developing plans for it, but it was postponed because of World War I. Thus, the 1925 Exposition was really the culmination of many years of innovative French design.

Poster by Robert Bonfils
for the 1925 Paris Exposition.
Author's collection.
Photo by Robert Four.

In the exhibition pavilions hosted by the large French department stores—Les Grands Magasins du Louvre, Bon Marché, Les Galeries Lafayette, and Le Printemps—furniture, lamps, mantel clocks, glassware, and jewelry reflected the new style. It was the exaltation of everyday objects into the realm of art. In fact, the rules for the exhibition explicitly forbade artists from displaying any object that relied on any historic European designs or patterns.

The exhibition was by no means comprehensive, although it included work by some of the most notable architects and designers of the time: architects Robert Mallet-Stevens and Melnikoff; painters Léger and Robert and Sonia Delaunay; sculptors Laurens and Lipchytz; and designers Pierre Chareau, Pierre Legrain, René Lalique, Jean Dunand, Paul Iribe, and Jean Puiforcat.

However, Le Corbusier's and Ozenfant's Pavillon de l'Esprit Nouveau, or "Pavilion of the New Spirit," named after a review they founded in 1920 to disseminate their pure Modernist views, was only begrudgingly included. The artists who had influenced Corbusier—the Bauhaus, Deutscher Werkbund, and Dutch De Stijl movements—were completely excluded. Josef Hoffmann and some of his contemporaries worked on the Austrian Pavilion, but the French pavilions had little to do with the Modern style.

France as a nation had not yet felt the economic imperatives that caused other nations to more readily adopt Modernism and new materials, as it would in the years ahead. Socially, the early deluxe style still held great sway. The new style was considered less "tasteful," and the French were not eager to part with macassar ebony cabinets, inlaid ivory, carved tassels on Süe et Mare furniture, and the flowery textiles of Paul Follot.

The exposition was a showcase for the art of the *ensemblier*, or "interior designer," who had come both to design and to commission fine works and to create "an ensemble" for a room with a single vision or "look." This was in spite of the fact that most people could not afford the services of *ensembliers* and had to make do with what they bought in the department stores.

The site chosen was at the heart of Paris and embraced a huge area including the banks and bridges of the river Seine and the Esplanade des Invalides where Napoleon is entombed. The pavilions of other countries were spread along the river and included Turkish, Danish, Swiss, Italian, Japanese, Austrian, Swedish, Polish, Belgian, Dutch, and British exhibits, and those of many other nations. The French sections were the largest, with almost a hundred pavilions, and were spread on the South Bank, centering on the pavilion called Ambassade Française, or "French Embassy."

The Eiffel Tower, which had been seen as scandalous and vulgar when it was built, had now become a symbol of the modern world. It was illuminated with changing patterns of lights created as a promotional effort by Citroën Corporation.

The Ambassade Française held the most prominent position and was put together to showcase the true geniuses of French design. Every room was completely furnished, carpeted, curtained, and fitted with glass and silver, ivory and jade ornaments, sculptures, and paintings. The reception rooms contained textiles by Raoul Dufy, metalwork by Edgar Brandt, and glass by Lalique. The series of rooms ended with a winter garden designed by Robert Mallet-Stevens overlooking the court and adjoining music room. Mallet-Stevens also designed the Pavilion de Tourisme.

Another of the most admired buildings at the exposition was the Hôtel d'un Riche Collectioneur, designed by Emile-Jacques Ruhlmann, built by Pierre Patout, and filled with Ruhlmann furniture of the most luxurious kind, as the "Home of a Rich Collector" should be.

Ruhlmann went to great lengths to obtain rare and precious materials for his clients, and his work was expensive even for the times. He collaborated with the leading artists to execute his designs. He furnished homes for many wealthy manufacturers, and had pieces purchased by the French government for the Elysées Palace, the French equivalent of the White House.

Of almost equal prominence to his pavilion was the Lalique Pavilion. Of course, Lalique would exploit the use of glass to its fullest, and even created a public fountain in the shape of an obelisk which was illuminated at night.

The Galeries Lafayette Pavilion was designed in their own studio known as La Maîtrise, under the direction of Maurice Dufrène. Dufrène's style used curved forms, discreet and indirect lighting, and subtle colors. The dominant color was rose, contrasting with the silver frames and black marble tabletops, and with lighter lemonwood or maple furniture.

The Magasins du Printemps and the work of their studio, Primavera, were housed in a building designed with a hyperbolic concrete dome encrusted with small circular pieces of glass.

By contrast, the Bon Marché Pavilion was more rectangular and monumental, and was furnished to perfection by Paul Follot, the director of Pomone, Bon Marché's studio.

The work of Studium Louvre of the Grands Magasins du Louvre was housed in a building with a balcony full of flowers, and windows where mannequins were seen with bobbed hair and cloche hats modeling dresses from *Vogue*. The door to this pavilion was pure Deco, with multiple moldings stepped back in a frame-within-a-frame pattern.

It is difficult for someone today to feel as people did in 1920. "The war to end all wars" was over. An entire generation which had seen misery on a greater scale than ever before in history now turned to color and luxury with a greater appetite than ever before. They also had an optimism about the future that no generation has so completely shared since.

Art Deco appealed to an emerging upper-middle-class population that was reaping the benefits of industrialization and evolving from "tasteful" to "progressive" in their tastes and habits. The Great Depression was years ahead, and many felt no need even to look at the mass-produced works of the Germanic nations.

Even more than the movements that had preceded it, Art Deco conceived of a room as a harmonious whole in which each object, functional or artistic, contributed to the overall work of art. Style was seen as the spirit of the era, and the role of the interior decorator was to gain great wealth by giving people a full complement of their own personal brand of style. Much individuality characterizes the production of this era.

The right of the decorator to an equal status with the painter, sculptor, and architect rested on the ability to recreate the effect of art through decoration—that is, to emotionally and intellectually impact the viewers, and make them feel they had glimpsed something for the very first time.

Perhaps the greatest in achieving this effect was Paul Poiret, who displayed his work on three barges anchored in the Seine River. Although Poiret's real genius lay in fashion design, his barges were among the most popular features of the exposition, although they were a financial disaster. Poiret succeeded in what had become a highly intellectual and sophisticated art form—achieving a quality described best by that often overused word, "chic."

LE PAVILLON DE L'ESPRIT NOUVEAU

Le Corbusier's pavilion and its contents were pivotal to the Modern movement in architecture and the decorative arts in France.

Le Corbusier had been influenced by Walter Gropius of the Bauhaus, as well as by Josef Hoffmann and the Wiener Werkstätte. In addition, he was an intelligent, articulate writer, and the leading French proponent of the new style. He was the architect who would replace the interior designer as the trendsetter. His pavilion faced bitter opposition for its design from the director of the exposition. It was only in the last minutes before opening, because of the direct intervention of the Minister of Fine Arts, that a thirty-foot fence that had been constructed to hide the pavilion was dismantled.

The purpose of the building, bluntly, was to deny the need for decorative art. Furniture, in Le Corbusier's estimation, was "household equipment that a building needs." He also successfully exploited the new possibilities of steel and concrete architectural construction. According to one chronicle of the period, after the French Embassy, this pavilion was "like a cold plunge after a Turkish bath."

The first half of the building was designed and furnished as a living space. The second part was an exhibition gallery where Le Corbusier set up his model for his Plan Voisin de Paris, or "Neighborhood Plan for Paris." His model showed the ideal city: a series of evenly placed tall buildings that could provide housing for three million people, as well as shops, offices, stores, and theaters.

Today, we may look at this design and feel lucky that it never came to pass. We already have enough "canyons" of tall buildings in our cities. However, the Plan Voisin was not a developer's get-rich-quick scheme, but rather a thoughtful interpretation of a socialistic utopian future, where the machine served humanity, and all persons were equally served.

Although others may have feared that the machine would enslave people by taking away individuality and craftsmanship, Le Corbusier saw the machine as a new liberator toward an even better society. In his 1926 book, *L'Art Décoratif d'Aujourd'hui*, Le Corbusier summarized his thinking on decorative arts and their place in the Machine Age:

> The past is not infallible. It had some things that were beautiful and some that were ugly. There are today, and more will emerge, consequences of the crisis that separates the pre-mechanistic society from the new mechanistic society. Decorative art is an imprecise and inexact term. The decorative arts are simply equipment, beautiful equipment. The machine, that modern phenomenon, is bringing about a transformation of the spirit in the world. Architecture is a spiritual system which fixes in a material way the sentiment of an era . . . and everything is integrated into an architectural system. We are no longer in an era of dilettantism, but rather a difficult and epic era, serious and violent, hasty and productive, fertile and economic. Decorative arts were basically anti-technical. They were going in the opposite way as the general direction of the epoch.

In practice, Modernism proved not to be as sterile or as undecorative as it may have sounded in theory. Le Corbusier's now-famous tubular steel chair with stretched pony-skin seat and built-in footrest today seems elegant and refined.

The extremes of Modernism would not hold sway except perhaps in the field of industrial design. As the movement gained momentum in the United States, it acquired the American taste for color and boldness, and was transformed once again into something that was "stylish," but decidedly American.

ART DECO AND AMERICA

In 1925, the year of the Paris Exposition, fashion designer Erté set sail for Hollywood, there to influence the film industry through his elaborate designs for sets and costumes for Metro-Goldwyn-Mayer. In consequence, he set new tastes for the American public. Well-known to American fashion-followers, he had been under exclusive contract to illustrate for *Harper's Bazaar* for ten years.

However, the first foothold gained by Art Deco in America had really been because of the work of committed museum curators and others who had recognized the importance of the style long before the public. A fund created in 1922 for the Department of Decorative Arts of the Metropolitan Museum of Art, New York, enabled it to purchase and commission examples of modern decorative art in Europe and America.

Joseph Beck, curator during 1922–1923, built up a collection of quality examples of Art Deco style. In 1926, the museum presented the "International Exhibition of Art in Industry," featuring some of the best of the 1925 Paris Exposition. The exhibition, sponsored by R. H. Macy, toured several cities in the United States, including Boston, Philadelphia, Cleveland, Detroit, St. Louis, Minneapolis, and Pittsburgh.

In 1927, commerce followed art, and Macy's hosted an exhibition and sale of contemporary decorative arts under the name "Art in Trade." Other department stores in New York, Los Angeles, and Chicago followed suit with their own exhibitions and "moderne" boutique departments.

The French style of Art Deco was not readily adopted in America, however. Art Deco had to pass through the American lifestyle and be transformed by both social and cultural influences: the need for mass production, jazz, and Hollywood. It would also be greatly transformed by Modernist designers already at work in the United States, already borrowing on a more Germanic, Bauhaus philosophy and idiom. Urbanization meant smaller living quarters, and the new Industrial Age would redesign Americans' entire surroundings to fit.

The year 1927 gives a very good picture of how America had changed. In that year, for the first time in history, hemlines rose above women's knees—fashion was keeping pace with the popularization of a new image for women as jazz-loving, cigarette-smoking, short-haired, independent, and slim. Symbolically and physically bringing America and Europe closer together, Charles Lindbergh made the first solo flight to Paris. Meanwhile, in other things American, Babe Ruth hit sixty home runs, Jack Dempsey and Gene Tunney met in one of the greatest prizefights ever, and Al Jolson and *The Jazz Singer* brought talking pictures to Hollywood.

**Bronze andirons
by Eliel Saarinen,
c. 1929.**
*Courtesy of the
Cranbrook Academy
of Art Museum,
Michigan.*

Prohibition had been in place for seven years, and numbers of people were flouting the law and going to speakeasies. Flappers drank champagne from high heels, and middle-class Americans were having "private" parties at home.

Sacco and Vanzetti were executed in the electric chair in Charlestown, Massachusetts, causing unrest among the working class in this country and rioting in London and Paris. The Ford Model A was introduced, and radio sales were booming. George Gershwin's "American in Paris" premiered.

The great stock market crash of 1929 was just two years away.

Starting in the mid-1920s, avant-garde American designers quietly but persistently moved toward a Modern style in architectural and household design. A host of talented immigrants from many countries made their impact felt: Bruno Paul, Walter von Nessen, and Lucien Bernhard from Germany; Joseph Urban, who headed the Wiener Werkstätte Gallery in New York; Paul Frankl from Austria; Alexander Archipenko from Denmark; and Eliel Saarinen from Finland were working in America before the impact of French Art Deco arrived on the scene.

Saarinen, an architect and designer, had emigrated from Finland in 1922 and became the first director of the Cranbrook Academy of Art near Detroit. This academy provided a nurturing ground for American Art Deco design, and many years later was the site of one of the major revival exhibitions in the early 1970s. Major artists of Cranbrook included Eliel Saarinen's wife, Loja Saarinen, who used geometric natural forms in her textiles; ceramist Maija Grotell; and sculptor Carl Miles.

In the Midwest, R. Guy Cowan's pottery studio near Cleveland was making a direct connection with Vienna through its talented artists like Russell Aitken and Viktor Schreckengost.

**Worker retouching
figurine at Cowan
Pottery, Ohio, c. 1928.**
*Courtesy of the Cowan
Pottery Museum, Ohio.*

In 1926, Norman Bel Geddes traveled to Europe to study the work of Le Corbusier, and returned with a commitment to streamlining and modern materials.

The early Modernists in America were secure enough in their own ideas to absorb and transform the impact of French Art Deco. When the more than four hundred works from the 1925 Paris Exposition made their tour of the United States over the next two years, American designers absorbed much of the aesthetic of Art Deco, but radically transformed the final product through the use of new materials, industrial techniques, and, ultimately, streamlining for mass production.

In many ways, a streamlined industrial product is about as far away as you can get from a sideboard in macassar ebony with ivory inlay. Yet perhaps today they are both called "Art Deco" because of what they share: a studied coolness, a self-conscious stylishness, and a concern for form meeting function that mandates a decorative rationality—with just a touch of Coco Chanel's daring.

As had happened in Europe, Modern design in America met with initial resistance, and artists banded together to promote their new vision in such groups as the American Designers' Gallery and Contempora. Unlike European design, American design received no official or governmental patronage. The American Designers' Gallery hosted its first exhibition of all-American designers in 1928.

Early French Art Deco had become so expensive and so "establishment" that designers such as Ruhlmann and Dunand survived on official commissions from the government, banks, hotels, and other institutions.

For example, when the luxury French ocean liner *Normandie* was outfitted in 1935, it was like a commissioned floating museum of the best in French Art Deco design. Jean Dupas sculpted wall murals that were lacquered by Jean Dunand, and there were textiles by Rodier and furniture by Jules Leleu. Other ocean liners, such as the *Ile de France* and the *Atlantique*, also had commissioned Art Deco interiors.

By that time, international travel had become more affordable and more tempting, and the grand ocean liners became everyman's floating dream of Hollywood. Travel posters recapture the marketed grandeur of ocean travel. Today, many collectors focus their attention on the Art Deco furnishings, souvenirs, and ephemera from the great ocean liners. However, the lavish early Art Deco was soon to be abandoned entirely by a world faced with grim economic and political realities.

The United States rivaled and then surpassed France for preeminence in the design field as the world turned increasingly toward industrialization. Architects such as William Van Alen, who designed the Chrysler Building in 1930, and Raymond Hood, one of the designers for John D. Rockefeller, led the way. The skyscraper was the dominant motif, and Paul Frankl created his "Skyscraper" line of furniture from 1925 to about 1930.

Other architects and designers like Donald Deskey, Kem Weber, Walter Dorwin Teague, Norman Bel Geddes, Henry Dreyfuss, and Raymond Loewy gained increasing recognition for their furniture, decorative, business, and industrial designs.

Loewy created some designs for the English firm Practical Equipment Limited, or PEL, one of the leading manufacturers of Modern furniture in England. It should be noted that England had never really accepted the early Art Deco style, but moved forward quickly with 1930s Modern design. This was especially true in the area of porcelain and ceramics, where the English successfully bridged the gap between studio and mass-produced work with designers such as Keith Murray for Wedgwood, Susie Cooper for Crown Works, and Clarice Cliff for the Arthur J. Wilkinson Company.

Between 1927 and 1932, the year that the famous Radio City Music Hall and the Empire State Building would be built, the new design style raged through American fashion and life, in spite of the stock market crash and the ensuing bad times.

In 1929, the Metropolitan Museum of Art hosted its own exhibition to show the best of what was being done in America and to encourage the creation of a new decorative style adapted to the needs of urban modern life. Entitled "The Architect and the Industrial Arts," it displayed a series of interiors by architect-designers.

In 1931, the American Union of Decorative Artists and Craftsmen, or AUDAC, held an exhibition at the Brooklyn Museum, and the range of design shown was broader than that shown at any museum exhibition previous—fabrics, radio cabinets, architectural models, furniture, and decorative and graphic arts. The show caused a marked progression toward a machine aesthetic, promoted by such designers as Russel Wright.

By 1931, the annual exhibition at the Metropolitan included industrially produced objects. By 1934, perhaps because of the Depression, it emphasized objects that could be easily and cheaply mass-produced, like Chase Chrome designs by Walter von Nessen, in an exhibition entitled "Contemporary American Industrial Art." The same year, the "Machine Art" exhibition debuted at New York's Museum of Modern Art.

Art Deco had survived the Wall Street crash of 1929 by becoming more functional and more readily mass-produced, but by retaining its stylishness. The Depression brought with it the new profession of industrial designer, someone whose job it was to create products that not only worked, but were good-looking enough to tempt the public to start buying again.

With the end of Prohibition, an array of bars, bar stools, cocktail shakers, ashtrays, and glasses were produced for "stylish entertaining." Over the next few years, handcrafting declined, and mass-produced industrial items flooded the market in the Streamline style and jazzy tilted angles. Jazz affected the design of everything from tea sets to ladies' hand mirrors to ceramic decoration.

Streamlining was an essentially American development. It changed the emphasis of Art Deco from vertical to horizontal lines. Smooth, rounded curves replaced most of the Cubists' geometric influence in design, and they were better suited to industrial manufacture.

The Art Deco style in America was transformed in yet another way—regionally. In a country this size, the regional transformation of the style resulted in distinct styles within the style.

In Florida and Cuba, a so-called Tropical Deco prevailed. Miami Beach was the place to go, or to stop on your way to the casinos and nightlife of Havana. Not surprisingly, Tropical Deco emerged with a softer palette and a sunnier face. It had a vacationer's vision of the grimier "Industrial Deco" of New York and Chicago, with its constant theme of progress via the machine.

Hollywood Deco or "Screen Deco," as it has been called, used and exaggerated Art Deco styling for its films, and continues to call on its appeal to sell tickets in films today. "Pueblo Deco" incorporated Modern design with Native American influences in elaborately beautiful structures in places like Tulsa, Oklahoma.

The Chicago "Century of Progress" Exposition in 1933 marked a high point of art in industrial design, and souvenirs of this exposition are very collectible today. Many feel that the last great expression of the Modern style in America came with the New York World's Fair of 1939. Some say that the more than twenty-five thousand different types of souvenirs of the 1939 New York World's Fair, sold to millions, signaled the end of Art Deco as a predominant design style.

By 1940, Art Deco was almost *too* stylish for a world faced with rationing, and lost its appeal to unadorned concrete, steel, and glass. In addition, the adoption by the German Nazi and Italian Fascist regimes of extremely stylized geometric patterns and designs for their propaganda posters and graphics did little to help maintain the style's popularity.

The Art Deco patterns and color combinations seemed to be repeated so often that they lost their appeal, but there were only drab wartime colors to replace them. Photographic effects increasingly began to replace the bold, strong graphics of Art Deco advertising art and illustration. The kitsch quality of Art Deco designs and novelties increased, and was vaguely and superficially perpetuated in cheap ceramics and other dime store items through the 1950s.

Many apartment blocks had fan-shaped hallway lights and fake square columns with Deco-motif cornices, but painted plaster moldings had replaced those made from wood or metal. Chrome and stainless steel were replaced with the even cheaper aluminum.

So broad and universal was the kitsch application of Art Deco motifs that many people are still conditioned against "liking" Deco, and many more remain unaware of the mastery and high quality of the style in its heyday.

It was thus more than the onset of World War II that finally ended the Art Deco fever: people's attitudes toward the production of the era changed as its products were produced in abundance. Designers and artists stopped working in the style and sought new frontiers. The Art Deco era had come to an end.

After the war, it was as if Art Deco had never existed. For example, when he died in 1950, the French artist Louis Icart was practically unknown. His etchings, which had been produced in extremely large quantities by the Louis Icart Society in New York, could be bought for pennies.

In the post–World War II years, French Art Deco seemed dated, perhaps a bit too elitist, and was largely ignored or forgotten. The later phases of the style appeared too cold, too mechanistic for a world that now realized that the machine did not necessarily lead to peace and prosperity—it could also lead to war.

Modern materials still were used, but "Biomorphism," a more organic style that had begun to emerge in the 1930s, gained popularity.

In the 1950s, after the war was over, America went on a binge. The whimsy of the period is best seen in coffee tables that looked like enormous bohemian artists' palettes, outrageous plastic sunglasses, clear plastic high heels, plastic handbags, and plastic everything.

The flying saucer became the most popular speculation and a popular symbol, and was quickly turned into bedroom lamps, space heaters, and other everyday objects. The molecular structure entered the general consciousness and found its way into design, especially in items such as kitchen wall clocks. Television, popular music, and "Negro" motif lamps replaced America's wonderment with the radio, smoky urban nightclubs, and sleek cigarette lighters.

THE ART DECO REVIVAL

Not until the late 1960s and early 1970s did Art Deco begin to enjoy a renaissance. At the time, some people felt that its resurgence was tied to a sort of historicism, tempered with a touch of nostalgia. Few expected the repopularization of Deco to last or to be so strong.

As with the early popularization of Art Deco, the revival owes much to museum shows. As opposed to its promotion by manufacturers in the 1920s and 1930s, Art Deco's popularity today is due in large measure to the research and promotion done by collectors, dealers, auction houses, and Art Deco societies—and to the dozens of books that have appeared in the last two decades.

The Musée des Arts Décoratifs in Paris launched a retrospective exhibition entitled "Les Années 25" in 1966, sending Art Deco shock waves through the design world once again. In 1970, Finch College Museum hosted the first revival exhibition of Art Deco in the United States, and was followed the next year by an expanded version of the exhibition at the Minneapolis Institute of Arts, which awakened contemporary collectors to the importance of Art Deco.

The Finch College Museum exhibition presented over 550 objects, from furniture to costume jewelry, and helped America rediscover Art Deco from many different countries. The Minneapolis exhibit increased that number to close to 1,500 objects. These exhibitions opened wide the doors of nostalgia for Art Deco and embraced the widest interpretation of the term for collectors.

Among the wide variety of works that were included at the Finch exhibition alone were bronze and ivory ("chryselephantine") statues of dancing and Egyptian figures by D. H. Chiparus; sculpture by Edouard Marcel Sandoz; gouaches from the flamboyant Erté; London subway posters by E. McKnight Kauffer; rare bookbindings; and jewelry by René Lalique, Georges Fouquet, Van Cleef & Arpels, and Cartier, including a rare lapel brooch watch in jade, chimera, gold, platinum, rubies, diamonds, onyx, and black enamel.

The furniture displayed was by a wide variety of designers and reflected the great divergence of styles grouped under the name "Art Deco": lacquered screens by Jean Dunand; a chair and dressing table by Paul Frankl; pieces by Léon Jallot, Armand-Albert Ratteau, and Emile-Jacques Ruhlmann, such as his sideboard in burled walnut with black marble top and bronze medallions, which had been exhibited in 1925 in Paris.

Many additional well-known designers were represented, including metalwork craftsman Edgar Brandt; glass artist Antoine Daum; and English potter Clarice Cliff.

Of course, no exhibition of Art Deco glass would have been complete without the work of Gaston Louis Vuitton and René Lalique, whose "Carthage" vase of clear glass with matte finish exterior and carved bird motif on each of eight buttresses, created in 1932, still made viewers gasp.

The exhibition included a chrome tubular steel chair with cane back and seat by Mies van der Rohe; a side chair with octagonal seat and hexagonal back designed for the Imperial Hotel in Tokyo by Frank Lloyd Wright; and works from Wiener Werkstätte.

Silver on display included pieces from the Orfeverie Christofle and from the master silversmith Jean Puiforcat. Textiles included the exuberant floral designs of Raoul Dufy and a wide variety of wallpapers, draperies, and bedcovers.

Albert Cheuret's 1930 Egyptian-inspired mantel clock was there. Broadway's *Funny Girl* star Barbra Streisand, an early collector of Art Deco, lent a Cartier clock in crystal, mounted with enameled gold and rose diamonds. Streisand lent other objects to the collection, including a Czechoslovakian atomizer with etched ruby panels, a gouache by John Vassos, and a floral-designed glass lamp by G. Argy-Rousseau.

Still, Art Deco was far from popular when these museums began to pay attention to it. Many art and antiques dealers were skeptical of the resurgence of interest, and felt perhaps it was only a passing fad. It was individual vanguard collectors and museums which were most attracted to collecting Art Deco during the revival period—an attraction that was to pay off handsomely.

These early revival exhibitions paid less attention to American designers, who have since come into their own on the collecting market. They also did little to promote the mass-produced American manufactures during the Depression, or the Streamline design of industrial collectibles.

Today, more than twenty years after the Finch exhibition, the collecting field for Art Deco has expanded far beyond the well-known names of French Art Deco. It now actively includes a variety of productions of other nationalities, broadening it even more as a collecting field, and adding new interest.

THE REDISCOVERY OF AMERICAN ART DECO

Something about the Bicentennial of 1976 refocused our attention on things American and rekindled an interest in our own heritage that has affected the collecting market ever since. At about that time, knowledgeable Art Deco collectors started buying American Art Deco in earnest.

In 1983, Yale University hosted "At Home in Manhattan: Modern Decorative Arts, 1925 to the Depression." The same year, another exhibition, "Design in America: The Cranbrook Vision 1925–1950," organized by the Metropolitan Museum of Art and the Detroit Institute of Art, in conjunction with Cranbrook Academy of Art, made a somewhat bigger splash. In 1986 and 1987, major exhibitions and shows had an impact on the Art Deco collecting market in a tremendous way.

In 1986, the Whitney Museum hosted "High Styles," the first in-depth exhibition of American 20th-century decorative arts. It included Tiffany and Art Nouveau, but also emphasized major Modern designers like Joseph Urban, Donald Deskey, Raymond Hood, and Kem Weber.

The same year, the Brooklyn Museum hosted "The Machine Age in America, 1918–1941," and vigorously reintroduced the industrial design and mass-produced furnishings of Walter Dorwin Teague, Walter von Nessen, Raymond Loewy, Russel Wright, and many others. In 1987, the Renwick Gallery of the Smithsonian Institution hosted "American Art Deco," which strongly focused the attention of the market on the best of our own Art Deco design heritage.

In the late 1980s, the Art Deco market surged forward at numerous specialized shows and dealer exhibitions. New Art Deco societies were created, focusing more public attention on preserving buildings, the largest examples of Art Deco, and broadening appreciation for the style. A continuing stream of important museum exhibitions take place both here and abroad.

While sales of Art Deco, like all areas of collecting, were affected by the economic downturn of the late 1980s and early 1990s, the collecting base continued to expand. Some areas, in which there was tremendous overspeculation, literally crashed in price, and it will take some time for them to recover. Other collecting areas stabilized within a year or two, and others are today back on the climb, with a host of new collectors who bought when the market was down. In addition, new collecting specializations emerged. (See "Today's Market.")

An important role in this expansion has been played by the dozens of books that have appeared since 1985. These include many new books on the more expensive Art Deco production as well as reissues of manufacturers' catalogues, and books focusing on inexpensively produced and more widely available collectibles: chrome, ceramics, plastics, ephemera, glassware, costume jewelry, graphics, industrial design, and other collecting fields that are still accessible to beginning Art Deco collectors.

As we fast approach the 21st century, the design of the early 20th century takes on an added importance. Today, there is an active, mature market for the vast array of "high-end," "mid-range," and "low-end" objects in the Art Deco style. We are sure that there are still some discoveries to be made and that the market will redefine itself further, but no matter what your collecting interest or financial resources, you can find something in Art Deco that fits your personality and your pocketbook, and you can start collecting for the 21st century.

ARCHITECTURE AND THE ART DECO PRESERVATION MOVEMENT

PRESERVING OUR ARCHITECTURAL HERITAGE

In January 1991, the Fourteenth Annual Art Deco Weekend, sponsored by the Miami Design Preservation League (MDPL), took place, once again thrilling "Decophiles" with a daily dose of streamlined chic: entertainment from the age of Cole Porter, trolley tours of the Art Deco District from Flamingo Park to the seaswept Ocean Drive, a rowing regatta, the "Moon Over Miami Ball," and even an exhibition of Art Deco toys at the Bass Museum

Yet not everyone had come to Miami Beach with just fun and festivities in mind. Earlier the same week, the MDPL had hosted the First World Congress on Art Deco, a groundbreaking conference attended by concerned individuals and representatives from Art Deco societies and preservation organizations throughout the world.

The dream of activist/preservationist Barbara Baer Capitman, who sadly had died in 1990 before seeing it come to fruition, the First World Congress was an international forum of exchange. Presentations focused on efforts to document and save Art Deco architecture in Australia, New Zealand, Canada, Indonesia, Argentina, England, and numerous cities in the United States, including Dallas, Tulsa, and San Diego.

The MDPL, founded in 1976, is the oldest Art Deco society in the world, and has been the driving force behind the preservation of the Art Deco District of Miami Beach. As the country's largest concentration of Art Deco architecture, containing about eight hundred

Logo illustration.
Courtesy of the Miami Design Preservation League.

significant buildings in both the Art Deco and Mediterranean Revival styles, the district was named to the National Register of Historic Places in 1979, enhancing, but not assuring, its chances for survival.

A growing appreciation and awareness of Art Deco decorative arts in the late 1970s paralleled the rise of the preservation movement. Shortly after the creation of the MDPL, Art Deco societies were started in New York, San Francisco, Chicago, and Washington, D.C., followed by cities such as Detroit, Los Angeles, Palm Beach, and Boston. More recently, Art Deco societies have been launched in Sacramento, Cleveland, and Charleston. Societies also exist in Australia, New Zealand, Canada, and England. (See the list of active Art Deco societies in the "Resource Guide.")

What clearly emerged from the congress was a picture of Art Deco as a significant worldwide movement in architecture and in the efforts to preserve it. A map of the world created for the congress was pinned with photos showing Art Deco architecture on every continent of the globe except Antarctica. Future world congresses were announced for October 1993, hosted by the Art Deco Society of Western Australia, and for 1995, hosted by the Twentieth Century Society in London.

What also emerged from the First World Congress was a need and desire to bring together the Art Deco societies in the United States to share information and preservation strategies, and to support one another's local efforts.

The following January 1992, MDPL sponsored a three-day Art Deco symposium, hosted by the Barbara Baer Capitman Archive Committee of MDPL, headed by Dennis Wilhelm. The symposium included a session called a "Presidents' Council," where representatives from U.S. Art Deco societies had a round-table discussion with concerned individuals representing cities without active societies. The flurry of exchange and discussion led to a unanimous decision to create the National Coalition of Art Deco Societies (NCADS).

The goal of NCADS is to explore new ways to promote the understanding, appreciation, and preservation of Art Deco. It is also a network of mutual support for Art Deco societies, most of which are nonprofit or membership organizations working with all-volunteer boards and staffs.

The National Coalition serves as a forum for the exchange of news and information, supports each organization's local preservation efforts, and encourages the creation of Art Deco societies in other cities. Its long-range goal is to have a voice in national preservation policy issues.

Much of the success story in Miami lies in the MDPL's ability to advocate for preservation ordinances, design controls, and zoning matters. However, it has also faced the bottom-line economics of development by demonstrating, through such activities as Art Deco Weekend, the significant economic impact gained by using Miami Beach's Art Deco heritage as a focus for cultural tourism, and by showing developers that preservation and economic revitalization can go hand in hand.

This success has in turn bred other challenges as a revitalized Miami Beach, talked about constantly in the national press, is now increasingly desirable to developers seeking to capitalize on the region's appeal, causing the MDPL also to take up the battle to promote affordable housing and stave off the negative aspects of "gentrification."

In spite of MDPL's success, some battles to preserve Art Deco architecture are still lost. Take the case of the Sands, the 1939 hotel, which met the wrecker's ball on March 2, 1992. Although the building was included in the National Register District, because of the politics of development (the hotel occupied a prime beachfront area), the city had

The Sands Hotel, 1939,
Miami Beach—gone but
not forgotten.
Photo by Robert Four.

refused to give it protection on a local level. Two weeks after demolition started, in place of the Sands, there was an empty lot. Next door, another lot, once the site of the New Yorker hotel, has stood vacant for ten years.

This loss has pushed Miami Beach preservationists to work even more diligently for the inclusion of the entire National Register District into local preservation ordinances.

As Christine Knop Kallenberger, associate curator of Tulsa's Philbrook Museum of Art, stated at the end of her presentation at the First World Congress, "Obviously recognition and enthusiasm for Art Deco architecture is not enough. Its survival is not assured. We must all be caretakers of that history."

Everywhere in this country and abroad, preservationists are struggling to save Art Deco buildings from demolition or alteration.

The Art Deco Society of Washington, D.C., can be credited with saving both the outstanding Greyhound Bus Terminal and the giant Hecht Warehouse. In Los Angeles, the Art Deco Society was one of the forces that rallied to save the May Company store on Wilshire Boulevard. In Rochester, New York, the Hallman's Chevrolet Building was saved through the work of the Landmark Society of Western New York. The Art Deco Society of Western Australia in Perth has been fighting its preservation battles in the media as much as in the street.

Many people immediately think of the Chrysler Building or Rockefeller Center when Art Deco architecture is mentioned, but most Art Deco structures were relatively small by today's standards. Other cities are now rediscovering their Art Deco banks, theaters, cinemas, schools, and stores, and the Art Deco preservation movement will continue to expand.

Meanwhile, the publicity that these preservation efforts have generated serves two purposes: to focus attention on Art Deco as an important part of our design heritage, and to increase both the support for preservation and the base of Art Deco collectors.

Not only are Art Deco societies actively engaged in preservation issues, they offer lectures and programs on decorative arts, jewelry, posters, and other design of the period. Several host annual Art Deco sales or entire Art Deco weekends with walking tours and gala balls. For over fifteen years, they have been an important force behind the expansion of interest in Art Deco.

ART DECO: AN ARCHITECTURAL STYLE

Early French Art Deco was essentially a style created by furniture designers and fashion illustrators. However, the Modern design movements that would transform the style were led by architects. Today, many people feel that the Art Deco style in America and elsewhere is really shown at its best in architecture.

One early influence was architect/designer Charles Rennie Mackintosh of the Glasgow School, whose use of clear, geometric form in architecture also extended to the design of furniture, mantel clocks, and graphic designs for wallcoverings.

Otto Wagner and Adolf Loos were architects who had a profound influence on Austrian designers, the De Stijl group of Holland, and the German Bauhaus. Joseph Maria Olbrich (1867–1908) was a leading Viennese architect who began following Modern principles. Josef Hoffmann (1870–1956), one of the leaders of the Vienna Secession and an admirer of Mackintosh, was chosen to design the Austrian pavilion for the 1925 Paris Exposition. Peter Behrens, the teacher of Walter Gropius (1883–1969) at the Bauhaus, designed an Expressionist greenhouse attached to Hoffmann's pavilion.

When one thinks of the architecture of the 1930s, one almost automatically thinks of Le Corbusier or of Walter Gropius, Mies van der Rohe, Marcel Breuer, and the Bauhaus School. However, in actuality, Gropius and his followers were banned from the 1925 Paris Exposition and had to set up their own pavilion to show their wares. The French were so embarrassed by Le Corbusier's Pavillon de l'Esprit Nouveau that they tried to hide it behind a thirty-foot fence. Robert Mallet-Stevens (1886–1945) and Andre Lurcat were two other French architect/designers who had taken up the Modern style.

It was not until the 1930s, and its move to the United States, that the Bauhaus School of architecture and design gained true popularity. Many talented European architects emigrated to America. Here their ideas met those of American industrial designers and architects such as Frank Lloyd Wright (1867–1959).

In England, where Breuer lived and worked before joining Gropius at Harvard University, he influenced an entire generation of 1930s architects such as Wells Coates (1895–1958). German architect Erich Mendelsohn (1887–1953) also worked in England before coming to America, where his work helped popularize the "Streamline" style of Modern design.

Another architectural pioneer in America was Austrian-born Joseph Urban, who played a crucial advocacy role for Modern design in America. His career as a set designer first brought him to live in America, and he moved from Boston to New York in about 1917, where he became associated with the Metropolitan Opera Company.

Returning to architecture in 1925, he had six or seven very prolific years that included the design of Palm Beach residences, restaurants, cabarets, retail stores, and the Ziegfeld Theater in New York. By 1930, he was in the vanguard of American architecture along with Raymond Hood (1881–1934), Ely Jacques Kahn, and others, many of whom were creating in the "Skyscraper" style.

The Art Deco "Skyscraper" style in the 1920s and 1930s was itself greatly influenced by ancient styles of architecture, including Egyptian, Mayan, and Aztec stepped temples. Another influence was the "ziggurat" or temple tower of the ancient Assyrian and Babylonian cultures, where each step was smaller than the one below it. (*See the chapter "Other Influences."*)

When people say "Art Deco architecture," they are usually thinking about stepped-back skyscrapers. However, Art Deco was not really a specific "style" of architecture, but rather a distinctive style of modern architectural ornamentation.

As the contour of buildings changed, the ornamentation was often used to draw the viewer's eye to those changes. For example, vertical decorations, the use of piers and bays, or the vertical alignment of windows draw the eye upward, help diminish the feeling of massiveness, and give even looming buildings a sense of speed and sleekness. Horizontal ornamentation on the step-backs, or horizontal banding in the stone, painted or created by the placement of spandrels or moldings, gives the building a rhythmic quality as it rises.

Other ornamentation, such as window moldings, grillwork, sculptural details, cast stones, doors, and tile work on these buildings often have the same stylized motifs that were used in the decorative arts. (*See the section "Motifs."*)

The 1920s and 1930s heyday of Art Deco architecture in America produced some of the most revolutionary and exciting architecture our country possesses. The skyscraper was a truly American phenomenon and the American answer to urban development. There were no skyscrapers in Europe.

America had a history of multistory metal frame buildings starting before the turn of the century. The ever-increasing height of buildings was leading to concern over congestion and the loss of sunlight in American cities, and in 1916, New York passed the first zoning act, which in fact may have helped create the "Skyscraper Style."

This act allowed a building to be built higher, provided it was set back from the street, and it could only rise to the maximum height on one-quarter of its lot. Some say it was this law which forced architects to adopt the new style; others say the new style came along just in time. Whatever the case, the Art Deco stepped-back skyscraper design fit perfectly, and the skyline of urban centers more than doubled in height. Designers began to use the skyscraper motif in everything from vases to coffee pots, cigarette cases, earrings, mantel clocks, furniture, and even textile designs.

The New York City Landmarks Preservation Commission was established in 1965 to protect the city's most important architectural sites from demolition and alteration. In 1974, the first Art Deco building to be named a landmark was the American Radiator Building at 40 West 40th Street, designed by Raymond Hood. Today, numerous Art Deco buildings have landmark designation.

Radio City Music Hall, which celebrated its sixtieth anniversary in 1992, was the first of the buildings forming Rockefeller Center to be completed. It represents an extraordinary concentration of talents: John D. Rockefeller was the developer of the entire center, with three major architectural firms involved in its creation. In addition, René Chambellan (1893–1955) was the architectural sculptor for the Music Hall and Donald Deskey was the interior designer. The well-known precision dance team, the Rockettes, has been an integral part of Radio City Music Hall since its opening night in December 1932.

The interior was named a landmark in 1978, meaning that all public areas of the theater, as well as carpets, drapes, wallcoverings, and furnishings had to be maintained in their original design, fabric, color, and style, setting off a nationwide search for original components. The original plates for the silver- and gold-toned wallpaper were located in Germany, and over ten thousand yards of floor coverings were rewoven. Its whirlwind restoration was remarkably completed in about one month's time in 1979.

The whole of Rockefeller Center is resplendent with Art Deco sculpture, murals, figural terra cotta, and glass by dozens of talented designers of the day. It is also perhaps the all-time favorite Art Deco walking tour. Whether you are a Rockefeller or not, you can

One of the many stunning architectural ornamentations at Rockefeller Center, New York. *Photo by Robert Four.*

Panel in aluminum by René Chambellan for Alcoa. *Author's collection. Photo by Robert Four.*

enjoy a tour past Paul Manship's monolithic sculpture *Prometheus* in the Lower Plaza; *Atlas*, a seven-ton bronze, and outstanding relief sculpture by Lee Lawrie; magnificent glass relief and limestone incision designs by Attilio Piccirilli; fountain heads by sculptor René Chambellan; huge wall murals by Jose Maria Sert and Dean Cornwell; and the streamlined stainless steel sculpture by Isamu Noguchi (b. 1904) over the door of the Associated Press Building.

Many people feel that the Chrysler Building epitomizes the American Art Deco architectural style. Both the building and the interior have landmark status. Designed by William van Alen (1883–1954), it features remarkable nickel-chrome-steel cladding, dome, and spire that make it an attraction for tourists from all over the world, even though it was quickly eclipsed as the tallest building in the world. Its direct connection with the automobile is emphasized by the enormous ornamental Chrysler radiator caps at the corners of the thirty-first floor.

New York has many other fine examples of Art Deco architecture and architectural decoration—the Waldorf Astoria Hotel, the McGraw-Hill Building, the Empire State Building, and the Daily News Building by Raymond Hood. The Chanin Building, with its stylized flora and fauna bronze relief panels by René Chambellan, is also well-known. Many other less well-known buildings, such as department stores, schools, theaters, banks, apartment and office buildings, and even prisons were designed or decorated in the new style.

Every major city acquired outstanding examples of Art Deco architecture. The San Francisco Telephone Building was the first skyscraper to be built outside New York, but was soon followed by the Guardian Building in Detroit, the Northern Life Tower in Seattle, and the Richfield Building in Los Angeles.

San Francisco has a number of architectural designs in the Art Deco style, notably by architect Timothy Pflueger (1892–1946), who created the Oakland Paramount, which was restored in 1978 as a civic center. Pflueger also created many of the buildings at the Golden Gate International Exposition of 1939, I. Magnin's, the Castro and Alhambra Theaters, and the San Francisco Stock Exchange with its colorful murals by Diego Rivera.

Washington, D.C., has more Art Deco detailing on government buildings than people usually imagine, although the style has been called "Greco Deco" or "Federal Deco." Apartment and office buildings, stores, restaurants, and churches in Washington also display Art Deco motifs.

In Boston, the stepped-back United Shoe Machinery Building was named a landmark in 1980 by the Boston Landmarks Commission. The completely renovated office building, now called the Landmark, was built in 1928 by the firm Parker, Thomas, and Rice. Almost 10 percent of its brickwork had to be restored, requiring locating and pressing back into service the original quarry in the Midwest. Most of the eighteen hundred cast stone panels in thirty-four different designs had to be replicated. One of its most stunning features is the recessed bronze doorway and transom grillwork where two stylized women are leaning on a shoe-lasting machine—the machine that built the corporate fortune.

So many other American cities have outstanding Art Deco architectural examples: the original art museum in Seattle, the Wisconsin Gas Building in Milwaukee, Cincinnati's Union Terminal, the Kansas City Power & Light Building, Egyptian-inspired commercial and residential buildings in San Diego, the Butler Mansion in Des Moines, the American Laundry Building in Grand Rapids, the National Guard Armory in Minneapolis, the Reynolds Building in Winston-Salem, Tulsa's Boston Avenue Methodist Church, and the Tulsa Fire Alarm Building, to name just a very few.

It is beyond the scope of this book to describe or show the magnificent breadth of Art Deco architecture in America, but in the bibliography you will find numerous volumes focusing on different aspects of Art Deco architecture. An important national survey of Art Deco architecture has also just been completed. Before she died, preservationist Barbara Baer Capitman had begun the task of writing a book entitled *Rediscovering Art Deco U.S.A.* for the publisher E. P. Dutton, a project that was taken up by the MDPL's Dennis Wilhelm and Michael Kinerk, chairman of Art Deco Weekend.

Smaller cities and suburbs felt the impact of the new style as well: bridges, train depots, silos, warehouses, and similar structures were among the first to be affected. Soon, post offices, schools, suburban banks, and so-called taxpayer blocks of one-story

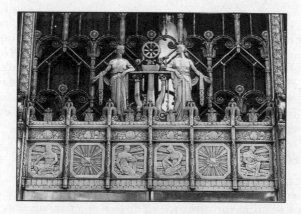

Grillwork on the United Shoe Machinery Building, Boston, 1928. *Photo by Robert Four.*

commercial buildings adopted an Art Deco style, not to mention the shiny "Sterling Streamliner" diner at the edge of town.

What many people know about Art Deco architecture they know because of John Eberson and his son Drew, who built Modern-style movie theaters all over the world. Born of the nickelodeons in 1906, the movie houses adopted the gaudiest features of opera house architecture, with gold gilt, marble, and cut-glass chandeliers. In the early 1920s, the "Atmospheric" style predominated, and movie theaters looked like palaces with plaster and ornamental wrought iron. The 1930s brought stepped-back façades, Deco murals, mirrors, and lighting. The few original theaters by the Ebersons, Fox, Loewe and Paramount theaters from the era are finding new advocates and being preserved more than ever before.

The impact of the Bauhaus School of architecture, which has its own vocabulary of form, is felt in Modern-style homes around the country. The term "Long Island Modern" was coined to describe the many structures built there mostly during the 1930s, with outside spiral staircases in metal, decks, and flat or geometric roofs. Beach homes seemed to be the perfect place to experiment with the new style, and their design was well-suited to furnishings by Donald Deskey, Paul Frankl, or Walter von Nessen.

"Pueblo Deco" is the name given to the Deco-inspired architecture of the Southwest, which was also heavily influenced by Native American design, ornamentation, and color palette. The pueblos, or "Indian towns," were like large terraced apartment buildings built from adobe bricks. After 1900, hotels and office buildings began to spring up in places like Fort Worth, Tucson, and Albuquerque. The motifs of Indian pottery, jewelry, and basket work soon appeared on storefronts and city halls throughout the Southwest and Texas.

"Tropical Deco" is the name given to the architectural design, and later the furnishings and decorations, of Florida, cities in the South, and much of the Art Deco architecture of Havana.

It drew on Art Deco motifs such as zigzags and stylized patterning, but it added to the list native plants; birds such as flamingos, herons, and pelicans; and ocean images of waves and sea grass. Sunbathing became popular in the 1920s and 1930s, and the radiating sun became a favorite Art Deco motif while Miami was becoming a favorite vacation spot.

Miami Beach's hotels have stylings like rounded corners, banding or "racing stripes," "eyebrows" over the windows, and etched glass. Stepped parapets and façades, decorative moldings, and patterned friezes abound. Many buildings are in a "Nautical Deco" style, and look like ocean vessels coming into port, complete with ship's towers, portholes, and deck rails. Materials include terrazzo floors made from imbedding granite or marble chips in concrete, glass block, and glass tile, which most often came under the trade names "Vitrolyte" and "Carrara." These buildings also evidence the impact of the Bauhaus on American architecture.

COLLECTORS ARE PRESERVATIONISTS, TOO

Recognizing the forms, motifs, design styles, materials, and sensibilities of Art Deco as expressed in architecture will help you train your eye for the collecting field. Many architects' names will reappear when you read about the furniture, clocks, glass, and other household and decorative objects they designed. Similarly, many of the outstanding Art Deco decorative and fine artists received architectural commissions.

Ceramic relief by Viktor Schreckengost on the
pachyderm building at the Cleveland Zoo.
Photo by Robert Four.

Often, the architect of a building was also the interior designer, and designed the mirrors, lighting fixtures, rails, gates, and metalwork ornaments of a building. Architectural sculptors were commissioned to design reliefs and friezes in bronze, terra cotta, and other materials.

Today, you will increasingly see architectural details and fragments from both residential and commercial buildings on the Art Deco market: windows, lighting fixtures, mantels, doors, spandrels, sconces, mailboxes, grates, and more. The same is true of Art Deco nightclubs, theaters, and cinemas, with their ornate fixtures, door frames, lighting, and mirrors.

These kinds of elements are today being salvaged by knowledgeable dealers and collectors. Salvage companies are doing a stronger business in Art Deco elements than in previous years.

Buying or collecting architectural elements is a means of preserving pieces of our architectural history, but it unfortunately means that another building has been lost or drastically altered.

Of course, not all Art Deco buildings can or will be saved for many reasons, and not all buildings of the period are so distinctive that they are worth saving. Often, landlords feel they must renovate apartment complexes or lose tenants. Commercial storefronts constantly change to attract customers and accommodate the demands of retail merchandising. However, sometimes Art Deco architectural salvage reminds us of going to an art museum to view the capital from a Greek temple column—all that was saved from the rubble. We'd much rather have the temple itself.

The Art Deco preservation field and collecting field fuel each other in many ways. The collecting field, which is now worldwide, is creating an even larger body of individuals who understand and appreciate Art Deco design and artistic output. When collectors begin to see the connections between the decorative arts and the architecture around them, they often also begin to see themselves as preservationists, and as stewards of a rich design history.

2

COLLECTING
ART DECO

HOW TO USE THIS BOOK

Note: *This book is a market survey—not a bible. Our goals are to report on the market, to offer an overview of Art Deco collecting, and to provide a wide variety of resources. Our hope is that you will come away with both some specific information and a broader knowledge and appreciation of many collecting fields, and get a sense of the market in those fields. Then put this book aside, go out, and explore the field that suits your interest and your pocketbook: go to museums and shows, visit dealers, buy reference books and auction catalogues, and experience the market firsthand.*

IF YOU CAN'T FIND IT HERE

We have introduced each collecting area covered with a narrative. Our "Special Focus" sections are written by, or are based on interviews with, outstanding collectors, dealers, and leading authorities. Unfortunately, we could not cover all the fields of Art Deco collecting, nor could we mention all the talented and skillful artists, designers, and manufacturers. In other words, if a particular name you are looking for is not included here, it does not necessarily mean the category is not worth collecting.

We concentrated our market survey on those objects, artists, designers, and manufacturers that a collector is most likely to see on the market in the United States. Some early French Art Deco designers' work is so rare that an important piece may come onto the market only once every few years. Some pieces are more likely to be found on the Art Deco market in countries other than the United States. However, the Art Deco output of numerous countries has found its way to markets here.

TO FIND A PARTICULAR DESIGNER OR MANUFACTURER

If you are looking for information on particular designers or manufacturers, look first under the subject for which they were best known: furnishings, ceramics, industrial design, etc. However, many designers of the Art Deco period worked in several fields, and information on their work may be included in several chapters.

ABOUT THE "RESOURCE GUIDE"

For collectors with particular interests, or those who just want to learn more about Art Deco, we created the extensive "Resource Guide" at the back of this volume.

The "Resource Guide" gives you the names, addresses, and phone numbers of dealers, auction houses, museums, periodicals, associations, and individuals whom we've consulted in putting this book together. There is also a bibliography that will help you find other books. Not all of the books listed are in print, and you may need the help of a book dealer in finding some that are of interest to you.

One great advantage to Art Deco collectors is that the era in which they are interested has been increasingly chronicled in the past two decades. There are still exceptions, but generally it is not too difficult to find information about the artists; designers; personalities; ateliers, or "workshops"; illustrators; and other key players.

This was not always the case. Because much of what Art Deco produced was "popular" in nature—such as posters, fashion, inexpensive housewares, advertising design, industrial goods, and the like—much of it lapsed into relative obscurity until its revival in the 1960s. Even some designers whose genius is recognized today had faded out of memory.

If you'd like to find out more about any of the areas in this book, the "Resource Guide" can help. In addition, the dealers, auction houses, Art Deco societies and others who are listed in the "Resource Guide" are generally willing to answer questions and guide you to other sources of information that will enhance your knowledge of Art Deco.

IMPORTANT NOTES
ON THE PRICE LISTINGS

Note: *We advise you to read this chapter closely. It includes important information on how the prices in this book were established, and other things to watch for in determining values for buying and selling Art Deco.*

As is often true of any collectible object, the value of many Art Deco pieces depends on what the buyer is willing to pay. We know more than one avid Art Deco collector who will pay just about any amount for a rare piece in fine condition that he or she "really needs" for a collection.

To a beginning collector, at first glance, some of the prices given in the following pages may seem high. Some areas of the Art Deco market are now firmly established. The best and often the highest-priced designers are bought by leading collectors of 20th-century decorative arts. In the context of prices achieved for fine arts and for the decorative arts of earlier periods, even the highest prices for Art Deco can appear modest.

Even with the overall setback to prices in the late 1980s and early 1990s, some pieces still break records at auction. However, many original Art Deco objects and collectibles that are very good or fine examples of the style are still within the reach of average collectors.

In each category, we have offered a sampling of prices, and not necessarily an exhaustive list. If you do not find exactly the object you are looking for here, the prices given can still be used for comparison. Also, reputable dealers and auction houses will always be willing to quote what they feel a particular object is worth on the market. If you feel that you have acquired a particularly valuable piece or collection, you may want to pay for a professional appraisal.

HOW WORKS ARE DESCRIBED AND LISTED

For each listing, we give the following information, where it is known or was available to us:

- Name of the designer or manufacturer.
- Country of origin.
- Year or approximate year it was made.
- Size.
- Description, including materials used, and any additional background on the designer or the piece.

- Condition, and any information on condition that may affect value on the market. (*See also "A Key to Collectible Value."*)
- Any notes on the collectibility of the piece (whether it represents an average, good, very good, or fine example of a particular designer, type of object. etc.).
- Any information on stamps, marks, signatures, patent numbers, etc., by which the piece may be identified, and any information on known fakes or forgeries. (*See also "A Key to Collectible Value."*)
- Retail price range or auction price realized.

There is no universal standard for describing the myriad of objects which are bought and sold on the Art Deco market. You will see several methods used. However, for this volume, we have combined a few of the methods which are used by better auction houses and dealers.

For Most of the Listings in This Book

When it is our opinion or the opinion of our resources:

1.   That a piece is the work of a certain designer or manufacturer, by virtue of some documentation, signature, mark, or other means of positive identification, we list the work under the designer's name, may describe it as being **BY** that designer, or simply **DESIGNED FOR** a certain company.
2.   That it is very likely that a piece is the work of a designer or manufacturer, but cannot definitely be confirmed, we list the work under the designer's name, but describe it as being **ATTRIBUTED** to the designer.
3.   That a piece might be the work of a certain designer or manufacturer by virtue of its resemblance to other known works, we list the work under the artist's name, but describe it as being **IN THE STYLE OF** the designer.

For Bronzes and Statues

When it is our opinion or the opinion of our resources:

1.   That a statue is made from an artist's original model, and was cast during the lifetime of the artist or shortly thereafter, we describe the work as being **CAST FROM A MODEL** by the artist.
2.   When it is our opinion that a statue is a later copy, we describe the work as being **CAST AFTER A MODEL** by the artist. (*See the chapters "Fakes Alert!" and "Decorative Sculpture" for more information.*)

HOW GIVEN PRICES WERE ESTABLISHED

The vast majority of price listings in this book were observed by us, or reported to us primarily by collectors, dealers, and auction houses during 1991 and 1992. We also anonymously gathered information about pricing at dealer shops, exhibitions, and antique shows.

Price Ranges

The price ranges given represent a retail price range in which you are likely to find the listed item. However, retail prices can vary greatly depending on the condition of the item, the dealer from whom you are buying, whether the item has been restored, and many other factors. (*See the chapter "A Key to Collectible Value" for more information on condition.*) The price ranges in this volume are offered as a guide only, and are based on prices reported to us by collectors, dealers, and others all over the country.

Auction Prices

When the price given for an item is followed by the word (Auction), it means that this price was reported to us by one of the auction houses listed in the "Resource Guide." These prices represent the final bid, not the final purchase price. That is, they do not include the "buyer's premium" charged by most auction houses, which is usually 10 percent, plus any applicable sales tax or other charges.

Multiple Prices

Where more than one auction price, or where both an auction price and a retail price are known, the description may be followed by more than one price indication. In some instances, you will see that an auction price exceeded the retail price at which the item is generally available on the market.

In evaluating Art Deco, whether you are buying or selling, there are a few additional points to consider in setting prices:

Prices in the market can change rapidly

Some areas cool off, other trends pop up. It seems that there are always at least a handful of Art Deco collecting fields that are "hot"—marked by a flurry of buying and selling activity—and prices spiral upward.

Important discoveries, new books, exhibitions, auctions, and other factors can send prices up or down almost overnight. The designer of a previously "anonymous" object might be identified. It might be discovered that fewer—or many more—examples of a work exist. A rash of fakes can send prices tumbling as collectors become wary of a particular field.

The Art Deco market was not immune to the economic woes of the late 1980s and early 1990s. After the buying frenzy in the late 1980s, some areas tumbled 20 to 25 percent. A few crashed to 50 percent of their previous value, and will take some time to recover. Prices held stable in some areas, and others just continued climbing.

At the same time, new collecting specializations emerged, attention was focused on new aspects of Art Deco production, and a host of new collectors were drawn to the market by a variety of influences and lower prices.

We feel that this means that the collecting base for Art Deco has increased, and, with an economic recovery, collecting competition will be stronger than ever and will force prices upward again. (*See "Today's Market."*)

The best advice we can offer is to use this book as a starting point, and then go out into the market and find out what is happening to prices in your area of interest today.

Prices for Art Deco have not "nationalized"

Prices are not standard across the country, and there can be variations on the retail price of any given item depending on where and from whom it is bought. Generally speaking, New York and California tend to have the highest retail prices, with other major metropolitan areas not far behind: Chicago, Washington, D.C., Philadelphia, Boston, Miami, Atlanta, Detroit, Baltimore, Denver, Minneapolis, etc.

The Art Deco market, though, is becoming increasingly "self-conscious." Information on the going price and on prices realized at auction is more readily available than ever before. There are still bargains to be found in out-of-the-way shops, smaller towns, less "urban" parts of the country, and through dealers who do not specialize in Art Deco. However, this is changing as the field matures.

Selling to or buying from a dealer

The retail prices in this guide do not necessarily represent the price at which a specific dealer will either buy or sell an item. If you are looking to sell to a dealer, do not expect to get the retail price range represented here. Dealers can't pay retail prices because they are in the business of "brokering" Art Deco, and need to mark up the price to make a profit.

In buying from a dealer, you should also be aware that dealers have costs other than their purchase cost which impact the retail price—the costs of carrying inventory, overhead, salaries, rent, shipping costs, and more. Dealers may have already incurred the time and expense of restoring, repairing, or cleaning, or of researching and documenting the piece.

In addition, high-quality material is getting more and more difficult for dealers to find, and many report having to spend increased amount of time at auctions and elsewhere to obtain it, including travel to distant parts of the globe. As with any service, the price you will pay reflects these "service" costs as well.

Many collectors prefer to let the dealers do this legwork, and also rely on the dealers' expertise, with the reassurance that reputable dealers will stand behind what they sell.

Buying or selling at auction

More individual collectors are attending auctions, and auction house personnel are happy to advise private buyers as well as dealers. However, many collectors still do not understand the auction process.

First, each auction is a unique event that will never be re-created. The price realized depends largely on who is bidding. If there are two individuals who desperately want an item for their collections, you can bet the price will soar. If there is just one person in the room who wants a certain item, he or she may get it at a price lower than retail. However, many auction houses have "reserves," the price they guarantee the consignor they will not go below.

When the bid runs very high at an auction, it is more likely to be a collector rather than a dealer who is willing to go the distance. A dealer who pays the highest possible price for an item may not be able to resell it at a profit. When a dealer places the highest bid, chances are the dealer already knows a collector who might buy it or has actually received the go-ahead from a collector who has agreed in advance to purchase the item.

Auction prices in a guide such as this are generally lower than retail prices because dealers acquire inventory at auctions for resale. So don't expect to purchase an item from a dealer at the auction price listed here. Remember, too, that the auction prices included here do not necessarily always represent the best or most important work of any given artist, designer, or school, or the best condition in which an object might be found.

Prices realized can also depend on how well the auction is promoted. For example, one dealer complained that a major auction had not been advertised broadly enough, and that those most likely to buy the objects which were offered were not in attendance. Of course, this was great news for those who were at the auction, but for those who consigned the items, the results were disappointing.

Remember, too, that almost all items at auction are sold "as is." That means it is your responsibility to completely inspect the piece you intend to buy; to be the judge of its condition, authenticity, and importance; and to be responsible for having it restored, repaired, or cleaned.

While you can be fairly confident about the catalogue descriptions given by major auction houses, to limit their liability, even they state that the descriptions are "their opinion."

Less experienced auctioneers and out-of-the-way auctions miscatalogue Art Deco all the time. Sometimes this is to the benefit of the buyer because an auctioneer has not recognized the importance of the piece or identified the designer. More often, however, it is to the buyer's detriment. We have seen numerous fakes and forgeries being sold as the real thing at these auctions.

A note on hunting for Art Deco at auctions: because Art Deco was so popular and widespread, smaller auctions or estate auctions may feature a few pieces of Art Deco. Generally speaking, not as many Art Deco collectors or dealers will attend these auctions, preferring those that offer a wider selection for sale. If you are confident about your ability to judge an item and buy at auction, you can still acquire some real bargains.

A KEY TO COLLECTIBLE VALUE

Note: *Many factors come into play when determining the value of Art Deco furnishings, objects, works on paper, collectibles, and industrial design. Of course, in many ways, value is determined by the market: auction records, average prices in the marketplace, or just the price that a collector is willing to pay for an item for a collection. In many of the chapters and "Special Focus Sections," you will find additional information on how value in those particular fields is determined. This chapter outlines some of the overall key factors that affect collectible value in the Art Deco field.*

DESIGN ACHIEVEMENT

In all categories of Art Deco collecting, works by recognized designers will always have a higher value than those by lesser known or anonymous designers.

Designers such as Emile-Jacques Ruhlmann, Edgar Brandt, Donald Deskey, Paul Frankl, René Lalique, Charles Schneider, Charles Catteau, Clarice Cliff, Jean Puiforcat, Norman Bel Geddes, A. M. Cassandre, Ludwig Hohlwein, François-Louis Schmied, Henry Dreyfuss, and numerous others are widely recognized as innovators whose work stands head and shoulders above the work of their contemporaries.

Most designers of this stature were considered important contributors to the world of design during their lifetimes, and most of them produced significantly large bodies of work with consistently high quality to earn that recognition.

Remember, however, that an "unknown" artist today can become a celebrated "rediscovered" artist tomorrow. The past twenty years has brought to light numerous designers who were previously unrecognized for their design achievements, so use your instincts.

DESIGN AUTHENTICATION

As you read in the chapter "Important Notes on the Price Listings," some designs have evidence that they are *by* a specific designer, some are *attributed* to the designer, and others, lacking verification, are simply considered to be *in the style of* the designer. These indications can greatly affect the value of any work on the market. A dealer might feel "certain" that a piece is the work of a specific designer, but unless there is a signature or written evidence, it is really only an attribution.

Signatures, Stamps, and Other Marks

Signatures, stamps, marks, patent numbers, and other means which collectors rely on to help authenticate a piece can also add value to a work in some cases. However, this whole area can be confusing in the world of Art Deco, and in some cases it can also be used as a means to defraud collectors.

Hand Signatures

Few decorative arts, with the exception of some studio pieces and special commissions, were signed by hand by the designer, as an artist would sign a canvas. In those rare instances, you might hear a signature described as "hand signed," a "hand-painted signature," a "pencil signature," or an "original signature." However, in some fields, such as rare books, when an item is described as "signed by the author" or "signed by the artist," this generally means "hand signed." In these instances, a signature can add significant market value.

Other Signatures

Most often, when a work is described as "signed" in the decorative arts, it implies some other means of applying the artist's signature or name to the piece. Signatures can be cast, incised, etched, molded, stamped, or printed. Sometimes descriptions offered by dealers and others will be precise: "an ink-stamped signature," "an etched signature," etc. Sometimes the piece will simply be referred to as "signed."

For example, in the world of posters, "signed" usually means that the artist signed on the lithographic stone, or signed the original design that was later printed in multiple copies. Henry Dreyfuss did not hand sign his now famous thermos; a "facsimile" signature was stamped into the metal. Russel Wright did not hand sign all of the "American Modern" ceramic pieces he designed—they were ink-stamped with his signature.

In instances like these, while the signature can increase value over anonymous pieces by authenticating the work, it does not in itself add any significant value.

In each field, designers used different marks, stamps, and other means of identifying their work. In fine silver, each country used a different "hallmark" or stamp to identify its production. Get to know the marks and signatures of the field you are most interested in to help you avoid deception. Industrial manufacture often carries a trademark, logo, patent number, or other means of identification. However, even a patent number is no guarantee of authenticity, for as you will read in our chapter on Art Deco telephones, Korean replicas are often stamped with the original patent numbers.

DESIGN QUALITY

Within a designer's body of work, there will always be some pieces that are prized more than others for their design achievement. Even when designers reach the ranks of "the best," not all of their work will be considered fine examples of their style or use of materials. This is also true for the output of manufacturers, for entire collecting fields, or for specific areas.

For example, furniture designer Paul Frankl created innovative studio work early in his career, and also went on to design pieces for machine production. While his production furniture may still be considered a good or very good example of his work, his earlier pieces and special commissions will always be more highly regarded, and have a higher value.

Manufacturers, such as Chase Brass and Copper, produced a wide variety of items, a handful of which are today considered the finest examples of Chase design.

Determinations such as these can only be made by comparing a wide variety of works by a particular designer or in a particular field.

Other factors, too, will affect the judgment of quality of a piece: for example, whether the work was handmade or machine-produced, whether it is signed, and the materials from which it is made.

In our listings, although there are exceptions, when we say the quality of a piece represents a "fine," "very good," or "good" example of a designer or type of object, we generally mean:

Fine: An example showing the finest attributes of the Art Deco style or the designer's work; known maker or designer, with signature or mark and known provenance; recognized as an important work by a leading designer or maker; highly original or unique in use of materials, design, and overall aesthetic; handmade, perhaps one of a kind, or a rare surviving example of a small edition; rarely seen.

Very Good: A well-executed example of the Art Deco style or the designer's work; distinguished in some way by the originality of the design, application of materials, or technique; identified maker, designer, or manufacturer, perhaps with original label or patent number; perhaps produced in a small edition, numbered and signed, or details finished by hand; if mass-produced, recognized as one of the best examples of design for its category; not easily found.

Good: A collectible example of the Art Deco style or the designer's work, but not really unique or distinguished; perhaps unsigned, unidentifiable maker or designer, or date of manufacture unknown; or, if maker is known, perhaps one of the many mass-produced American or European designs of the period; commonly found, or still readily available on the general antiques and collectibles market.

RARITY

Rarity or scarcity can affect the value of work in many ways, and in different collecting areas, different measures of rarity are used.

As we have seen, much of the early Art Deco production was handmade, while later work tends to be machine-made or described as "mass-produced." However, handmade does not necessarily mean one-of-a-kind, and just because some objects were mass-produced does not mean they aren't rare.

Take for example the Catalin radios of the 1930s and 1940s. While they were machine-made and mass-produced, in reality very few survived, and in some cases only one or two examples of a particular radio are known to exist.

Notice we say "known to exist"—it is always possible that more will be found.

In addition, rarity alone will not necessarily increase value, unless other key factors also exist. For example, one might purchase an apparently handmade lacquered box at a flea market, and the dealer will assure you it is "probably one of a kind," but unless the designer can be authenticated or unless it is a superb example, it will have no more value than hundreds of other anonymous lacquered boxes on the market.

If a piece is truly rare—a special commission, a known small edition, one of a few surviving examples—it will attract more interest, and a collector will pay more to have it.

INTRINSIC VALUE OF MATERIALS

In some areas of Art Deco collecting, the intrinsic value of the materials used will play an important role in helping to determine value.

This is most obvious with precious gems and metals: gold, silver, platinum, diamonds, sapphires, and the like. Furniture, too, can have a value based on its materials: rare woods, ivory inlay, and other precious materials will always have a greater intrinsic value than chrome-plated steel or plastic. However, in the collecting world, usually only a small portion of an item's value is based on the intrinsic value of the materials used. You'll pay more for a Norman Bel Geddes "Manhattan Cocktail Set" in chrome than you will for many diamond brooches, and some Catalin plastic radios can cost more than sterling silver tea sets.

SUBJECT

In certain collecting areas, the subject being depicted can impact the value of a piece. For example, in the world of Art Deco posters, all other things being equal (artist, condition, etc.) trains, ocean liners, and cabaret/theater subjects will generally bring more than product posters for items like cough drops, shoes, or toothpaste. In bronze and ivory sculpture, exotic figures of women dancers, performers such as Josephine Baker, and similar subjects tend to command higher prices than sculptures of children or animals.

CONDITION KEY

The condition of a piece has a lot to do with its value on the market. Again, condition is judged in different ways in different collecting fields, so you will find additional information about condition in many of the chapters and "Special Focus Sections."

Condition should certainly be a key factor in judging what you are willing or unwilling to pay for a specific piece, given that you may have to spend time and money restoring, repairing, or cleaning it.

It is always best to purchase items in "excellent" or "fine" condition, or in the very best condition that you can find them. This will help ensure the value of your collection over time. For very rare pieces, sometimes collectors will lower their standards and purchase an item which is only in "good" condition. However, a common mistake beginning collectors make is to purchase an item in "good" condition because they think it is rare, only to find out later it is still available on the market in "fine" condition.

"Mint" and "Poor" Condition

The term "mint" should be used only to refer to items which are in the same condition as they were when originally made. In some Art Deco collecting fields, "mint" condition pieces are still found on the market, for example, a set of dinnerware in its original box. However, in most cases, Art Deco pieces have been used, if only to a limited degree, and the term "mint" should not apply.

You will see many items on the market that are really in "poor" condition. That is, they fall below the standards described as "good" condition. In most cases, you should pass up these items, unless you have repair expertise or are collecting items to use as parts. In the price listings in this book, we have not included any prices for items known to be in "poor" condition.

In the vast majority of Art Deco collecting fields, there is no universally accepted code to describe condition, so we have combined several different standards for condition into the following descriptions:

FOR FURNITURE

Fine or Excellent Condition: In its original finish, with original hardware, and structurally in excellent shape; only very minor scratches or nicks; or minor professional repairs, refinishing, reupholstery, rechroming, etc., using original materials of the period.

Very Good Condition: Retaining the original hardware and wood and structurally in good shape; scratches and nicks, but not very noticeable; minor repairs or refinishing needed or well executed but somewhat noticeable; or totally refinished, but very well-executed; reupholstery or rechroming needed or well-executed using appropriate modern materials.

Good Condition: Structurally somewhat less than stable; fairly major repairs needed or obvious; surfaces with obvious dents, nicks or scratches; may be missing some hardware; refinishing, reupholstery, or rechroming needed or only fairly well-executed or using inappropriate materials.

FOR OTHER FURNISHINGS

Fine or Excellent Condition: No loss of mirror silvering; no chips, cracks, or other damage in glass components; clocks in working order; rugs with very little wear, very minor high-quality repairs, and no permanent staining; lamps in working order with original shades; metalwork with original patina, only very minor repairs, scratches, or dents.

Very Good Condition: Small loss of mirror silvering but not in image area; only very minor chips, cracks, or other damage in glass components; clocks that can easily be restored to working order; rugs with some wear or somewhat noticeable repairs, but no permanent staining; lamps that can easily be restored to working order, but still with original shades; metalwork with some loss of the original patina, or noticeable repairs, scratches, or dents, but no missing parts.

Good Condition: Loss of mirror silvering in image area; some damage in glass components; clocks that cannot easily be restored to working order, or with several missing parts; rugs with visible signs of wear, small noticeable holes or needed repairs, or minor permanent staining; lamps that cannot easily be restored to working order, or missing original shades; metalwork with repairs needed or obvious, obvious scratches or dents, or missing parts.

FOR SCULPTURE AND STATUES

Fine or Excellent Condition: Unaltered patina with no degradation; marble without chips or nicks; ivory aged but not worn or damaged in any way; cast metal with no flaws, scratches, or loss of paint or electroplating.

Very Good Condition: Unaltered patina, but with some degradation or loss of color; minor scratches or nicks on marble; ivory with some signs of wear; cast metal with minor flaws, scratches, or loss of paint or electroplating.

Good Condition: No missing pieces; unaltered patina, but degraded or somewhat heavy loss of color; small dents or nicks in metal surface, but not broken through;

small chips and cracks on marble; ivory perhaps overly aged from drying, or with visible cracks or pulled away from bronze, but no missing pieces; cast metal with some flaws, dents, scratches, or loss of paint or electroplating, but not distracting from the overall design.

FOR GLASS
Fine or Excellent Condition: No apparent wear to glass or patina; no chips, cracks, or other damage; signature or mark clearly readable.

Very Good Condition: Minor flaws or bubbles within the original glass; some wear to bottom of the piece, or to patina; no chips, cracks, or other damage; signature readable.

Good Condition: Noticeable flaws within the piece; heavy wear to bottom of the piece, or heavy loss of patina; signature or mark readable but obscured; very slight but not noticeable chips, cracks, or other damage.

FOR CERAMICS
Fine or Excellent Condition: No apparent wear to surfaces or paints; no chips, cracks, or other damage; glazing of consistent quality and color; signature or mark clearly readable.

Very Good Condition: Original glazing slightly flawed or uneven; some wear to surfaces or paints; no chips, cracks, or other damage; signature readable.

Good Condition: Noticeable flaws within the original glazing; heavy wear to surfaces or paints; signature or mark readable but obscured; very slight but not noticeable chips, cracks, or other damage.

FOR POSTERS AND GRAPHICS
Fine or Excellent Condition: Fresh colors and no paper loss; no staining; only marginal blemishes; minor restorations to museum specifications; folds not apparent.

Very Good Condition: Fresh colors overall; very slight paper loss or staining, but not in any crucial design area; high-quality restoration but not apparent; folds somewhat visible.

Good Condition: Image clear; good but somewhat faded colors; some staining, restoration, folds, or paper loss, but not overly visible, and not in image or critical area; small, somewhat noticeable repairs; folds apparent.

FOR INDUSTRIAL DESIGN
Fine or Excellent Condition: In almost original condition; very minor scratches or surface wear, but no dents or other damage; in working order.

Very Good Condition: Some scratches and surface wear; very minor dents or other damage; no parts missing; easily restored to working order.

Good Condition: Obvious scratches, surface wear, or dents, but not distracting from the overall design; some parts missing, but can be restored to working order.

Knowing the key factors that impact collectible value in the world of Art Deco can help you understand the prices you will see in this book and in the marketplace, and should also help you determine whether a dealer is offering a "fair price" for something you wish to buy.

FAKES ALERT!
REPLICAS, FORGERIES,
AND OTHER DECEPTIONS

Note: *Unfortunately, the revitalization of interest in Art Deco in the last twenty years has also seen a flood of both expensive and cheaply produced reproductions on the market. Today's collector has to be very wary, or very well-educated in a chosen area, when purchasing Art Deco objects from other than reputable dealers. In many of the chapters and "Special Focus Sections," we have included additional information on fakes, forgeries, and reproductions. Here we describe some of the more common problem areas.*

A RULE OF THUMB

Remember that Art Deco is no longer an unknown style, and most of the time dealers will know exactly what an object is worth. In collecting Art Deco, the best rule of thumb to follow is that if the price looks too good to be true, it probably isn't true.

ART DECO ISN'T THE 1940S OR 1950S

One of the first problems to overcome in collecting Art Deco is to be clear on what is meant by the term, how broadly it is used, and what production actually warrants the name. Uninitiated collectors who are beginning an Art Deco collection should be aware that often things sold in flea markets and antiques fairs as "Art Deco" are really from the 1940s and 1950s. This is due in part to the fact that the influence of Art Deco lasted much longer in the United States than elsewhere, and in part because many dealers aren't knowledgeable.

FURNISHINGS

There are today elegant reproductions of furniture using almost exactly the same materials used by early French designers. One company was producing a noted Ruhlmann desk for about $10,000. The original now brings in the six figures.

In addition, because the Art Deco era was not that long ago, some companies are still issuing or licensing the same designs they produced over fifty years ago—for example, Josef Hoffmann's bentwood "Fledermaus" chairs; Mies van der Rohe's chairs such as the "Brno Chair," still sold through Knoll; Cassina's licensed reproduction of a famous chair by Le Corbusier; and Nessen Lighting's reissues of designs by Walter von Nessen.

Design America has reissued Paul Frankl designs for chairs and sofas. We hasten to add that all of these pieces are being manufactured or reproduced with very high-quality materials and standards.

Even 1930s American furniture in chrome and aluminum is being produced, and other companies are re-creating chairs and couches based on the numerous American and English living room designs that were popular.

Sometimes these designs are commissioned by dealers who sell them through their shops. If you are in doubt, don't be afraid to ask. If you don't fully trust the person with whom you are dealing, pass it up. If your love of Art Deco is really just for decorating your home, then go ahead and purchase a 1990 wall sconce rather than the 1930 original, and it may serve your needs better. But don't expect it to have any long-term value on the collecting market.

Most of the production we are talking about is well-made. The true deception comes when someone tries to sell it as the original item, at a price that is unwarranted for new production.

BRONZE AND BRONZE AND IVORY DECORATIVE SCULPTURE

No matter how often the warnings go out on bronze and bronze and ivory statues, people get taken on their purchase of these every day. Recastings and reproductions of Art Deco, Art Nouveau, Remington, and other statues proliferate on the market today, sometimes sold side by side or in the same shop with originals. Since the early 1970s, it has been the hardest hit area in Art Deco collecting. In many cases, these recastings are very good, and even experts have problems detecting fakes with chemically aged patina, real ivory, foundry marks, and expert attention to detail.

You see the ads in antiques trade journals headlining "Big Profits to Be Made Selling Bronze Sculptures!" Because most of these designs are in the public domain, nothing can prevent reissues, and now about five foundries in the United States put out large quantities.

Moreover, one company has even claimed (privately, of course) that buyers can sell these at auction at great profit—which of course constitutes fraud. Perhaps the ivory importation ban will help cut down at least on the numbers entering the market. When a bronze and ivory statue by Chiparus can sell for tens of thousands of dollars, the temptation to spend $2,000 to $5,000 on a fake from Hong Kong with real ivory is great.

Some recastings are more obvious fakes: cheaply cast, patinated colors, and bases that look too new, and ivory faked by the use of "ivorine" or "ivoria," a plastic that does not yellow or age like ivory.

A reputable auction house or dealer will describe original bronzes as "cast *from* a model by the artist" and later recastings as "cast *after* a model by the artist." (*See the chapter "Important Notes on the Price Listings."*)

The foundries that produce these works do not claim they are original castings, but they often tiptoe around the language they use. In addition, once the piece has left the hands of the foundry, it is not responsible if the piece is misrepresented in the market. One manufacturer explained to us that all of its reproductions were tagged as such—but tags can easily be removed! If they were being entirely above board, they would cast the date of reproduction directly into the bronze.

This was done, for example, by Child's Gallery in Boston, which posthumously issued forty-three magnificent bronzes from original plaster maquettes of Boston artist

Donald DeLue (1897–1988). These works, ranging in height from 8" to 60", were for the most part models for large monumental works that had never been produced in the artist's lifetime. One of DeLue's best-known sculptures is *Quest Eternal* in the Prudential Plaza on Boylston Street. Child's dating of the castings in this way has not hurt their sale at all.

"The Usual Suspects"

Here we list by name some of the most frequently seen bronze and bronze and ivory recasts on the market:

Marcel Bouraine: Stylized figures of Amazons.

D. H. Chiparus: By far the most often recast artist of the Art Deco period. The fakes are named with either the real name for a Chiparus design or a fabricated name: *Antinea, Starfish Dancer, Thais, The Book Lady, Hindu Dancer, The Entrance, Girl with a Parrot, Dancer of Kapurthala, Egyptian Dancer, Temple Goddess, Dancer With Raised Skirt*, and others.

Claire Jeanne Roberte Colinet: *The Oriental Dancer, Anhora Dancer, Thebian Dancer*.

Joe Descomps: *Masked Dancer*.

John Bernard "Descombes": Several figures of nudes.

Gori: Several figures of women.

Louis Icart: *Freedom* and *Fountain*.

Pierre Le Faguays: *Diana the Archer, Message of Love*, and other figures of women.

Lorenzl: Several statues of dancers.

Louis Moreau: Many works without specific titles.

Paul Phillipe: *Russian Dancer* and *Girl With Parrot*.

Prof. Poertzel: *The Aristocrats* and *Snake Charmer*.

Fritz Preiss: *Spring Awakening, Con Brio, Flame Dancer, Autumn Dancer, The Flame Leaper, Girl Sitting on a Wall*, and *Charleston Dancer*.

Bruno Zach: *Riding Crop*.

FRANKART

Numerous Frankart designs for statues and lamps have been recast using the original molds, and many have already made their way onto the secondary market from the gift shops where they were first sold. The quantity of pieces which were remade affected the resale value of Frankart when buyers became wary of all Frankart production. The market seems to be coming back to Frankart slowly, but collectors shy away from pieces which simply look "too new," and prefer to buy pieces with the original finish or paint even if somewhat degraded.

GLASS

A frequent deception in glass is forging a signature or mark, so inspect pieces carefully, and get to know the mark of the designer or maker you want to collect. A well-done fake signature is hard to detect, and the best bet if you are collecting signed glass is to arm yourself with a scholarly book in which signatures of glassmakers are reproduced. One of the best of these is *Glass: Art Nouveau to Art Deco* by Victor Arwas.

Another word of caution about collecting glass. Repairs and damage are generally hard to hide in glass, but sometimes a chip on a rim will be repaired by the entire rim being cut down. A dealer may "forget" to tell you if there is a small chip or crack, so run your fingers carefully over the surfaces and the rim.

There is an abundance of contemporary glass that imitates Art Deco styles. In addition, artists such as René Lalique were imitated in their own day. Etling, Sabino, and other manufacturers produced Lalique-like frosted glass, which is both collectible and in some cases superb. American imitators included Consolidated Lamp and Glass Company and Phoenix Glass Company in the 1930s. These makers are today collected on their own merits. The only deception is when an unscrupulous dealer offers these or any other frosted glass piece as Lalique.

René Lalique glass can bring such high prices that it is easy to see why it is a favorite target for reproduction and forgeries. An excellent guide to detecting fake Lalique is to be found in Nicholas Dawes's book, *Lalique Glass*. Also, with very rare exceptions, Lalique glass is marked, so be wary of someone offering you "unsigned Lalique."

Recently, there was also a rash of well-made reproductions of Lalique and other famous glassmakers emanating most probably from Brazil. To skirt charges of fraud, some of these crooks simply misspelled "Lallique."

CERAMICS

Some of the same warnings given about the condition of glass also apply to ceramics. It may be easy to spot a chip in a color ceramic glazing, but it is sometimes impossible to tell if the glazing has been repaired. Watch, too, for brightly colored pottery that has been simply overpainted to hide problems. Generally, the overpainted area will be either a little too dull or a little too glossy to match the original glaze.

Hairline cracks are harder to notice in ceramics than in glass because you can't see them by holding them up to the light. Tap the ceramic lightly but sharply with your finger, and if there is a dull thud instead of a ring, the ceramic may well have a hairline crack somewhere.

Some Art Deco dinnerwares are being reproduced. A department store advertisement declared, "Art Deco Is Back!" and announced a sale of new Hall China. What is being reproduced and sold today includes the common "Ball Jug," produced in 1938, as well as the "Rhythm" and "Airflow" teapots, and "Doughnut" water pitcher.

The Hall China Company in Ohio is casting these pieces from the original molds, and new ones are just as nice as the originals. The best way to tell the difference is by knowing the company trademark, stamped on the bottom of the piece, which changed over time. In addition, today's Hall, with its pastel shades of pink, blue, and white, is also quite different from its original production in Chinese-red, delphinium-blue, lettuce-green and other colors.

The same "color theory" holds true somewhat for Homer Laughlin's "Fiesta" ware, produced from 1936 through 1972, and reintroduced in 1986. To the original colors of red, blue, yellow, green, and ivory, turquoise was added in 1938. Red ceased production in 1943, when the uranium oxide needed to create it went to wartime use, but it returned in 1959. After World War II, new colors were added, and the 1986 colors are apricot, rose, cobalt-blue, black, and white; a sea-mist green was added in 1991 for sale through Bloomingdale's. Confused? Then buy only through a reputable dealer.

Ceramic reproductions and imitations of Art Deco abound: lamps, vases, teapots, statues, ashtrays, bookends, clocks, and more, selling at all price ranges. Some of the companies that have or are continuing to produce them include Silvestri, FF (Japan), Saspirilla, Five & Dime, Mann (Japan) and Keramik (Italy). In fairness, it should be noted that *most* of these reproductions are plainly marked with the names of the manufacturers. However, that does not stop people from trying to sell them as vintage. In some cases, all it takes is the peeling off of a label. It is up to you to know the difference.

Some Art Deco ceramics are very expensive, although most still have a long way to go before reaching the heights of Arts and Crafts pottery. Still, as prices increase, ceramics will increasingly become targets for reproduction and downright fraud.

SILVER

Sterling silver is difficult to fake, but, again, it is best to buy from a reputable dealer. Some of the fine silver designs of the day have been remanufactured, such as the Christolfe coffee set from the *Normandie*, but these are often sold registered and numbered, and from what we've seen are worth the retail prices asked.

Again, it is best to get to know the maker's marks, country hallmarks, and other stamps used on fine silver. Even tiny earrings will usually carry a silver mark. Firms like William Spratling are still operating, and have re-created some of Spratling's most outstanding designs. The company, however, has changed the mark that is stamped into the silver.

FASHION

Fashion from the Art Deco era has never stopped being imitated. Open any fashion magazine today, and you are sure to see the influence of Art Deco design.

In fashion, generally speaking, the prices for nondesigner "vintage" clothing are about the same as you would spend for modern designs. Because most people who collect in this category collect clothing to wear, they concern themselves more with the fit and the price than with collectible value. A few years ago, skinny men's silk ties with geometric designs were in vogue, but the new ones were often nicer because they didn't come with old gravy stains.

Generally speaking, forgers in this field choose items that are "hot" in today's fashion market—like Vuitton bags and Gucci designs.

JEWELRY

Some jewelry pieces are today reproduced as exact duplicates of the originals, using the same quality precious stones and metals. One company has spent enormous time and money creating exact costume replicas of Cartier, Van Cleef & Arpels, and other outstanding high-end jewelry, which is retailed through finer department stores. This is ironic in some ways, because it was during the Art Deco period that costume jewelry became popular, through the influence of designers such as Coco Chanel.

Jewelry, especially fine jewelry, is another area where you should trust a reputable jeweler or estate jewelry dealer, unless you happen to be a gemologist yourself. Because often jewelry prices are based on the intrinsic value of the materials used, the prices you will pay for "lower-end" Art Deco jewelry is about the same you would pay for similar modern designs. However, outstanding Art Deco designs, even in semiprecious stones or enamel, will have prices that far exceed their intrinsic value.

The most commonly faked costume pieces are those that include marcasite. Marcasite is not rhinestones, but faceted metal polished to appear like diamonds. In early marcasite jewelry, the "stones" were individually set in silver, not glued.

Our resources tell us that a lot of fake Bakelite and Catalin jewelry is on the market. There is a test using a hot pin which one can use to "smell" whether the plastic is really Bakelite, and sometimes the same smell can be raised by rubbing your fingers on the jewelry until it is hot. However, since both of these tests would be embarrassing to perform in a dealer's shop, it is best simply to buy from a dealer you trust.

Another piece of advice on jewelry: don't buy a Cartier or Rolex watch from a vendor on the corner of a busy intersection.

ART DECO ON PAPER

Icart and Erté

Thousands upon thousands of Louis Icart reproductions have been sold through frame shops and retail galleries over the past five years. The boom in Icart prices in the late 1980s, which saw prices rise to over $20,000 at auction in some cases, was accompanied by a corresponding boom in fakes. Though that market crashed to about 50 percent of its value (*see chapter "Today's Market" for more information*), many reproductions found their way to the Art Deco market, and into the hands of unwitting buyers who thought they had made a find.

Erté is reproduced as well, but less so, mainly because most of his serigraphs (and sculpture) date from the 1960s through the present, and are under copyright to publishers such as Chalk & Vermillion and others. Even though Erté died in 1990, new Erté issues continue to appear.

However, the most common deception for both of these artists is the sale of a photo-offset reproduction of a work that was originally an etching, lithograph, or serigraph. The same holds true for posters.

Printing Processes

Louis Icart's original works were etchings which he generally signed in pencil. In etching, an artist draws through wax laid on a metal plate; then, in an acid bath, the lines become etched into the plate. The ink that is applied settles in these lines, and a sheet of paper is laid down over the plate and pressed to lift the ink onto the paper.

Before World War II, most posters were printed lithographically, and it is these that most dealers and collectors today refer to as "vintage." A lithograph is printed from a stone or a metal plate. The design is drawn on the surface with a greasy medium, and the entire surface is dampened with water. Since grease repels water, when a greasy colored ink is then applied, it adheres only to the drawing. Paper is laid down, and the whole is run through a scraper that presses the colored ink into the paper.

A serigraph is a screenprint process, like silkscreening, in which the ink is forced through a mesh screen onto the paper.

Under a jeweler's lens or a very strong magnifying glass, an etching will look like the series of tiny lines that it is, and lithographs and serigraphs will generally have an evenness in their colored areas. In lithographs, lines often look as if they have been drawn by a crayon, and spatter areas look like spattered paint.

In photo-offset, a photograph is taken of the original art and turned into negatives. The negatives are used to photochemically etch into the plate from which the poster will be printed. To make etching possible, the negative must be turned into a series of very tiny, regular dots in neat straight lines that often can't be seen with the naked eye. Use a jeweler's lens or a very strong magnifying glass, look at any photograph in this book, and you will see the dots in straight lines (called a "dot matrix") of photo-offset printing.

Perhaps the easiest thing to look at on an Icart or an Erté is the signature itself. It should be in pencil, and should not appear "broken up" by the dots of photo-offset printing.

The copyrights on many vintage posters, if they had them to begin with, ran out long ago. Anyone with a printing press can print and distribute for sale a vast number of poster titles by notable Art Deco artists. Dozens of lithographic posters have been reproduced by photo-offset by commercial poster publishers.

For example, a catalogue of Poster Originals, Limited, of New York City has reproductions of Ludwig Hohlwein's poster for the delicatessen Wilhelm Mozer, with its bright red lobster; "East Coast by LNER," a British rail poster designed in the 1920s by Tom Purvis; and others.

Other favorites for reproduction are Cassandre's famous 1935 *Normandie* ocean liner poster and his 1927 "Étoile du Nord" train poster. The well-known 1932 "Exactitude" poster by Pierre Fix-Masseau is widely available in photo-offset.

This area is such an ongoing problem that poster dealers will often say that they sell "original" posters or "vintage" posters to distance themselves from the later reproductions.

Lithographic Forgeries

Fortunately, the lithographic process is a difficult and expensive one to re-create, so reprinted posters are almost always done using photo-offset means. Unfortunately, a few posters, such as the 1925 "Avranches" poster by Albert Bergevin, the 1928 "Bal Tabarin" poster by Paul Colin, and the "Rayon des Soieries" opera poster by Maurice Dufrène, have been targets of lithographic counterfeiting in the recent past.

These attempts to defraud are so well executed that only subtle differences in color from the originals have tipped off the poster community. Word about these kinds of forgeries tends to travel quickly through the trade, and reputable dealers will avoid any questionable poster.

INDUSTRIAL DESIGN

The newest area of problems and potential problems is industrial design. Since the 1986 Brooklyn Museum exhibition, prices on some of the collectible industrial designs of the period have climbed upward, spawning reproductions in the wake of the publicity they caused.

For example, Walter Dorwin Teague's blue mirrored glass Sparton "Bluebird" radio was reproduced and sold at $250. One magazine, which was actually applauding the reproduction, headlined its story "Deco on the Outside—Sony on the Inside." It has been reported to us that fake Catalin radios are now appearing. Also on the market is a reproduction of the well-known but anonymously designed blue glass and chrome airplane lamp, vintage examples of which score well on the market.

In industrial design, perhaps the easiest thing to look for is typical wear, rust, discoloration, and other signs of age that tell you an object is old. If it is shiny new, but the dealer claims it is an original, it may also have been rechromed or repainted. Look for maker's marks and metal plates with patent numbers. However, some replicas, such as telephones, have been issued with the original patent numbers stamped into them. (*See "Special Focus: Telephones" for more details.*)

WHAT IS BEING DONE ABOUT FAKES?

Professionals in the antiques business have been taking the problem of fakes and forgeries into their own hands in recent years. Members of the Professional Show Managers Association (PSMA) are trying to find new ways to identify and keep reproductions out of shows. One show manager, Irene Stella, even created a traveling exhibition to educate the public about fakes.

At a show, if you feel you have identified a fake or forgery, or have been a victim of a deception, you should report it to the show management. If they don't seem to care, or brush you off, it's best not to attend that show again.

Connie Swaim, editor of *Antique Week*, has crusaded against fakes for some time by frequently publishing articles about fakes in different fields. The newly formed American Antique Association (AAA) has made the war on fakes the launching pad for their organization.

While these efforts will not stop deception in its tracks, and may not focus specifically on Art Deco, all collecting fields stand to benefit. Even more, such efforts reflect well on the professionalism and ethics of the antiques profession.

Throughout this book, you'll find additional information on fakes, forgeries, and reproductions, along with special "Fakes Alert!" notes, which we hope will help you become a "Confident Collector" of Art Deco.

TODAY'S MARKET

Art Deco continues to enjoy increasing popularity among collectors. The past ten years have seen a wealth of museum exhibitions, books and magazine articles, and successful shows and publicity generated by prominent dealers and auction houses, which have added fuel to the fire, and expanded the market. Even people who don't consider themselves "collectors" are buying Art Deco furniture, lamps, glassware, ceramics, posters, radios, and other decorative and household objects because they are easy to integrate into modern homes.

Hollywood is once again playing a role in popularizing Art Deco design as it did in the 1930s. Movies such as *Batman*, *Dick Tracy*, and others with Art Deco scenic design have helped to repopularize the style, and neo-Deco advertising abounds.

The Art Deco market, especially what is called the "high-end" market, is mature and competitive. Art Deco has taken its place with the most valued 20th-century decorative arts, the broader collecting field of which it is part. The resurgence of interest in all 20th-century decorative arts, such as Arts and Crafts, has benefited Art Deco collecting immensely.

Like almost all collecting fields, Art Deco was affected by the economic downturn of late 1989 and the early 1990s. In some categories, prices fell 20 to 25 percent, while in a few areas prices crashed as much as 50 percent. The areas that were most affected were those which deal with items produced in multiples, such as Lalique and Icart. In some cases, prices have already started to recover, while in others, it will take a much longer time for prices to rebound to where they were at the end of the 1980s, if they ever do, especially areas in which there was rampant overspeculation.

Of course, new "hot" areas have come along to replace them and capture the collecting fervor. Over the past few years, the appreciation of Art Deco has broadened so greatly, along with an expanded collecting base, that even areas that suffered some setbacks still have strong demand.

What are some of the influences that are fueling the Art Deco market today?

THE GROWING BASE OF COLLECTORS

Collectors of Art Deco and the entire range of 20th-century design are more numerous than ever, a trend that will no doubt continue as we move toward the 21st century. They are also more knowledgeable than ever, and learn more about the field through books and other publications every day. Areas that were once considered "low end" have surged ahead due to the number of people who are actively collecting. Chase Chrome, Depression glass, mass-produced ceramics, World's Fair memorabilia, industrial design, and other areas have seen prices increase due to the growing demand.

Clearly, most of us may never personally afford to own pieces in the higher price ranges of the market. However, Art Deco is such a vast field that many very good examples of the style are still affordable, especially pieces that were produced in some quantity.

Interestingly, the quantities in which these items were produced have actually helped to create active collecting fields around them. In other words, enough was made for them to become broadly known and sought-after by a number of collectors. Affinity groups and collectors club in specialized areas now abound. At the same time, collectors are becoming more discriminating.

Comments Bill Meisch, owner of the shop Of Rare Vintage in Asbury Park, New Jersey, "Most of my collectors are in their late thirties to early forties. They have gotten more serious, and want only the best. They aren't being as frivolous, and they are looking for better styling and designer pieces."

ART DECO SOCIETIES

Art Deco societies in the United States and abroad have helped to expand interest and awareness in the style. Today, there are more than a dozen active societies in the United States and several others in Canada, England, New Zealand, and Australia. While generally Art Deco societies are concerned foremost with architectural preservation, their members are often also avid collectors of decorative arts, graphics, industrial design, or fine arts of the period. Societies often offer lectures and programs in the decorative arts, as well as lobbying for the preservation of the built environment.

This ever-growing awareness of the need to preserve our Art Deco architectural heritage has strengthened people's desire to own the furnishings and decorative arts of the period, and vice versa.

MUSEUM EXHIBITIONS

Museum exhibitions continue to educate the public and bring new collectors to the field each year. In the late 1980s, two groundbreaking exhibitions and their accompanying books helped to widely promote awareness of America's Art Deco heritage: "The Machine Age," the Brooklyn Museum exhibition of 1986, and "American Art Deco," which opened at the Renwick Gallery of the Smithsonian Institution in Washington, D.C., in April 1987. These two exhibitions fueled the already expanding market for Art Deco in the late 1980s.

Other specialized exhibitions, also often with accompanying books, have drawn attention to other areas. For example, the Fashion Institute of Technology in New York presented "Lalique: A Century of Glass for a Modern World" in 1989, a traveling exhibition and the most comprehensive retrospective of Lalique's work since 1933. In 1990, "The Art of Van Cleef & Arpels," organized by the Los Angeles County Museum, also traveled to the Smithsonian and Honolulu. The Museum of Modern Art presented both "The Modern Poster" in 1988, and "High & Low: Modern Art/Popular Culture" in 1990. Also in 1990, the Hudson River Museum in Yonkers, New York, organized and hosted "The Sphinx and the Lotus: The Egyptian Movement in American Decorative Arts, 1865–1935."

The same year, the Brooklyn Museum presented "Czech Modernism: 1900–1945," the first exhibition in America to document the evolution of Czech art during the first half of the 20th century. With the improved relations between the former Soviet republics and the West, one can anticipate that the outstanding contributions of Czechoslovakia, Hungary, Poland, and other countries to early 20th-century design will become better known and more widely appreciated in the future.

In 1991, the Montreal Museum of Fine Arts presented "The 1920's: Age of the Metropolis," a stunning overview of both fine and decorative arts of the period. The same year, "Design 1935–1965: What Modern Was," an exhibition comprising objects from the collection of the Montreal Museum of Decorative Arts, was hosted by the IBM Gallery in New York. This latter exhibition, accompanied by an important book of the same title, provided tremendous insight into a broad range of modern design. It will undoubtedly have a strong impact as collectors in greater numbers begin to consider the 1940s, 1950s, and 1960s as serious collecting arenas.

These special museum exhibitions, coupled with existing and newly created permanent collections in American museums, have vastly increased the appreciation of Art Deco and related design styles.

AUCTIONS

Although many collectors still rely on dealers as their source for building collections, the number of individuals buying at auction continues to increase.

Numerous auctions focusing on 20th-century design now take place regularly across the country. Auction houses with long-standing specialties in 20th-century decorative arts continue to host regular sales: the New York houses of Christie's, Christie's East, William Doyle Galleries, and Sotheby's, and San Francisco/Los Angeles's Butterfield & Butterfield.

Larger, and sometimes smaller, regional auction houses have also jumped into the Art Deco market. In 1989, the Massachusetts-based Skinner, Inc., became the first auction house in New England to make commitment to sales including 20th-century design. Savoia's Auction of South Cairo, New York, continues to have catalogued sales of 20th-century design, usually emphasizing machine-made and mass-produced Art Deco designs. Other auction houses that have entered the field include Michael Myers Auction Gallery in St. Petersburg, Florida; Leslie Hindman Auctioneers in Chicago, which has also announced plans to expand to St. Louis; Wolf's Fine Arts in Cleveland; and Treadway Gallery, in Cincinnati, which now incorporates modern design with Arts and Crafts in its auctions.

In spite of the increased buying by individual collectors at auction, an auction can be a minefield for beginning collectors, who must rely on their own judgment as to the value and condition of a work. Even authenticity can be a question. Although collectors can usually rely on the word of reputable auction houses, all auction houses publish disclaimers in their catalogues, and all items are sold "as is," with very little recourse should the buyer discover later that the item purchased is a reproduction or forgery.

"You have to be fairly knowledgeable," states Eric Silver, the 19th- and 20th-century decorative arts specialist at William Doyle Galleries. "Know the values and check the auction records before you buy, and educate your eye.

"Examine all items carefully before you bid on them," Silver continues. "There are a lot of fakes out there, and some of them are very good and could be sold at auction. Read the catalogue language carefully, too. If something is sold at auction as 'Art Deco *style*,' there is no guarantee it is actually from the period."

The auction arena can also be highly speculative, with dealers bidding (read: *betting*) they can resell a piece at a higher price than they pay. However, in spite of these caveats, the auction arena for Art Deco is more active than ever, and activity is bound to increase as time goes on.

Hélène Petrović, Art Nouveau and Art Deco specialist at Christie's East, comments, "I always try to advise my clients on a personal basis. I disagree with speculation where taste doesn't mean anything. You must put taste before investment considerations if you are going to live with the things that you buy."

Although specific areas have fallen at auction, in general the auction prices for very good and fine examples of Art Deco have remained strong.

States Nancy McClelland, senior vice president at Christie's New York, "On the whole, because there was not a great and unreasonable rise except in certain areas, the auction market is fairly solid, although there is less being offered on the auction arena today because there is a concern as to whether or not there will be a buyer for it."

Petrović echoes her sentiments. "The auction business is significantly different today. I am more selective in what I offer. If someone is willing to consign an object, I really have to study it and know that I have a buyer for it."

"If you are interested in buying at auction, you should try to find an opportunity to introduce yourself to the specialist in charge," McClelland notes. "They can help you understand the choices that an auction offers. It is also a good idea to subscribe to the auction catalogues so that you can closely follow the market in which you are most interested."

SHOWS

Collecting for the 21st century can now take place at numerous Art Deco and 20th-century design shows each year.

Some Art Deco societies have hosted "Art Deco Weekends" for many years, which include sales of 20th-century designs. These include notably the annual Miami Beach Art Deco Weekend in January, sponsored by the Miami Design Preservation League, and spring shows sponsored by the Art Deco Society of Washington, D.C., and the Art Deco Society of California in San Francisco. The Miami Beach weekend now draws as many as a half million people who come to enjoy both the festivities and the splendor of the Art Deco district with its hundreds of Art Deco hotels. Another long-standing show is the "Indianapolis Art Deco and Vintage Clothing Show," nicknamed the "Indy Deco Show," which has taken place twice each year for fifteen years at the Indiana State Fairground in Indianapolis.

In 1986, a new show was launched by Sanford Smith in New York. Called "Modernism—A Century of Style and Design," this annual show has gone seven rounds as of this writing. It brings together the finest examples of the entire gamut of 20th-century design from various movements that were taking place internationally and sometimes simultaneously: Art Nouveau, Bauhaus, Arts and Crafts, Art Deco, Vienna Secession, the Aesthetic movement, and more.

In 1988, the show management firm of Caskey Lees & Olney entered this arena with "L.A. Modernism." In 1990, Chicago became the third major city to launch an annual high-caliber show, "Winnetka Modernism," organized by the Winnetka Community House.

Other major annual shows with strong reputations for featuring Art Deco include the "Manhattan Antiques and Collectibles Show," organized by Irene Stella, who holds her huge "triple pier" events in New York City in March and November, and the "20th Century Design Show and Sale," held twice yearly in Los Angeles, organized by Modern Times.

The impact that shows and sales such as these have had on the Art Deco collecting field is immense, and no doubt other specialized shows will continue to be created.

TRENDS OVER THE PAST FEW YEARS

As you read through this volume, you'll find a wealth of detailed information relating to the market for specific collecting fields, particularly in our "Special Focus" sections and the chapters we group together under the title "Modern Living." But here, in a brief overview, are some of the current trends and some tips on how the market is performing.

Furnishings

Early French Art Deco furniture continues to gain very high prices, and the most advanced collectors focus on its pantheon of gifted and popular designers including Emile-Jacques Ruhlmann, Jules Leleu, Paul Poiret, Jean-Michel Frank, Maurice Dufrène, Pierre Legrain, Edgar Brandt, and others.

Prices for works by these artists in some cases rose dramatically in the late 1980s. In the past few years, due to the economic downturn, increases in this market have not been as dramatic, but the market has held steady.

"Prices are holding," comments Gary Calderwood of Calderwood Gallery in Philadelphia. "Furniture prices have not gone up tremendously, but they are continuing to rise slowly. There has always been a scarcity of fine French furniture in the United States, and I still travel to Europe a lot to buy, as well as spending a lot of time on the phone. Outstanding material is much harder to find today."

A few major Art Deco "estates" have come onto the market in recent years, including the 1988 Sotheby auctions of the Andy Warhol and Elton John collections, both of which sent prices spiraling on early Art Deco treasures.

In 1989 and 1991, two successive auctions of the collection of French author and early Art Deco collector Alain Lesieutre took place in Paris. The collection took twenty-five years to assemble and was hailed in the press as "the most important collection of Art Deco in private hands in the world."

The vast array of furniture offered included lacquer panels by Jean Dunand; over sixty pieces of furniture by Emile-Jacques Ruhlmann; furniture by Pierre Charreau, Jean-Michel Frank, and Süe et Mare; early gouaches by Erté and Georges Lepape; ceramics by Decoeur, Buthaud, and Simmen; decorative metalware by Linossier; silver by Desny and Puiforcat; jewelry by Max Ernst, Van Cleef & Arpels, Gerard Sandoz, Georges Fouquet, and Cartier; glass by Maurice Marinot and René Lalique; paintings by Marie Laurencin and Paul Jouve; sculptures by Gustav Miklos, Edouard Sandoz, Demetre Chiparus, and others; lighting by Edgar Brandt with shades by Daum Nancy, lighting fixtures by Albert Cheuret and René Lalique; and several rugs by Ivan Da Silva Bruhns.

If the preceding list reads like an encyclopedia of high French Art Deco design, it is, and the catalogues from the sales have already become valuable out-of-print reference books.

More recently, in January 1992, Christie's New York held an important auction of the estate of William McCarty-Cooper, which included outstanding work by Ruhlmann, Leleu, Legrain, Jean-Michel Frank, and other early French designers.

"Most major collectors are still relatively young," comments Christie's Nancy McClelland. "It will be some time before we see their estates at auction." Yet each time a major estate collection comes to the auction arena, it gives collectors and dealers a chance to acquire important, often one-of-a-kind pieces. The rarity of many of these works on the market means that when they do come up, they are strongly vied for.

Even though the early French Art Deco style was largely replaced by a more Modern style that incorporated metal and other new materials in furnishings, some French designers continued to create in luxurious materials for a wealthy clientele into the 1930s and 1940s. These designers are now enjoying a resurgence of popularity.

"Designers such as Jacques Adnet and André Arbus have bigger reputations right now in Europe than they do in the United States," comments Calderwood. "However, they are increasingly popular today, both because of price and because they continued to use richer materials."

The work of a few notable Art Nouveau designers whose firms continued to produce into the Art Deco period are also receiving renewed attention. Robert Aibel, owner of the shop Moderne, also in Philadelphia, believes that the work of Louis Majorelle's studio is currently undervalued.

"Majorelle is the leading name in Art Nouveau furniture," Aibel explains. "After he died in 1926, his studio continued to produce furniture, but in a more Modern style. Not enough research has been done on Majorelle's Art Deco designs, but my clients find it interesting, and I am certain we'll see it rise in the market in the years ahead."

In addition, well-designed but anonymous furniture has climbed in the market, perhaps due to the high prices for designer pieces. "In one of our 1992 sales we had a good selection of Art Deco furniture," notes Jon King, senior vice president at Butterfield & Butterfield. "Although it was unattributed, it was so well-designed that it was bringing double and triple the estimates.

"Now is really a good time to buy furniture," King continues. "Prices have stabilized for the most part. Buy the best pieces you can afford in the best condition you can find them, but remember, it might be quite a while before you will see an appreciable increase in values again. Let your taste guide you. You can't store furniture away and wait for it to go up; it is something you have to live with."

American furnishings, especially designs by the leading designers such as Paul Frankl, Kem Weber, Donald Deskey, Gilbert Rohde, and others, continue to show solid prices and steady appreciation.

Paul Frankl's early "Skyscraper" furniture, produced in small quantities, is a leader in the collecting field for early American Modernists. At Christie's New York in June 1992, a pair of his lacquered wood and metal "Skyscraper" bookcases brought $50,000 plus buyer's premium, one of the highest auction prices ever paid for American Art Deco (*see color section*). "The underbidder was a museum," notes McClelland. "And, ironically, the buyer was a European client."

Furnishings by the leading designers, even examples of their mass-produced designs, are today frequently included in the finest auctions and shows across the country. In particular, Gilbert Rohde's designs for the Herman Miller Company have enjoyed a resurgence of interest in recent years. (*See "Special Focus: Gilbert Rohde" for more details.*)

Decorative Sculpture

While the bronze and bronze and ivory decorative sculptures of the 1920s and 1930s have been hard hit by fakes and forgeries (*see "Fakes Alert!" for more information*), the market for original works continues to be very strong, with Demetre Chiparus and Ferdinand Preiss leading the way overall.

The June 8, 1990, sale of Art Deco bronze and ivory sculpture at Christie's New York set a new auction record in this arena with Chiparus's *Semiramis* selling at $160,000 plus buyer's premium against an estimate of $80,000 to $120,000. Also scoring high at the same auction was *Nordica* by Maurice Guiraud-Rivière, which brought $52,000 plus buyer's premium against an estimate of $20,000 to $25,000.

The market has continued to be strong for works by these artists, and in June 1992, Christie's posted very high prices on three works by Chiparus—$30,000 for *Starfish*; $70,000 for a rare, large version of *Thaïs*; and $42,000 for *Russian Dancers*, with several smaller works by Chiparus selling in the healthy range of $9,000 to $15,000, all plus buyer's premium. (*See "Decorative Sculpture" and color section.*)

Glass

In the world of Art Deco glass, while there is a growing appreciation for the work of many glassmakers, that of René Lalique is still far and away the most actively traded, with rare pieces commanding tens of thousands of dollars.

"While the prices on Lalique have come down in the past few years, the demand has remained strong," comments Nicholas Dawes, an author and dealer who served as curator for the Fashion Institute of Technology's 1989 exhibition. "Collectors are still willing to pay strong prices for a piece that is outstanding in one way or another.

"The recession affected disposable income," he continues. "But more importantly, Japanese collectors were buying huge quantities of Lalique, and when they stopped, dealers were left with large inventories. Collectors should not be afraid to buy now, while the prices are good."

One specialized area of collecting in the world of glass which has enjoyed a growing base of collectors is that of commercial perfume bottles and boudoir items. One of the largest dealers in this country is Madeleine France in Plantation, Florida.

"Every great glass designer created perfume bottles or boudoir pieces—Lalique, Gallé, Daum, Moser, Decorchement—the list is very long," she states. "Advanced collectors seek perfumes which are factory fresh, with their original labels and boxes. We say 'FSLB,' meaning 'filled, sealed, labeled, and boxed.'"

Although prices in this field make it still accessible to novice collectors, France advises, "Beginning collectors are still not discriminating enough in this field, and seem to want to accumulate rather than collect. Accumulators want an instant collection, and will often make the mistake of buying, say, four more common perfumes at $250 each than a rare and sought-after perfume for $1,000."

Another area of glass collecting which has seen an enormous resurgence of interest is the stylized cameo glass of Charles Schneider called "Le Verre Français." Dealers Mark Feldman and Corey Warn of Brookline, Massachusetts, are the leading specialists in this field, and their shop is filled with hundreds of examples of fine pieces.

"While you can still buy a good example of 'Le Verre Français' for under $2,000, fine and rare pieces can now command $8,000, $10,000, and more," comments Feldman.

"This is especially true for monumental pieces of rare geometric designs. Also adding to the value are pieces with applied stems and handles.

"These works were created in far smaller numbers than works by Lalique, which left France by the trainload," he says, "which makes them much harder to find. As the collecting base for 'Le Verre Français' continues to increase, its value will continue to climb."

American glass by Steuben, Phoenix, Consolidated, and American Depression glass in the "Manhattan," "Pyramid," "Tearoom," and "Cubist" styles continue to be sought after by Art Deco collectors.

Phoenix and Consolidated collecting got a big boost in 1990 with the publication of *Phoenix and Consolidated Art Glass 1926–1980*, by Jack D. Wilson. Of particular interest to Art Deco collectors is information he provided on "Ruba Rhombic," Consolidated's jazzy asymmetrical line introduced in 1928 with the marketing slogan, "An Epic in Modern Art."

The first major exhibition and sale of "Ruba Rhombic" was held in September 1992 at the Philadelphia gallery Moderne, headed by Robert Aibel. Comprising four hundred pieces from private collections, with prices ranging from $100 to $3,600 for individual pieces, it included many rare examples.

"But all 'Ruba Rhombic' must be considered rare," Aibel comments. "In all, we think that less than 1,500 pieces of 'Ruba Rhombic' still exist, so when you are talking about a piece with only two known examples or a piece with eight known examples, rarity becomes a matter of semantics. I think this will prove to be a benchmark show for 'Ruba Rhombic.' "

Ceramics

In the world of ceramics, Clarice Cliff continues to fetch high prices, followed closely by another English ceramist, Susie Cooper. (*See "Special Focus: Susie Cooper."*) The auction house of Christie's South Kensington in England leads the way with specialized auctions of Cliff, Cooper, and other English Art Deco ceramics such as Poole Pottery and Carlton Ware.

Cloisonné enameled pottery by the French firm Longwy and the Belgian firm Boch Frères continues to build its audience, although prices remain moderate when compared to designers such as Cliff. "Longwy is the only company still producing cloisonné enameled pieces," states Richard Fishman, owner of the San Francisco shop As Time Goes By, which has a strong specialization in Longwy. "It is a labor-intensive and expensive process, and in the long run the company may not be able to survive."

Fishman commissioned Longwy to create ceramic tiles which decorate his shop-front, and also had a line of reproductions of Longwy's Art Deco designs made specifically for his shop. "Understanding people's concern with reproductions, we had each piece stamped 'Reproduction' on the bottom," he explains. "However, the process by which they were created remains the same, and all of the designs are original to the period. Many of these pieces would never be seen again otherwise, and the new pieces can make buying very good examples of Longwy more affordable to average collectors."

Boch Frères pottery, especially pieces designed and signed by Charles Catteau, continues to gain in the market, with the best pieces bringing very high prices. While dealers such as Morton Abromson of Brookline, Massachusetts, have specialized in Boch Frères pottery for many years, the collecting base is still small enough that good and very good examples can be acquired at affordable prices.

This may not continue to be the case for too much longer, as Boch Frères is the subject of a book which was released in France in 1992. We were unable to obtain a copy of it prior to our deadline for this volume, but our sources say that it will definitely increase interest in the field by helping dealers and collectors categorize and identify works in a way that has been impossible until now.

Also in the ceramics field, an area which came up quickly over the past few years is the "Argenta" line produced by the Swedish firm Gustavsberg. "Argenta" is usually a mottled green glaze, with silver overlays in various designs of fish, mermaids, and other motifs. Just a few years ago, "Argenta" rarely appeared on the market, but now is found frequently at Art Deco shows and auctions, with prices ranging from under $200 to much higher ranges.

Right now there is a question, however, whether an increased market for Gustavsberg "Argenta" can be maintained, or if the market for it will come back stronger after the current economic doldrums have passed. At the June 1992 auction at Christie's East, several lots of "Argenta" failed to sell.

"Unfortunately, except for rare and unusual pieces, it is not selling very well," commented Hélène Petrović. "There seems to be no market for it for the moment, but in general ceramics aren't doing as well because of the recession."

Fashion and Jewelry

Jewelry and fashion from the 1920s and 1930s continue to be popular both with collectors and with those who simply buy it to wear.

Fine jewelry from the period continues to fetch record prices at auction, although fine jewelry is more likely to appear in jewelry auctions than in the Art Deco arena. We have not included a chapter on fine jewelry in this volume, but those who are interested should visit some of the outstanding dealers listed in the "Resource Guide" to get a better sense of the market in this arena.

Costume jewelry, introduced by Coco Chanel, became very popular during the Depression, as did Bakelite plastic jewelry. Carved and colored for high fashion, Bakelite jewelry is available at many Art Deco shops and vintage clothing stores, and a bracelet can sell for as little as $30 up to $500 and more, depending on the design.

Marsha Evaskus, owner of the shop Zig Zag in Chicago, observes, "People enjoy wearing Bakelite jewelry every day, and not just with vintage fashions. There are people who have been collecting for ten years or more, and they tend to look for very special pieces, or unusual figural pieces. Many new collectors are also entering the field, which has been given a boost by the publication of books of the subject."

Remarking on changes in this arena, she adds, "Recently, I've noticed less interest in the fanciful Bakelite pieces and increased interest in combination chrome and Bakelite pieces that have a 'Machine Age' look, with a strong geometric design. Many of these were made in Germany, and some in France, and probably some were made in England as well. They are hard to find, but worth the trouble to search for them."

There is also greatly increased interest in two areas for which we offer "Special Focus" sections in this volume: "Mesh Purses" and "Mexican Silver Jewelry." Mesh handbags with enameled Art Deco designs, especially from Whiting & Davis, are very collectible, and some can sell very high. Mexican silver jewelry is enjoying an immense renaissance of appreciation, especially works by William Spratling, Antonio Pineda, Margot de Taxco, and others. These artists have been expertly promoted in recent years by Carole

Berk, owner of Carole A. Berk, Ltd., of Bethesda, Maryland, and the public response has been very strong.

Vintage Books and Other Publications

As interest in the Art Deco field has grown, there has been a corresponding increase in interest in the books and other publications of the period. Collectors, dealers, and institutions are actively buying the early books, magazines, and publications that document the creative work, innovations, and thinking of the era's preeminent designers.

In addition, collectors of furniture, glass, ceramics, and other Art Deco objects are rediscovering the wealth of finely designed books, treasured for their bindings, striking illustrations, covers, dust jackets, typography, and other decorations. Thomas Boss of Thomas G. Boss Fine Books in Boston has provided a "Special Focus" section for this volume which overviews the vintage book market and provides numerous tips for collectors.

Posters and Graphics

Art Deco posters, magazine covers, and graphics from all countries continue to attract attention. The most sought-after and highest-priced Art Deco posterist continues to be A. M. Cassandre. However, Art Deco poster artists from other countries such as England, Germany, Holland, Switzerland, and Italy are also attracting collectors. Magazine covers for *Fortune*, *Vanity Fair*, *Asia*, and other magazines, while still very affordable, have gained in the market.

The poster market has remained relatively strong during the economic downturn. Although there was some softening of prices in the auction arena, especially for those posters previously sought-after by Japanese collectors, such as those of the Art Nouveau artist Alphonse Mucha, the poster collecting field has "internationalized" to a very large degree. This means that competition for the very best posters and recognized artists is broad-based and remains quite high.

By the 1920s and 1930s, advertising had become a significant international industry. Happily, this was also the first era of international travel, and the lithographic travel posters of the Art Deco period, whether for resorts, sports-related travel such as skiing, ocean liners, trains, or early airplanes are highly collectible and very popular. Good and very good examples of Art Deco travel posters can still be found at affordable prices.

Icart

The best Icart news in recent years has been the publication of *Louis Icart: The Complete Etchings*, by William Holland, published by Schiffer Publishing, which has given collectors and dealers a new reference tool for identifying over 500 etchings, including 125 more than the book previously used as a primary research tool.

The bad news for Icart collectors and dealers has been the precipitous drop in prices since the autumn of 1990. Generally speaking, Icart's etchings have fallen in the auction arena overall by 35 to 50 percent and more, and one internationally important collector reported to us that the only reason he could smile is that it allowed him to lower the insurance on his collection by 50 percent as a result.

The auction record for Icart of $24,000 was set for his 1936 etching "Mardi Gras" at Christie's New York in June 1990, but prices have been spiraling downward ever since. Even by October 1990, another impression of the same print failed to sell when presented at Christie's East with a low estimate of $15,000, and by March 1991 was still passed with an estimate of $8,000 to $12,000.

Japanese collectors were the major driving force behind the Icart market in the late 1980s, and when they stopped buying—as they did in other fields such as Lalique and paintings—the bottom fell out of the price pyramid. Icart etchings moved so quickly into the international auction arena that it is doubtful that a large enough base of collectors was ever formed in this country to ensure a rebound in prices in the near future.

Just as no two auctions are ever alike, two different impressions of the same etching can be different in terms of quality and condition. A few examples of how prices on the Icart market have gone are enough to demonstrate.

"Coursing III," which had sold as high as $12,000 at auction, brought only $3,000 at Christie's East in June 1992. "Love's Blossom," which had sold as high as $9,000 at auction, now brings in the range of $5,000. In 1990, the charming "Pink Slip" shot up to $7,000 in March, but had fallen back to $3,500 by December, and sold at Butterfield & Butterfield for only $2,250 in April 1992. "Thais," a 1927 etching, crashed from $8,000 in March 1990 to $3,300 in October of the same year, and has only brought about $2,500 in three auctions since then.

Christie's East, long known as a major venue for the Icart market, has steadily reduced the number of pieces it has offered for sale. Hélène Petrović advises, "If you own Icarts today, I would hold on to them and wait to see what happens. There were just too many on the market, and people are now relatively blasé about them. As you know, however, all things in this market tend to be cyclical, and eventually Icarts will come back into popularity."

Due to the continuing instability of this market, we have not included a chapter or price listings on Icart in this volume. We advise collectors who are interested in this market to closely watch the auction arena for signs that prices have either stabilized or are making a rebound. At this point, how long it will take this market to recover is an open question. Remember, after World War II and Icart's death in 1950, his works fell so far out of popularity that they could be bought for only a few dollars, and it took almost forty years for them to reach the heights from which they have fallen.

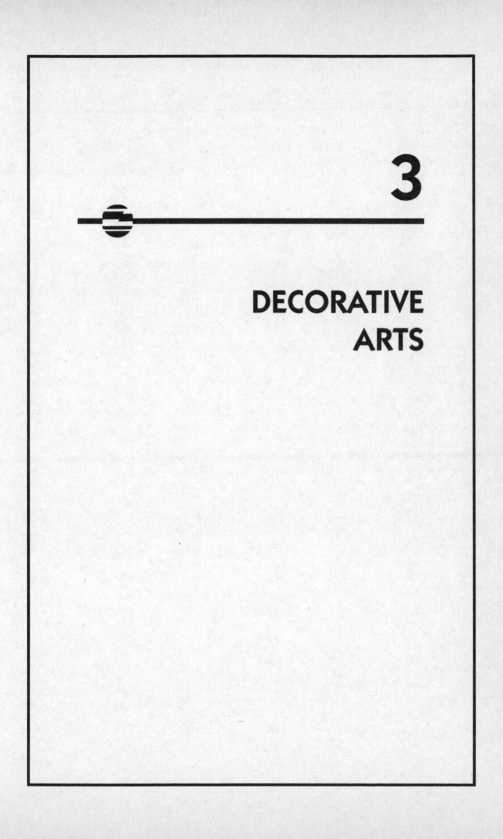

3

DECORATIVE
ARTS

FURNISHINGS

The design of furnishings reflected the profound transitions that were taking place in fashion, style, and society in the 1920s and 1930s. They were transformed not only by new design ideas, but by new lifestyles, technical advances, and new materials and inventions.

FURNITURE

Tradition-loving French *ébénsites*, or "cabinetmakers," while abandoning the overly ornamental Art Nouveau, still used highly refined materials. Woods such as *ébène de macassar*, or "macassar ebony"; Brazilian *palissandre*; rosewood; palmwood; zebrawood; mahogany; amboyna; amaranthe; violet wood; and other rare woods were popular. Other materials and finishes such as lacquer; *bronze doré*, or "gilt-bronze"; ivory; mother-of-pearl; and tortoise shell were also frequently used. Wrought iron eventually came to surpass bronze in popularity in furnishings, due in part to the talents of the artists who chose the medium.

Another favorite material was galuchat, the skin of a dogfish, specially treated to be used and tooled like leather on desk tops and other furniture and decorations. Today, you'll often hear galuchat called sharkskin, and it is also substituted as a term for *peau de chagrin*, which translates as "shagreen."

There were numerous notable designers of furniture during the early French Art Deco period. For the most part, their work is highly prized and highly priced today. Often, they created their furniture for wealthy clients who commissioned them to design unique pieces.

Designers who are in the top of the collecting market include Emile-Jacques Ruhlmann, Eileen Gray, Pierre Legrain, Eugene Printz, Armand-Albert Rateau, Jules Leleu, Louis Süe and André Mare, André Groult, Clement Rousseau, and André Domin and Marcel Genevrière's company Dominique, and the master lacquer artist Jean Dunand.

Others who are well-known from this era include Maurice Dufrène, Paul Vera, Clement Mère, Léon Jallot, Paul Follot, Paul Iribe, and Paul Poiret and his firm Atelier Martine. Perhaps less well-known but equally talented are designers such as Jean-Michel Frank, Gabriel Englinger, Eric Bagge, André Frechet, and George Champion.

A few designers successfully made the transition from Art Nouveau to the more Modern style. Several of these designers are from the Nancy region, including Louis Neiss. The workshops of the leading Art Nouveau furniture designer Louis Majorelle (1859–1929) produced outstanding Modern designs in the 1930s. While these were produced after his death, they still tend to be undervalued in terms of their quality.

Furniture by many of these designers can bring very high prices. The highest quality works, which auction houses like to call "important" pieces, are often found only in museums, and in many instances rarely appear on the open market.

Overall, Emile-Jacques Ruhlmann remains the undisputed master of the Art Deco furniture market. He was known as a maker of luxury furniture, and was expensive even in his own time. His furniture has elegant lines, discrete curves, or slightly *bombé* fronts. The plinth, a base on which furniture may rest, is a favorite Ruhlmann motif, and added more majesty to his already sumptuous pieces. Ruhlmann also was the master of modern veneering in exotic woods. Veneers were laid down with grains in opposition to the wood below it, to lessen warping. This allowed Ruhlmann to create his broad, flat surfaces for doors, cabinets, and other furniture.

Ruhlmann enjoyed the patronage of private clients such as textile magnate David-Weill, the automobile manufacturer Voisin, and even princes from India. Later in his career, he received numerous commissions from the French government for the decoration of embassies, town halls and luxury ocean liners such as the *Ile de France*.

Armand-Albert Rateau was really an independent artist who followed no particular movement. He was influenced by Oriental art, often used lacquers, and preferred to work in oak. In 1920, he was commissioned to design the apartment of fashion designer Jeanne Lanvin, for whom he created bronze furniture.

Eileen Gray, who was Irish but worked in Paris, created floor lamps, benches, and tables using asymmetrical designs that echo Cubist patterns. Her style was also very individual, and more Modern than that of many of her contemporaries.

Louis Süe and André Mare were the most traditional designers of the period in many ways, and were influenced by provincial styles. Their Compagnie des Arts Français created dignified furniture highly prized today for its refinement and restraint.

Jean Dunand perfected the art of lacquer, especially eggshell lacquer. The lengthy lacquering process of layer upon layer requires extreme skill and patience if a high-quality finish is to be obtained. But, by the 1930s, lacquer, too, had become modernized, and industrial lacquer and enamel in design extended right down to designs on cheap cigarette cases.

Fashion affected furniture design. Just as the previous generation's hoop skirts and crinolines necessitated certain proportions for chairs, the new fashion meant new furniture. To wear an Oriental-inspired robe or long stylish dress with the required casual slinkiness, a low-slung couch or chaise longue, literally "long chair," was needed instead of a straight-backed settee. To go with low chairs, tables became low cocktail or coffee tables.

The impact of Les Ballets Russes on early Deco furniture was an Orientalism which some have dubbed a "boudoir style." There was a fashion for pattern-on-pattern textiles and cushions with long silk tassels. Furniture was redesigned for comfort, including deeper armchairs and dining room tables with a single pedestal instead of legs.

Interior designers paid as much attention to tapestry, curtains, chair covers, and wall hangings as they did to furniture. Fountains, flowers and multicolored brocades were typical designs.

Paul Follot used abstract shapes and stylized flowers in textiles to create a rich effect. Follot liked "beautiful" materials and techniques such as marquetry, lacquer, and bronze work. In 1923, he became director of Pomone, the workshop for the department store Au Bon Marché, and was in charge of its pavilion at the 1925 Exposition. He defended a tradition of luxury and was opposed to mass-produced furnishings.

Maurice Dufrène, who in 1904 had been a founding member of the Salon des Artistes Décorateurs, became the director of La Maîtrise, the workshop for the department store Galeries Lafayette. He designed a multitude of furnishings, ceramics and decorations that were executed by numerous companies. His furniture designs are outstanding, and highly individual.

These specialized workshops in the department stores had a huge impact on furniture design, and their pavilions at the 1925 Paris Exposition were among the most popular. Along with those already named, Claude Levy, who directed the Primavera workshop at Au Bon Marché, commissioned numerous designers in all of the decorative arts for their stores.

Even after the use of tubular metal in furniture design gained popularity at the end of the 1920s and early 1930s, some French designers remained loyal to traditional materials, although they often adopted modern form and design. Today, they are gaining increasing recognition and popularity with collectors who enjoy the warmth of wooden furniture.

Included in this category are André Arbus, Ruhlmann's nephew Alfred Porteneuve, Jean Pascaud, Jean Royère, and Jacques Adnet, who took over the direction of Süe et Mare's Compagnie des Arts Français in 1928, where he remained until 1959. Also sought after are works by René Prou, who succeeded Follot as director of Pomone from 1928 to 1932, and Michel Dufet, whose company Meubles Artistiques Modernes created stunning designs that were produced in series by Le Bucheron.

In 1927, metal furniture was first exhibited at the Salon des Artistes Décorateurs. The new furniture designers were greatly influenced by the Bauhaus, where, in 1924, Marcel Breuer had introduced the first furniture made in tubular steel, and modular furniture the following year. Sometimes called the "Moderns," they regarded furniture as "interior architecture" or "household equipment." They further simplified the lines, volume, and decoration, making it easier to mass-produce and reflecting social and economic changes in the world.

Thonet began to mass-produce tubular steel frames in 1928. Concert halls, restaurants, and other commercial establishments were quick to realize the practicality of the new stacking chair. With the rise of urban centers, especially after the Wall Street crash of 1929, the demand for fine furniture was not as great as the demand for less costly furniture for everyday use by middle-class families.

In 1930, inspired by the Bauhaus and Modern theories of Charles Edouard Jeanneret (1887–1965), who called himself Le Corbusier, a number of artists created the Union des Artistes Modernes (UAM) and declared a radical departure from the style of their contemporaries. These artists included some already mentioned, such as Jacques Adnet and René Prou, as well as Francis Jourdain, Raymond Templier, and architects René Herbst, Robert Mallet-Stevens, André Lurcat, Pierre Chareau, and others.

Le Corbusier set the philosophical tone of the Modern movement, declaring that furnishings should be made in the service of people and not art. In 1927, he designed chairs and tables of various types that were manufactured by Thonet in tubing, metal, and glass. The chair coverings were simple pieces of canvas held taut by spring fastenings. However, his best-known chair uses pony skin stretched between metal tube supports.

René Herbst was one of the main people responsible for the split that led to the Union des Artistes Modernes. He was openly hostile to all decoration, and made prolific use of metal, steel, aluminum, and other new materials. Robert Mallet-Stevens also used chromed and painted metal tubing.

Francis Jourdain was one of the first to face the problem of smaller living spaces with the design of his furniture. He was determined, in a socialistic way, to produce low-priced furniture for the masses. Like Pierre Chareau, he looked at furniture with the eye of an architect.

In France, Décoration Interieur Moderne (DIM), founded by René Joubert in 1919, became one of the first French companies to start producing chrome furniture a few years later. In 1931, Practical Equipment Limited (PEL) opened in England, obviously influenced by the idea of furniture as "equipment." The leading designers of furniture in England were Serge Chermayeff and Welles Coates, both architects.

American furniture design, which had been evolving on its own in the 1920s, was much more influenced by the Bauhaus and the "Moderns" than by Ruhlmann and Süe et Mare. Many designers, in fact, had emigrated to the United States from Austria, Germany, and Scandinavia.

Furniture designers such as Bruno Paul came to America because they felt their ideas would be readily accepted in the country which was moving the fastest toward industrialization. Paul's work was praised at the 1928 Macy's exhibition.

The Bauhaus, founded by Walter Gropius in 1919, relocated to the United States in the 1930s. Gropius became a professor of architecture at Harvard University. Ludwig Mies van der Rohe (1886–1969) and Marcel Breuer also came to America. Many of their designs were issued, and have been reissued by Knoll International, founded in 1938, and well-known for their office furniture systems.

Scandinavian countries were quick to develop simplified Modern design when faced with the austerity of the global Depression. Perhaps the best-known Finnish designer was Alvar Aalto, known for his streamlined designs for chairs, armchairs, and tables. Eliel Saarinen, who emigrated to America from Finland, became the first director of the Cranbrook Academy of Art in 1922, and influenced countless American designers. The impact of Scandinavian Modern design would be strongly felt in the 1930s and into the 1940s in the work of Charles and Ray Eames, George Nelson, and Eero Saarinen, Eliel's son, who designed bent plywood furniture that was marketed through Knoll.

America really had had no strong native style of furniture since the American Colonial style. Many movements had their heydays: Chippendale, Tudor, Victorian Gothic, Rococo, Eastlake, and Arts and Crafts among them. However, when the new European design reached America, the forces of the Prairie School and Frank Lloyd Wright (1867–1959) were already at work, transforming the shape of both architecture and furnishings in America.

Another architect, Joseph Urban (1872–1933), who emigrated from Vienna, had a strong influence on both architecture and American decorative arts of the period. He was director of the Wiener Werkstätte Gallery in New York, where he displayed a variety of furniture.

It is Paul Theodore Frankl (1878–1962) who stands out as the first major Modernist in America. Born in Vienna, he studied in Berlin and Copenhagen before coming to America in 1914. It was he who noted that the 1925 Exposition in Paris would have been markedly different if America had been able to display a skyscraper or two.

Skyscrapers were the inspiration for his extraordinary desks, wardrobes, and bookcases introduced in 1926, custom-made at Frankl Galleries in New York. Generally made in California redwood with nickel-plated steel or lacquered trim and interiors, these met with immediate acclaim, and can sell for tens of thousands of dollars today—when they can be found on the open market.

Although some criticize Frankl's work for its use of cheaper materials and sometimes less than elegant finishing and enameling, his conceptual strength shows through. Frankl was also a great advocate for the Modern movement, and a prolific writer who spread his design ideas by example and by the written word. Later, Frankl contributed his talents to designs for production furniture for Johnson Furniture, Brown and Saltzman, and Barker Brothers department store in Los Angeles.

Eugene Schoen was another early Modernist designer in America, establishing an architectural practice in New York in 1905. He produced only one-of-a-kind items which have traces of both French and German influences, and his pieces are rare and expensive on the market. His work has been compared to Ruhlmann's in that it is monumental and unadorned, and often relies on the grain of the wood for its design.

Urban living spaces and the American lifestyle called for furniture to change dramatically once again. Built-in closets and cupboards eliminated the need for wardrobes and kitchen stands. Dining room tables were given drawers for silverware. Even baby grand pianos were designed by Chickering, Steinway, and others in the new Modern style. Fireplace chairs disappeared with fireplaces. Metal and glass increasingly replaced wood. Upholstered "easy chairs" and sofas became popular, and modular furniture could be arranged to fit smaller spaces better. With the end of Prohibition in 1933, liquor cabinets, bars, stools, and other furniture proliferated. Also, a host of synthetic industrial materials came into use, known by their familiar trade names such as Formica, Bakelite, and Plexiglas.

For design pioneers in America like Donald Deskey, the use of plastics, steel, and aluminum to create low-cost furnishings that could be easily mass-produced was a way to satisfy the twin goals of quality and quantity.

Donald Deskey is a giant in many fields of American design. He founded his own design firm, Deskey-Vollmer, with partner Phillip Vollmer in 1927. His first furniture designs were private commissions, and he went on to design for manufacturers such as Ypsilanti Reed Furniture Company, Widdicomb, S. Karpen & Company in Chicago, and others. Over four hundred pieces of his work were put into production in the four-year period of 1930–1934, and many feel his crowning achievement was the interiors and furnishings for Radio City Music Hall.

Another notable designer is Kem Weber, born Karl Emmanuel Martin Weber in Berlin, where he studied under Bruno Paul. He was a proponent of a streamlined style in furnishings and other designs, and even streamlined his own name, taking his initials K. E. M. as a first name.

He went to San Francisco in 1914 to work on the German pavilion for the Panama-Pacific Exposition, and was forced to remain there when war broke out. After the war, he moved to Los Angeles and soon became art director for Barker Brothers, and opened his own design studio there in 1927. He was perhaps the only notable Modernist designer on America's West Coast, where he became friends with Modernist architect Richard Neutra. Weber also designed for S. Karpen & Company and created tubular metal designs for Lloyd Manufacturing.

Other important American furniture designers include Gilbert Rohde and Wolfgang Hoffmann. Rohde was chief designer for Herman Miller, and his work was also manufactured by Troy Sunshade in Ohio, Heywood Wakefield, Kroehler Manufacturing in Chicago, and others. (*See "Special Focus: Gilbert Rohde."*) Wolfgang Hoffmann, the son of Vienna Secessionist Josef Hoffmann, designed a sought-after line of metal, enamel, and glass furniture for the Howell Company in Geneva, Illinois.

Russel Wright created a number of designs for his own "American Modern" furniture line, as well as for the Massachusetts manufacturer Heywood-Wakefield, for whom he created the "Flexible Modern Line."

While Walter Dorwin Teague and Norman Bel Geddes are both towering figures in American design of the era, they are best known for their industrial designs. Both did some furniture design: Teague designed for S. Karpen & Company, and Bel Geddes designed metal furniture for Simmons.

At first, the industry was focused on wooden furniture, and centered mostly in Grand Rapids, Michigan, where it had the resources of numerous European immigrant cabinetmakers and workers who had settled in the Midwest. Other Grand Rapids manufacturers included the Imperial Furniture Company and Grand Rapids Chair and Bookcase Company, among others. One line of furniture by Grand Rapids Chair and Bookcase Company, called "Sculptured Modern" is particularly notable. (*See description and photo in the "Furniture Price Listings," page 115.*)

Grand Rapids lost its preeminent place in American furniture making in part because it was slow to respond to the surge toward production of furniture in metal.

There were numerous American metal furniture manufacturers in the 1930s, including the already-mentioned Herman Miller, Widdicomb, Troy Sunshade, Simmons, and Lloyd, as well as Mutual Sunset Company and Royal Metal Furniture. Many of the designs of these companies look alike, and unless there is a company mark or label, or you are armed with original catalogues, it is often hard to tell the difference. Another notable metal furniture designer, Warren McArthur, designed for his own manufacturing company in New York, which used spun aluminum extensively in furniture.

One of the most common types of anonymously mass-produced American Art Deco furniture used blue mirrored glass for tops of tables, coffee tables, bars, and more. Much of this production is unidentifiable, and in the late 1960s and early 1970s, numerous cheap reproductions were manufactured.

Mass-produced English furniture of the 1930s is also sold in this country, and the most notable examples on the market are the bar cabinets, armoires, and other furnishings designed by Ray Hille. Of course, the most valuable collectible furniture will always be that designed by recognized designers. However, there is an increasing market for the overstuffed American mohair furniture that was popular during the Depression. Today, this furniture is being refinished and reupholstered, and many people find it stylish, functional, comfortable, and durable—the very reasons it was popular in the 1930s.

METALWARE

In metalware, there is no question that the dominant artist of early Art Deco is Edgar Brandt. Brandt's work is remarkable for the combination of traditional skills and the use of new technology. He used autogenous welding, a process that permits two different metals to be welded together, and the new power hammer. These tools also allowed for greater production and lower costs. Today, his gates, lamps, andirons, wrought-iron mounted tables, fire screens, and other works are very expensive.

In 1926, Brandt did the metalwork for the Cheney Building in New York City, where he opened a branch of his company. Other French designers who are sought-after for their work in metal include Raymond Subes, Paul Kill, and Nic Frères.

Known for his metalwork in a more traditional way was William Hunt Diederich. Born in Hungary in 1884, Diederich emigrated to America like so many of his contemporaries. He worked primarily on Long Island, and died in 1953. Diederich was noted for his weathervanes, fireplace screens, and other metalwork.

The metalwork of Oscar B. Bach, who emigrated to New York City from Germany, is increasingly drawing attention on the market, in particular his designs for mirrors, lighting, and other furnishings. Bach did the metalwork on the Empire State Building and for interiors of the Chrysler Building and Radio City Music Hall, and his work is bound to have an increased following in the years ahead. Metalware such as andirons by Donald Deskey and Russel Wright also command attention on the market.

LIGHTING AND LAMPS

Many noted lamp designers were glassmakers, such as René Lalique, Daum Nancy, Charles Schneider, and Degué. (*See also* "*Glass.*") Sought after today for their finely designed and still affordable chandeliers is the French firm Muller Frères. One of the leading figures of early Art Deco design for lighting is Albert Cheuret, whose works are expensive and who often used alabaster for the shades.

Several of the metal designers named also designed lighting fixtures incorporating metal. Edgar Brandt worked with Daum to create luxurious table lamps and torchères, literally "torches," or floor lamps. Today, they are sought after by glass collectors as well as by Brandt collectors.

Figural and sculptural lamps also increased in popularity. Another noted artist was Jean Goulden, who was influenced by Byzantine enameling and who created visually appealing geometric and abstract designs for lamps, as well as other furnishings. Jean Perzel, a Czechoslovakian who emigrated to France, also created fine designs for lighting.

Collectors should take note of the many wonderful anonymous designs for chandeliers and other lighting fixtures produced in a French style in the United States in the 1920s. Created by such companies as Lincoln, Lightolier, and Markel, they were often produced in painted or patinated cast base metals instead of wrought iron, but are well-designed and affordable. Both Consolidated Lamp and Glass and Phoenix Glass also produced chandeliers and wall sconces.

Perhaps the best-known American lighting designer is Walter von Nessen. After studying in Berlin under the progressive architect Bruno Paul, he settled in New York in 1925 and opened his own studio two years later. He received commissions for architectural lighting, as well as doors, vestibules, and elevator cabs.

While he is also known for his houseware designs for Chase Brass and Copper, as well as for small metal furnishings, he is most highly regarded for his design of lamps, using chrome, aluminum, glass, Bakelite, and other modern materials. Nessen Lighting continues to manufacture many of his innovative swing-arm designs today. Some have attributed the outstanding design of the Pattyn Products table lamp featured in our color section to von Nessen.

Lamps and lighting fixtures had undergone a change. With the perfection of Edison's incandescent bulb in the 1920s, lighting had become more of a science. The form of the lamp depended more on the type of lighting desired than on a shape of a lamp as sculpture.

Other residential and commercial lamp designers of the day include Donald Deskey; Walter Dorwin Teague; Kem Weber, for Miller Lamp Company; Gilbert Rohde; Kurt Versen, who designed for Lightolier; and Carl Sorensen. Through the 1920s and 1930s, dozens of companies produced decorative and commercial lighting fixtures. A new term, "illuminating engineers," came into being, and many unique designs were created.

CLOCKS

No pun intended, but one can watch the evolution of the Art Deco style ticking away in the design of the clocks that were always a part of furnishing a household, from key-wound models to later digital electric alarm clocks.

In the early Art Deco period, French clocks were often made of gilt bronze and marble, and designed with fruit, flowers, and stylized birds or veiled nudes. Süe et Mare created mantel clocks in gilt-bronze, one of which has a case formed as a pair of doves. Albert Cheuret, mentioned previously for his lighting designs, was a leading designer of clocks, such as a 1930 silvered bronze and onyx clock that was reminiscent of a Cleopatra headdress. Luxurious glass clocks were made by Lalique, fabulous jeweled bedside and mantel clocks were made by Cartier, and silver designer Jean Puiforcat contributed some stunning designs. (*See color section.*)

In France in the 1920s and 1930s, for middle-class customers many manufacturers produced mantel clocks with garniture. Literally translated as "garnish," these were two additional pieces placed on either side of the central clock to decorate the mantel. Clock garnitures had been made previously, but the Deco style made use of marble or onyx set in geometric patterns. In addition, the clock itself may be surmounted with bronze or brass figures. Some had figures of Cleopatra, Amazons, or distinctively styled animals.

American manufacturers of clocks which are sought-after today are Herman Miller, Pennwood Numeron, Seth Thomas, J. E. Caldwell, and Manning Bowman, which still produced clocks in wood and/or marble before switching to chrome.

Gilbert Rohde created several clock designs for Herman Miller Clock Company (later Howard Miller Company) of Zeeland, Michigan. Paul Frankl's "Skyscraper" clock for Telechron is also a fine example by a leading designer. In the 1930s, American clock faces changed dramatically as digital clocks came into use, or as designers replaced numerals with chrome balls or squares of plastic. Kem Weber's digital clock designs for Lawson time, such as his "Zephyr" clock, are among the most notable of the era.

FURNITURE PRICE LISTINGS
(Alphabetically by designer or manufacturer)

ANONYMOUS

Armchairs, American, c. 1935, 35" high, 40" wide. Pair of mohair overstuffed armchairs with two-tone burgundy, with gray and blue mohair; overall bulbous form. Good quality and condition.   **$800–$1,000**

Armchair, Austrian, c. 1930. Walnut reclining armchair, the adjustable back above sharply rounded arms continuing to form the feet, with back and seat cushions. (*See photo, opposite.*)   **$2,250 (Auction)**

Armchair, English, c. 1930s. Maple framework with black lacquer. Seat depth 27", and arms in four horizontal planes from back to arm support. Two cushions, restored in original pink satin. (*See photo, opposite.*)   **$1,500–$1,650**

Armchair, French, c. 1930. Rosewood armchair, the rectangular back above downswept arms, the suede-upholstered square seat raised on square front legs joined by a rounded base stretcher. (*See photo, opposite.*)   **$1,700 (Auction)**

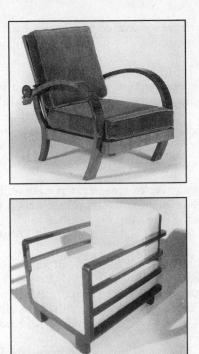

Austrian walnut reclining armchair. *Courtesy of Butterfield & Butterfield, California.*

French rosewood armchair. *Courtesy of Butterfield & Butterfield, California.*

English armchair with maple frame-work and black lacquer. *Courtesy of The Warehouse, Pennsylvania.*

Armchairs, American, c. late 1930s. Various living room chairs with deep seats, wide arms. Overstuffed look, with rounded edges and occasionally with wood veneer trim.

Unrefinished and unrestored	**$500–$600**
Restored and reupholstered	**$1,500–$2,000**

Armchairs, French, c. 1930, 32" high. A set of eight zebrawood and palissandre arm-chairs with padded backs and seats into an angular frame, the tapering legs of square section terminating in gilt-bronze sabots, some with tag inscribed "S.A.L.T./Lyon 30 rue Crequi." **$9,000 (Auction)**

Armoire, English, c. 1930s, 70" high, 46" wide, 20" deep. In walnut veneer, two doors with Bakelite handles, fitted interiors. Inside compartments with glass doors have metal labels marked "Shirts," "Collars," "Sportswear," "Pajamas," etc. **$700–$900**

Armoire, French, c. 1925, 72" long. Burl wood veneered armoire, the fluted doors with ivory escutcheons. A very good example in fine condition. **$2,400 (Auction)**

Bar, American, c. 1930s, 49" high, 59" long. Black lacquered, gilt, and airbrushed. Triangular form, divided in sections by "skyscraper" side relief; original gilt and airbrush design of repetitive circles. **$2,000–$2,200**

Bar cabinet, 55" high, 43" wide. Stepped round front with roll doors opening to an illuminated mirrored top and fitted base. Dark brown finish.   **$425 (Auction)**

Bar cabinet, American, late 1930s, 44" high, 73" wide, 14" deep. In polished walnut, two-door storage with shelves below, upper portion opening to reveal mirrored bar with light, ashtray, and toothpick holder. In excellent condition.   **$800–$1,000**

Bar cabinet, American, c. 1935, 33½" long. Rectangular surface and hinged lid opening to sunken mirrored interior, with semicircular chromed metal shelf and rail. Good condition.   **$1,300 (Auction)**

Breakfront, American, c. 1935, 70" high, 45" wide. Burled veneered stepped front, featuring orange Bakelite pulls and round knobs of simulated wood. Three-section top with two glass doors flanked by two on angle; the base with two doors flanked by two curved doors. Very good condition.   **$700–$900**

Breakfront, French, c. 1925, 72" high, 60" wide. In French oak, with an Italian verdi marble counter. In three sections, with two side cabinets with beveled glass windows and a center section with a beveled glass mirror. The oak carved with the stylized fruit and flowers motif of early French Air Deco. An excellent example of the style, albeit anonymous. (*See photo, below.*)   **$2,500–$3,000**

Buffet, French, 36" high, 70" wide, 17½" deep. The three central short drawers flanked by two cupboard doors with chrome pulls and escutcheons, bears metal tag of Dinner, Paris.   **$2,300 (Auction)**

Cabinet, American, c. 1935, 46" high. Mahogany cabinet with D-shaped curved cut-glass panel door with three-section round glass panel sides. In good condition.   **$275 (Auction)**

French oak breakfront. *Courtesy of Sambeau's Ltd., Missouri.*

Pair of French walnut club chairs. *Courtesy of Butterfield & Butterfield, California.*

Cabinet, French, c. 1925, 90" high, 42" wide. Case is diagonally laid African ebony, with brass banded trim at the top and bottom, double curved doors; opening to reveal three adjustable shelves below two recessed lighting fixtures; with a center rollout shelf above a drawer and a lower shelf. (*For photo, see section on "Materials and Techniques," page 17.*)
$3,800–$4,000

Cabinet, *curio*, English, c. 1935, 45" high, 40" wide, 14" deep. Curved walnut glass-front case with mirrored back, glass shelves, painted decorated glass-front doors.
$800–$900

Chair, American, c. 1933. Circular seat and spiral-design back that spirals down in front below seat level. Upholstered in new mohair with a feather cushion and hand-tied spring units. May have been designed to be shown at the 1933 World's Fair furniture exhibit in Chicago.
$2,500–$2,700

Chairs, 35" high. Side chairs, with gondola backs and ivory sabots on the front legs, upholstered in cream striped fabric. Pair.
$1,600 (Auction)

Chairs, American, late 1930s. Probably designed for an office or a nightclub in original leather, with solid, rounded dark brown arms, and rounded backs and seats in burgundy or tan leather. Pair.
$1,500–$1,600

Chairs, *club*, French, c. 1930. Mahogany club chairs, each angled velvet-upholstered back and cushioned seat enclosed by sloped and angled arm supports; raised on a plinth base. Pair.
$4,000 (Auction)

Chairs, *club*, French, c. 1930. Walnut club chairs, each barrel-shaped back with block-stepped sides, raised on molded platform feet; upholstered in moire satin. Pair. (*See photo, above.*)
$7,000 (Auction)

Chair, *side*, English, c. 1930s. Mahogany framework, refinished and upholstered in original green leather with white and red leather trim and piping.
$1,200–$1,300

Chair, *side*, French. Eight walnut side chairs, each with a curved rectangular back and raised on tapering square legs, upholstered in gold cut-velvet fabric with a swirling design.
$4,000 (Auction)

Console in chrome and ebonized wood.
*Courtesy of Butterfield & Butterfield,
California.*

Chest of drawers, French, 35" high, 46" wide, 19" deep. Lacquered chest of drawers, the three long drawers with large chrome pulls.   **$1,500 (Auction)**

Console, American, 34½" high, 36" wide. After a design by Donald Deskey. In chrome and ebonized wood, the shaped rectangular ebonized top raised on three scrolled chrome supports on a rectangular base. (*See photo, above.*)   **$950 (Auction)**

Console, French, c. 1930, 31" high, 58" wide, 21½" deep. Inlaid wood, with rounded front corners and wide reeded legs, the folding top opens to double surface.

$800–$900

Consoles, probably French, c. 1925, 40" high, 23½" long, 12½" deep. In wrought iron and marble, with faceted rectangular tops of beige marble, the wrought-iron supports of grid design with beaded aprons. Pair.   **$3,000–$4,000**

Credenza, French, c. 1935, 35½" high, 60" long. Overall curved design in ebonized wood with blond maple interior. A very good example, in excellent condition.

$3,500 (Auction)

Desk, American, c. 1935, 32½" long, 21" wide. Rectangular top over single drawer with copper pull, one end rounded with three open shelves for books.   **$500–$600**

Desk, French, 29½" high, 54½" wide, 25½" deep. Lacquered desk, the pedestal with four drawers, each with a chrome pull raised on a chromed metal base and footrest, lacquered with a tortoise-shell design.   **$1,500 (Auction)**

Desk, French, c. 1925, 29½" high, 59" long. Walnut "bureau plat" or "flat bureau"; rectangular top with beveled edge above a single center drawer, raised on tapering square legs. Fine condition.   **$3,750 (Auction)**

Desk, French, 30" high, 75" long. Rosewood pedestal desk, the slightly curved rectangular top raised on two pedestals, one fitted with three drawers, the other with a cupboard door.   **$3,500 (Auction)**

French black-lacquered
desk. *Courtesy of
Butterfield & Butterfield,
California.*

Desk, French, c. 1930, 30¾" high, 59" long. Black-lacquered desk, the rectangular top with slightly clipped ends above a cupboard door enclosing a slide-out liquor chest flanked by open shelves at one end, three conforming drawers at the other end, raised on chrome with plinth feet. (*See photo, above.*)   **$1,400 (Auction)**

Dining suite, French, c. 1930, table: 30½" high, 41½" long. Circassian walnut nine-piece dining suite comprising a dining table with two leaves, extending to 82", six chairs, a buffet and credenza; the chairs with rounded backs above black simulated leather seats; the buffet with gold-veined black marble top above a central beveled glass door; the credenza with marble top. Very good quality.   **$7,000–$10,000**

Love seat and chair, English, c. 1930s. In original cut mohair. Brown, orange, and beige with both straight lines and contrasting large stylized triangles. (*See photo, below.*)
                $3,000–$3,200

Magazine rack, American, c. 1930, 14" deep. In maple, with four compartments, each divider cut in a skyscraper form, topped with an ivory Bakelite decoration.   **$150–$200**

Magazine rack, American, c. 1935, 10½" deep. Overall circular design with three co partments for magazines, in blond wood painted with a geometric design.   **$50–$75**

**English love seat
and chair in original
cut mohair.** *Courtesy
of The Warehouse,
Pennsylvania.*

Sideboard, 42¼" high, 19" deep, 49½" long. A marble-top sideboard, the curved rectangular top set with gray marble, above a central short drawer and cabinet, flanked by two long cabinets.   **$300 (Auction)**

Sideboard, American, 40" high, 42" long, 20" deep. In ebonized wood with maple interior, designed with two drawers above a central cabinet, the cabinet also fitted with a pull-out tray for silverware. A good example of an American Art Deco dining room piece.   **$800–$1,000**

Sideboard, French, 38½" high, 72¼" long, 23" deep. A burlwood and macassar ebony sideboard, the central section with convex two-door front, flanked by side cabinets, the cabinets fitted with shelves, unsigned.   **$1,000 (Auction)**

Sideboard/bar, English, c. 1925, 37½" high, 54" wide, 19¾" deep. In various open grained wood veneers, with the center of top opening to reveal a mirrored and lighted compartment, over three drawers, top drawer fitted for implements. Two long cabinet doors, with interior median shelf, on a rectangular cut-out base. Metal tag "P & S Woods Ltd."
In good condition, in need of refinishing   **$300 (Auction)**
In very good condition, refinished   **$700–$900**

Sofa, American, c. late 1930s. High back and overstuffed cushions. Central cushion is higher than others, which are vertically cut in three sections each. Rounded edges and wood veneer trim. Deep-seated.   Unrefinished and unrestored   **$700–$800**
Restored and reupholstered   **$2,500–$2,750**

Sofa, Austrian, c. 1930, 92½" long. Walnut sofa, one end fitted with a raised cupboard door enclosing shelves, the side with open shelves, raised on rounded square feet. (*See photo, below.*)   **$2,000 (Auction)**

Austrian walnut sofa.
Courtesy of Butterfield & Butterfield, California.

Sofa in tubular chrome and leather.
Courtesy of Savoia's Auction, Inc., New York.

Sofa, American, c. 1935, 32" high, 68" wide. In tubular chrome and leather, with three thick sectional cushions, the backs in green and the seats and arms wrapped in deep red. Very good condition. (*See photo, above.*)   **$800–$1,200**

Table, 29½" high, 44" diameter; leaf: 21¾" wide. Circular with tapered, curving legs ending in gilt bronze sabots, with one leaf.   **$1,500 (Auction)**

Table/bookcase, French, c. 1925, 34" diameter. Parcel-gilt and red-lacquered marble-top bookcase table.   **$1,500–$1,600**

Table, card, French, c. 1930, 30" high, 29½" diameter. Rosewood circular card table, top with inset glazed surface with two handles, the reverse with baize-lined playing surface, raised on slightly flared tapering square legs joined by an X-form stretcher.
                  $1,700 (Auction)

Table, coffee, American, late 1930s, 17" high, 32" long, 17" wide. Stained blond wood; top has slight curve and inset blue mirrored glass. Legs are vertically banded, two tiers. In good condition, but in need of refinishing.   **$200–$225**

Tables, end, American, c. 1930, 22" high, 25" wide. Pair of end tables; designed as a wide circular band supporting two rectangular shelves, supported overall by a rectangular footed base, in blond wood veneer. Fine condition.   **$275 (Auction)**

Tables, end, American, c. 1935, top: 30" wide, 12" deep. Black lacquer and chrome end tables, each with three shelves. In very good condition.   **$1,250–$1,300**

Table, occasional, American, c. 1935, 32" high, 22" deep. In black lacquer and chrome, in very good condition.   **$950–$1,000**

French calamander occasional table.
Courtesy of Butterfield & Butterfield, California.

Vanity designed for the Dutton House.
Courtesy of Skinner, Inc., Massachusetts.

Table, occasional, French, c. 1930, 25" high, 24" diameter. Walnut occasional table, the circular top supported on three cabriole legs joined by a circular platform stretcher.
$2,750 **(Auction)**

Table, occasional, French, c. 1930, 23" high, 34½" diameter. Calamander occasional table, the circular top raised on four curved rectangular supports joined by a coved platform base. (*See photo, above.*)
$2,250 **(Auction)**

Vanity, American, c. 1930. 29¾" high, 39¾" wide, 13" deep. Designed for the Dutton House, Walpole, Massachusetts. Rectangular black marble top on a pair of scrolled flat steel supports, continuing to convex base accompanied by vanity seat and flush mounted circular wall mirror. Very good quality. (*See photo, above.*) $1,400 **(Auction)**

Vanity, American, c. 1935–1940, 58½" high, 59½" long, 18" deep. In blond wood, with large circular glass mirror set on long pedestal, flanked on left with four-drawer dresser with glass knobs.
$400–$600

Vanity, French, c. 1928, table: 30" high; mirror, 80" high. Rectangular metal-framed mirror held by shaped wood support, each side flanked by shaped and stepped top over pie-shaped drawer with open shelf over lower drawer joined by long vertical cabinet, with round pulls, raised on rectangular base.
$800–$1,000

Vanity and stool, American, c. 1935, 42½" high, 52" wide, 15½" deep. Central circular mirror flanked by two graduated drawers, on curving support and sled base, with matching stool. In very good condition.
$1,500–$2,000

Vitrine, French, c. 1925, 65" high, 30" wide. Zebrawood vitrine, the rectangular top above a glazed door, sides and mirrored back, raised on tapering cylindrical legs; with glass shelves.
$2,000 **(Auction)**

Vitrine, French, 65" high, 31½" wide. Fruitwood vitrine, the rectangular top above a beveled glass door, sides and mirrored back and base, over two cupboard doors opening to five drawers, raised on tapering rectangular feet.
$1,600–$2,000

Wall unit, Austrian, c. 1930, 73" high, 98¾" long. In walnut, in two sections, the rectangular top above open shelves, cupboard doors, a fall-front desk and liquor cabinet, the lower section with cupboard doors and slides, raised on shaped block feet. A fine example, albeit anonymous, in very good condition. (*See photo, below*.)   **$5,000 (Auction)**

ALVAR AALTO (Finnish, 1898–1976)
Armchairs, c. 1935, pair of laminated maple armchairs, each square back and seat flanked by broad rectangular arms curving to form the feet.   **$2,500 (Auction)**

Chair, lounge, c. 1932, 24" wide, 27" deep, 30" high. Designed for Artek. In bentwood, with laminated birch arm/legs, padded and reupholstered seat, arms are original finish, very good condition. Stamped "Artek."   **$800–$900**

"C" chair, c. 1930, 31" wide, 32" deep, 27" high. Designed for Artek. In bentwood and upholstery. Stamped "Artek." In excellent original condition.   **$1,500 (Auction)**

Stacking stools, 15" diameter, 17" high. Set of four stacking stools, black-lacquered tops, legs of laminated and molded birch. In excellent condition and original finish.
$1,200–$1,400

ANDRÉ ARBUS (French, 1903–1969)
Cabinet, c. 1935. An exquisite and important cabinet, presented at the 1937 Paris International Exhibition. It is covered in parchment and has nine drawers with ivory pulls and an ivory lacquered base.   **$40,000–$45,000**

Secretary, c. 1937. Created in parchment, with ivory fittings and the interior in parchment and sycamore, it is from the series of designs shown by Arbus at the Exposition Internationale de 1937. Arbus felt that a house should satisfy the material comforts of the inhabitant and should "compensate for the century of iron and reinforced concrete."
$40,000–$45,000

Austrian walnut wall unit. *Courtesy of Butterfield & Butterfield, California.*

Secretary by André Arbus. *Courtesy of Calderwood Gallery, Pennsylvania.*

NORMAN BEL GEDDES (American, 1893–1958)

Desk and chair, c. 1930, Desk: 30¼" high, 33¾" wide. Designed for Simmons; lacquered back and red, with a single drawer supported between curved ends. Good quality and condition.   **$350 (Auction)**
                                                                           $500–$600

Bedroom set, chest: 44½" high; dresser: 34½" high. Designed for Simmons, and including chest, dresser with mirror, and a pair of twin beds. Black enameled steel rounded at the top corners, fronts trimmed with a band of chrome; polished nickel pulls. Chest carries paper Simmons label.   **$1,200 (Auction)**

Bedroom set, c. 1925, vanity: 30" high, 43¾" long, 19¼" deep. Designed for Simmons, and including a vanity table with mirror, a chest of drawers, and a single bed. Black enameled steel, chrome trim, with paper Simmons label.   **$1,800 (Auction)**

COMM FIXTURE COMPANY (American)

Table, conference, c. 1930, 30" high, 15" long, 62" wide. Executed for the Los Angeles Pacific Stock Exchange Building in 1930, massive ebony-inlaid and bronze-mounted walnut conference table. Rectangular top with wide canted corners. Superior quality and fine condition.   **$10,000–$15,000**

DONALD DESKEY (American, b. 1894)

> **Among many other accomplishments, Donald Deskey designed the interior and furnishings of the Radio City Music Hall.**

Bedroom set. Designed for Widdicomb Furniture Co. Five-piece bedroom set in pale birdseye maple and black lacquer, includes tall chest, low chest, vanity with mirror and stool, and bedside table.   **$12,500–$15,000**

Console, c. 1930, 34" high, 20" wide. In Bakelite and chrome, with rectangular Bakelite top raised on three scrolled chrome supports on a rectangular base. A very good example of the designer's style, in excellent condition.   **$1,900 (Auction)**
                                                                         $2,800–$4,000

Console, c. 1932, 30" high, 24" wide, 12" deep. In Formica and aluminum, the black rectangular top supported by three aluminum legs curved at top and bottom, all on a smaller black rectangular base, stamped "Formica For Furniture Fixtures" and "14.23.1." (*See color section.*)   **$2,200 (Auction)**

Desk, c. 1930, 52" long, 36½" high, 21" deep. Designed for Valentine-Seaver, Chicago. In walnut veneer, wood, Bakelite, and chrome. Two drawers on the left above a cabinet, a single drawer in the center, and a cabinet on the right, orange Bakelite handles on cabinets and drawers, with maker's tag.   **$1,100 (Auction)**

Desk and chair by Norman Bel Geddes.
Courtesy of Savoia's Auction, Inc., New York.

Chest by Maurice Dufrène. *Courtesy of
Calderwood Gallery, Pennsylvania.*

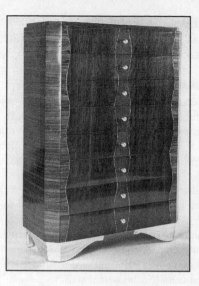

Table, c. 1928–1929, 24" diameter. Designed for Ypsilanti Reed Furniture Company. In
tubular chromed steel and black lacquer. **$1,500–$1,750**

Table, side, c. 1932, 21" high, 28" wide, 14" deep. In Formica and aluminum, the black
rectangular Formica top supported by continuous U-shaped aluminum legs, on two narrow rectangular feet, stamped "Formica For Furniture Fixtures." (*See color section.*)
$2,200 (Auction)
$2,500 (Auction)

DIM

*(Décoration Interieur Moderne, French firm founded by René Joubert and Georges Mouveau in
1918, operated through the 1940s)*

Desk, c. 1927, 31½" high, 40½" wide, 23¼" deep. In figured birch galuchat and ivory,
Cubist in conception. Tapering legs support a writing surface inlaid with nine panels of
center-cut galuchat, flanked on either side with angular lift-top wells lined in macassar
ebony veneer and fitted with ivory block knobs, all above one shallow central and two
deeper flanking drawers fitted with hidden release mechanisms. **$12,000 (Auction)**

MICHEL DUFET (French, b. 1888)

Bookcase/cabinet, 1930. Designed for Au Bucheron. In light rayed wood, center opening
bordered in macassar ebony. Two drawers with large cylindrical chrome pulls. Shown at
the Dufet Retrospective at the Musée Bourdelle in 1984. (*See color section.*)
$23,500–$25,000

MAURICE DUFRÈNE (French, 1876–1955)

Chest, c. 1927. Created from violet wood, purpleheart, abalone, and silver leaf, this
model was exhibited at the prestigious 1927 Salon des Artistes Décorateurs in Paris.
$18,000–$20,000

JEAN-MICHEL FRANK (French, 1893–1941)

Table, side, 16½" high. A wood and parchment side table, the slab foot and top joined by a scrolling X-frame support.   **$32,000 (Auction)**

PAUL FRANKL (American, 1878–1962)

Bookcase, c. 1930, each 75" high, 27" wide, 11" deep. A pair of lacquered wood and metal "Skyscraper" bookcases, each with slender ascending shelves above wider base, painted black with brick and red trim and cylindrical metal accents, each with metal tag "Sky/Scraper/Furniture/Frankl Galleries/4 East 48th Street/New York." An outstanding example of Frankl's early designs. (*See color section.*)   **$50,000 (Auction)**

Chair, side, c. 1930, 27½" high, 22¼" wide, 19¾" deep. Production furniture design in black lacquer and purple leather upholstery. In excellent condition.   **$2,500–$2,750**

Desk and bookcase, 1931, desk: 30¼" high, 42" long; bookcase: 66" high, 66" long. In painted wood, the bookcase surrounding the desk, with compartment interiors painted red, and silver pulls on the desk drawers. A good example of the designer's style, in good condition. (*See photo, below.*)   **$3,500 (Auction)**
                                                                     $5,000–$8,000

Dining set, American, dining table: 72" long, 42" wide, 32" high. Designed for Johnson Furniture. In mahogany and cork, comprising a rectangular table on double-pedestal base; a rectangular breakfront fitted with three drawers, and two doors enclosing fitted interiors surmounted by similar structure for three glass shelves, stamped "#22510193" with paper label; sideboard of rectangular form fitted with five central doors enclosing shelves, stamped "#2250–418," each stamped "Johnson Furniture Co, Grandrapids, MI."
                                                                     $2,400 (Auction)

**Desk and bookcase
by Paul Frankl.**
*Courtesy of Christie's
East, New York.*

**Rattan sofa and armchair
in the style of Paul Frankl.**
*Courtesy of Treadway
Gallery, Ohio.*

Rattan sofa and armchair, c. 1935, sofa: 75" long, 33" deep, 31" high; armchair: 34" wide, 33" deep, 31" high. In the style of Paul Frankl. Sofa in three sections; both sofa and armchair with a six-banded frame in natural finish; both reupholstered in a black wool fabric. In very good condition.

Sofa **$3,000 (Auction)**
Armchair **$1,000 (Auction)**

Tables, end, c. 1930s, each 18½" high, 20" wide, 26½" deep. Designed for Brown & Saltzman. In blond mahogany with bronze handles on composition drawers. A good example of Frankl's production furniture, in very good condition. Pair.

$2,500–$2,750

GRAND RAPIDS CHAIR AND BOOKCASE COMPANY (American)

Bedroom suite, "Sculptured Modern," c. 1939. In white oak, English brown oak, and white birch knobs with small aluminum inserts. Consisting of tall chest, low chest, vanity, nightstand, two mirrors, two twin beds. Figural reliefs carved in white birch adorn the chest and bed. The original advertisement for the set read, "A type of Decoration that will be instantly recognized by any student of Modern Decor." A fine example of an American Modern bedroom suite. **$3,600–$4,000**

**"Sculptured Modern" bedroom
suite, by Grand Rapids Chair
and Bookcase Company.**
*Courtesy of Of Rare Vintage,
New Jersey.*

WOLFGANG HOFFMAN (American, 1900–1969)

Console with mirror, 1930s, 70¾" high, 31" wide, 13½" deep. Designed for Howell Manufacturing. In black lacquer and chrome, with mirror. In very good condition.

$2,900–$3,200

Console table, c. 1930s, 27½" high, 12" long, 28¾" deep. Designed for Howell Manufacturing. In black lacquer and chrome. In excellent condition. $1,750–$2,000

Desk, American, c. 1935, 31" high, 43¾" long, 24½" deep. Designed for Howell Manufacturing. Black-lacquered desk with chrome base and pulls and black glass top. With Howell paper label, and in excellent condition. $4,500–$4,750

PAUL IRIBE (French, 1883–1935)

Bergère, c. 1913, 43¼" high, 29" wide, 23" deep. In carved walnut, the delicate black rail delineating an exaggerated, scalloped upholstered back, terminating at either side in elaborate nautilus spiral detailed with linear bead and foliate carving, all on a shaped frame. Seated on four tapering legs elaborately carved as pendant berries, blossoms, and leaves, inscribed signature, "Paul Iribe." $55,000–$75,000

PIERRE LEGRAIN (French, 1887–1929)

Tabouret, 20½" high. A tabouret in the African style, the rectangular seat and back a continuous arc canted on the sides and carved with series of pyramidal clusters of triangular devices further enhanced with gilding, the stool raised up on faceted conical legs terminating in faceted horn feet. $95,000 (Auction)

JULES LELEU (French, 1883–1961)

Cabinet, c. 1927. In Brazilian rosewood with ivory inlay and ivory mounts. Shown at Lord & Taylor 1927 exhibition. Script signature. A superb example of the artist's style which used the finest materials available. In excellent condition. $89,000–$95,000

Chiffonière, c. 1935, 63" high. Rectangular with two doors above the five-drawer set, opening to a shelved interior. With gilt bronze lock escutcheons, pulls, and cabriole leg edges. Paper label "Ce meuble dessine par J. Leleu a ete execute sous sa direction." Superior quality and fine condition. $20,000–$25,000

Cabinet by Jules Leleu, c. 1927.
Courtesy of Calderwood Gallery, Pennsylvania.

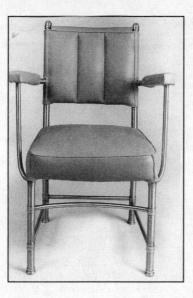

Warren McArthur armchair, c. 1935. *Courtesy of Treadway Gallery, Ohio.*

Dining table, c. 1938, 28¾" high, 58" diameter. A circular dining table, the pedestal base encircled by three bronze bands and raised up on three broad but slightly arching feet terminating in bronze sabots, with the firm's ivory tag.   **$16,000 (Auction)**

Table, games, and chairs, 1938. Square games table and four armchairs in palissandre rosewood, with nickel-plated bronze feet. Also, a nickel-plated bronze cupholder/ashtray pulls out from underneath the table on each side. Chairs covered in a red fabric to match the red felt of the tabletop.   **$12,500–$14,500**

WARREN MCARTHUR CORPORATION (American)
WARREN MCARTHUR (1885–1961)

Armchair, c. 1935, 32" high, 23" wide, 23" deep. In aluminum tubing, cast iron, wood frame spring cushion. In very good condition, but with recent beige upholstery to original specifications.   **$800 (Auction)**
    $1,800–$2,000

Armchair, c. 1935, 33" high. In aluminum tubing, with original red leather seat, arms, and back. A very good example of McArthur furniture, in excellent condition.
    $2,500–$3,000

Settee, c. 1935, 33" high, 48" wide. In aluminum tubing, with original salmon upholstery on the seat, back, and arms. A fine example, in excellent condition.   **$6,000–$8,000**

LOUIS NEISS (French, work: late 19th–early 20th century)

Table, side. In quilted mahogany, satinwood, and ebony, designed as a central pedestal on a square base, with overall angular design complemented by the inlaid wood. Neiss made the transition from Art Nouveau to Art Deco.   **$3,800–$4,000**

Side table by Louis Neiss.
*Courtesy of Moderne,
Pennsylvania.*

PITTSBURGH PLATE GLASS (American)

Armchair, 1939, 29½" high, 23¼" wide, 22¾" deep. Made from a single sheet of glass, with etched border, wrapped around an upholstered snakeskin seat. (*For photo, see section on "Materials and Techniques," page 17.*)   **$3,000 (Auction)**

PAUL POIRET (French, 1879–1944) and ATELIER MARTINE

Bed, c. 1928, 36¼" high, 82" long, 94" wide. Retailed by Lord & Taylor. The headboard with overlapping triangular panels in gilt and silvered wood, and matching footboard continuing on either side to circular seats; flanked by a square night table with circular shelves.   **$10,000–$12,000**

Cabinet, c. 1925, 46½" high, 38" wide, 19" deep. Designed by Poiret as a special commission for an American client. In black lacquer and silver-leaf, the doors opening to reveal two top drawers and four below. A very good example of Poiret's style, in good condition.   **$4,000–$6,000**

Cabinet by Paul Poiret,
c. 1925. *Courtesy of
Christie's East,
New York.*

Commode, c. 1923, 33¾" wide, 16¼" deep, 29½" high. Decorated by Leo Fontan. In silver-leafed wood and onyx, the front and sides of gently serpentine form, incised with outlandish designs of a roadster with a goggled driver, a woman in a hat with a gardening spade, a large flower holding a slumbering woman, and two women in a classical garden. The front feet of tassel form, the keyholes of onyx, with original silvered bronze key. Incised "Leo Fontan, 1923." An exquisite design.   **$70,000 (Auction)**

PRIMAVERA (French)
(Boutique in the department store Printemps headed by Claude Levy)

Table, c. 1925, 31" high, 31" square. In painted wood, the square beveled mirror top supported by two molded square sides, painted with a blue and green geometric design. Marked "Primavera."   **$7,000 (Auction)**

EUGENE PRINTZ (French, 1889–1948)
Cabinet, 31" high, 79" wide, 16½" deep. A mahogany and bronze mounted cabinet, the rectangular case fitted with a central bank of four doors, three with arched brass pulls, flanked on either side by rectangular cabinet doors, all resting upon reverse arched bronze mounted feet, stamped "E. Printz."   **$17,000 (Auction)**

ARMAND-ALBERT RATEAU (French, 1882–1938)
Table, c. 1922, 13" high, 34½" wide, 15" deep. In bronze and marble, with four finely cast birds of highly stylized form and feathers, grasping spheres supporting a rectangular marble top with conforming white marble stringing, the bronze with a green patina, each bird stamped "A A Rateau INVR 5545 1272," one additionally stamped "Paris."

$110,000 (Auction)

SPECIAL FOCUS
GILBERT ROHDE
by Ric Emmett

Ric Emmett is a certified fine arts appraiser, a nationally known speaker, and the president of Modernism Gallery in Coral Gables, Florida, which specializes in American designer furniture, other furnishings, and fine art from 1925 to 1965. You can contact him at: Modernism Gallery, 1622 Ponce de Leon Boulevard, Coral Gables, FL 33134, (305) 442-8743.

By the summer of 1930, the Depression had hit home, and a young New York City furniture designer named Gilbert Rohde made a trip to Grand Rapids, Michigan, to obtain business for his three-year-old firm. Grand Rapids was the hub of American furniture at the time, mainly due to the large number of German and Scandinavian furniture makers who emigrated there.

Rohde had already had several prestigious private commissions, and his studio furniture was collected by a number of wealthy New York clients, both private and commercial. He was producing his own furniture designs, which sold through Lord & Taylor department store. He had also designed a chair for the Massachusetts firm of Heywood Wakefield which had become a best-seller. He was certain that he could sell his skills to the mass producers of furniture in Grand Rapids.

However, Rohde's designs were considered avant-garde. He had visited Paris in 1927 and was influenced by the designers who had made the 1925 Exposition such a watershed of new form and use of nontraditional materials. The same year, he traveled to Germany and studied the work of the Bauhaus designers.

The Herman Miller Company was one of hundreds of furniture companies in Grand Rapids. Like those of its competitors, its designs were basically reissues of traditional designs, promoted as "This Year's Sheraton" or "Our New Chippendale Line."

Rohde convinced D. J. DePree, owner of Herman Miller, that the future lay in "Modern" furniture. Since Herman Miller Company was close to bankruptcy, DePree took a gamble. The fact that Herman Miller remains one of America's furniture giants sixty years later is testimony to the success of that gamble.

Rohde produced new lines for Herman Miller through 1941. Most of his case goods pieces were marked with a metal or metallic paper tag. Collectors can still find these tags sometimes, but, unfortunately, many of them were lost over the years. Almost all of Rohde's Herman Miller furniture has a four-digit code on the back. For many of his lines, the first two digits indicate the year that the line was designed.

A review of Herman Miller catalogues from the 1930s and early 1940s shows that Rohde changed not only his basic design from year to year, but the materials and veneers he used as well.

During his short career, cut off by his untimely death in 1944, Rohde also designed individual pieces and furniture lines for Kroehler Manufacturing, Heywood Wakefield, Thonet, John Widdicomb, and Troy Sunshade.

He originated the modern sectional furniture concept for seating and case goods while at Herman Miller. He also influenced Herman Miller to enter the lucrative field of modern office furniture, an area where home furniture manufacturers had never ventured.

Rohde went on to introduce a "Contemporary Juvenile Furniture Group" for Kroehler, the first children's furniture in the United States in the new Modern design style. For Troy Sunshade, his line of chrome furniture in 1933 brought Modern tubular chrome furniture into American homes. Today, many Art Deco collectors are familiar with his innovative tubular chrome "Z" stool for Troy Sunshade, which uses a single chrome-plated tube to form the base, support, and seat base. Apart from furniture, he lent his talents to designs for clocks and lighting fixtures for Herman Miller as well.

As with most Art Deco collecting fields, as public awareness of Gilbert Rohde's furniture increases, so do prices for his work. Ten years ago, as a Deco dealer, I recall telling a customer that there were no great American 1930s designers, only French ones. Even five years ago, the name "Rohde" would draw a blank stare from Deco dealers.

But things have changed. In 1981, Washburn Gallery in New York held a retrospective of Rohde's designs. Ralph Caplan's book *The Design of Herman Miller*, now out of print, and more recent books such as *American Art Deco* by Alastair Duncan, the Brooklyn Museum's *Machine Age*, and the American Federation of Art's *Bentwood and Metal Furniture*, have all featured designs by Rohde.

While Rohde's production furniture has not yet reached the price level of some other Modern American designers such as Donald Deskey, Kem Weber, or Paul Frankl, his prices are generally higher than those of George Nelson, who followed him as chief designer at Herman Miller.

There are numerous reasons that Rohde's designs are both worth collecting and will probably never go "out of style." His designs were not only original, they were most often innovative as well. He used exotic veneers such as paldao wood, acacia burl, rosewood, East India laurel, sequoia burl and white holly inlaid with paroba. Rohde's work was and still is scaled for American Modern living. In addition, happily, his designs were executed with the superb craftsmanship that was the basis of Herman Miller company's reputation.

For a few years after he was "rediscovered" by a wider base of collectors in the late 1980s, numerous pieces of Rohde furniture surfaced on the collecting market. Today, the amount of his furniture fresh to the market is slowing to a trickle, and the relative rarity of some lines and items is becoming apparent. Even with his more common pieces, not many were originally made and even fewer survive.

FIVE GILBERT ROHDE SHOPPING TIPS

1. Study the Rohde designs illustrated in recent reference books, and try to acquire the Herman Miller catalogues, some of which have now been reprinted, to help you identify pieces by Rohde and decide which styles you like.
2. Visit dealerships that specialize in Rohde and other American designers, as well as antiques shows, to see firsthand as much of his work as you can.
3. Realize that pieces which Rohde produced as commissions and in small series in his New York studio will probably always be more valuable than his designs for mass-produced furniture. However, many of his mass-produced designs weren't produced in the quantity we think of today when we say "mass-produced" and are quite hard to find on the market.
4. Remember, not all designs made by Rohde are marked. Those which were marked with metal tags or metallic paper labels may have lost their labels. The existence of a tag or a label does not in itself increase the price of a piece if it can be documented as a Rohde design in another way.
5. Try to buy pieces in the best condition you can find them, and only allow experts to handle any necessary restoration. Don't be afraid to ask a dealer if a piece has been restored, repaired, or refinished.

Note: *With special thanks to the Chicago Art Deco Society for the portions of this article which originally appeared in their newsletter* CADS News.

Detail of Rohde label.
Courtesy of Treadway Gallery, Ohio.

GILBERT ROHDE (1894–1944)

(Also, see additional listings for Rohde under "Clocks.")

Cabinet, c. 1933, 34" wide, 18" deep, 42" high. Walnut veneered cabinet with burled wood inlay stripe, mahogany pulls with satin chrome overlay, door opens to reveal shelving. In good condition, with some veneer loss, needs refinishing.   **$600 (Auction)**

Desk, c. 1934, 29" high, 42" long. Designed for Troy Sunshade. In chrome-plated steel, plastic, and wood. Simple tubular frame design, with two drawers suspended on right, in fine condition.   **$1,200–$1,500**

Desk, fall front, c. 1935, 48¼" high, 36¼" long. Designed for Herman Miller. The drop front with pigeonholed interior over a cabinet on the left and four drawers on the right, on pedestal feet. In good condition, needs refinishing.   **$900–$1,000**

Ottoman, c. 1934, 17" diameter, 16" high. Designed for Herman Miller. Cushioned ottoman in black leather, in excellent condition. (*See photo, opposite.*)   **$500–$600**

Stool, "Z," 1934, 24" high. Designed for Troy Sunshade Company. Red vinyl upholstered round seat, on a tubular chrome base with a single tube bent into a "Z" form to support the seat. In good condition, but needs rechroming.   **$400–$450**

Stool, "Z," as above, but rechromed and with reupholstered/repadded seat. **$750–$900**

Table, coffee, c. 1931, 17" high, 29" long, 18½" wide. Designed for Heywood Wakefield. Palissandre wood veneer, rectangular top on double molded U-shaped base raised on two cross stretchers. Overall good condition, with some restoration. Rohde's designs for Heywood Wakefield were generally not as finely executed as those for Herman Miller.   **$400–$600**

Tables, end, each 32" long. Designed for Herman Miller. In paladio wood, in excellent condition. Pair.   **$3,500–$3,750**

Table, end, approximately 30" long, model #3461. Designed for Herman Miller. In East Indian laurel wood. A very good example of a Rohde end table, in fine condition, refinished.   **$2,500–$2,750**

Games table by Gilbert Rohde, c. 1932, designed for Herman Miller.

Vanity and ottoman, c. 1934 by Gilbert Rohde, designed for Herman Miller.
Courtesy of Treadway Gallery, Ohio.

Table, games, c. 1932. Designed for Herman Miller. In inlaid fruitwood, with inlaid chess/checkerboard with circular tapered legs. Inset in each corner is an ashtray with mesh screens, small drawer for cards, game pieces, etc. In good condition, in need of refinishing. (*See photo, above.*)   **$2,500–$2,800**

Vanity, c. 1935, 56" high, 52" wide. Central mirror held with stylized clips; three-tiered Streamline bookshelf on left, three drawers on right, golden oak and dark walnut finish, signed on paper label in top drawer "Gilbert Rohde." Overall good condition with minor chips on mirror, some wear on veneer, in need of refinishing.   **$1,000 (Auction)**

Vanity, c. 1940, 53" wide. Designed for Herman Miller. A suspended top with slant sides and an arched front, above two- and three-drawer fronts on each side; large round pulls in black; rounded corner mirror with a deep black frame; chair with angular back slats and black seat upholstery wrapped over the front. A very good example of Rohde's style, in very good condition.   **$3,000–$4,000**

Vanity, c. 1934, 52" wide, 16" deep, 66" high. Designed for Herman Miller. In white holly and red ash, with tubular chrome base, full-length mirror flanked by circular cabinets, Bakelite amber-colored pulls on drawers, in very good condition. (*See photo, above.*)   **$3,250 (Auction)**
                                                                  $5,000–$6,500

Vanity, c. 1935, model #3920. Designed for Herman Miller. In rosewood and burl redwood veneers, brass-plated steel, glass, and ebonized plywood. Three drawers on each side, supported on a semicircular base, a semicircular central area for the chair; with three round mirrors, each individually supported on brass rods. (Illustrated in Duncan, *American Art Deco*, p. 52). An outstanding Rohde design, with only three known examples, in fine condition.   **$10,000–$12,000**

ROYAL METAL FURNITURE COMPANY (American)
Desk and chair, c. 1935, desk: 30¼" high. Three-drawer desk framed in tubular chrome, with black steel surfaces on the desk and chair covered in red. Good condition.
$350–$400

JEAN ROYÈRE (French)
Tables, side, 24" high, 18½" wide, 11¾" deep. A pair of mahogany and rosewood side tables, the continuous angular and free form rosewood frame supporting a rectangular mahogany box with depressed top and fitted with single drawer with circular brass pull.
$5,000 (Auction)

EMILE-JACQUES RUHLMANN (French, 1879–1933)
Banquette, 49" wide, 19" high, 13" deep. In upholstered macassar ebony, the seat lifting to reveal a storage area, branded "Ruhlmann."   **$10,000 (Auction)**

Beds, 37" high, 43½" wide, 81" long. In amboyna and ivory, sleigh-form on scroll feet, the molded side rails inlaid with ivory bands, branded "Ruhlmann" and "A" encircled. Pair.   **$15,000–$20,000**

Bed, "Lit Soleil" ("The Sun Bed"), 76½" high, 71" wide, 89½" long, mattress 67½" wide. In macassar ebony, the huge semicircular headboard featuring a stepped sunburst effect from the radiating veneers, the mattress set into a low Modernist base with slightly higher outturned footboard, branded "Ruhlmann." An outstanding design.
$120,000 (Auction)

Blotter, 7⅞" wide. A rocker-blotter, the base with oak inset panel surmounted by macassar ebony of shaped, stepped form and attached to the base by a large spherical device, branded "Dessiné Par Ruhlmann Edité Par Porteneauve."   **$850 (Auction)**

Bookcase, c. 1930, 67½" vectored. A mahogany corner bookcase, constructed of two four-level cases joined by a central three-level case, branded "Ruhlmann."
$15,000–$20,000

Cabinet, c. 1920, 71½" high, 55¼" wide, 18" deep. In macassar ebony, ivory, and silvered bronze. The two doors are ivory inlaid with an intersecting "oyster" design within a hexagonal reserve above two silk tassel pulls with ivory surround, the whole raised up on silvered-bronze fluted feet resting on a plinth, the interior fitted with adjustable shelves, branded "Ruhlmann" once on the cabinet and again upon the plinth base.
$70,000 (Auction)

**Cabinet by Ruhlmann, c. 1930
in macassar ebony and ivory
inlay.** *Private collection.*

Cabinet, c. 1930, 52" high. In macassar ebony with two doors, both with ivory inlay, in an intersecting diamond pattern, the gracefully curved legs ending in silvered sabots. Branded "Ruhlmann."   **$40,000–$50,000**

Chair, "Tivo," c. 1925, 27½" high, 15" wide, 17" deep. In macassar ebony and ivory. The back inlaid with an ivory Ionic scroll design, the slightly outturned legs ending in ivory pad feet, the seat with inset upholstered cushion, branded "Ruhlmann."
                                                                  $12,000 (Auction)

Chair, side, "Chaise Gondole," 37¼" high. In macassar ebony, with fluted back splat and drop-in upholstered seat, the front legs ending in silvered-bronze sabots, branded "Ruhlmann."   **$7,500 (Auction)**

Chaise longue, "Morozeau," 27½" high, 28" wide, 73" long. In macassar ebony, the sloping daybed with slightly scrolled backrest, upholstered and raised up on four fluted silvered-bronze feet.   **$32,000 (Auction)**

Dressing table and chair, "Red Head," dressing table: 48½" high, 35½" wide, 18" deep; slipper chair: 27" high. In aboyna, galuchat, and ivory, the central surface and drawer front inset with diamond-pattern galuchat and ivory banding; the pivoting bronze mirror surround supported by a semicircular frame; the rounded kneehole flanked on either side by a bank of three short drawers, the entire construction on a U-form base, branded "Ruhlmann" and "A" encircled.   **$62,000 (Auction)**

Easel, c. 1925, 71" high, 13" wide, 17½" deep. In macassar ebony of attenuated stele form on scrolled plinth foot, the picture brackets of chromed-bronze, branded "Ruhlmann" and "A" encircled.   **$48,000 (Auction)**

Mirror, 17" high, 15¾" wide. The shaped mahogany stand supporting a circular mirror, branded "Ruhlmann" and stamped "Deroubaix."   **$1,400 (Auction)**

Mirror, "Antilope," 18¼" high. A bronze table mirror, with circular face inset with mirrored glass and raised up on two outturned feet with fluting on upper section, supported behind with an easel back.   **$4,800 (Auction)**

$2,600 (Auction)

Mirror, "Psyche à Trois Feuilles," c. 1920, 79" high, 29¾" wide, 18¾" deep. A three-part macassar ebony and ivory standing mirror. Articulated panels each fitted on their interior with mirrored glass, the stele form resting on an undulating foot with ivory Ionic scroll design, further ivory on the front and back panels featuring a diaper in a diamond repeat within a rectangular reserve, branded twice "Ruhlmann." An outstanding example of Ruhlmann's style.   **$75,000 (Auction)**

Table, c. 1929–1930, 25½" high, 39½" diameter. In macassar ebony, the round dish top supported on three tapering scroll legs, joined by a central hexagonal terminus, branded "Ruhlmann."   **$25,000–$30,000**

Table, bedside, 23" high, 19" deep, 14¾" wide. In amboyna and ivory, oviform, on a stylized Ionic scroll base, with sliding pocket shelf and drawer below, branded "Ruhlmann" and "A" encircled.   **$7,500 (Auction)**

Table, reading, "Liseuse Cla-Cla," 30" high, 31½" wide, 24" deep. In macassar ebony, the articulated rectangular top attached by ratchet mechanism to a stele-like pedestal supported by two attenuated scroll feet, branded "Ruhlmann," stamped "Deroubaix," and branded "B."   **$46,000 (Auction)**

Tables, side, 23¾" high, 15¼" wide, 18" deep. Each in macassar ebony, oval, fitted with three false drawers on the verso, and on the recto having one drawer with open shelf below, each raised up and swiveling on a pedestal base further supported by a scrolled plinth, one branded "Ruhlmann." Pair.   **$48,000 (Auction)**

Tabouret, 17¼" high, 27" wide, 19½" deep. In upholstered macassar ebony, the legs of X-form, the feet silvered-bronze sabots.   **$19,000 (Auction)**

PAUL SAIN (French, b. 1904)

Screen, 69" high, each panel 17¾" wide. Lacquered four-panel screen, decorated with geometric motifs in gold leaf, eggshell, and colored lacquer, signed lower left.

$3,200 (Auction)

SÜE ET MARE (French)

LOUIS SÜE (1875–1968) and **ANDRÉ MARE** (1887–1932)

Bergères, c. 1920, 32¾" high. Upholstered acajou bergères, with gondola back and arms sweeping down to a circular seat on four legs; the scrolled back carved to resemble gathers of fabric; the aprons also carved as fabric with a fringed border; the legs each carved with a tassel, upholstered in tufted green velvet. A rare and fine example of the Süe et Mare style. (*See color section.*)   **$32,000 (Auction)**

Chair, 1920. Designed for the French ocean liner *Paris*. This beautifully sculpted chair is in mahogany and was pictured in *La Sculpture Décoratif Moderne* in 1925. $8,000–$10,000

Chairs, side, c. 1920, 33½" high. In upholstered acajou, with gondola back sweeping down to a circular seat on four legs; in the same design as the bergères listed above; upholstered in deep green tufted damask. $40,000 (Auction)

KEM WEBER (American, 1889–1963)
Armchair, c. 1935, 32" high, 29¼" wide. Designed for Barker Brothers in wood with brown leather upholstery. $6,500–$7,000

Chair, "Airline," 1934–1935, 25" wide, 30" deep, 30" high. The "Airline" chair designed for Walt Disney Studios in an edition of only three hundred and produced by the Airline Chair Company, a local Los Angeles furniture maker. This aerodynamic chair came unassembled in molded birch. Though discussions took place between Weber and manufacturers, the chair never went into production beyond the first edition. In the original finish, in very good condition with only minor chip in arm. $7,500 (Auction)

Sofa, c. 1930, sofa back: 21" high; seat: 60" wide, 21½" deep. Designed for Lloyd Manufacturing, with chrome frame and original pattern upholstery. $2,700–$3,000

WIDDECOMB COMPANY (American)
Cabinet, after 1930, 60" high. Tall cabinet piece, the case inset with three horizontal black bands, curved front with elongated pulls. Overall good condition. $600–$800

RUSSEL WRIGHT (American, 1904–1976)
Armchair, c. 1936, 28¾" high, 27" long. The back and seat cushion upholstered in leather. Branded "American Modern." Good condition. $600 (Auction)
$550–$850

Chair by Süe et Mare, 1920, for the ocean liner *Paris*. *Courtesy of Calderwood Gallery, Pennsylvania.*

Kem Weber "Airline" chair, 1934–1935. *Courtesy of Treadway Gallery, Ohio.*

METALWARE PRICE LISTINGS
(Alphabetically by designer or manufacturer)

ANONYMOUS

Andirons, American, c. 1930, 18" high. Raised chrome geometric pattern against textured black iron. Good quality and fine condition. $200–$300

Andirons, American, c. 1935, 17" high. In brass, with square poles terminating in angular and geometric designs. $325–$375

Andirons, figural. Man: 18" high. Silvered bronze shaped as a man and a woman; the woman has three movable brass bangle bracelets. Unsigned (possibly Hagenauer). (*See photo, below.*) $3,200–$3,400

Balcony guard, French, c. 1920s, approximately 72" long, 16" wide. Wrought iron with floral design. (*See photo, below.*) $575–$650

Console/mirror, French, c. 1925, console: 31" high, 19¾" wide; mirror: 49½" high. A wrought-iron and marble console and mirror with hexagonal peach marble top raised on openwork support wrought with scrolled design, the flared rectangular mirror surmounted by conforming scrolled crest.   **$2,800 (Auction)**

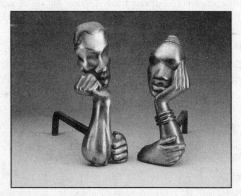

Silvered-bronze andirons with African motif.
Courtesy of Of Rare Vintage, New Jersey.

French wrought-iron balcony guard.
Courtesy of Salvage One, Illinois.

Wrought-iron fireguard in the style of Paul Kiss.
Courtesy of Skinner, Inc., Massachusetts.

Gates, possibly French, c. 1930, 33¾" high, 13¼" wide. In wrought iron, signed with maker's initials "F.T.," consisting of four vertical supports separated by vertical, decorative supports alternately undulating top and bottom, and surmounted with a repetitive circle design.   **$600–$800**

Fireguard, French, c. 1925, 26" high, 83" long. In wrought iron, two rectangular sections with fluted crest rail over a series of square spindles and foliate work; ends square with stands, Egyptian gray and beige marble top above two shelves. Possibly by Paul Kiss. (*See photo, above.*)   **$2,000 (Auction)**

Mirror, 31⅓" long. Oval with faceted edges and wrought-iron trim around the bottom and sides, the sides with decorative openwork panels and strips for hanging.

$600 (Auction)

Mirror, French, c. 1930, 24" long. Wrought-iron frame with stylized floral patterns. Mirror in good condition, with minor loss of silvering.   **$500–$650**

Pedestal, French, 48¼" high, 10¼" wide. In wrought iron, the textured rods supporting a square pale green marble top with canted corners. A very good example in fine condition

$2,200–$2,400

Pedestal, French, 28¾" high, 28" diameter. In wrought iron, the circular mottled red, gray, and white marble top within a textured wrought-iron band, raised on a textured rod support on a circular base decorated with scrolled and textured bars interspersed with circular coils.   **$2,000 (Auction)**

OSCAR B. BACH (German/American, 1884–1957)

> **Oscar Bach also executed metalwork on the Empire State Building, the Chrysler Building, and Radio City Music Hall.**

Bronze mirror by Oscar B. Bach.
Courtesy of Wolf's Fine Arts Auctioneers, Ohio.

Rooster andirons by Edgar Brandt.
Courtesy of Wolf's Fine Arts Auctioneers, Ohio.

Mirror, 39" high, 22" wide. The rectangular beveled frame in bronze with a notched border, the top edge cast with stylized scrolls centering a nude female form. Signed "Oscar B. Bach, N.Y."   **$1,300 (Auction)**
$1,600–$2,000

EDGAR BRANDT (French, 1880–1960)

Andirons, c. 1925, 13" high. In wrought iron, each in the form of a crowing rooster, with stylized widespread wings, on a rectangular base with two curling circular form feet. Stamped "E. Brandt."   **$7,000–$9,000**

Firescreen, *"Le Paon"* (*Peacock*), c. 1926, 51" high, 48" wide. In wrought iron, the elaborate peacock placed against a scrolling, foliate background, all within a reticulated, rectangular frame, stamped "E. Brandt."   **$13,000 (Auction)**

Gates, 78" wide, 30½" high. Wrought iron and bronze, the end post supports with curving and brace and medallion pattern, the two doors with framed scrolling ironwork, each with a central bronze figure, one of a maiden with tambourine, the other a male piper, stamped "E. Brandt."   **$14,000 (Auction)**

Mirror, *"Les Roses,"* 51" wide, 36" high. In wrought iron, the molded, circular frame supporting a beveled mirror, both sides adorned with scrolling rosettes and leafy foliage, stamped "E. Brandt."   **$40,000 (Auction)**

DONALD DESKEY (American, b. 1894)

Andirons, c. 1960, 19½" high, 9" deep. Chrome-plated and cast iron, modeled as a tapering spear form on a curved base with angled feet.   **$1,200 (Auction)**
$1,800–$2,000

HUNT DIEDERICH (Hungarian, 1884–1953)

Wall bracket, 23½" high. Wrought iron, in the form of a rooster. $5,000–$7,000

HAGENAUER (Austrian, 1920s–1930s)

Andirons, c. 1930, 6" wide, 4" deep, 21" high. Elegant stylized Art Deco leaf motif on heavy tiered chrome base, original finish, signed and with Hagenauer Werkstätte monogram, excellent condition. $850 (Auction)

NIC FRÈRES (Hungarian/French brothers Jules and Michel)

Vitrine, c. 1925, 56½" high, 24½" wide, 12" diameter. In wrought iron and glass, hexagonal, raised on four feet, with three shelves, unmarked. Fine quality and excellent condition. $3,000–$5,000

RAYMOND SUBES (French, 1893–1970)

Console, c. 1927, 33" high, 43" wide, 16½" deep. In wrought iron and marble, the black, forest-green, and white-veined marble top supported by scrolling legs adorned with ropelike bunting, all on a similarly shaped black base. $16,000 (Auction)

Console, 34½" high, 24½" deep, 76" wide. Wrought iron and marble on a white variegated, stepped marble base, the scrolling reticulated iron elements supporting a similarly shaped marble top. $13,000 (Auction)

Wrought-iron wall bracket by Hunt Diederich. *Courtesy of William Doyle Galleries, New York.*

Vitrine by Nic Frères, c. 1925. *Courtesy of Christie's East, New York.*

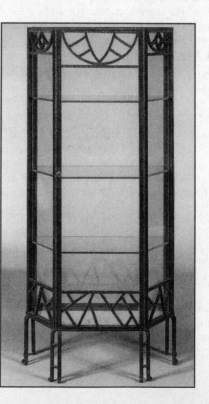

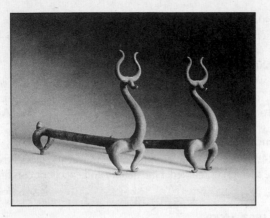

"Fire Deer"
cast-iron
andirons by
Russel Wright.
Courtesy of
Of Rare Vintage,
New Jersey.

Table, 29½" high, 92" long, 44½" wide. Wrought iron and marble, the buff marble slab top supported by a rectangular iron frame on scrolling legs joined by further tight, repeated scrolls and straight cross members, all on block feet.   **$12,000 (Auction)**

SÜE ET MARE (French)

LOUIS SÜE (1875–1968) and ANDRÉ MARE (1887–1932)

Console, 34" high, 36½" wide, 18" deep. In wrought iron and marble, the molded pink, green, and gray marble top supported by a banded apron with two curved, tapering legs terminating in a stylized floral basket, all seated on a marble base.   **$13,000 (Auction)**

RUSSEL WRIGHT (American, 1904–1976)

Andirons, c. 1930, 16" high, 23" long. Cast-iron "Fire Deer," signed "Russel Wright 1930."
$2,800–$3,000

LIGHTING AND LAMPS PRICE LISTINGS
(Alphabetically by designer or manufacturer)

(See also the chapters and price listings on "Glass" and "Ceramics" for additional descriptions of lighting fixtures.)

ANONYMOUS

Chandelier, American, mid-1920s, approximately 28" long. A highly stylized design, with openwork gilded base metal, and with five amber frosted shades with stylized floral motifs. A very good example of an American 1920s Art Deco chandelier. (*See photo, opposite.*)   **$600–$650**

Chandelier, American, mid-1920s, approximately 18" long. A stylized design that borrows from a more ornate French style, the stem and flush ceiling mount in an openwork fountain motif. In copperplate with five frosted glass shades and a central glass disk, all with stylized flowers. Perhaps made by Lightolier Company. In very good condition.
$800–$850

**American
chandelier,
mid-1920s.**
*Courtesy of
Vintage Modern,
California.*

Chandelier, American, mid-1920s, approximately 14" long. Base metal painted a metallic blue-gray, with three frosted glass shades in a dramatic wing-shaped form. In very good condition. $300–$350

Chandelier, probably Czechoslovakian, c. 1930, 16" wide. Glass and metal in the form of a star with etched and polished projections. A stunning fixture and a fine example of workmanship, albeit anonymous. $9,000 (Auction)

Chandelier, French, c. 1930. 16" high, 23½" diameter. Chrome, frosted and blue-tinted glass with a widely flared metal circular fixture with four quarter-circular blue glass fins. Central chromed tubular shaft with eight lights. Good condition. $275 (Auction) $500–$600

Chandelier and sconces, American, c. 1935, chandelier: 19" high; sconces: 17⅛" high. Blue and green glass and patinated metal star-form chandelier and pair of matching sconces, the chandelier in the form of a twelve-pointed star, each five-paneled arm in blue and green textured glass, the sconces with seven four-paneled arms. $800 (Auction)

Lamp, airplane, American, c. 1935, 7½" high, 11½" long. Blue glass body, accented in silver paint, with nickel-plated wings, tail, and base; resting on a looped metal support on a flat, rectangular base with rolled ends. (*Fakes Alert!* Reproductions of this lamp are on the market. Watch out for airplane lamps that look "too new.") In very good condition. $900 (Auction)

Airplane lamp, c. 1935.
*Courtesy of Skinner, Inc.,
Massachusetts.*

French table lamp, c. 1930.
Courtesy of William Doyle
Galleries, New York.

Chrome and copper table lamp,
c. 1935. *Courtesy of Vintage Modern,*
California.

Lamp, fan, American, c. 1925, 13⅜" high, 17" wide, 5½" deep. Fan-shaped mica-covered metal shade with painted metal standard and base. Somewhat transitional in style from Art Nouveau boudoir lamps.   **$400–$450**

Lamp, table, French, c. 1930, 26" high. Hexagonal shade and openwork decoration of stylized nude woman walking dogs. Mica panels and circular copper base. Fine condition. (*See photo, above.*)   **$1,600 (Auction)**

Lamp, table, American, c. 1935, 14" high. In chrome and copper, with an arching semi-circular stem supporting the rounded stepped-back shade. In very good condition. (*See photo, above.*)   **$275–$325**

Torchère, French, c. 1930, 70½" high. In chromed metal, glass, and burl wood, in fine condition.   **$1,000–$1,500**

Torchère, American, c. 1930, 66" high. Urn-shaped shade on cylindrical standard, held by two metal supports in brass finish with copper accents, on stepped circular wooden base, stamped "MS1C4375," in good condition.   **$400–$550**

Torchères, 65" high. In gilded bronze, Egyptian-influenced design, base with geometric scales surrounding ribbed axle leading to tricolor V-shaped ornamental cobweb design supporting crested fan-shaped mica shade.   **$2,200 (Auction)**

Torchères, c. 1930, 81" high, 24" wide, 24" diameter. High-style pair in anodized aluminum, with two-tiered shades, tiered base with floating disks and suspended tubes. In excellent condition, with one requiring rewiring. Large and dramatic fixtures.   **$3,000–$4,000**

Chrome mantel
torchères,
c. 1935.
*Courtesy of
Vintage Modern,
California.*

Torchères, mantel, French, c. 1930, 10½" high. Pair of mantel torchères, orange glass cylinders with black hand-painted silhouette scenes of women and children dancing.

$350 (Auction)

Torchères, mantel, American, c. 1935, 14" high. Pair of mantel torchères in chrome, with overall flaring form. In fine condition. Pair. (*See photo, above.*) $450–$500

JACQUES ADNET (French, b. 1900)

Sconces, 22" high, 5" wide, 3¾" deep. In metal, each of Modernistic geometric design, fitted for two lighting tubes. A very good example of lighting design by Adnet, known best for his furniture. $2,600 (Auction)

OSCAR B. BACH (German/American, 1884–1957)

Lamp, table, c. 1930, 26" high. Three standing bronze bird figures atop a ball on hexagonal stand; with sides of openwork plant form, flaring to larger hexagonal base; signed on plaque "Oscar B. Bach, New York." In fine condition. $1,200–$1,500

Lamps, table, c. 1930, 23⅝" high. A pair of parcel-gilt bronze, steel, and mica figural lamps, cast from a model by Oscar Bach, stamped on the underside in raised letters "Obaso Bronze c. Oscar B. Bach Studios." $1,800 (Auction)

Torchère, 59¾" high; shade: 12½" diameter. Mica shade, the ribbed brass stem in a circular base with four feet, the shade suspended from a scrolled arm. A very good example of Bach's style, in fine condition. $3,000 (Auction)

NORMAN BEL GEDDES (American, 1893–1958)

Torchères, 99" high. Pair of chrome ten-light torchères, each cylindrical shaft interspersed with alternating black and chrome circular disks, supporting a central and five curved arms ending in single lights, four larger curved arms below, all with frosted cylindrical shades, raised on ten scrolled legs; electrified. $11,000 (Auction)

EDGAR BRANDT (French, 1880–1960)

Chandelier, 29" high, 27" wide. Wrought iron and Daum glass with eight arms supporting upright domed crystalline glass shades, the arms joined by repeated V-shaped sections surmounted by upright tassels, the cylindrical center shaft terminating in a stepped conical finial, the shades inscribed "Daum Nancy France," the frame stamped "E. Brandt." A fine example of a Brandt-Daum collaboration.   **$16,000 (Auction)**
$22,000–$30,000

Lamp, table, c. 1925, 11¼" high. Wrought iron and Daum cameo glass, with the domed shade cut with stylized leaves and berries in enameled red on a white mottled background frosted with splashes of pink and green. Spherical lamp base resting on a square mount stamped "E. Brandt." A good example of a Brandt-Daum collaboration. (*See photo, below.*)   **$4,000 (Auction)**

Lamp, table, c. 1925, 19¾" high. Wrought iron and Daum glass, with three conical shades of mottled glass, etched "Daum Nancy." The base in elaborate wrought iron with applied leaves and scrollwork on a square mount.   **$8,000–$10,000**

Sconces, 14½" high. In wrought-iron wall, the circular mount with stylized tulip and foliage supporting two curved arms terminating in flared bobeches, stamped "E. Brandt."
$8,000 (Auction)

Torchère, 71" high, 17" wide. Wrought iron and alabaster, the tapering shaft joined at the center by a stylized floral band and ending in four rolled feet, all supporting a turned alabaster shade, stamped "E. Brandt."   **$18,000 (Auction)**

**Lamp by Edgar Brandt
and Daum Nancy.**
*Courtesy of Butterfield
& Butterfield, California.*

Chandelier by Hugue.
*Courtesy of Butterfield
& Butterfield, California.*

ALBERT CHEURET (French, work: 1910–1940)

¢ Cheuret is a recognized master of lighting design and often used alabaster for shades. Important pieces by Cheuret can bring over $100,000.

Lamp, table, 9" high, 13" wide. In alabaster and metal, the lozenge-shaped metal base decorated with a geometric pattern, supporting the shade formed from four triangular pieces of alabaster, with conforming metal finial, stamped "Albert Cheuret." In average condition, with cracks to the alabaster shade.   **$4,000 (Auction)**

Sconces, 16" long, 9" wide. In bronze and alabaster, modeled as a stylized bird in flight with extended legs, a conical alabaster shade suspended from its beak, inscribed "Albert Cheuret." A dramatic and very good example of the artist's work, in fine condition.
$30,000 (Auction)

DEGUÉ (French, 1920s–1930s)

Chandelier, 32¼" long. Silvered metal and glass, with central cylindrical globe in mottled yellow, orange, and blue held in a three-arm floral mount, each arm with matching bell for shade, one shade signed "Degue."   **$850 (Auction)**

Chandelier, 29" long. In silver-patinated metal, with three arms ending in bell-shaped shades in a honey-colored glass, surrounding a central dish-shaped glass shade of the same color. Central shade molded "Degue." In very good condition, and a good example of Degué's chandeliers.   **$1,800–$2,000**

DOMINIQUE (French, founded 1922, by André Domin and Marcel Genevrière)

Sconces, 13¼" long. In chrome and alabaster, the mounts of V-form, inset with a curving panel of alabaster, unmarked.   **$1,000 (Auction)**

JEAN-MICHEL FRANK (French, 1893–1941)

Lamp, table, 11¾" high, the base of intersecting wood X-form, fitted with a silk chiffon-covered card shade.   **$4,500 (Auction)**

HUGUE COMPANY (French)

Chandelier, c. 1925, 34½" high, 16" wide. Molded and frosted glass and chrome; striking design with geometric patterning of the glass and stepped metal supports, the glass signed "Hugue." Good quality and fine condition. (*See photo, opposite.*)
$1,200 (Auction)

L. KATONA (French)

Torchère, 56¼" high. In wrought iron and Daum glass, the cruciform base wrought with spiraling vines and berries, the cylindrical standard with scrolled vine and berry finial and adjustable arm holding flared, frosted bell-form shade, base impressed "L. Katona Made in France," shade engraved "Daum Nancy France" with Daum's Cross of Lorraine mark.   **$5,000 (Auction)**

JEAN LUCE (French, 1895–1964)

Lamps, table, 14¼" high, ceramic, the rectangular base supporting two curved arms forming a U-shape, each arm surmounted by a small shallow square "drip-pan" with circular bobeche fitted with light fixture, glazed in pale gray, with silver glazed edging, printed with the artist's monogram and "France."   **$3,000 (Auction)**

MAJESTIC LIGHTING COMPANY (American)

Torchère with tray, c. 1935, 57" high. An aluminum tubular standard, topped with a black paper shade. The standard loops to support a black lacquered tray table on a domed circular base stamped "MLSC 4579." A good example of later Art Deco floor lamps, in very good condition.   **$450–$600**

MULLER FRÈRES (French, 1910–1939)

Chandelier, 34" long. In glass and wrought iron, with central light bowl and three matching side shades of yellow shading to pink and blue mottled frosted glass, signed "Muller Frères Luneville," scrolling foliate ironwork.   **$800 (Auction)**

Chandelier, approximately 40" long. In nickel over bronze and frosted glass with stylized flower patterns. Central shade hangs from a circular mount that supports six scrolled arms, each in turn supporting a glass shade. The arms are also interspersed with frosted glass panels, signed "Muller Frères Luneville." A very good example of Muller Frères' chandeliers. (*See color section.*)   **$3,500–$4,000**

Chandelier, 41" long. Wrought iron and glass, the central circular frosted glass panel surrounded by six side panels, each molded with a stylized bouquet of flowers and signed "Muller Frères Luneville." In good condition, with restoration to one panel.
    $2,000–$2,750

Chandelier, 42" high. Wrought iron and molded glass, dish-shaped central shade with geometric leaf design. The wrought iron formed as grapes and leaves, with three scrolled arms, each suspending glass shades signed "Muller-Frères, Luneville."
    $1,500 (Auction)

Lamp, 15" high, 13" long. "Stork Lamp," designed by Muller Frères and Chapelle. The form of the stork shaped by a wrought-iron reticulated cage, with the blown glass body in silver-flecked bright pink, red, and blue glass. The bird perched on one leg above stepped square iron and marble platform marked "Chapelle Nancy France," glass signed "Muller Frères Luneville France." An outstanding example of a Muller figural lamp.
    $7,500 (Auction)

PATTYN PRODUCTS COMPANY (American, Detroit)

Lamp, table, c. 1935, 20" high. In aluminum and frosted glass, cylindrical, the multi-stepped base with a multidisk shade enclosing a frosted glass cylinder, the base decorated with rust and black bands. An outstanding example of an industrial design lamp, featured in the 1986 Brooklyn Museum's "Machine Age" exhibition. (*See color section.*)
    $4,200 (Auction)

Muller Frères "Stork Lamp."
Courtesy of Skinner, Inc., Massachusetts.

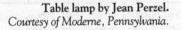
Table lamp by Jean Perzel.
Courtesy of Moderne, Pennsylvania.

JEAN PERZEL (Czechoslovakian/French, b. 1892)

Lamp, table, c. 1930, 22" high. In brass, with a flaring white-lacquered shade and black-lacquered base and stem, with overall simplified lines.   **$2,500–$3,000**

Sconces, c. 1937, 5" high, 15¾" wide, 7¼" deep. A pair in chromed steel and glass, conceived as a section of core molding interrupted by stepped "chipped" glass, circular motif, illuminated from behind, stamped three times.   **$1,800 (Auction)**

JEAN ROYÈRE (French)

Sconces, c. 1934, 23¾" high, 24¾" wide, 13" deep. A pair in gilt-metal, the domed mounts issuing five slender ogee arms of square section, the point of each ogee supporting a light fixture.   **$8,000 (Auction)**

EMILE-JACQUES RUHLMANN (French, 1879–1933)

Chandelier, 28" wide. Glass and metal of star form with etched and polished projections.   **$17,000 (Auction)**

Lamp, table, 24½" high, shade: 17¾" diameter. In metal, the hunter-green silk shade supported by tapering shaft on circular beaded foot.   **$24,000 (Auction)**

Lamp, table, c. 1928, 28¼" high. In silvered bronze, three reeded branches surmount a circular base with dentated border at the lower edge, the shade of black painted metal and the finial of elongated reeded form.   **$25,000 (Auction)**

ELIEL SAARINEN (Finnish/American, 1873–1950)

Torchère, c. 1930, 55¾" high. Brushed aluminum, circular adjustable disk shade supported by a U-shaped tubular bracket, raised on adjustable tubular standard, terminating in a circular base. Superior quality.   **$2,000–$3,000**

CHARLES SCHNEIDER (French, 1881–1962)

Chandelier, c. 1930, 37" high. Wrought iron and glass, the central dish-shaped shade heavily molded with stylized flowers. Elaborate stylized wrought-iron mount, with three additional pendant shades, each molded "Schneider France." A very good example of Schneider's chandeliers.   **$3,000–$4,000**

Chandelier, 21¼" diameter. Wrought iron and glass, a circular platform hung from four chains, from which five shades are suspended. Each shade is red, spotted with blue, and inscribed "Schneider." In good condition.   **$1,100 (Auction)**

Torchère, 68½" high. In wrought iron and glass, with a hexagonal base designed with stylized leaves. The standard supports a single frosted glass shade in mottled yellow, inscribed "Schneider."   **$2,000–$2,500**

WALTER VON NESSEN (American, 1889–1943)

> **Nessen, Inc., is still a major supplier of table, wall, floor, and other lamps for the residential and commercial design industry, with many of the designs using the swing-arm concept Walter von Nessen originated in 1927.**

Torchère, c. 1928, 67½" high. In chrome-plated metal, designed with a fluted column resting on a circular base. The chrome-plated shade has a concentric, conical shape.   **$6,500 (Auction)**

KURT VERSEN (American, b. 1901)

Torchère, c. 1935, 48½" high; shade: 12" diameter. Chrome and black and white lacquer with satin finish shade.   **$800–$1,200**

Torchère, c. 1935, 60" high, design #30793. Designed for Herman Miller Company. Two-tiered flared shade on a slender stem; black-banded brushed stainless steel on a brushed cast base. A very good example of the artist's work in fine condition.   **$550 (Auction)**

Torchère, c. 1935, 68¼" high. Designed for Herman Miller Company. In chrome, with cylindrical stem and dished shade. A good example of the artist's work, in average condition.   **$400–$600**

CLOCKS PRICE LISTINGS
(Alphabetically by designer or manufacturer)

ANONYMOUS

Clock, American, c. 1935, 5¼" high, 4½" wide, 4" deep. In painted brass. Within the glass globe, the second hand and minute hand are designed as angelfish. One ticks, the other revolves. The hour is indicated on a red ball in the center. A highly unusual and unique design, excellent example of American Tropical Deco. (*See photo, below.*)
$1,500–$2,000

Clock, French, 7" high. In chrome and illuminated glass, the square face with rounded glass sides and glass top, molded with radiating panels with amber patina, on footed base.
$400 (Auction)

Clock, probably French, c. 1935, 14" high. In aluminum, rectangular with stepped sides and floral decorative pattern, the top mounted with a floral bouquet in a vase.
$175–$200

Clock sets with garniture, various, French, 1920s–1930s, clocks: 12"–16" high, 16"–20" wide. In marble or onyx with distinctive angles and designs achieved through layering different colors. Sometimes surmounted with a reclining woman, a greyhound, or other figure usually in gilt base metal, and sometimes in brass. Accompanied by a pair of "garnitures," which translates literally as "garnish." These are decorative pieces, sometimes formed as vases, in the same design and materials as the clock to "garnish" the mantel. Price range depends on design and working condition.

In good condition, working	$500–$800
In good condition, not working	$400–$600

Clock set with garniture, French, clock: 9½" high. A rouge marble and onyx clock set, comprising a clock and matching pair of vases, clock face marked "L. Pecheux Chateau Thierry." **$375 (Auction)**

Angelfish clock, c. 1935.
Courtesy of The Florida Picker, Florida.

Marble three-piece clock garniture.
Courtesy of Butterfield & Butterfield,
California.

Telechron mantel clock, 1929,
by Paul Frankl. *Courtesy of*
Butterfield & Butterfield, California.

Clock set with garniture, French, c. 1935. In marble, the circular cream marble clock face mounted with green-patinated arms and hours, within foliate-carved black and marble curved supports surmounted by four green striated marble disks and flanked by two marble balls, mounted on a rectangular slate base. A fine example of this type of clock set. (*See photo, above.*)   **$1,000 (Auction)**

J. E. CALDWELL COMPANY (American)

Clock, table, c. 1935, 7" high, 9" long. In green onyx with arched casing and rectangular plinth. Wood inset to complete the design at the angle of the base and casting. In very good condition, working.   **$175–$200**

PAUL FRANKL (American, 1878–1962)

Clock, mantel, 1929, 7¾" high. Designed for Warren Telechron Company. Rectangular chrome and black-enameled metal case; face with radiating brush-burnished brass in a sunray pattern. A good example of the artist's industrial design for furnishings, which has become something of an icon for Art Deco collectors. Price range varies widely, depending on source and condition.   **$800–$1,400**

GENERAL ELECTRIC COMPANY (American)

Clock, mantel, "Skyscraper," c. 1935, 7½" high. Design similar to the skyscraper Catalin radios of the period. Mint-green stepped geometric form with gold-tone vertical inlaid banding and round illuminated dial. Good condition.   **$250–$300**

"Deux Figurines" clock by René Lalique.
Courtesy of William Doyle Galleries, New York.

RENÉ LALIQUE (French, 1860–1945)

(For additional listings of clocks by Lalique, see "Glass.")

"Deux Figurines," c. 1925, 14" high. Frosted and clear crystal arched frame with recessed molded design of two women in diaphanous gowns centering clock insert, mounted on luminar base of gilt metal.

Good condition, clock and light need restoration   **$9,000 (Auction)**
In excellent condition   **$11,000 (Auction)**

MANNING BOWMAN COMPANY (American, Meriden, CT)

Clock, mantel, c. 1930, 9½" high, 10" long. Square chrome body with scroll feet, inlaid with green marbleized Bakelite outlining the windowed clock face, the clock face silvered with black numbers. Resting on rectangular Bakelite slab, raised on stepped chrome base, with four flat square Bakelite foot rests. Good condition.   **$350 (Auction)**

Clock, mantel, c. 1930, 10" high. In wood and chrome, in a stepped-back pyramid style with three colors of wood veneer inlaid in geometric patterns. Rectangular face with stylized Roman numerals. Good condition, some repair needed.   **$400–$450**

Clock, mantel, "Empire State," c. 1935, 18½" high. Designed as a stepped architectural structured form topped by an orange Bakelite inset finial. A very good example of Manning Bowman's mantel clocks in good condition.   **$650 (Auction)**

PENNWOOD NUMERON COMPANY (American)

Clock, bedroom, "Imperial," c. 1935, 4½" high, 10½" long. Digital clock with oval face; three ivorine plastic fins which extend from the front around the sides, giving the appearance of slicing through the clock. Good condition.   **$250–$325**

JEAN PUIFORCAT (French, 1897–1945)

Clock, c. 1932, 7½" high. Chrome-plated bronze and marble, the cylindrical metal housing surrounded by twelve circular rings intersecting with cylindrical sections of white marble set with conforming metal rings with cut-out numbers and supported by a rectangular marble column raised on a small reversed arch metal foot, stamped "Gubelin Swiss." (*See color section.*)   **$15,000 (Auction)**

REX ART PRODUCTS COMPANY (American)

Clock, mantel, c. 1930, 10" high, 16½" long. Central rectangular glass panel with Arabic numerals flanked by a stylized nude and large flowering plants, set against an ebonized panel. The glass is held in place by two silvered metal architectural forms, raised on a stepped rectangular ebonized base, electrified. In good condition, with minor chips.

$1,100 (Auction)

GILBERT ROHDE (1894–1944)

(See our "Special Focus" section on Rohde in the "Furniture" Price List.)

Clock, 6¼" high, 8" wide. Designed for Herman Miller. Chrome finish, square frame, resting on two square feet, on a rectangular base. Stamped "Herman Miller" on face and back.   **$250–$350**

Clock, c. 1932, 13⅛" long. Designed for Herman Miller. Rectangular bird's-eye maple veneered case, with square face and black Arabic numbers. Three horizontal chrome bands extending from the face around the curved end of the clock. Face marked "Herman Miller Clock Co., Zeeland, Mich." A very good example of a Rohde clock design, in fine condition.   **$2,000–$2,200**

Clock, c. 1933, 6½" high, 6" diameter. Designed for Herman Miller. Circular blue-mirrored glass face, with chromed metal hands, and twelve chrome balls to mark hours, on a rectangular brushed chromium base. Stamped "Herman Miller."   **$1,500–$2,000**

KEM WEBER (American, 1889–1963)

Digital clock, 7¼" long. Designed for Telechron, in copper, with rectangular footed form and central ivory dial. Telechron metal tag.   **$220 (Auction)**

Mantel clock by
Rex Art Products.
Courtesy of Butterfield &
Butterfield, California.

Digital clock, "Zephyr," 1933, 3" high, 8" long, model #304. Designed for Lawson Time; rectangular digital face set in a sweeping rounded and curved rectangular gunmetal case. Another clock that has become sought-after by collectors of industrial design. In good condition.   **$800 (Auction)**
$700–$1,000

Digital clock, 13" long. Designed for Lawson, rectangular, in brass with stepped sides of chrome and glass on white onyx base. With Lawson tag.   **$850 (Auction)**

Digital clock, 13" long, model #350. Attributed to Kem Weber. Created by Lawson Time, in gilt metal and green onyx. In rounded rectangular form with applied streamlining on stepped base. With Lawson marks.   **$320 (Auction)**

DECORATIVE SCULPTURE

In Europe especially, the Art Deco era saw a closer rapprochement, or "coming together," like never before of the fine arts and the decorative arts. Fine artists were commissioned to create designs for the applied arts, and designers borrowed concepts and innovations of form from the world of fine arts. In consequence, or as part of that process, decorative sculpture came more into demand, building on a popularity that had started in the Art Nouveau period.

In sculpture, as in certain other areas, such as works on paper, it is sometimes difficult (and sometimes arbitrary) to delineate between what is "decorative art" and what is "fine art." In the world of Art Deco, this confusion has been further caused by the terminology used.

For example, in the field of prints, lithographs, woodcuts, and etchings, especially those which are hand signed by the artist, the pieces are generally considered "fine art." However, Icart's hand-signed etchings are sold at "decorative art" auctions, and advertising posters of the 1920s and 1930s, which were also usually lithographs, will often be described as "fine art posters," emphasizing the high quality of their design. Conversely, there has been a trend in recent years to call some paintings that reflect the stylizations of the decorative arts field as "Art Deco paintings," such as the work of Tamara de Lempicka.

Perhaps the best way of distinguishing decorative sculpture from fine art sculpture of the period is the intent behind its creation. Decorative sculpture was commissioned expressly for commercial production and distribution. Its goal was not to break new ground in an artistic way, but rather to be visually appealing, even purposefully beautiful, to function as a decorative component in interior design. Their breathtaking qualities, however, gave rise to the term "decorative works of art," which seems to bridge the gap.

Happily, in the Art Deco period, advances in bronze casting made it possible to more easily produce and distribute statues to satisfy the new markets. Many artists, such as Belgian Claire Jeanne Roberte Colinet, began in the tradition of fine arts and were later commissioned for works that would be produced in larger quantities.

Underscoring the commercial intent of the manufacturers who produced them, in addition to larger quantities and recastings as the market grew, many of these works were also produced in different sizes. Some were mounted on bases and others on trays. The higher-priced models might be mounted on marble, and the lower-priced ones on quartz.

Where fine artists most often did not paint the bronze beyond overall patination in green, brown, or black, many of the new decorative statues were polychromed in bright colors and mounted on bases of colorful marble or onyx.

After World War I, decorative bronze sculptures were produced for and distributed through major department stores. For example, Pomone at Au Bon Marché commissioned artists to create works specifically for their stores. Many were sold through the Phillips & MacConnal Gallery in London. Marcel Bouraine created cast bronze bookends and paperweights designed as stylized small animals which were distributed through Alfred Dunhill in New York.

Art Deco sculpture reflected the new design style with lithe nude and seminude maidens, most often dancing, and sometimes flying through the sky. The female figure—real, mythical, or exotic—was the most popular subject for decorative statues. Often the subject was a well-known singer, actress, or personality, such as Josephine Baker or Nijinsky. The costumes and cultures of India, Egypt, Africa, Persia, and elsewhere were also favorite subjects.

Sporting figures, often of women, also became popular: archers, tennis players, golfers, swimmers, fencers, javelin throwers—few sports activities were missed. Other sculptures were cast as figures of children, jesters, schoolmasters, and other "characters."

Not far behind women in popularity was the animalier movement in modern sculpture. No longer restrained by the Beaux Arts tradition of realistic portrayal of animals, the Art Deco period elongated, streamlined, and otherwise "tamed" wild beasts into the modern idiom.

Gone were the wild boars ferociously attacking a stallion. In their place appeared greyhounds, gazelles, and the large cats, perfect subjects for the sleek new look. Edouard Marcel Sandoz was noted for his sculptures of animals, and François Pompon is one of the best known artists of the modern animalier movement. In 1922, at the Salon d'Automne in Paris, he exhibited a marble statue of a polar bear which is credited with starting the modern depiction of animals using smooth lines and frozen poses.

CHRYSELEPHANTINE—BRONZE AND IVORY

By far the most popular statues of the Art Deco era are "chryselephantine," or bronze and ivory. Popular for at least two decades before the Art Deco period, they reached their peak of production during the late 1920s until the mid-1930s.

The term "chryselephantine" was first used to describe the statues that used both gold and ivory in ancient Greece. During the Art Nouveau era, the Belgians, the most prolific producers of bronze and ivory statues, extended the meaning to encompass any statue fashioned in combination with ivory.

Ivory has always held the interest of sculptors for its beauty and ease of carving. Ivory also ages and yellows in attractive ways. In the middle of the 19th century, however, ivory was being used primarily for everyday items: brushes, doorhandles, and the like.

When the Congo was conquered by the Belgians, ivory tusks were shipped back to Europe in quantities that far exceeded household uses, and that would enrage conservationists today. In 1894, the Secretary of State for the Congo Free State called on Belgian artists to use more ivory, and it was further officially encouraged by commissions and competitive exhibitions.

However, the basic materials that were used—bronze, ivory, and marble—changed as the market for the statues grew. Cheaper metals, such as spelter, a type of zinc that is more akin to pewter and molds more easily, came into use for less expensive statues. A plastic composition, ivorine, which only sometimes actually contains a small amount of powdered ivory, replaced the real thing.

The bases, which at first were made from high-quality marble and even lapis lazuli, and which had increased the status of the statues as precious objects, changed to cheaper marble and finally to onyx or other marblelike stones. The best onyx came from Brazil and was a favorite material for other decorative objects as well.

These statues, along with many decorative bronze-only pieces, were ignored for many years but there was a strong resurgence of interest in the early to mid-1970s. At that time, leading scholars and dealers such as Brian Catley, Victor Arwas, and Alain Lesieutre reawakened the collecting market's interest in them.

Prices rose dramatically until about 1983, when a flood of reproductions created both in the United States and abroad hit the market, setting prices back considerably. Since then, prices not only have recovered, but have risen higher than ever. (*See the chapter "Today's Market" for more information.*) However, the reproductions are still a scourge, and unwary collectors get taken every day. Bronze-only statues have also been reproduced in quantity. Because most of these statues are not protected by copyright, a manufacturer can simply cast a mold from one and start production. (*For details on the reproductions, see the chapter "Fakes Alert!"*)

The reproductions are often sold for a few hundred dollars to a thousand dollars or so. Authentic castings of bronze and ivory figures command thousands of dollars, or even tens of thousands of dollars in today's Art Deco market, depending on design, size, materials used, artist, subject, and workmanship. Price alone is not the best indicator to use in discerning a fake, as a fake can also be sold with a high price tag.

The best auction houses and dealers use standardized language to indicate the casting of statues. When a bronze is made from the artist's original model and was cast during the artist's lifetime or shortly thereafter, they will describe it as "Cast from a model" by the artist. When it is a later casting, they will describe it as "Cast after a model" by the artist. If the dealer you are speaking with does not make this distinction, the best advice is to move on.

FRENCH

In Paris, the firm Etling, known to many for its frosted Lalique-like glass, was the largest "éditeur" of decorative sculpture, employing artists such as Colinet, Demetre H. Chiparus, Joé Descomps, A. Becquerel, Maurice Guiraud-Rivière, and Marcel Bouraine. The Goldscheider firm in Paris was also a large manufacturer, and issued works by artists such as Alexander Kelety, Pierre Traverse, and Pierre Le Faguays.

Demetre H. Chiparus leads the market as the foremost name in decorative sculpture of the period (and is the most often forged as well). Chiparus came to study in Paris from his native Rumania, and exhibited at the Salon des Artistes Français from 1914 to 1918. He is best known for his bronze and ivory figures of exotic dancers, with subjects often taken from the contemporary performing arts, such as his *Russian Dancers*, identified as Nijinsky and Ida Rubenstein of Les Ballets Russes. (*See color section.*) Chiparus is recognized for the spectacular design and elaborate treatment and patination of the costumes his figures wore.

Chiparus's early figures, on relatively simple bases, were primarily cast by Etling. Later pieces were made by the LN & JL foundry, which appears to have specialized in making the more elaborate and zigzagged marble and onyx bases. Chiparus's figures, though not as "Deco," also include adorable children and little clowns.

Claire Jeanne Roberte Colinet also worked in bronze and ivory. A native Belgian, she moved to Paris and was elected to the Société des Artistes Français in 1913. Later, she would exhibit at the Salon des Indépendants from 1937 to 1940.

Maurice Guiraud-Rivière was also a prolific sculptor, contributing models of dancers in a variety of materials to Etling, as well as models for porcelain figures to Sèvres and Robj. Guiraud-Rivière is also known for subjects relating to speed, such as motorcar racing, charioteering, and steeplechasing, which allowed him to significantly use horizontal styling. One of his most outstanding works is an allegorical figure of a woman called *The Comet*. (*See "Decorative Sculpture Price Listings" for description and photo.*)

Apart from the bronze figures of animals for bookends and paperweights already mentioned, Marcel Bouraine is perhaps best known for his figures of battling Amazon women, which appear to have been produced in a series. Alexander Kelety, a Hungarian who came to live and work in France, was also an outstanding artist of the period, working more in bronze than in bronze and ivory. Joé Descomps is another talented bronze and ivory artist. Born at Agen, he exhibited his work as early as 1903 and 1904 at the Société des Artistes Français.

In the 1920s, another noted French artist, Pierre Le Faguays, also exhibited his work there. Le Faguays is best known for his lithe nude dancers, archers, and other figures of women in bronze. Le Faguays also designed models for the shop of sculptor Max Le Verrier.

Le Verrier specialized in statues, figural lamps, and bookends, and other decorative, functional sculpture often cast in cheaper metals. He created his own pieces and also commissioned Le Faguays and other artists such as Raymond Guerbe, Fayral, and Marcel Bouraine. Le Verrier's production, and the artists associated with him, were probably the inspiration for Frankart, the American manufacturer of inexpensive sculptural bookends, lamps, ashtrays, and other objects in the 1920s.

GERMAN

In 1906, the ivory carver Ferdinand Preiss and his partner, Arthur Kassler, started the firm Preiss-Kassler in Berlin, and soon came to control the market for bronze and ivory sculpture in Germany.

Preiss was and is as popular as Chiparus, and his work was widely distributed by the Phillips & MacConnal Gallery of Arts in London, as well as others. He created ivory-only sculptures as well as bronze and ivory, and made his reputation on the finesse with which he carved the ivory. He is perhaps best known for his sportily clad men and women, who really mirrored modern life. He also often used a cooler metallic color palette of blues, silvers, and grays.

He, too, created figures from the world of entertainment, such as Brigitte Helm as the human heroine of Fritz Lang's *Metropolis* and his *Bat Dancer* from the Hollywood film *Flying Down to Rio*.

Preiss commissioned other sculptors to create for his firm, such as Otto Poertzel and Paul Phillipe. The Preiss-Kassler "PK" monogram within a circle is often found stamped on the bronze portion of these statues.

"Professor Poertzel," as he was called, created bronze and ivory sculptures of cabaret and burlesque performers and circus stars. Phillipe's chryselephantines are usually women with elongated bodies and sharp-pointed features. He designed several statues in ivory only, as did Preiss, and these tend to be far less expensive than the chryselephantine sculptures.

VIENNESE

In Vienna, the firm of Frederich Goldscheider manufactured bronze and ivory sculpture, mostly by Joseph Lorenzl. Lorenzl's figures of dancers and fashionable women are very stylized, and were also produced in ivory alone or in spelter. Decorative bronzes were also made by the Bergman and Argentor foundries in Vienna, the latter issuing several works by Bruno Zach.

Zach was also commissioned by Preiss, but worked mainly in Austria, and is best known for his erotic sculptures in bronze and ivory. He often depicted his women in leather trousers, smoking cigarettes, or wearing garters. Zach also designed a few bronzes with "exotic" American Western themes—cowboys and Indians on horseback, sleekly galloping across plains he had never seen.

With its emphasis on functionality, the Vienna Secession did not produce many decorative sculptures for their own sake. However, one Austrian name does stand out on the collecting market: Atelier Hagenauer. Sculptures by this workshop, mostly from the late 1920s and early 1930s, were often retailed through department stores as well, and at times were commissioned by the Wiener Werkstätte

Franz Hagenauer used a wide variety of materials to fashion his work, including chromed metal, wood, silver, nickel, brass, and painted bronze. His work ranges from two-foot-high chromed metal busts to knickknack-sized animals and figures of jazz musicians only a few inches high.

In recent years, his work has seen greatly renewed interest on the market both for its own sake and perhaps because it is more affordable than the chryselephantine statues. Some interesting design comparisons can be made to his work and the figural bookends and other pieces designed by Walter von Nessen and other designers for Chase Brass and Copper.

FINE ART SCULPTURE

Both fine art and monumental sculpture attracted numerous talented artists in the Art Deco era, both in Europe and in America. Affected by the same forces that shook the world of painting—Cubism, Fauvism, and Futurism—sculpture took on new form.

In Europe, artists working in several media, such as Alexander Archipenko (1887–1964), Gustav Miklos (1888–1967), and Josef Csaky, a Hungarian who worked in France, would translate into sculpture the new dimensions that Cubists were reflecting on the two-dimensional plane. Early fine sculpture of the period was also inspired by African masks and motifs from other ancient cultures as the Western world opened up to new influences.

Today, the work of these artists is represented in "fine art" as opposed to "decorative art" auctions. Because many of the sculptures created by these artists were produced in very small editions, prices are correspondingly high. For example, Archipenko made bronzes usually in editions of no more than twelve, and Miklos sometimes made editions as small as four.

In America, fine sculptural artists include many who were commissioned for public monuments and architectural sculpture. Distinguished sculptors include Paul Manship (1885–1966), Anna Hyatt Huntington (1876–1973), Carl Milles (1875–1955), Elie Nadelman (1882–1946), Carl Paul Jennewein (1890–1978), and Lee Lawrie (1877–1963), whose Atlas at Rockefeller Center is well-known. Manship's Prometheus, created in 1934, is another famous Rockefeller Center sculpture. Other notable American sculptors include Sidney Waugh, the avant-garde John Storrs (1885–1956), William Hunt Diederich, Boris Lovet-Lorski (1894–1973), and Waylande Gregory.

Some of these artists are known to collectors of other Art Deco items: Waylande Gregory designed ceramic pieces for Cowan Pottery; Diederich created metalware such as weathervanes and fireplace screens; and Waugh designed glass for Steuben.

AMERICAN

Roman Bronze Works and Gorham Foundry were the foremost bronze foundries in America, and executed both fine art and monumental sculptures for many of the leading artists, including some already named. In many ways they helped put the bronze sculptures of America on a par with those of Paris and Rome. They had the ability to cast very large garden statuary in bronze for the country estates of wealthy families such as the Whitneys and the Vanderbilts, and often produced pieces based on mythological subjects treated in a Modernist fashion.

Several sculptors, many of them women, distinguished themselves through their work for this kind of garden sculpture: Harriet Whitney Frishmuth, Edith Parson, Janet Scudder, Malvina Hoffman, Eugenie Schonnard, and others.

Models by some of these and other artists were reduced in size for commercial distribution. Gorham Foundry had its own store in New York, and other works were sold through the Grand Central Art Gallery and Tiffany & Company. Among the most sought-after on the market today is Harriet Frishmuth (b. 1880), who created numerous bronze statues, and even an electroplated bronze radiator car mascot of a nude woman. True to the Art Deco style, her hair streams behind her as she flies through space.

DECORATIVE SCULPTURE PRICE LISTINGS
(Alphabetically by designer or manufacturer)

Note: *Unless otherwise noted, all bronze and bronze and ivory figures below are cast from the original model by the artist named. See the chapter "Fakes Alert!" for additional information on fakes in this market. See also the chapter "Important Notes on the Price Listings" for an explanation of terms used to describe these figures.*

LUCIEN ALLIOT (French, work: c. 1905–1940)

Pierrot, 6½" high. In bronze and ivory, cast and carved from a model by Alliot, standing with hands clasped as if in prayer, signed in the bronze "L. Alliot." Alliot's figures are generally more in the Art Nouveau than Art Deco style.   **$500 (Auction)**

DOMINIQUE ALONZO (French, work: 1912–1926)

Young Girl, 11" high. A gilt bronze and ivory figure, the bare-breasted figure standing on a rock, her dress blown by the wind, signed in the bronze "D. Alonzo."

$2,800 (Auction)

A. V. BEQUEREL (French, work: 1915–1925)

Bowl of Milk, 10" high. A bronze and ivory figural group of a young girl drinking her milk, surrounded by her dog and cat companions, signed in the bronze "Bequerel" and "Etling Paris," on green marble base.   **$2,500–$3,000**

Bronze figure of an Amazon, by Marcel Bouraine.
Courtesy of Christie's, New York.

MARCEL BOURAINE (French, work: 1918–1935)

Amazon, c. 1925. In bronze, with a rich greenish-brown patina, the stylized figure leaning back on one knee, preparing to throw a lance, and holding a shield. Inscribed "M. Bouraine." Bouraine created a series of models of battling Amazons. (*Fakes Alert!* Amazon figures by Bouraine are favorites for reproduction.)   **$10,000 (Auction)**

Young Girl, 17¾" high. Bust in bronze, signed in the bronze "M. Bouraine" and "Cire perdue Etling—Paris."   **$1,800–$2,200**

Dancer, 26¾" high. In bronze, the female nude posing with a hat and a fan, a rose between her teeth, on black marble base, base inscribed "Bouraine Etling Paris."   **$1,700 (Auction)**

Fish lamp, 10⅝" high, 20¾" long. In bronze on a green onyx base. The fish is a stunning parcel-silvered and gilt-bronze lamp.   **$9,000 (Auction)**

Ravens, bookends, c. 1930, approximately 8" high. In bronze, the stylized ravens with ivory bills perched on stepped veined black marble bases, their feet hanging over the first step. One inscribed "Bouraine" and one marked "456."   **$1,500–$2,000**

Bronze and ivory raven bookends by Marcel Bouraine.
Private collection.

DEMETRE H. CHIPARUS (Rumanian/French, work: 1915–1935)

Bayadère, a dancer, 20⅞" high. A cold-painted bronze and ivory figure, in a balloonlike skirt, on tiptoe, with her hands above her head, her hands and face in ivory. Standing on a triangular black veined marble base, which has a cold-painted and gilt bronze relief of two dancers inscribed "D.H. Chiparus." Base inscribed "Made in France." (This statue was also edited in bronze only.) (*See color section.*)   **$12,000 (Auction)**

Carnival, 16⅜" high. A cold-painted bronze and ivory figure of a woman wearing her outlandish carnival costume and pointed hat, her hands, shoulders, and face in ivory. Standing on a brown onyx base with veined black marble and green onyx band. Base signed "D.H. Chiparus" and inscribed "Etling. Paris." (*See color section.*)   **$14,000 (Auction)**

Dancer of Kapurthala, 20¼" high, including green and brown onyx base. A cold-painted bronze and ivory figure of a dancer, wearing a tight-fitting body suit and cloche hat, with hands and face in ivory. (Two other versions of this statue exist, one 14¾" high in bronze and ivory and one 20¼" high in all bronze.) Stamped "Made in France" and "89," onyx base signed "Chiparus." (*Fakes Alert!* Replicas are on the market, usually cast in bronze only.)   **$26,000 (Auction)**

Everlasting Love, 27⅛" high, including brown onyx base. A cold-painted bronze and ivory group, the man on one knee before his intended, their hands and faces in ivory. Stamped "Made in France," "7," and "1," base signed "Chiparus." This is a rarely seen figural group by Chiparus.   **$45,000 (Auction)**

Exotic Dancer, 15" high. A cold-painted bronze and ivory figure of an exotic dancer, her costume in Egyptian style, her legs, torso, shoulders, arms, and face in ivory; standing on a small rounded green onyx base signed "D. Chiparus" and inscribed on the underside "Made in France."   **$7,000 (Auction)**

Indiscreet, a girl with a parrot, 17¼" high. A cold-painted bronze and ivory figure of a young girl in a full dress and hat, her arm outstretched, holding a parrot, her arm and face in ivory. Stamped "Made in France" and indistinct numbers. Mounted on a brown-veined onyx based signed "Chiparus."   **$9,000 (Auction)**
                                                                                        $12,000–$15,000

On the Beach, 17¾" high. Cold-painted bronze and ivory figure of a woman in a long cloak, holding a small parasol, her hands and face in ivory, standing on a variegated brown marble base signed "Chiparus." (*See color section.*)   **$15,000 (Auction)**

Pajama Lady, 18½" high. A cold-painted bronze and ivory figure of a woman in long-belted pajamas, her arms and head in ivory, stretching as she awakens. Standing on a veined black marble base signed "D. H. Chiparus" and inscribed "Etling. Paris." Base has cold-painted bronze relief of a stretching cat. (*See color section.*)   **$14,000 (Auction)**

Russian Dancers, 22" high. A cold-painted bronze and ivory group of a man and woman in exotic costume, dancing with tambourines, their hands, arms, and faces in ivory. Standing on a very elaborate variegated black and rouge marble and brown onyx base signed "D. H. Chiparus" and inscribed "Etling Paris." The two dancers have been identified as Vaslav Nijinsky and Ida Rubenstein dancing in the Russian Ballet's production of *Scheharazade*, which was first performed in 1910. A fine example of Chiparus's work, one of his rare statues with two figures. (*See color section.*)   **$42,000 (Auction)**

Starfish, a dancer, 19½" high. In cold-painted bronze and ivory, figure of a woman in a tight-fitted body suit decorated with stylized starfish, her hands entwined above her head, hands and face in ivory. (This statue was also made in an edition 15¼" high.) Base is an elaborate green and brown onyx and marble, signed "D. H. Chiparus" and inscribed "Etling. Paris." (*Fakes Alert!* Recastings of this statue using both real and fake ivory have been identified on the market.)   **$30,000 (Auction)**
$35,000–$45,000

Tendres Promesses, (*Tender Promises*, also sometimes called *The Secret*), 14⅞" high, 31" long, including elaborate variegated onyx base. A cold-painted bronze and ivory group of a young harlequin whispering tender words into the ear of a young woman wearing a high collar and cloche hat, their hands and faces in ivory, stamped with the LN & JL foundry seal and "Made in France," base signed "Chiparus," with paper label on the underside inscribed in ink "893/1641/1 Tendres Promesses." One of very few double-figure works by Chiparus. (This statue was also issued in 10¼" high.)   **$32,000 (Auction)**

Thais, a dancer, 22⅛" high. In cold-painted bronze and ivory, the dramatic figure on one knee, her arms extended, her dress and headpiece of exotic fashion; her feet, hands, arms and face in ivory; on a brown onyx base signed "D.H. Chiparus." Thais, a courtesan and actress in early Christian Alexandria, is the subject of an opera by Jules Massenet, based on a story by Anatole France. See also *Thais*, a glass sculpture by René Lalique. A rare, large figure and a fine example of Chiparus's work. (*Fakes Alert!* Replicas of this statue are on the market, usually cast in bronze only.)   **$70,000 (Auction)**

Thais by Demetre Chiparus.
Courtesy of Christie's, New York.

Top Hat, a dancer, 18⅛" high. Cold-painted bronze and ivory figure of a woman holding a top hat and cane, stamped "71," standing on a stepped brown-veined onyx base, which carries a cold-painted relief of four dancers inscribed "D. H. Chiparus." (*See color section.*)
$15,000 (Auction)

SYLVESTRE CLERC (Paris, work: 1915–1930)

Female Nude, 12" high. After a model by S. Clerc. In bronze on a black marble base, the seated figure with her head leaning on her hand. Inscribed "S. Clerc" and "Susses Frs Edts Paris cire perdue" and impressed with Susses Frères foundry seal. $800 (Auction)

CLAUDE JEANNE ROBERTE COLINET (Belgian/French, work: 1910–1930)

Andalusian, a nude dancer, 28⅞" high. In polychrome bronze on a gray marble base, inscribed "Cl. JR. Colinet 6" and stamped "8." A good example of Colinet's romantic Art Deco style. $3,800 (Auction)

DECOUR (French, work: 1920s–1930s)

Panthers, 19½" long. Two menacing panthers in silvered bronze, on black onyx base trimmed in green onyx. Inscribed "Decour." (*See photo in section "Motifs," page 16.*)
$2,800–$3,200

JOSEPH EMMANUEL DESCOMPS, called CORMIER (French, 1869–1950)

Nymph and Putto, 18¼" high, 22½" long. In parcel-gilt bronze on a green marble base, the two figures connected by a garland of stylized flowers. Inscribed "JD Cormier," with the artist's cipher and "425," and impressed with the Colin foundry seal. $4,800 (Auction)

JEAN-BERNARD DESCOMPS (French, 1872–1948)

Lion, 21" high. In bronze, with dark and golden-brown patina, the well-cast figure of a lion with its graceful lines. Signed "J.B. Descomps." $1,800–$2,200

Female Nude and Satyr, 23" long. After a model by Descomps. In bronze, mounted on a white marble base, signed "J. Descomps." $1,500 (Auction)

PIERRE LE FAGUAYS (French, work: 1920–1935)

Two Maidens, a lamp, 15⅞" high. A bronze group of two maidens in long flowing dresses, supporting a bowl-shaped alabaster lamp on their shoulders, with an elaborate marble base signed "Le Faguays." Le Faguays' work influenced the design of Frankart lamps. $12,000 (Auction)

Odalisque, 23½" high, on green marble base. A parcel-silvered bronze figure, with separate tag inscribed "Pierre Le Faguays Piece d'Art Deco Unique Odalisque." $8,000–$9,000

HARRIET WHITNEY FRISHMUTH (American, 1880–1979)

Allegra, 1929, 11⅝" high, plus base. In bronze, with a rich brownish-green patina on a Belgian marble base, modeled as a lithe nude woman with flowing hair, her face turned to one side, one arm outstretched. Inscribed "Harriet W. Frishmuth," and dated "1929."
$8,000–$12,000

Slavonic Dancer, 1921, 12¾" high, plus base. In bronze, with a brown patina, on a black base, modeled as a nude man in a strongly angular pose, his fists clenched by his head, one leg lifted. Inscribed "Harriet W. Frishmuth," dated "1921" and stamped "Roman Bronze Works, N-Y." Apparently an edition of ten.   **$7,750 (Auction)**

AMADEO GENNARELLI (Italian, work: 1915–1930)

Towards Destiny, a female nude, c. 1920, 7½" high, 13" long. A polychrome bronze relief plaque including an incorporated bronze frame, depicting a stylized figure of a woman rolling a large wheel. This figure was also edited as a three-dimensional figure in two sizes.   **$1,500 (Auction)**

A. GODARD (French)

Dance of the Rose, a dancer, 20⅝" high, including onyx base. Cold-painted bronze and ivory, signed "A. Godard" and inscribed "Etling. Paris."   **$4,000 (Auction)**

MAURICE GUIRAUD-RIVIÈRE (French, b. 1881)

The Comet, c. 1925, 21¾" high. Parcel-gilt and cold-painted allegorical figure on a stepped Belgian marble base. Inscribed "Guiraud-Rivière" and "Etling. Paris." A fine example of Guiraud-Rivière's work and an unforgettable image.   **$20,000–$25,000**

Charioteer, 1928, 13¾" high, 33½" long. A bronze figure of a racing charioteer and horses, which communicates its speed and power, on a variegated marble base. Stamped with the LN & JL foundry seal and inscribed "M. Guiraud-Rivière 1928."   **$7,000–$9,000**

ATELIER HAGENAUER (Austrian, 1920s–1930s)

Franz Hagenauer

Boxers, 16" high. A chromed metal figural group. Flat-sided, figures punching at each other, impressed with Hagenauer/Wiener Werkstätte mark, "Franz Hagenauer Wien Made in Austria 1087/88."   **$2,400 (Auction)**

Boxer, 8½" high. In nickel finish, the stylized figure throwing a punch, impressed "Hagenauer Wien, wHw."   **$1,800–$2,200**

The Comet by Maurice Guiraud-Rivière.
Courtesy of Christie's, New York.

Bust of a Woman, 24½" high. In chromed metal with elongated features, curly hair, and red enameled lips, impressed with Hagenauer/Wiener Werkstätte mark, "Franz Hagenauer Wien Made in Austria 1274."   **$6,500 (Auction)**

Bust, 11½" high. Wooden, modeled as an African woman wearing a coiled metal necklace, impressed "wHw, Made in Austria, Hagenauer Wien, Handmade."

$800 (Auction)

(Two) Dancing Figures, larger 11¾" high. In chromed metal, comprising a seminude female in a sweeping skirt, unsigned, and a frolicking female nude, impressed "wHw Handmade Hagenauer Wien Made in Austria Karl."   **$750 (Auction)**

Elephant, 6¾" high. Painted bronze, silhouetted with rear leg chained to a post, impressed "Hagenauer Wien" with Wiener Werkstätte/Hagenauer mark and "Made in Austria Handmade."   **$420 (Auction)**

Horse, 8⅝" high. In brass, the stylized animal rearing, impressed "Karl, Hangauer, Wien, wHw, Made in Austria."   **$600 (Auction)**

Horse, 12" long, 12" high, nickel-finish, impressed "wHw, Hagenauer Wien."

$1,600 (Auction)

Horse, c. 1935, 9" high, 2¾" wide. In nickel over brass. Rearing figure on elongated hind legs, on a circular base, impressed "wHw, Hagenauer Wien." A fine example of Hagenauer's modern animalier designs. (*See photo, below.*)   **$3,300–$3,600**

Javelin Thrower, 11½" high. In nickel-finish, impressed "Hagenauer Wien, wHw."

$800 (Auction)

Sculpture of a horse by Hagenauer. *Courtesy of Rosebud Gallery, California.*

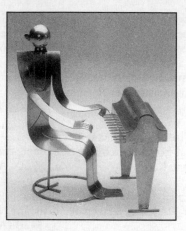

Hagenauer figure of a piano player. *Courtesy of Skinner, Inc., Massachusetts.*

Four Jazz Musicians, 9⅞" high. The flat, stylized figures playing a trombone, guitar, violin, and cello, each impressed "Franz Hagenauer Wien" and "wHw."   **$4,000 (Auction)**

Three Jazz Musicians. Two-dimensional, angular figures performing on brass, drums and saxophone. Wonderful details, in excellent condition. Impressed "Franz Hagenauer Wien." (*See photo in section "Motifs," page 14.*)   **$4,000–$5,500**

Piano Player, 8½" high. A nickel-finish, flat, stylized representation, impressed "Made in Vienna, Made in Austria, wHw."   **$1,000 (Auction)**

Three Polo Players, largest 5¼" high. In brass, showing different stages of play, two impressed "wHw" and "made in Austria," one impressed "wHw" and "Hagenauer Wien."   **$1,100 (Auction)**

Reclining Nude, 15¾" long, 5¾" high. In nickel-finish, the slender female relaxing on scrolled recamier, impressed "wHw, Hagenauer Wien."   **$2,800–$3,400**

Stylized Fox, 12¾" long. In brass, impressed with Hagenauer mark, "Franz Hagenauer Wien Made in Austria."   **$1,800–$2,000**

Wolfhound, 14⅝" high. In brass, impressed "wHw, Hagenauer Wien."   **$2,000 (Auction)**

MALVINA CORNELL HOFFMAN (American, 1887–1966)

Offraud, a figural group, 1919, 10⅜" high. In bronze with a green patina on a black base, modeled as a nude couple, kneeling before each other, his hands gently cupping her face. Each inscribed "M. Hoffman," and dated "1919," the man also inscribed "Roman Bronze Works, Inc., N.Y."   **$2,500–$3,500**

ALEXANDER KELETY (Hungarian/French, work: 1920–1940)

Birds in Flight, 21⅜" high. Three birds in silvered bronze, one whose wing stretches as support along a Belgian marble base. Inscribed "Kelety" and "Etling. Paris."   **$3,000 (Auction)**

Dancer, 19⅛" high. A polychrome bronze figure of a dancer, her head bent back almost touching her raised foot, her hands entwined in a circular garland larger than she, mounted on gray marble base. Inscribed "Kelety." $7,000–$9,000

ISADORE KONTI (Austrian/American, 1862–1938)

Bookends, 6½" high. In bronze, with a brown patina, modeled as two muscular men pushing, as if against a wall. Each inscribed "I. Konti," stamped "Gorham Co. Founders/0471," and numbered "#122." $2,500–$3,000

JACQUES LIPCHYTZ (1891–1973)

Exotic Dancer, 18" high. Gilt bronze figure, signed "Lipchytz," on a stylized mixed marble and onyx base. $1,300 (Auction)

JOSEPH LORENZL (Austrian, work: 1915–1930)

Dancer, c. 1925, 22½" high. In bronze, with a deep green patina, the figure on one foot, her arms and face uplifted, signed "Lorenzl," standing on a green onyx base, impressed "Austria." $2,500–$3,000

WILMA MENZEL (Belgian, work: early 20th century)

Cubist head, 15" high. In bronze, with a medium brown patina, the angular face with only one eye. Inscribed "Cire Perdue" and "4/4." $7,000 (Auction)

AUGUSTE MOREAU (French)

Wood Nymph, c. 1920, 24" high. In bronze with brown patina on a circular red variegated marble pedestal base, modeled as a young nude woman, her arm outstretched. (*Fakes Alert!* Moreau, whose style is somewhat romantic, is a widely reproduced artist, particularly because he worked in bronze only.) $2,000–$2,200

Bronze figure of a dancer by Lorenzl. *Courtesy of William Doyle Galleries, New York.*

FRANÇOIS POMPON (French, 1855–1933)

Owl, 10¾" high. In bronze, the smoothly stylized figure resting on an incorporated base. Inscribed "Pompon."   **$4,000 (Auction)**

FERDINAND (FRITZ) PREISS (German, 1882–1943)

Con Brio, a dancer, 15⅛" high, including green onyx and black marble base. A cold-painted bronze and ivory figure of a woman with one leg raised, her arms stretched in front and behind her. Her body in ivory, she wears shorts, a halter top, and a cloche hat, all in patinated bronze. Retailed in London by Phillips & MacConnal Gallery in the 1930s, which also sold the same figure mounted on tray. (*Fakes Alert!* This is perhaps the most frequently replicated statue by Preiss.) Onyx base signed "F. Preiss."   **$10,000 (Auction)**

Hoop Girl and Sonny Boy, 8¼" high and 8⅛" high, including green onyx bases. Pair of cold-painted bronze figures of a little girl and little boy, with legs, arms, and heads in ivory. Each on a green onyx base signed "F. Preiss."   **$4,000 (Auction)**

Little Girl Dancing, 7⅛" high. Cold-painted bronze and ivory figure of a small girl raising her skirt delicately, her hands and face in ivory, standing on a green onyx base. Statue inscribed "F. Preiss" and stamped with the Preiss-Kassler foundry seal, onyx base also signed "F. Preiss."   **$2,600 (Auction)**

Mandolin Player, 23⅛" high. Cold-painted bronze and ivory of a woman with a mandolin, standing with one hand on her hip, hands and face in ivory. With an elaborate onyx and marble base signed "F. Preiss." Marketed in the 1920s in London by Phillips & MacConnal Gallery. A very good example of Preiss's figures.   **$18,000–$20,000**

Oar Lady, an athlete, 11½" high. Cold-painted bronze and ivory of a woman wearing a short silver-patinated skirt, holding an oar, and standing on a black patinated bench which rests on a green onyx base. Stamped with the Preiss-Kassler foundry seal, on a green onyx base signed "F. Preiss." In excellent condition.   **$2,600 (Auction)**
$4,000–$5,000

Torch Dancer, 15¼" high, including green onyx base. The dancer, with one leg raised, bends backward holding two torches aloft. Legs, body, and head in ivory. This statue was marketed in the 1930s in London by Phillips & MacConnal Gallery. Two variants, including the dancer mounted on a tray, and an all-bronze figure mounted on an onyx base, also exist. (*Fakes Alert!* A fake of this statue is sold under the name "Flame Dancer.")   **$12,000–$15,000**

FREDDY STOLL (Swiss, work: 1920—1940)

Young Girl, 32¼" high. In parcel-gilt bronze on a marble base, inscribed "F. Stoll."   **$3,000–$4,000**

PAUL TERESZCZUK (Austrian, work: 1895–1925)

Dancing Couple, 29½" high. Bronze and ivory group with dark patina, the faces of carved ivory, on a green onyx base and mounted as a lamp, stamped "P. Tereszczuk Made in Austria."   **$1,000 (Auction)**

Young Girl by Freddy Stoll.
Courtesy of Christie's East, New York.

**Bronze and ivory of an Amazon,
by Bruno Zach.** *Courtesy of
Wolf's Fine Arts Auctioneers, Ohio.*

BRUNO ZACH (Austrian, work: 1918–1935)

Amazon, 14¾" high without plinth. In bronze and ivory, the Amazon on horseback, her legs, body, and head in ivory, a bronze feather in her hair. The horse finely cast in bronze stepping forward with its foreleg held high, its stylized mane and tail falling in heavy straight plaits from its head. Raised on a marble plinth. Signed "Bruno Zach." A very good example of Zach's work.   **$7,500 (Auction)**

Bookends, 6¾" high. A pair, cast in bronze from a model by Zach, each cast as an animated jester mounted on stepped plinths in chocolate brown patina, signed in the bronze "Zach" and impressed "Argentor Wien."   **$1,000 (Auction)**

Dancing Couple, 16⅛" high. A polychromed bronze figural group of a dancing couple, with a white onyx base. Inscribed "B. Zach."   **$1,800–$2,200**

Indian on Horseback, c. 1930, 15⅞" high. In black patinated bronze, the American Indian riding his charging steed with only one hand on the reins. Mounted on a veined black marble rectangular base. Bronze signed "B. Zach" and impressed "Argentor Wein." A very good example of Zach's style and an unusual subject for a European artist.
$6,000–$6,500

Wrestlers, 10½" high. Cast in bronze from a model by Zach, with brown patina on a green onyx base, signed "Zach" in the bronze and impressed "Argentor Wien."
$2,500–$3,000

GLASS

The growing recognition of the decorative arts, coupled with the emergence of the individual decorative artist in the mid-1800s, was strongly reflected in the field of glass design. In addition, with the rise of urban areas, both art glass and functional glass were in high demand in the Art Nouveau and Art Deco periods.

As in the Art Nouveau period, the major center of glass production in France continued to be near the city of Nancy in the region of Alsace-Lorraine along the French border with Germany, with its rich forests to fire the furnaces. Czechoslovakia, where labor was cheap and raw materials abundant, became the other major center of European glass production.

In the United States, Art Nouveau glass is best known by the works of Tiffany and Steuben. Tiffany brought the United States unrivaled preeminence in stained and iridescent glass, and today Tiffany lamps gain astronomical prices on the market.

In the 1920s and 1930s, both in Europe and in the United States, mass-produced glass was needed to meet the demands of middle-class households. Handmade production increasingly became unfeasible, and was carried on by only a few designers.

Glass is usually made from powdered flint or fine sand, ashes or another alkali, salt or metallic oxide, and lime. The type and proportion of its ingredients give it its color, transparency, opacity, ability to distort light, and so on. Lead crystal has at least 24 percent lead oxide. Other metallic oxides are what give color to glass.

The field of glass collecting in the Art Deco period is particularly rich and wide-ranging. One can collect many different kinds of glass—hand-blown, *pâte-de-verre*, cameo, enameled, acid-etched, leaded crystal, or molded—from a variety of designers and manufacturers.

HAND-BLOWN

The leading studio artist in hand-blown glass of the Art Deco period is Maurice Marinot (1882–1960). Other notable studio artists are Henri Navarre (1885–1971), Andre Thuret (1898–1965), Jean Luce (1895–1964), and Jean Perzel (b. 1892), who was known primarily for his lamps and lighting fixtures.

Marinot's work was bought up by collectors and museums from the start. He was known as a Fauve artist, along with such painters as Matisse, Dufy, and Braque, and was the first fine artist to undertake making glass himself. From 1923 on he blew his own glass. Marinot's glass is often deeply etched, and the color effects are subtle; one of his hallmarks is the way he captured the air bubble in the glass.

His patterns are mostly geometric, and even natural motifs such as flowers are stylized geometrically. He used many methods for cutting the glass, using flint, a cutting wheel, or etching with acid. Typical patterns are series of triangles or circles in bold relief.

Marinot's style of glassmaking, in which the artist and perhaps one or two assistants created the works, soon gave way to an increasingly industrialized glass manufacture using molds and power presses. However, it is interesting to note that the success of some of Marinot's design creations—especially the deep, acid-etched geometric patterns—inspired others to create more Modernist designs to meet changing tastes and increasing demand.

PÂTE-DE-VERRE

Blown glass is given its shape while still molten. Afterward, surface decoration may be applied, painted, carved or acid-etched. In contrast, *pâte-de-verre*, literally "glass paste," is finely crushed glass crystals mixed with a binding agent. The paste is mixed with different metallic oxides for color and can be sculpted in its cold state like clay, and shaped into figures, plaques, bowls, or vases. The glass is then fired to re-vitrify the crystals. The result is a glass that can be decorated or colored throughout its mass, not just on the surface.

François Decorchement (1880–1971) was the leading artist of the *pâte-de-verre* method. Decorchement also produced an eggshell-thin *pâte-d'émail*, a "porcelain paste" of which little has survived. *Pâte-de-verre*, however, is thicker, heavier, and translucent rather than transparent. His work is rated on a par with that of the leading artists in other decorative arts of the period, and is rare and expensive on the open market.

Other notable *pâte-de-verre* artists are Gabriel Argy-Rousseau and Alméric Walter, both of whom made many different types of objects: bowls, vases, jewelry pendants, candlesticks, paperweights, sculptures, and *vide poches*, which translates as "empty pockets," a decoratively sculpted glass dish to be kept on a dresser to hold coins, pins, and the like.

Alméric Walter, who first ran the *pâte-de-verre* workshop at Daum, later set up his own company and commissioned several other artists to produce models for him, including Henrí Bergé, Jean Descomps, Henri Mercier, and even the well-known French posterist Jules Chéret. Today, the work of these *pâte-de-verre* artists is fairly high-priced on the collecting market.

CAMEO

Cameo glass was one of the first major types of glass to gain widespread popularity, and was revived in England in the 1870s. Cameo glass has two or more layers of superimposed glass, then the top layer or layers are carved to create the designs. At first it was carved by hand, but soon glassmakers were using cutting wheels or etching the layers using hydrofluoric acid.

In the Art Nouveau period, Emile Gallé, one of the first glass artists to sign his work, created a style and technique for cameo glass that would be widely copied. Both Gallé and another Alsatian glassmaker, Daum, were known for their cameo glass using naturalistic motifs. As the Art Deco style emerged in France, a few glassmakers continued to design using cameo glass, although it was far less adaptable to mass production.

Some glassmakers also experimented with or adopted the method of acid-etching designs into thick-walled vessels made of a single layer of glass. Enameled glass, often painted to appear as cameo-cut, also enjoyed some popularity.

The firm Degué made both cameo and acid-etched pieces, which in the last five years have started appearing more frequently on the market, and are beginning to find a collecting base. Legras produced some fine pieces using all three methods. Daum eventually largely abandoned cameo glass and became the leader in acid-etched designs.

The outstanding talent in cameo glass of the Art Deco period is Charles Schneider, who trained under both Gallé and Daum. He founded Cristallerie Schneider in 1913 with his brother Ernest Schneider (1877–1937), who ran the business operations.

At first, the firm produced tableware and toilet articles much in the naturalistic style of Daum. Soon, however, Charles's innovations in handcrafted design and color distinguished "Schneider" glass in its own right. Works thus signed generally tend to be uncarved pieces with a stylized simplicity of form and rich color, including deep greens, reds, blues, pinks, and an orange color he called "Tango." The company's line grew to encompass art glass, serving pieces such as compotes and bowls, light fittings, and glass panels.

Most sought-after by Art Deco collectors today is a specialized cameo glass line Schneider called "Le Verre Français," literally, "The French Glass." The line included vases, lamps, bowls, urns, and more, usually acid-etched in highly stylized natural patterns of flowers and plants. Rarer, and more expensive, are the company's striking geometric patterns. (*See color section.*) Bright colors, such as red and orange, are highly prized, and some pieces also have applied handles and bases, often in a contrasting color.

Usually signed "Le Verre Français" in cameo, this line was also sometimes signed "Charder," an abbreviation of "*CHAR*-les Schnei-*DER*." Occasionally, a piece will also be signed "Ovington," the New York department store that helped popularize the line in this country, and for which Schneider created special commissions.

While the company continued to produce some art glass until 1982, it really flourished in the 1930s until the start of World War II. The bright colors were discontinued in 1933, due to the Depression and the rising costs of the rare minerals, such as uranium, needed to produce them. This was the case in both ceramics and glass worldwide, especially as uranium, which is the mineral for the color red, was put to wartime use.

Though production of "Le Verre Français" was to some degree industrialized, the quantity produced was much smaller than the mass production of Lalique and other glassmakers.

While a major German traveling museum exhibition in 1981–1983 referred to Schneider glass as "The Art Deco Glass," interest in this country only surged ahead in the last five years or so. Much of the credit for its rising popularity recently is due to antique dealers Corey Warn and Mark Feldman of Antiquers III in Brookline, Massachusetts, the only dealers specializing in "Le Verre Français." (*See the chapter "Today's Market" for more information.*)

ACID-ETCHED

Although, as we have seen, acid-etching can be used to carve away the layers of cameo glass, acid-etching itself became a way of creating designs in thick-walled vessels made of a single layer of glass.

The leading firm in the production of acid-etched glass in a Modernistic style is Daum Nancy. Founded by the brothers Auguste and Antoine, Daum was one of the leading producers of art glass in the Art Nouveau period. They successfully made the transition to Art Deco with their new designs, which were influenced by artists such as Maurice Marinot.

The market for acid-etched Daum started to emerge in the early 1980s, and today is firmly established, with some pieces fetching very high prices on the market and the collecting base growing. Particularly striking are the acid-etched lamps produced by Daum. (*See color section.*)

CRYSTAL

From the Scandinavian countries came the best of yet another kind of glass: clear leaded crystal cut with Modernist designs. As in other decorative arts, Scandinavian modern design in glass had an impact in the United States. The leading Scandinavian crystal manufacturers were Orrefors, Leerdam, and Kosta.

Until World War I, Orrefors was a little-known company in the forests of southern Sweden. In 1915 and 1917, it became the first crystal company to allow individual artists to sign their works. Many talented designers worked for Orrefors during the 1920s and 1930s, including Simon Gate, Edward Hald, Vicke Lindstrand, and Nils Landberg. In 1950, Lindstrand joined Kosta as chief designer.

Engraved glass by these designers, often depicting mythological themes, is highly prized today. Orrefors also developed another stunning type of glass called "graal," a cased glass where colored relief decorations are covered with clear, smooth crystal. Even today, Orrefors advertises crystal that is "devoid of intricate cutting patterns" but also "devoid of flaws." This 250-year-old company continues to be recognized for its glass artistry.

French firms offered some competition to the Scandinavians, perhaps most notably Baccarat. Founded in France in 1764, the firm continues to this today. In the 1920s, it produced some fine Art Deco designs, notably for perfume flasks and tableware in both glass and crystal, particularly the designs by Georges Chevalier.

In the United States, Frederick Carder (1863–1963) established the Steuben Glass Company, absorbed by the Corning Glass Works in 1918. Carder's incredibly beautiful Art Nouveau iridescent designs wound up gathering dust on the shelves, as they were strongly challenged by the Scandinavians, and he was forced to make a transition to a new style. Some of Steuben's designs before 1930 fall broadly into what can be called an Art Deco style, such as its "jade glass" vases with "alabaster" handles, made around 1925.

However, the best Modern designs from Steuben came in 1931–1932, when Walter Dorwin Teague designed a series of crystal stemware patterns such as "Riviera," "Spiral," "Blue Empire," "Winston," and "St. Tropez." Teague was the firm's design consultant for only about two years, and his work for Steuben is highly collectible. Teague also designed for Libbey Glass Company, the leading producer of higher-quality everyday glassware in the 1930s.

In 1933, Steuben commissioned John Gates and Sidney Biehler Waugh to create engraved designs in crystal that could compete with the Scandinavians. Waugh created massive vases with bold facets. He also used stylized mythological motifs carved into crystal, such as his "Europa" bowl in 1935. His "Gazelle" bowl, also created in 1935, is one of the best-known examples of quality Art Deco glass in America. Among other things, Gates designed the World's Fair Cup for the 1939 New York World's

Fair, which incorporated the design of the Trylon and Perisphere on top. This, along with other designs, some monumental in size, were exhibited at the Steuben pavilion at the fair.

MOLDED

Molded glass was the most suited to industrial mass production, and the maker who rose to the very top of the industry was René Lalique, both because of his tremendous design talents and because he was the first to really accept and develop industrial mass production of glass, which helped lower prices and open up new markets. His real genius was in staying ahead of the times.

Lalique actually started as an Art Nouveau jeweler and had his first exhibition in Paris in 1890. His use of glass paste, enamels, rock crystal, and precious metals was immediately recognized for its genius, and brought him clients such as Cartier, Boucheron, and Sarah Bernhardt. Somewhere around 1900, he started to create studio works in glass. At first, he molded his designs in a *cire perdu* or "lost wax" method, and retained naturalistic motifs of humans, animals, and foliage in an Art Nouveau style. As he moved from this handcrafted style to more industrial production, his designs also changed to reflect the newer styles.

The turning point came in 1907, when he was commissioned by Coty perfumes to design a line of scent bottles. Roger Coty was an entrepreneur with a great idea. Until that time, customers had to bring their own bottles to the stores to be filled with perfume. What if, Coty thought, the perfume was sold in its own special bottle? For one thing, it would mean that perfume could be sold everywhere instead of in just a few places.

For Lalique, it was the right idea at the right time. Already very interested in glass, he now truly committed himself to it by founding a factory for glass production near Paris in 1909. Since that time, the bottle itself has been almost as important as the perfume inside in terms of making a sale.

Perfume and toiletry bottles have become a collecting field in themselves, and were produced by many notable Art Deco glassmakers including Gallé, Daum, Marinot, and Baccarat. Perfume bottles were also made in Germany, Sweden, Czechoslovakia, and other countries. Many of these were manufactured in large quantities for retailing through department stores. The market for commercial perfume bottles has grown rapidly in the past five years, and because the Art Deco style has persisted in perfume bottles to the present day, it is a field that is still very accessible to beginning collectors.

According to Florida-based Madeleine France, one of the leading dealers in commercial perfume bottles, collectors especially look for perfume bottles that are "FSLB"— "filled, sealed, labeled, and boxed." (*See the chapter "Today's Market" for more information.*)

Lalique's Coty commissions made him see the value of mass-producing glass, especially since the market for both housewares and decorative objects was expanding so quickly. In 1920, he acquired the company's present glassworks factory in Alsace, right in the center of glass production in France.

Generally, the shapes of Lalique's vases are simple, but the glass may be tinted in a variety of different colors, frosted, or enameled. Molded designs can be in low, medium, or high relief. Motifs range from gods to geometric patterns to insects and fish, but most of his designs were drawn from nature. Especially popular are his figures and figurines of draped or nude women.

He created an incredibly wide range of products: picture frames, inkwells, glass table services, clocks, lamps and chandeliers, car radiator mascots, and perfume and toiletry bottles, which expanded his market and his popularity. As he continually increased his production, his line became available in quantity in both American and European department and jewelry stores. Vases, sculptures, and other decorative objects were popular gifts for weddings, anniversaries, and holidays. By 1933, he had produced over fifteen hundred different items.

After his death in 1945, the family's artistic tradition was carried on by his son Marc, who reopened the factory which had closed in 1939 because of the war. Marc revived many of his father's designs and created his own. Marc also changed the production from glass to lead crystal. Crystal has a content of at least 24 percent lead oxide, giving it greater weight and sparkle.

When Marc Lalique died in 1977, he left the direction of the factory to his daughter Marie-Claude, who today designs a third generation of Lalique sculptures, vases, and other items for exclusive distribution. The newer Lalique is sold under the trade name "Cristal Lalique," and is engraved "Lalique France," while works by René Lalique are signed "R. Lalique" or "René Lalique." The company inscription has changed several times and helps date a piece. (*See the chapter "Fakes Alert!" for more information.*)

The collecting base for Lalique, already large, got another boost in 1989 and 1990 when a major retrospective exhibition "Lalique: A Century of Glass for a Modern World" was organized by the Fashion Institute of Technology in New York, and traveled to museums in Coral Gables, Florida, and Baltimore.

Curated by Lalique author and dealer Nicholas Dawes, it was the first major museum retrospective on Lalique since 1933. Serious collectors have access to several references on Lalique, including Dawes's book *Lalique Glass*, earlier works by Katherine McClinton, the Lalique catalogues themselves, and *Lalique par Lalique*, published by the Société Lalique in 1977. Many Lalique collectors also belong to a collecting society created by Marie-Claude Lalique. For additional information on the Lalique Society, call (800) CRISTAL.

Though collected and collectible in their own right, a host of other makers of molded glass in both Europe and the United States will perhaps always be considered "imitators" of Lalique. These include Sabino, Etling, Hunnebelle, Genet & Michon, Edouard Cazaux, Paul D'Avesn, Muller Frères, Henri Dieupart, Verlys, Consolidated Lamp and Glass, and Phoenix Glass. Other glassmakers who produced "Lalique-like" molded and frosted glass starting in the 1920s, continue to produce at the present.

Etling was an important manufacturer for the department store trade in the 1920s and 1930s, and was noted for its production of bronze and ivory statues, as well as glass. André Hunnebelle was a leading designer of tableware, and his designs tend to be more geometricized and abstract than Lalique's. After World War II, Hunnebelle became a noted French film director.

Marius Ernst Sabino was a talented designer who exhibited at the 1925 Paris Exposition. He became known for his opalescent glass, which can be confusing for collectors, as it continues to be produced today. Muller Frères, although perhaps best known for their chandeliers and other lighting fixtures, also produced some striking vases, especially those incorporating metallic foil in the designs.

In the United States, Consolidated Lamp and Glass Company and Phoenix Glass, both located in Pennsylvania, also imitated Lalique for their molded vases.

Under the direction of chief designer Reuben Haley, Consolidated introduced its "Martelé" or "hand-wrought" line of molded glass vases in 1926. The models reflected the influence of Lalique, and some, such as "Love Birds," were direct copies of the Lalique designs Haley admired. When Consolidated closed from 1933 to 1936 because of the Depression, as many as forty to forty-five Consolidated molds were transferred to Phoenix, which continued their production under the direction of Reuben's son, Kenneth Haley.

While the Consolidated and Phoenix molded vases were less well-executed both in color and quality than Lalique, they have created a fairly large collecting base that is certain to continue to expand. These Depression-era wares gained a popular market at the same time Lalique's works were selling at fine department stores.

The collecting field for both Consolidated and Phoenix got a major boost in 1989 with the publication of Jack Wilson's book *Phoenix and Consolidated Art Glass 1926–1980*, which describes in detail the company histories and offers profuse illustrations of the many lines and patterns they produced.

The most innovative and truly American design created by Reuben Haley for Consolidated was the "Ruba Rhombic" tableware line, introduced in 1928 and advertised as "An Epic in Modern Art." With its irregular Cubist-inspired geometric planes and angles, "Ruba Rhombic" reflected the influence of jazz music in American design. Created in colors such as "Jungle Green," "Smokey Topaz," "Sunshine" yellow, lavender, silver, and rarer clear opal and black, it has become the most highly prized of all Consolidated designs. (*See color section.*)

There were about thirty-seven items in the "Ruba Rhombic" line, and today many are so rare that only a few examples are known to exist, such as the 16½" vase, and a fishbowl and stand which was actually produced by Phoenix, apparently under Kenneth Haley's direction. However, all "Ruba Rhombic" must today be considered rare, as it is currently estimated that in total fewer than fifteen hundred pieces still exist. The line was never produced again after Consolidated shut down in 1933 for a three-year duration.

In 1928, Kopp Glass, also of Pennsylvania, introduced its "Modernistic" vases, which resemble "Ruba Rhombic" but have angular designs that are more regular. Reuben Haley also used the "Ruba Rhombic" design for pottery produced by the Muncie Pottery Company of Muncie, Indiana, which is difficult to find on the market today.

The first major exhibition and sale of "Ruba Rhombic," featuring over four hundred pieces, took place in September 1992 at Moderne, a dealership in Philadelphia headed by Robert Aibel. The enormous national publicity the exhibition created may bring to light more "Ruba Rhombic" examples, but the organizers doubt that any large numbers will be located. The small quantity of pieces that exist coupled with a high demand means that prices will probably continue to climb rapidly. (*See the chapter "Today's Market" for more information.*)

CARNIVAL AND DEPRESSION

In the 1920s and 1930s, carnival and Depression glass flourished in America. Carnival glass, so called because of its use as prizes at carnival booths, comes in a wide variety of shapes, patterns, and manufacturers. Carnival glass is not Art Deco in design. Rather, carnival, with its metallic surface finish, is the Tiffany of carnival-goers.

Depression glass is the name given to a whole range of glass tableware produced to sell inexpensively during the Depression. Usually in transparent clear, green, pink, amber, and other colors, it was produced by numerous companies, and sometimes whole sets of this everyday kitchenware were given away as premiums with the purchase of a refrigerator or stove. Among the many companies which produced it are Indiana Glass Company, Anchor Hocking, Westmoreland, Hazel Atlas, and Federal.

Most Depression glass is not in the Art Deco style, but a few patterns are now very popular with collectors, notably Indiana Glass Company's "Pyramid" and "Tea Room" designs, Anchor Hocking's "Manhattan," and a design called "Cubist" or "Cube" that may have been produced by more than one maker.

Depression glass is a collecting field unto itself, with many collectors, clubs, and newsletters. However, in general, the few Deco styles seem to bring higher prices with Art Deco collectors than they do with collectors of Depression glass.

GLASS PRICE LISTINGS
(Alphabetically by designer or manufacturer)

RENÉ LALIQUE (French, 1860–1945)
Car Mascots

"Cinq Chevaux," c. 1930, 4⅝" high. Molded clear glass figure of five overlapping rearing horses, with frosted glass highlighting. Molded "R. Lalique" and engraved "France," mounted on a chromed metal circular base. In fine condition.   **$8,500 (Auction)**

"Coq Nain," 8" high. In gray glass, in the form of a rooster, molded "R. Lalique France."
$2,800–$3,200

"Epsom," 5" high, 6" long. In gray frosted glass, stylized horse head attached to chrome radiator cap, marked in the mold "R. Lalique." In good condition, but with small chips to both ears.   **$650 (Auction)**

"Falcon," 6¼" high. In clear glass, molded as a falcon, molded "R. Lalique," wheel-cut "France" and engraved "No. 1124."   **$1,400–$1,700**

"Levrier," c. 1930, 3" high, 7¾" long. Flat clear glass demilune shape molded in intaglio with a frosted glass greyhound. Molded "R. Lalique France," and mounted on a chromed circular base. A very good example of a mascot in excellent condition.
$2,500 (Auction)

"Tête D'Aigle," 4½" high. Frosted and clear glass, in the shape of an eagle's head, molded "R. Lalique."   **$1,000 (Auction)**
$700 (Auction)

"Victoire," c. 1930, 6½" high. Colorless glass tinted with gray enamel, an allegorical figure of "Victory," her eyes and mouth wide open, hair streaming behind her. Molded "R. Lalique." One of the finest examples of a Lalique car mascot. This piece has sold as high as $10,000 at auction.   **$7,000 (Auction)**
$9,000–$12,000

"Victoire" car mascot by René Lalique. *Courtesy of Christie's, New York.*

Glass by René Lalique including "Ceylon" *(far left)*, "Deux Colombes" clock, and "Rampillon" *(front center left)*. *Courtesy of William Doyle Galleries, New York.*

Clocks

"Deux Colombes," 9½" high. Molded opalescent glass, the arched case with a pair of doves and flowers in relief, signed "R. Lalique."   **$3,600 (Auction)**

"Hirondelles," 5⅞" high. Frosted glass, rectangular, molded in relief with six swallows on draping floral branches surrounding a circular dial, molded "R. Lalique" and engraved "R. Lalique, France No. 70." In good condition, with small chips to base.

$2,500–$3,000

As above, but in blue enameled glass   **$4,500 (Auction)**

"Inseparables," 4¼" high. Frosted glass, square with a molded pair of love birds on each side of the clock face, molded "R. Lalique" and engraved "R. Lalique France No. 258."

$3,800 (Auction)

"Roitelets," 7⅞" high. Frosted glass, circular, modeled as wreath of wrens in flight supported on a circular foot, engraved "R. Lalique France."   **$3,500–$4,000**

Lighting

Chandelier, "Champs Elysées," 25¼" high, 18" diameter. In molded glass, the hexagonal platform applied with six upright maple leaves suspended by four slender cylindrical supports from a stepped circular ceiling cap.   **$3,250 (Auction)**

"Champs Elysées" chandelier by René Lalique. *Courtesy of Butterfield & Butterfield, California.*

Chandelier, "*Coquilles*," 12" diameter. In opalescent glass, the hemispherical shade molded with shells, and with four hook mounts, molded "R. Lalique," with ropes and ceiling mount.   **$3,000–$3,500**

Chandelier, "*Dahlias*," 12" diameter. In opalescent glass, with hemispherical shade molded with dahlia blossoms and leaves and with four hook mounts, molded "R. Lalique," with ropes and ceiling mount.   **$4,200 (Auction)**

Chandelier, "*Feuilles de Charme*," 19" diameter. In frosted glass, hemispherical, composed of ten radiating sections, each molded overlapping leaves, each section molded "R. Lalique." A fine example of Lalique's chandeliers.   **$7,000 (Auction)**

Chandelier, "*Ronces*," 27" high, 27½" diameter. In clear and frosted glass, a simple frosted domed shade surrounded by four highly geometric scrolled devices.   **$8,500–$9,000**

Chandelier, "*Villeneuve*," 12¼" diameter. Frosted glass, semispherical, molded with a garland of fruits, molded "R. Lalique France."   **$3,000–$3,500**

Lamp, table, "*Cardamine*," 16¾" high. The standard with frosted design of a stem with scrolling leaves, with fluted rectangular shade, engraved "R. Lalique France."   **$8,000–$9,000**

Jewelry

Brooch, 3⅞" long. Blue patinated glass, molded with a pair of birds flanking a wreath with central cabochon, the gilt metal back with design in relief of branches, impressed "Lalique."   **$3,000–$3,500**

Brooch, "*Faune*," 1¾" long. Frosted green glass, quatrefoil, molded as a satyr's head, the brass mount with pin stamped "Lalique."   **$2,600 (Auction)**

Brooch, "*Grenouilles*," 1⅝" diameter. Frosted glass, circular, molded with three crouching frogs facing one another to form a triangular pattern, with dark patina and backed with copper foil, the brass mount with pin, stamped "Lalique."   **$2,200–$2,600**

Brooch, "Blue Moths," 1¾" diameter. Frosted and clear glass, circular, with four flying moths against bright blue foil backing, mounted in gilt metal frame stamped "Lalique" with square "RL" trademark.   **$1,500–$1,700**

Medallion, "Fioret," 1⅜" diameter. Frosted glass, molded with a female nude and flowers, molded "R. Lalique Fioret Paris."   **$600 (Auction)**

Necklace, "Fleurettes," each bead 1⅜" long. In frosted, mauve-colored glass, beads of cylindrical form, molded with bands of stylized blossoms, with seventeen beads on a mauve silk cord.   **$3,500–$4,000**

Necklace, "Grosses Graines," each bead 1" long. In blue glass, cylindrical beads molded with berry clusters in deep blue, with eight beads strung on a blue cord.   **$2,800 (Auction)**

Perfume and Toiletry Bottles

Atomizer, 5¼" high. Cylindrical form molded in relief with four niches, each surrounding a female nude, molded "R Lalique Made in France."   **$500 (Auction)**

Atomizer, 4" high. Gilt-metal-mounted, green tinted frosted and clear glass, cylindrical in shape, molded in relief with pattern of flowers. The mount impressed "France," the bottle molded "R. Lalique" and "Made in France."   **$600–$750**

Perfume bottle, "Amphytrite," 3¾" high. In frosted colorless glass, in the form of a swirled snail shell, with a kneeling nude woman stopper. Script signature "R. Lalique France." In good condition, except with the insert on the stopper ground.   **$900 (Auction)**

Perfume bottle, "Calendal," 4½" high. In frosted glass, in a flattened ovoid shape, molded with nude figures and a ground of flowerheads; the stopper hemispherical in shape molded flowerheads, traces of peach enamel in the recesses, acid-stamped "Molinard/Paris France."   **$950 (Auction)**

Perfume bottle, "Cigalia," 5¼" high. In frosted glass, a tapering rectangular bottle molded with frosted winged locust at each corner, the lozenge-shaped stopper molded with stylized branches. An outstanding example, with the original decorated wooden box.
                                              $7,000 (Auction)

Perfume bottle, "Coeurs," 3¾" high. Frosted colorless glass, four hearts with gilt screw cap, molded "R. Lalique France," housed in hand-stitched red leather sheath.
                                              $175 (Auction)

Perfume bottle, "Dans la Nuit," c. 1930, 3" high. Designed for Worth Fragrances. The blue spherical body molded with tiny stars. A good, if more commonly found, example of Lalique perfumes. In fine condition.   **$650 (Auction)**
                                              $700–$900

Perfume bottle, "Imprudence," c. 1938, 3¼" high. Designed for Worth, with paper label and molded "R. Lalique." In the original box.   **$400 (Auction)**

"Leurs Ames," perfume bottle by René Lalique.
Courtesy of Madeleine France, Florida.

Perfume bottle, "Jardinee," 5" high. Molded glass, in a flattened circular shape, molded with overlapping flowerheads on an amber stained ground; disk stopper molded with a single flowerhead, molded "Lalique" on the bottom, molded "Volnay Paris" on the side. **$1,700 (Auction)**

Perfume bottle, "Leurs Ames," c. 1914, 5¼" high. In fine glass, in an inverted cone shape; fitted with a tiara stopper etched with female figures suspended from flowering tree boughs; the base molded "Leurs Ames D'Orsay" and twice "Lalique" and incised "78H." Extremely rare, the early first edition of one of only a few perfume bottles by Lalique with tiara stoppers. **$26,000 (Auction)**

Perfume bottle, "Leurs Ames," as above, but c. 1920, later edition created for broader distribution, the lower front molded "Leurs Ames d'Orsay." **$3,500–$5,000**

Perfume bottle, "Perles," 6¾" high. Tinted glass cologne in tapering cylindrical form, festooned in low relief with three tiers of beads in graduated sizes; the conical stopper with two rows, centering a cluster of beads, satin finish dusted in blue. Molded in intaglio "R. Lalique" and etched "France" in script. **$550 (Auction)**

Perfume bottle, "Roncier," 4¾" high. Clear and frosted glass, in a flattened semicircular form; conical stopper, molded with a design of blossoms amid briars. Molded "R. Lalique" and "Volnay Paris." In good condition, but with small chips. **$650 (Auction)**

Perfume flacon, "Eucalyptus," 1¾" long. Frosted glass, molded with slender leaves, on pomegranate-colored silk cord. Molded "Lalique." **$2,400 (Auction)**

Powder box, 4⅜" diameter. Circular, molded with Venus being dressed by two nymphs, etched "Lalique" and "Nina Ricci Paris." **$600–$750**

Powder box, "D'Orsay," 4" diameter. Flowered "Emiliane" box with brown patina, molded "R. Lalique—France." In good condition, the patina worn.   **$400–$500**

Powder box, "Moths," 3¼" diameter. Molded round box with trees below, four moths on cover, pale green patina overall, signed "Lalique."   **$1,200–$1,500**

Sculpture

Suzanne, a female nude, c. 1932, 8¾" high. An opalescent glass statue, molded as a standing female nude with a robe draped over her outstretched arms, molded "R. Lalique." (*See color section.*)   **$5,000 (Auction)**
$8,000–$10,000

Thais, a nude, c. 1925, 8¼" high. A clear and frosted glass figure of a draped nude, arms outstretched. Stamped "R. Lalique France." (This figure also came mounted as a lamp. For additional information on *Thais,* see the bronze and ivory sculpture of the same name by D. H. Chiparus in the chapter "Decorative Sculpture.") A fine example of Lalique sculpture, in excellent condition.   **$10,000–$12,000**
$8,000 (Auction)

Virgin and Child, c. 1930, 13¼" high. In clear and frosted glass, the figures molded in intaglio on the stele form, mounted on a rectangular wooden plinth. The glass acid stamped "R. Lalique/France."   **$1,600 (Auction)**
$1,500–$2,000

Vases

"Actina," 8¾" high. Patinated glass, everted tapering cylindrical form, molded with serrated undulating vertical bands, in brown patina, engraved "R. Lalique France."   **$1,800 (Auction)**

Glass by René Lalique (*clockwise from top*):
"Coqs et Plumes," "Deaux et Deaux,"
powder box for **"D'Orsay,"** and **"Lievres."**
Courtesy of Skinner, Inc., Massachusetts.

Thais by René Lalique, c. 1925.
Courtesy of Christie's East, New York.

"Bresse" by René Lalique.
Courtesy of Skinner, Inc.,
Massachusetts.

"Albert," 6¾" high, catalogue #958. Topaz glass, cylindrical form with molded handles formed as falcon heads, engraved "R. Lalique France No. 958."   **$2,000 (Auction)**

"Archers," c. 1930, 10½" high, catalogue #893. Oviform amber with nude hunters holding bows, pursuing large birds, inscribed "R. Lalique France No. 893." In fine condition.
$4,250 (Auction)
$2,500–$3,500

"Avallon," 6" high. Frosted glass, the flaring vessel molded with birds and berries, heightened with blue patina, engraved "R. Lalique France."   **$1,800 (Auction)**

"Bacchantes" c. 1930, 9⅝" high. In clear and frosted glass, molded with a continuous frieze in medium and high relief of nude women dancing arm in arm. The Bacchantes were the priestesses of the god Bacchus. Inscribed "R. Lalique."   **$5,500 (Auction)**
$7,000–$9,000

"Borromee," 9¹/₁₆" high. Blue patinated glass, ovoid molded in relief with a design of overlapping peacock's heads, engraved "R. Lalique France."   **$3,000 (Auction)**
$15,000 (Auction)

"Bresse," 1932, 4½" high, catalogue #1073. Amber with a flared raised rim and base, round body deeply molded with stylized roosters, accented with mustard-yellow matte enamel wash in recessed areas, acid-stamped "R. Lalique France."   **$2,100 (Auction)**

"Camaret," 5½" high, catalogue #1010. In frosted glass, a bulbous form, molded with fish and heightened with a light blue patina, engraved "R. Lalique France No. 1010."
$2,500–$3,000

"Canard," 5½" high. In amber glass, the bulbous body with a spiraling design of ducks, stenciled "R. Lalique France."   **$2,500–$3,000**

"Ceylon," c. 1921, 9½" high, catalogue #905. In opalescent glass, ovoid with a flattened rim, molded with four sets of lovebirds on arched branches; impressed "R. Lalique." Very good quality and fine condition. (*See photo in "Clocks" listing "Deux Colombes," page 170.*)

$4,500 (Auction)
$4,800 (Auction)

"Chardon," 8½" high, catalogue #979. In frosted green glass, with gently everted rim, the body molded with thistle plants, engraved "R. Lalique France No. 979."

$5,500 (Auction)

"Coqs et Plumes," 6⅛" high. In frosted glass with a blue wash, the conical form molded with twelve roosters in high relief. Inscribed "R. Lalique France." (*See photo in "Perfume and Toiletry Bottles" listing "Powder box, 'D'Orsay,'" page 174.*)   **$1,200 (Auction)**

"Dahlias," 4⅞" high. In black enameled glass, in a compressed spherical form, the blossoms with enameled centers, the design heightened with amber patina, molded "R. Lalique."   **$2,200–$2,500**

"Danaides," 7⅛" high. In smokey-amber molded glass, in an ovoid shape with a wide mouth, molded with the figures of six nude women pouring water from urns held on their right shoulders. The Dainaides were the daughters of Danaos, King of Egypt. Molded "R. Lalique," inscribed "France."   **$2,750 (Auction)**
$3,000–$4,000

"Dentelé," c. 1930, 7½" high. In frosted glass, the narrow cylindrical neck spreading out to a globular body molded in relief with knobbed ridges running vertically, molded "R Lalique." A good example of Lalique, in fine condition.   **$600 (Auction)**
$800–$850

"Deaux et Deaux," 7⅛" high. A flared goblet shape molded with repeating relief of paired daisies, colored in a yellow wash with orange centers and green stems, acid stamped "Lalique France." (*See photo in "Perfume and Toiletry Bottles" listing "Powder box, 'D'Orsay,'" page 174.*)   **$650 (Auction)**

"Deux Sauterelles," 9½" high. In clear glass, oviform in shape, molded on either side with a grasshopper, wheel-cut "R. Lalique."   **$8,000–$9,000**

"Escargot," 8½" high, catalogue #931. In frosted fiery opalescent glass, molded as a snail shell, colored strongly with blue-green patina, signed "R. Lalique France No. 931."

$2,800–$3,200

"Espalion," 7½" high, catalogue #996. In frosted blue glass, the spherical form molded with fern leaves, engraved "R. Lalique France No. 996."   **$3,800 (Auction)**

"Floride," 14½" high. In frosted glass, the flared cylindrical form molded with a row of large leaves about the bottom, the recessed areas washed with a brown patina, stenciled "R. Lalique."   **$5,000–$6,000**

"Formose," c. 1932, 6¾" high. In opalescent glass, the spherical form molded with swimming fish, with light blue patina in the recesses. Inscribed "R. Lalique France." Fine condition.   **$2,000–$2,500**

"Grande Boule Lierre," 14½" high. A large frosted glass vase, in spherical form, molded with delicate tendrils of ivy, engraved "R. Lalique." A rare and fine example of the artist's eye. **$20,000 (Auction)**

"Grimpereaux," c. 1930, 8¼" high. In molded glass, the widely conical form, on six slightly raised feet, molded with tiny birds perched on leafy branches, with blue patina in the recesses, inscribed "R. Lalique." **$1,600 (Auction)**

"Gui," c. 1935, 6¾" high. In clear molded glass, the spherical body molded with mistletoe, molded "R. Lalique." A good, albeit more common example of Lalique's style, in fine condition. **$750 (Auction)**
$600–$700

"Honfleur," 5⅝" high. In molded glass, the flaring cylinder with two applied molded handles, and heightened with brown patina, wheel-cut "R. Lalique France." **$1,000 (Auction)**

"Jardinère St. Hubert," c. 1925, 18" long. Boat form with oversized handles finely molded with antelopes among foliage; etched "R. Lalique France." **$3,500–$4,000**

"Lagamar," 7⅛" high. In frosted and enameled glass, the body carved with horizontal bands, with a black enamel pattern, wheel-cut "R. Lalique." **$8,000 (Auction)**

"Laurier," 7" high, catalogue #947. In opalescent glass, cylindrical form, molded in relief with laurel leaves and berries, engraved "R. Lalique France" and "No. 947." **$700 (Auction)**
$700–$900

"Lievres," 6¼" high. In frosted glass, spherical form with a flared rim, molded with a frieze of running rabbits, against gray-wash patina, with molded fern fronds above and below, molded "R. Lalique." (*See photo in "Perfume and Toiletry Bottles" listing "Powder box, 'D'Orsay,'" page 174.*) **$1,200 (Auction)**

"Martins Pecheurs," c. 1923, 10" high. In dark blue-green glass, ovoid, molded in low relief with martins perched and flying amid fuchsia branches, with light gray enamel highlighting in the recesses. The base molded in cameo "R. Lalique" and inscribed in script "Lalique." A fine example in a rare color. **$35,000 (Auction)**

"Jardinère St. Hubert" by René Lalique. *Courtesy of William Doyle Galleries, New York.*

"Mesanges," c. 1930, 12½" high. In clear and frosted glass, the conical shape molded with a glass medallion of a bird among blossoms. Inscribed "Lalique France." **$800–$1,200**

"Monnaie du Pape," c. 1925, 9¼" high. In molded, lustrous, red-amber glass, the oval body molded with overlapping honesty plant pods, leaves, and stems; impressed "R. Lalique." A very good example of Lalique's style, in a hard-to-find color. **$7,000–$9,000**

"Orans," c. 1927, 10½" high. In frosted glass molded in relief with large dahlias and leaves; inscribed "R. Lalique. France." **$7,500 (Auction)**

"Oursin," 7¼" high. In blue patinated frosted glass, the spherical shape molded as a sea urchin, heightened with blue patina, etched "R. Lalique France." **$900 (Auction)**
$750 (Auction)

"Penthièvre," c. 1932, 10¾" high, catalogue #1011. In topaz glass, spherical with everted rim, molded with rows of angular stylized fish, each row swimming in an opposite direction than the previous one, engraved "R. Lalique France No. 1011."
$6,000 (Auction)

"Penthièvre," as above, in amber glass. **$14,000 (Auction)**

"Pérruches," c. 1932, 10¼" high. Deep blue ovoid form, molded in medium and low relief with lovebirds perched on blossoming quince branches. Rim molded "R. Lalique," base engraved "R. Lalique France." A rare color in fine condition. **$15,000 (Auction)**
$18,000 (Auction)

"Pierrefonds," c. 1932, 6¼" high, catalogue #990. In butterscotch-colored glass, the central cylindrical vessel with two large scrolling thorny handles, inscribed "R. Lalique France No. 990." In fine condition. **$11,000 (Auction)**
$10,000–$13,000

"Rampillon," 5" high. Molded opalescent glass, the cone-shaped vessel with raised diamond-shaped projections against molded flat leaves and flowers, signed. (*See photo in "Perfume and Toiletry Bottles" listing "Deux Colombes," page 170.*) **$650 (Auction)**

"Sauterelles," c. 1932, 11" high. Deeply molded yellow with myriad grasshoppers among thick blades of grass. Inscribed "R. Lalique France." In fine condition. **$4,750 (Auction)**

"Sauterelles," c. 1932, 11" high. As above, but in sapphire blue glass. **$25,000–$30,000**

Other Glass Items

Ashtray, *"Feuilles,"* 6⅞" long. Amber glass, oval, molded with leaves, engraved "Lalique."
$700–$800

Beverage service, *"Setubal,"* tray: 18" long. Seven pieces, frosted and clear glass, comprising six flared tumblers with leaf and berry design and matching tray, each piece marked "R. Lalique." **$700 (Auction)**

Bottle, "*Douze Figurines Avec Bouchon,*" 11½" high. In frosted glass, the cylindrical body with narrow neck, molded in high relief with six nude embracing couples; the stopper molded as a kneeling female nude figure, stenciled "R. Lalique."   **$4,500–$5,000**

Bowl, "*Cernuschi,*" 10⅝" diameter, catalogue #392. In frosted glass, semispherical with flat everted rim, molded with a band of blossoms and foliage, wheel-cut "R. Lalique France" and engraved "No. 392."   **$650 (Auction)**

Bowl, "*Nemours,*" 3⅞" high, 10" diameter. In frosted glass, the hemispherical bowl molded in intaglio with concentric rows of flowerheads, with a beige tint, and raised flowerhead centers enameled in black, lightly molded "R. Lalique/France."   **$1,500–$1,800**

Bowl, "*Ondines,*" 8" diameter. Opalescent glass, molded with mermaids amid bubbles, engraved "R. Lalique France."   **$1,400–$1,700**

Bowl, "*Pérruches,*" 4" high, 9⅜" diameter. In molded opalescent and clear glass, molded with parrots in high relief, on a ground of overlapping branches and blossoms, the recesses washed in blue. Acid-stamped "R. Lalique."   **$2,500–$2,750**

Box, "*Cigales,*" 10½" diameter. In opalescent glass, plain glass bottom, the lid molded with cicadas, molded "R. Lalique" and engraved "France No. 44."   **$1,500 (Auction)**

Box, "*Dahlias,*" 8½" diameter. In opalescent glass, blue leather-covered box bottom, the lid molded with three stylized blossoms, molded "R. Lalique."   **$750 (Auction)**

Box, "*Geneviève,*" 4" diameter. In patinated frosted glass, molded with two doves on a branch, surrounded by pine branches, heightened with blue patina, engraved "R. Lalique France No. 65."   **$480 (Auction)**

Box, "*Hirondelles,*" 4" long. In molded glass, rectangular, bottom molded with chevrons, lid molded with swallows, molded "R. Lalique" and etched "Lalique."   **$750–$900**

Charger, "*Martiques,*" c. 1930, 14½" diameter. In molded glass, with a shoal of swimming fish, molded "R. Lalique."   **$2,700 (Auction)**

Charger, "*Sirènes,*" 14½" diameter. In frosted glass, molded with a sinuous nude maiden amid the surf, with blue patina, molded "R. Lalique."   **$3,200–$3,800**

Decanter set, "*Pouilly,*" decanter: 11¼" high. In blue patinated glass, decanter base and stopper molded with leaping fish, with six matching cordials. Decanter stamped "R. Lalique."   **$1,300 (Auction)**

Door handles, "*Gros Bourdon,*" 3" long, 3¼" deep. In clear and frosted glass, molded as a bumble bee, engraved "R. Lalique." Rare and unusual Lalique item. **$15,000 (Auction)**

Frame, "*Naiades,*" 4½" square. In clear glass, molded with mermaids, molded "Lalique."
$1,200 (Auction)
$1,500–$1,600

"Bahia" lemonade set by René Lalique.
Courtesy of William Doyle Galleries, New York.

Goblets, "Epines," 4" high. A group of eight, patinated glass with flaring cylinders, molded with thorn branches and heightened with brown patina molded "R. Lalique."
$700 (Auction)

Lemonade set, "Bahia," glasses: 4½" high; tray: 17" diameter. The tray and nine glasses in amber-colored glass, molded with a flat leaf design, signed "R. Lalique."
$1,000 (Auction)

Mirror, table, 14½" high. In frosted molded glass, rectangular, molded in high relief with a double scalloped border, acid-etched "R. Lalique France," mounted with a silverplated backplate and easel support. In good condition, with two small chips to lower back corner of frame.
$3,500 (Auction)

Wine coaster, c. 1930, 6¼" diameter. In clear glass, round saucer form colored with sepia patina enamel; molded with a portrait of St. Odile for the cloister winery; signed "R. Lalique."
$500–$600

OTHER GLASS DESIGNERS

(Alphabetically by designer or manufacturer)

GABRIEL ARGY-ROUSSEAU (French, 1885–1953)

Bowl, 3⅝" diameter. Low bowl, molded with entwined leafy vines in tones of indigo and purple, raised on a slightly flaring ring foot, signed "G. Argy-Rousseau." **$1,500–$2,000**

Covered box, 3⅞" diameter. Cast as a cluster of fuchsia blossoms with black and white centers, molded "G Argy-Rousseau" and numbered "21484." **$5,000 (Auction)**

Covered box, 3¾" diameter. With domed cover, mottled all over with rich red poppy blossoms, signed in the mold "G. Argy-Rousseau" and "5997." **$5,800–$6,000**

Pendant, 2" long. Oval, molded with a locust in gray, green, lavender, and blue on a pale green ground, molded "GAR," on a black cord. **$1,500–$2,000**

Pendant, "Coccinelles," 2½" long. Oval, molded with three red ladybugs on lavender scrolled vines, with a charcoal border, signed "G.A.R.," on a charcoal cord. An outstanding example of an Argy-Rousseau pendant. **$4,200 (Auction)**

Pendant, "Edelweiss," 2⅝" diameter. A central stylized blossom in blue-green and purple, molded "GAR," on a purple cord.   **$900 (Auction)**

Pendant, "Papyrus," 2½" long. Oval, molded with stylized curling blossoms in blue, purple, and green, surmounted by a single green glass bead, molded "GAR," on a pink and taupe tasseled cord.   **$1,400–$1,500**

Perfume bottle, c. 1920, 5" high. A conical mottled earth-tone colored body, decorated with molded frieze of forsythia blossoms; signed "G. Argy-Rousseau." A very good example in good condition, missing atomizer fittings.   **$1,900 (Auction)**

Vase, 6" high. Cylindrical, with waisted neck and wide mouth, molded around the body with four thistle plants in raspberry and green on a yellow and amber streaked frosted ground, signed "G. Argy-Rousseau" in intaglio, "France" on the base.   **$3,500–$4,000**

Vase, 8⅛" high. Ovoid, molded around base with four overlapping rows of lappet bands, the slightly everted rim with a crenelated band, the sides with handles in the form of unfurling ferns, in deep raspberry changing to deep purples streaked with pink, signed "G. Argy-Rousseau" in intaglio.   **$4,250 (Auction)**

Vase, "Fougères," 8¼" high. Ovoid, mottled mauve and apricot glass molded with rows of dentils at bottom and rim, and with coiled fern leaves at each side forming handles, molded "G. Argy-Rousseau."   **$5,000–$5,500**

Vase, figural, "Jaunesse," 6" high. Flattened oviform, everted rim, each side molded with a seated nude female figure in white with a circular frame, reserved against radiating dentils in mottled brown and orange, signed in the mold "G. Argy-Rousseau" France.
                                                                $14,000 (Auction)

Vase, figural, "Le Jardin des Hesperides," 9½" high. Oviform, everted rim, purple and plum-streaked translucent ground with three fuchsia and plum-colored women gathering orange-red apples from three deep violet trees, all above a large Greek key pattern motif in plum and fuchsia, molded "G. Argy Rousseau."   **$35,000–$40,000**

Vase, figural, 9¾" high. Cylindrical with everted rim, the pale ground mottled with violet and fuchsia, molded with two Grecian harpists in bright terra cotta and violet, with stylized circular motifs below, signed in the mold "G. Argy-Rousseau." A rare and outstanding example of a figural Argy-Rousseau.   **$40,000 (Auction)**

PAUL D'AVESN (French, work: 1920–1933)

Vase, 8½" high. In pink glass, footed ovoid form, molded all over with rosettes, molded "P. D'Avesn France."   **$600 (Auction)**

Vase, 8½" high. In gray glass, cylindrical, molded with pheasants nestled together, their plumage crisscrossing in a fanned pattern, molded "P. D'Avesn, France."   **$800 (Auction)**

Vase, 9" high. In amber glass, ovoid with large mouth, molded with a design of overlapping poppies, heightened with blue patina, molded "P. D'Avesn France."   **$800–$1,200**

Vase, 10⅝" high. In gray glass, spherical with everted rim, molded with a design of stylized fish, with blue patina in the recesses, painted "P. D'Avesn."   **$1,000 (Auction)**
$1,500–$2,000

BACCARAT (French, founded 1764)

Perfume bottle, c. 1935, 4¼" high. Designed for Guerlin. Tapering oval form with
molded facets and faceted head-form stopper labeled "Guerlin Parfum des Champs
Elysees Paris." In fine condition.   **$1,500–$1,800**

Vase, 8¼" high. In clear and frosted glass, a tapering rectangular form, molded with
flowers, supported between the wings of a grasshopper resting on a foliate-molded
domed rectangular base, signed "Baccarat" in relief.   **$700 (Auction)**

CARILLO (French, late 1930s–1950s)

Vase, c. 1940, 7½" high, 7½" diameter. Full round body molded with overlapping leaf
design selectively polished in the Lalique manner; molded "Carillo."   **$250–$400**

Vase, c. 1940, 8" high. Ovoid form in white frosted glass, molded with overlapping leafy
branches, molded "Carillo."   **$150–$300**

CONSOLIDATED LAMP AND GLASS COMPANY
(American, Coraopolis, Pennsylvania 1894–1967)
"Martelé" Line—Introduced in 1926
Designed by Reuben Haley (1872–1933)

> **C** The direct impact of René Lalique can be seen in several of
> the "Martelé" ("hand-wrought") designs. Some of these
> were also reproduced by Phoenix Glass, under the direction
> of Reuben's son Kenneth, using Consolidated molds when
> Consolidated closed from 1933–1936 during the Depres-
> sion. (See chapter "Glass" for additional information on the
> relationship between Phoenix and Consolidated.)

Vase, *"Dragon-Fly,"* 6" high. Molded with dragonflies and reeds in yellow cased glass, in
fine condition.   **$225–$250**

Vase, *"Dragon-Fly,"* as above, but molded with dragonflies in green on green and brown
reeds on satin milk glass, in fine condition.   **$100–$125**

Vase, *"Katydid,"* 7" high. Molded with grasshoppers on stalks of grass in frosted glass against a
brown patina ground, flattened ovoid shape with oval mouth, in fine condition. **$200–$225**

Vase, *"Katydid,"* 8" high. As above in coloration but slightly flaring conical shape, in
fine condition.   **$225–$275**

Vase, *"Love Birds,"* 10½" high. Directly copied from the Lalique "Perruches" design.
Molded with pairs of lovebirds highlighted in blue, perched on branches highlighted in

brown with lavender berries, against a ground of satin custard-colored glass, ovoid form with round mouth, in fine condition. $500–$550

Vase, "Screech Owls," 5¾" high. Designed by Kenneth Reuben. Molded with owls highlighted in blue, perched on reeds highlighted in salmon color, against a ground of satin custard-colored glass, flattened ovoid form with oblong mouth, in fine condition.

$200–$225

Vase, "Tropical Fish," 9" high. Molded all over with goldfish in frosted glass against a blue patina ground, flattened square shape with rounded shoulders and oblong mouth, in fine condition. $300–$350

Vase, "Tropical Fish," as above, but molded entirely in green cased glass, in fine condition.

$400–$425

"Ruba Rhombic" Line—Introduced in 1928
Designed by Reuben Haley (1872–1933)

> Produced in a number of colors including jade (light green), jungle-green, smokey-topaz, lilac, and sunshine (yellow), as well as a white opalescent and a silver. Under fifteen hundred pieces of "Ruba Rhombic" are known to exist. *(See color section.)*

Ashtray, in white opalescent. $700–$800

Cigarette box, in sunshine. $800–$900

Creamer, in jungle-green. $250–$300

Candle holder, in lilac. $200–$250

Decanter set, in smokey-topaz. Stoppered whiskey decanter, six tumblers, and tray. An outstanding example of the style, very rare, especially the tray. $5,000–$5,500

"Ruba Rhombic" decanter set (tray not shown), 1928. *Courtesy of Moderne, Pennsylvania.*

"Ruba Rhombic" pitcher, 1928. *Courtesy of Jack D. Wilson.*

Fishbowl and stand, fishbowl: 12" wide, 8" deep; metal stand: 24" high. Designed by Kenneth Haley for Phoenix Glass Company, the only "Ruba Rhombic" design produced by Phoenix. The large fishbowl in a vaseline glass (not a Consolidated color), supported by a three-footed pedestal base in wrought iron with stylized motifs. Extremely rare; only four examples known to exist. **$5,500–$6,500**

Pitcher, 9" high, in smokey-topaz. **$4,000–$4,500**

Plate, 10" diameter, in jungle-green. **$325–$375**

Sugar bowl, in jungle-green. **$250–$300**

Tumbler, flat, 9 oz., in lilac. **$325–$375**

Tumbler, footed, 3¼" high, in jade. **$250–$300**

Vase, 9½" high, in jungle-green. **$3,000–$4,000**

DAUM FRÈRES
Antoine Daum (1864–1930) and Auguste Daum (1853–1909)

Bowl, 6" high. In acid-etched glass, conical form on circular foot, in yellow, engraved "Daum Nancy France" with Cross of Lorraine. **$1,000–$1,200**

Lamp, 15½" high; shade: 15½" diameter. In acid-etched glass, the domed shade and footed cylindrical base in pale salmon, deeply etched with stylized geometric pattern, base and shade acid-etched "Daum Nancy France." A fine example of a Daum lamp. (*See color section.*) **$19,000 (Auction)**

Vase, c. 1930, 3¾" high. In pale amber glass, spherical with flared flattened rim, with three textured acid-etched rings against the polished surface, signed "Daum Nancy France." **$700–$800**

Vase, c. 1930, 4" high. In pale blue, ovoid body, deeply acid-etched with circles and semicircles; engraved "Daum Nancy" with the Cross of Lorraine trademark.

$450–$600

Vase, 4½" high. In pale yellow glass, conical form on circular foot, deeply acid-etched with a pattern of vertical ribs beneath squares, engraved "Daum Nancy France," with Cross of Lorraine.

$950 (Auction)

Vase, 5⅝" high. In gray-blue glass, spherical, acid-etched with stylized square-petaled blossoms, engraved "Daum Nancy France" with Cross of Lorraine.

$1,100–$1,200

Vase, 9½" high. In dark gray glass, footed gourd form, with smooth vertical ribbing, engraved "Daum Nancy France" with Cross of Lorraine.

$750 (Auction)

Vase, 10½" high. In dark gray glass, baluster-form, acid-etched with a "confetti" design, engraved "Daum Nancy France" with Cross of Lorraine.

$900–$1,000

Vase, c. 1930, 12" high. In golden-yellow, conical form, with deeply acid-etched banding. Engraved "Daum Nancy France," with Cross of Lorraine trademark.

$1,700 (Auction)

Vase, 13" high. In smokey-topaz glass, a flared bowl with waisted foot, deeply acid-etched with stylized geometric design, engraved "Daum Nancy France." A fine example of a Daum acid-etched vase.

$5,000 (Auction)

Vase, 13" high. In pink flecked glass, baluster form, acid-etched with vertical ribbing, engraved "Daum Nancy France."

$2,300–$2,500

Vase, c. 1930, 14¼" high. In icy aqua-blue glass, in squared baluster form, deeply acid-etched with circles and stripes. Signed "Daum Nancy France," with Cross of Lorraine trademark. A very good example of a Daum acid-etched vase.

$2,350 (Auction)

Vase, 14¾" high. In gray glass, baluster-form with smooth vertical ribbing, engraved "Daum Nancy France" with Cross of Lorraine.

$1,500 (Auction)

DEGUÉ (French, 1920s–1930s)

Vase, c. 1925, 6¼" high. In clear glass, flared oval form on disk pedestal, with etched geometric medial frieze, signed "Degué," in fine condition.

$600–$700

Vase, 7⅞" high. In pale green glass, ovoid body, etched with a repeating triangular motif, signed "Degué."

$750 (Auction)

Vase, 9½" high. In lime-green glass, the ovoid form with wide mouth, acid-etched with swallows flying under stylized flora, signed "Degué" in relief.

$900–$1,000

Vase, 13½" high. In yellow mottled glass overlaid in orange and black, waisted oval body, etched in stylized floral repeating design, incised "Degué."

$800–$900

Vase, 16" high. In plum-colored glass, large pear form, acid-etched with stylized deer and foliage, signed "Degué" in relief. A very good example of an acid-etched Degué design. **$2,500–$3,000**

Vase, 16¼" high. In clear glass overlaid in green, etched with stylized large palm fronds and fruit, signed "Degué" in cameo. A very good example of a Degué Art Deco cameo vase. **$3,000–$4,000**

Vase, c. 1930, 17½" high. In red glass overlaid with black, the large, two-handled baluster form cut with abstract carved decoration. Signed "Degué" in cameo. **$2,500–$3,000**

ETLING (French, 1920s–1930s)

Car mascot, 8¾" high. Molded fiery opalescent nude figure with arm outstretched, holding drape and standing on raised platform, permanently mounted to chrome-plated radiator cap, glass marked "Etling France 50." **$1,500 (Auction)**

Bowl, c. 1930, 5¼" diameter. In opalescent frosted glass, the deep bowl formed as three intersecting flowers, the centers of which form three rounded feet. Molded "Etling France 23." **$400–$450**

Vase, c. 1935, 8" high. In frosted glass, spherical shape, molded with nasturtium blossoms, molded "Etling France." **$600–$650**

Vase, 11" high. In green glass, the tapered cylindrical form molded in relief with thistles, molded "Etling France 13." **$700–$900**

Vase, figural, 10⅛" high. In frosted glass, diamond-shaped on a circular foot, each side of the panel molded with a draped nude in relief, molded "Etling France 38." **$800–$1,000**

HUNNEBELLE (French, 1920s–1930s)

Vase, 8" high. In clear and frosted glass, ovoid form, molded with diamond shapes, molded "A. Hunnebelle & R. Cogneville France." **$800–$1,000**

Vase, 9¼" high. In opalescent glass, conical shape, with five opalescent vertical ribs, etched with a stylized snowflake design, molded "Hunnebelle." A very good example of a Hunnebelle vase, in fine condition. **$2,000–$2,500**

Vase, c. 1930, 13" high. Spherical, molded with stylized garlands cascading down the sides, heightened in brown patina, with faint molded marks. Good condition. **$900 (Auction)**

LEGRAS (French, founded 1864)

Vase, 9" high. In pale green glass, the ovoid form with waisted neck, etched with a ground of stylized flora, enameled with blue and gray garlands, enamel signature "Legras." **$600–$800**

Vase, 11" high. In mottled red and orange glass, cylindrical in form, tapering to a triangular rim, enameled and gilt with blue, yellow, and green floral garlands, gilt signature "Legras." In very good condition, with small flake at base. **$750–$900**

Pair of Legras acid-etched vases.
Courtesy of Butterfield & Butterfield,
California.

Vase, c. 1930, 12½" high. In clear glass, the extended ovoid form etched with leafy blossoms, and enameled with a design of stylized flowers and vines in orange and black, enameled signature "Legras."   **$1,000–$1,500**

Vases, c. 1930, 25¼" high. Ovoid, with waisted necks and slightly flaring mouths in olive green. Acid-etched with stylized roseheads in frosted glass, leaf tips and shell forms on a clear ground, signed in cameo "Legras." A very good example of Legras's acid-etched design. Pair. (*See photo, above.*)   **$2,500 (Auction)**

LIBBEY GLASS COMPANY (American, founded 1878)

Stemware, "Embassy," 1939. Designed by Walter Dorwin Teague and Edwin W. Fuerst for 1939 New York World's Fair (without World's Fair crest). Thirty pieces, each piece marked "Libbey," ten each: goblets, champagnes, and wines. In excellent condition with only one minor chip to one piece.   **$3,250 (Auction)**

Libbey stemware by
Walter Dorwin Teague and
Edwin W. Fuerst. *Courtesy of*
Skinner, Inc., Massachusetts.

MULLER FRÈRES (French, 1910–1939)

(See also listings for Muller Frères under "Lighting and Lamps Price Listings.")

Vase, 8¼" high. In mottled burgundy and blue glass, ovoid form with everted rim, with silver and gold foil inclusions descending in "drips" from the rim, engraved "Muller Fres., Luneville." **$400 (Auction)**

Vase, 9" high. In clear glass, decorated internally with silver speckled inclusions, orange, green, and blue swirls and striations, signed "Muller Frères Luneville." **$700–$900**

Vase, 9¾" high. In frosted glass, gourd form, molded with a design of stylized leaves and blossoms, molded "Muller Frères Luneville." A very good example of a Muller Frères vase. **$1,200–$1,500**

Vase, 10¾" high. In light blue glass with silver foil inclusions, pear form, overlaid in deeper blue and etched all over with a confetti-like pattern of dots, with scalloped borders, cameo signature "Muller Frères Luneville." A fine example of Muller Frères' style. **$2,200 (Auction)**

ORREFORS (Swedish, founded in 1726, began producing glass 1898)

> **¢** Orrefors employed several designers for their glass who individually signed or initialed pieces.

Simon Gate (1883–1945)

Bowl and stand, c. 1925, 4¾" high, 15¼" long. In clear glass, elongated form, engraved all around with stylized figures holding drapery among foliage, the stand with similar foliate motif engraved "Orrefors Gate 147–25W.E." **$2,500 (Auction)**

Bowl and underdish, 11½" diameter. In clear glass, engraved glass, the flaring conical bowl seated upon a circular liner profusely engraved with bands of geometric designs and bacchantes, inscribed "Orrefors" and "G. 122–19." An outstanding example of Gate's early work for Orrefors. **$10,000 (Auction)**

Edward Hald (1883–1980)

Vase, c. 1935, 5" high. In clear glass, globular form internally decorated with green fish swimming amid marine plants trailing from the circular base, clear glass infused with green, engraved "Orrefors, Graal, Nr. 228, Edward Hald." **$850 (Auction)**

Vase, 5" high. In colorless glass with green fish and seaweed decoration, the bulbous form inscribed "Orrefors Sweden Edward Hald, Graal n. 474B." **$1,200–$1,300**

Vase, c. 1936, 6¼" high. Oviform, internally decorated with fish among seaweed, engraved "Orrefors Sweden Graal No. 332H Edward Hald." In fine condition. (*See photo, opposite.*) **$1,300–$1,550**

Orrefors "Graal" vase,
designed by Edward Hald.
*Courtesy of William Doyle
Galleries, New York.*

Vase, 6½" high. In clear glass, internally decorated with fish and marine plants, swollen teardrop form, engraved "Orrefors, Graal, Nr. 249–G. Edward Hald."

$1,100 (Auction)

Vicke Lindstrand (1904–1983)

 Lindstrand came to Orrefors in 1928 and left to join Kosta in 1950, where he became senior designer.

Vase, c. 1939, 11" high. In clear glass, flared cylindrical form, on black base, engraved internally with a male figure swimming toward bottom, trailing bubbles, engraved "Orrefors Lindstrand 1343 AB" and with monogram. $1,300 (Auction)

Vase, c. 1955, 7¼" high. Designed for Kosta Glassbruk, Sweden. Ovoid with orange spot on one side, engraved with a leaping deer, signed "Kosta 46683 Lindstrand."

$600 (Auction)

Nils Landberg (b. 1907)

Landberg's early glass was engraved; later, and into the 1950s, he created free-blown glass for Orrefors.

Vase, c. 1940, 12" high. In clear engraved glass, the flattened cylinder depicting Poseidon and a mermaid in turbulent waters supporting a massive sailboat, inscribed "Orrefors Landberg Expo 3541 L2Ei." An excellent example of an Orrefors engraved vase. $6,500 (Auction)

PHOENIX GLASS COMPANY
(American, founded 1880s, acquired by Anchor Hocking 1970)

> The "Sculptured Line" was produced from 1933 to about 1957. Color variations help determine dates. This line was designed by Kenneth Haley (1905–1987), son of Consolidated Lamp and Glass Company designer Reuben Haley. (See "Glass" chapter for additional information on the relationship between Phoenix and Consolidated.)

Bowl, *"Diving Girl,"* 14" long. Molded in frosted glass against a blue patina ground, on either side a lithe nude swimming underwater, bubbles trailing, wave forms, and a fish swimming beside her, oblong shaped bowl, with self-handles. A very good example of a Phoenix design, in fine condition.   **$450–$500**

Vase, *"Daisy,"* 9¼" high. Molded with daisy blossoms and leaves in milk glass against a sky-blue patina ground, ovoid shape with waisted neck. In good condition, with some loss to patina.   **$225–$275**

Vase, *"Ferns,"* 7" high. Molded with repeating ferns in frosted glass against a green patina ground, ovoid shape with wide mouth. In excellent condition, with paper label.   **$125–$175**

Vase, *"Star Flower,"* 7" high. Blue patina, with molded flowers and raised repetitive ridges. Original paper label "Phoenix Glass Co." A good example of Phoenix, in fine condition.   **$175–$200**

Vase, *"Wild Geese,"* 9¼" high. Molded with Canadian geese in flight, in opal-white against a pastel blue patina ground. In very good condition, with paper label remnants.

$150 (Auction)
$300–$350

"Star Flower"
vase by Phoenix.
Photo by
Robert Four.

SABINO (French, 1920s–present)

Bowl, 9½" diameter. In frosted glass, etched with a large band of antique figures, molded "Sabino Paris." In fine condition.   **$800–$1,200**

Figure of a female nude, after 1935, 6¼" high. Opalescent glass figurine of a kneeling female nude, surrounded by three doves, engraved "Sabino Paris," with paper label.
                                        $350–$400

Figure of a maiden, 7¾" high. Opalescent glass figurine, the draped maiden in contraposto with raised right arm, engraved "Sabino Paris."   **$800 (Auction)**

Vase, c. 1935, 7" high. In black glass, spherical form, molded with overlapping artichoke leaves, engraved "Sabino Paris." In fine condition.   **$900–$1,200**

Vase, 7½" high. In blue glass, spherical with six indented panels, molded with stylized sunflower blossoms, engraved "Sabino France."   **$1,200 (Auction)**

Vase, 7⅝" high. In opalescent frosted glass, cylindrical form with wide mouth, molded with overlapping artichoke leaves, molded "Sabino France."   **$400 (Auction)**

Vase, figural, 9⅞" high. In opalescent glass, rounded rectangular form, each side with a female nude, joining around the vessel, etched "Sabino Paris."   **$1,700 (Auction)**

Vase, figural, 14" high. In opalescent glass, ovoid with everted rim, molded in relief with a procession of partially draped women, inscribed "Sabino France." A fine example of a Sabino figural vase.   **$2,800–$3,500**

CRISTALLERIE SCHNEIDER (French, 1913–1982)
Charles Schneider (1881–1962)

> Founded by designer Charles Schneider and his brother, businessman Ernest Schneider (1877–1937). Schneider glass of the period generally falls into two categories: those signed "Schneider," and their cameo-cut line, "Le Verre Français," which is also sometimes signed "Charder," an abbreviation of "CHAR-les Schnei-DER." Those listed below are all "Le Verre Français." Those marked "Ovington" were special commissions for the New York department store. (See "Glass" chapter for further information.)

Bowl, 5⅞" high. In pale pink glass overlaid with deeper pink, on a purple cushion foot, carved with stylized blossoms, signed "Le Verre Français."   **$1,500–$1,800**

Bowl, 10" high. In burgundy to orange glass, footed conical form on circular foot, orange overlaid carved with long stems and stylized blossoms, signed "Le Verre Français" and "France."   **$2,400–$2,800**

Lamp, 14¼" high. Bright pink mottled glass overlaid in amethyst and burgundy red, cameo-cut stylized sunflower motif, mounted to wrought-metal fittings illuminating both base and shade, signed "Le Verre Français."   **$4,500–$5,000**

Vase, 7⅝" high. Pale orange glass overlaid in brown, spherical, carved with stylized mimosa branches, signed "Le Verre Français."   **$1,400 (Auction)**

Vase, 8¾" high. Mottled pale orange and white glass overlaid in lavender, cylindrical form with everted rim and two applied handles, carved with stylized blossoms, signed "Charder" and engraved "Le Verre Français."   **$1,800–$2,200**

Vase, 9¹/₁₆" high. In yellow overlaid in orange descending into a deep blue, compressed spherical form on cushion foot, carved with square-shaped blossoms, signed "Le Verre Français."   **$1,500–$1,800**

Vase, 9½" high. In mottled white overlaid in lavender with blue, flared cylindrical form with flared rim on cushion foot, carved with blossoms with trailing vines, signed "Le Verre Français."   **$1,400 (Auction)**

Vase, 10¼" high. In mottled white overlaid in red and green, flared cylindrical form on circular foot, carved with stylized palmettes, engraved "Le Verre Français," signed in cameo "Charder" and etched "France." A good example of the style.   **$2,000–$2,500**

Vase, 10¼" high. Yellow glass layered in mottled orange-brown, pedestaled oval, carved with two salamanders and groups of dragonflies above a stylized rocky ground; signed "Le Verre Français/France/Ovington New York." A very good example of the style.   **$3,500–$4,000**

Vase, 10½" high. Bright yellow overlaid in brown to orange, spherical with everted rim, carved with stylized curling leaves and blossoms, signed "Le Verre Français, France."   **$1,800–$2,300**

Rare geometric pattern "Le Verre Français." *Courtesy of Butterfield & Butterfield, California.*

Vase, 11" high. In white glass overlaid in orange, ovoid with two applied looped handles in purple glass, carved with stylized fern fronds, signed "Le Verre Français."

$3,500–$4,000

Vase, 11⅜" high. In mottled yellow and blue glass, overlaid in dark blue to red, baluster-form, carved with stylized orchids, signed "Le Verre Français."   **$2,100 (Auction)**

Vase, 11½" high. In mottled shades of pink layered in orange and maroon, footed flared oval body, carved with four repeating elements of foxglove blossoming stalks, inscribed "Le Verre Français." (*See photo, below.*) $1,500–$2,000

Vase, c. 1925, 11¾" high. Vivid mottled yellow ovoid body, overlaid in tortoise-shell brown spotted with royal blue, boldly acid-cut with abstract straight and curved bands and base and rim borders. Engraved "Charder" and "Le Verre Français." A fine example of a rare geometricized design, in fine condition. (*See photo, opposite.*)   **$6,000–$8,000**

As above, but in a rare, monumental size of 21½" high.   **$12,000–$15,000**

Vase, 12¼" high. In mottled yellow glass shaded to red orange and overlaid in green speckled brown, elongated goblet form with pedestal foot, carved with repeating blossom clusters, pedestal foot signed "Le Verre Français France" and "Ovington New York" on base. (*See photo, below.*) $1,500–$2,000

Vase, 12½" high. In mottled turquoise-blue glass overlaid in bright royal-blue, oval cylindrical body pedestal foot, carved with floral repeating designs, signed "Le Verre Français France." (*See photo, below.*) $2,000–$2,200

Vases by Schneider *(left to right)*:
Five examples of "Le Verre Français" and two examples of "Schneider."
Courtesy of Skinner, Inc., Massachusetts.

Vase, 14½" high. In pale pink glass overlaid in purple, carved with stylized garlands, ovoid with everted rim on cushion foot, signed "Charder" and "Le Verre Français."
$1,300 (Auction)

Vase, 15" high. In mottled white glass, overlaid with orange, bulbous cylindrical form, carved with floral garlands, signed "Charder," etched "France."   **$1,500 (Auction)**

Vase, 15¾" high. In mottled pale yellow and blue overlaid in purple and orange, flared trumpet form on circular base, carved with design of stylized thistles, engraved "Le Verre Français."   **$2,500 (Auction)**

Vase, 16" high. Swelled oval body of mottled red, orange, and yellow overlaid in maroon, cameo etched with stylized grape clusters and trailing vines, inscribed "Le Verre Français" on foot. (*See photo, page 193.*)   **$2,300–$2,500**

Vase, 16" high. In blue glass with black overlay, elongated ovoid body with wide mouth, carved in a geometricized pattern on sharp arches and half-circles, signed "Le Verre Français." An outstanding example of a rare geometricized design in a stunning color combination. (*See color section.*)   **$9,000–$10,000**

Vase, 16⅛" high. In milky-white glass overlaid in bright blue, baluster form on cushioned circular foot, carved with stylized palms, signed "Charder," engraved "Le Verre Français."   **$2,700 (Auction)**

Vase, 16¾" high. In mottled off-white glass overlaid in red, orange, and blue, elongated form, carved with repeating stylized poppy elements, signed "Le Verre Français." A very good example of the style.   **$3,500–$4,000**

Vase, 18" high. In mottled white glass overlaid in orange to burgundy red, long-stemmed goblet form with black foot, carved with design of stylized blossoms, tendriled vines and dots, signed "Le Verre Français, France."   **$2,000 (Auction)**

Vase, 18½" high. In mottled yellow and pink glass overlaid in orange to blue, ovoid on cushion foot, carved with hanging morning glories, signed "Le Verre Français."
$2,700 (Auction)

Vase, 20¾" high. In melon-red at the base shading to mottled red and gray, elongated ovoid body, carved with four stylized flowerheads and foliage. Signed "Charder," incised "Le Verre Français." A very good example in fine condition.   **$3,500–$4,000**

Vase, 21½" high. In mottled pink and white overlaid in shades of amethyst with occasional orange highlights, oversized baluster form carved with repeating blossoms, signed "Charder" and engraved "Le Verre Français" and "Charder." A large, very good example of "Le Verre Français."   **$5,000–$5,500**

Veilleuse, 7" high. In peaked form on a wrought-iron base, pale blue glass overlaid in darker blue, etched with balloonlike blossoms, engraved "Le Verre Français, France."
$1,800–$2,000

STEUBEN (American, founded 1903)
Walter Dorwin Teague (American, 1882–1960)

> **Œ** Teague was appointed as a design consultant at Steuben in 1931, but only remained with the firm for about two years.

Smoking set, 1932, box: 1¾" high, 4½" wide. Designed for Steuben; rectangular covered box fitted with ashtrays; box lid engraved with vertical and horizontal repetitive lines at right angles. Very good quality and condition.   **$375 (Auction)**

Vase, 1932, 10" high. Designed for Steuben, model #7494; a 4½"-diameter base supporting the vessel on a short column; engraved with vertical and horizontal repetitive lines at right angles. Superior quality and fine condition.   **$1,200 (Auction)**

VERLYS (French, then American until 1951)
Bowl, after 1935, 20" long. In opalescent glass, oval shape, molded with fantailed fish, engraved "Verlys." In fine condition.   **$600–$800**

Bowl, after 1935, 19¼" long. In opalescent glass, the oval bowl molded on the exterior in relief with a continuous frosted and clear underwater scene of large goldfish with fantails, with feathered end handles, molded "Verlys" in relief, pseudo Lalique signature incised on the base.   **$700 (Auction)**

Dish, after 1935, 13⅝" diameter. In clear and frosted glass, molded in relief with butterflies and blossoms, engraved "Verlys."   **$300–$500**

Vase, c. 1935, 9" high. In topaz glass, ovoid in shape with flattened rim, molded with selectively frosted repeats of large sunflower blossoms amid broad leaves; inscribed "Verlys" in script on base. A very good example of Verlys, in fine condition.   **$600 (Auction)**

Steuben vase by Walter Dorwin Teague. *Courtesy of Savoia's Auction, Inc., New York.*

Verlys vase in topaz glass, c. 1935. *Courtesy of Skinner, Inc., Massachusetts.*

Vase, figural, after 1935, 10¾" high. In electric-blue glass, baluster form, molded in relief with mermaids and dolphins amid seaweed, inscribed "Verlys." In good condition, but with minor chips.   **$900–$1,200**

ALMÉRIC WALTER (French, 1859–1942)

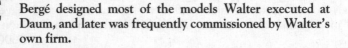

Walter headed the *pâte-de-verre* workshop at Daum Nancy and opened his own firm after World War I, retaining the copyright to his Daum models and also employing numerous Daum and other designers to create new models.

Covered box, 6¼" high. A mottled green and blue ground, flaring cylindrical shape, slightly ribbed, with a stepped circular pyramid with geometric pattern on the top, signed in the mold "A. Walter Nancy."   **$3,500–$4,500**

Pendant, 2½" long. Triangular, molded with a plum and green scarab on a mottled rust and pale yellow ground, signed in the mold "AWN."   **$400 (Auction)**

Tray, 9¼" long, 5½" wide. Molded oval green dish centering darker green figural fish with fanned gill fins in naturalistic detail, signed "A. Walter Nancy." In good condition, with small rim hairline crack.   **$2,000 (Auction)**

Vide poche, 7½" long. In lime-green, triangular shape, with a mallard duck in mottled shades of green and white, signed in the mold "A. Walter Nancy."   **$3,000 (Auction)**

HENRI BERGÉ

Bergé designed most of the models Walter executed at Daum, and later was frequently commissioned by Walter's own firm.

Box, 3½" high. Square, blue with green leaves, red berries and beetles at each corner, the final signed "A. Walter Nancy" and "Bergé, SC." In good condition, with chips to finial.   **$1,000 (Auction)**

Inkwell and cover, 4" high. The bulbous base with slender neck molded with a slithering lizard in sea-green and a bee amid moss-green foliage and deep violet berries, the circular cover molded with foliage and berries, molded "A. Walter" and "Bergé SC." A fine example of a Bergé-Walter collaboration.   **$5,500 (Auction)**

Paperweight, 3¾" high. Molded as a gray mouse nibbling on a nut atop a naturalistically shaped grassy mound, molded "A. Walter Nancy" and "Bergé."   **$2,200–$2,400**

Pendant, 2" long. Oviform, molded with a scarab in shades of brown and green on a mottled yellow ground, on silk cord, signed in the mold "AWN HB."   **$800–$850**

Vide poche, 4⅜" diameter. Low triangular dish in mottled mauve, the apex with a realistically molded bumble bee in green, yellow, and black, molded "A. Walter Nancy" and "h Bergé Sc."   **$1,500 (Auction)**

Vide poche, 7" long. Oviform mottled in shades of buff, orange, and umber, molded with a dark blue and green salamander among ivy leaves with small blossoms, molded "A. Walter Nancy" and "Bergé SC." A fine example in excellent condition.
                                                                                       $5,000 (Auction)

Jules Chéret (1836–1932)

Paperweight, 10" long. Modeled as a sea nymph rising amid the pale green and peach surf, molded "A Walter Nancy" and "Jules Chéret." A rare example of a work designed for Walter by the famous French poster artist.   **$5,500 (Auction)**

Henri Mercier

Sculpture, 6½" high. In the form of a sea lion, in olive-green, signed "A. Walter Nancy" and "H. Mercier."   **$1,400–$1,600**

AMERICAN MASS-PRODUCED DEPRESSION GLASS
(Alphabetically by pattern)

Depression glass is the name given to a whole range of glass tableware produced to sell inexpensively during the Depression. Usually in transparent clear, green, pink, amber, and other colors, it was produced by numerous companies including the ones listed below. Other Depression glass patterns not listed below may also reflect the impact of Art Deco design.

"Cubist" Depression glass bowls.
Author's collection. Photo by Robert Four.

"Cubist" Pattern—Maker Unknown

(Also called "Cube," possibly more than one maker, in pink, clear, or green)

Bowl, 4½" deep, pink.	$10–$15
Butter dish, covered, pink.	$45–$50
Creamer, 2" high, green.	$8–$10
Pitcher, 10" high, pink.	$40–$50
Salad bowl, 8" diameter, pink.	$40–$50
Salt and pepper shakers, pink.	$25–$30

"Manhattan" Pattern, c. 1930—Anchor Hocking

(Horizontal ribbing in clear, pink, or green)

Candy dish, 6" diameter, ball feet, clear.	$10–$15
Cup and saucer, pink.	$20–$25
Cookie jar, 9" high, with cover.	$75–$85
Fruit bowl, 10" diameter, pink.	$50–$60
Relish tray, 12" diameter, clear.	$30–$40
Relish tray, 14" diameter, five-part, clear with ruby red inserts.	$60–$75
Sherbet glass, on a thin ribbed stem, clear.	$10–$12
Tumbler, 10 oz., footed, pink.	$20–$25
Vase, 8" high, clear, the base encircled with clear glass balls.	$25–$30

**"Pyramid" bowl by
Indiana Glass Company.**
Author's collection.
Photo by Robert Four.

"Pyramid" Pattern, c. 1933—Indiana Glass Company
(Stepped-back inverted triangular pattern in pink, clear, green, and more rarely, an icy yellow)

Bowl, 3" high, 9½" diameter, pink.	**$60–$80**
Bowl, 6" diameter, pink.	**$40–$50**
Candy dish, covered, 6" diameter, pink.	**$60–$70**
Ice bucket, 8" high, in yellow, rare.	**$200–$250**
Salad or berry bowl set, in pink, including large bowl: 8½" diameter; 6 small bowls: 4½" diameter.	**$350–$450**
Tumbler, 7" high, pink.	**$50–$65**

"Tearoom" Pattern, c. 1930—Indiana Glass Company
(Inverted stepped design, in pink, green, or clear)

Banana split dish, 7½" long, clear.	**$40–$50**
As above, but in pink.	**$100–$125**
Bowl, 8" diameter, pink.	**$40–$50**
Candlesticks, pair, clear.	**$30–$40**
Creamer, green.	**$20–$25**
Cup and saucer, pink.	**$40–$45**
Pitcher, 64 oz., green.	**$125–$150**
Salt and pepper shakers, pink.	**$45–$55**
Sugar bowl, covered, green.	**$25–$30**
Tumbler, 8 oz., footed, pink.	**$30–$35**

CERAMICS

The Art Deco style in ceramics underwent the same transition as the other decorative arts, from artists creating new forms and decorations in the studio, to small-scale commercial production for the department store trade, and finally to mass-produced and mass-distributed inexpensive kitchenware.

The diversity of the ceramics field in Art Deco makes it one of the most popular areas for collecting: from high-quality china and porcelain to earthenware pottery, from cloisonné enameled vases to industrially produced refrigerator water jugs, fired and glazed in one step. And, while prices on some ceramics can be very high, it remains an area that is still accessible to beginning collectors looking for good examples of the Art Deco style.

Art Deco brought a breakthrough in form, color, and subject. Not only were potters no longer limited to traditional vessels, jugs, bowls, tea sets, and the like, they could experiment with incised or painted decoration, angularity, and subject matter, just as sculptors of the time.

As painters had found inspiration in African art, potters found inspiration in exotic Japanese and Chinese cultures, both for simplified design and for glazing techniques. In addition, the influence of Vienna and the Wiener Werkstätte was also felt on vessels, figural ceramics, and tablewares, but perhaps even more in America than in Europe.

FRENCH AND BELGIAN

Early Art Deco ceramic artists and studio potters in France included Emile Decoeur (1876–1953), Emile Lenoble (1876–1940), Henri Simmen (1880–1963), and René Buthaud, whose painted figures of women were reminiscent of Jean Dupas. These artists are rare on the open market today, and can command very high prices.

Both Theodore Haviland's company and the French national manufacture, Sèvres, commissioned leading artists to decorate tablewares, usually of porcelain. Among the more famous are Jean Dupas, Jean Dufy, Robert Bonfils, Emile-Jacques Ruhlmann, and Suzanne Lalique, daughter of René Lalique. Jean Luce, who ran a shop where he sold his own designs, is also noted for his porcelain tablewares.

Other fine studio artists whose work is sought-after by collectors today include Robert Lallemant, Jean Mayodon, Raoul Lachenal, and André Méthey. Lallemant created innovative angular pottery, often with sporting motifs. Studio pottery by these artists can be acquired at reasonable costs even today, especially when compared to prices for more commercially produced pieces whose large base of collectors keeps prices high.

French department stores played an important role in popularizing ceramic production, as they had with other decorative arts. Maurice Dufrène, of La Maîtrise at the Galeries Lafayette, and Claude Levy, at the Primavera workshop of Printemps, both created and commissioned designs. Dufrène favored the ceramics of the Belgian company Boch Frères. Primavera carried so much Longwy that still many pieces on the market today are marked "Primavera Longwy." Other leading designers such as Jacques Adnet, known also for his furniture designs, also created ceramics for the department stores.

Figural ceramic sculptures distributed by the Parisian firm of Goldscheider and Fau & Guillard include Edouard Cazaux, André Fau, Lemanceau, and others. Some of these works are very good examples of the Art Deco style and can still be found at affordable prices today.

Etling, too, seized upon the popularity of ceramics to produce figural ceramics by artists such as Joseph Descomps, and some work in the style of Longwy. Etling was a prolific company which produced a great volume of decorative and functional glass, bronzes, and statues for the department stores.

Both Boch Frères and Longwy produced decorative ceramics using the cloisonné enamel technique, which had come into commercial production as early as 1870. Their highly stylized natural and geometric designs in striking colors, usually on a crackled white or ivory ground, were achieved by using enamel glazes. These glazes were separated from one another by a material that resists their running together when fired.

Until the Art Deco period, Longwy's work was largely influenced by Far and Near East patterns. Longwy is the only firm in France still producing ceramics in cloisonné enamel. Richard Fishman, owner of the shop As Time Goes By in San Francisco, has made a specialization in Longwy, and even commissioned the company to create ceramic tiles for his storefront, and special edition pieces in cloisonné enamel.

Charles Catteau was the chief designer for the Belgian firm Boch Frères during the Art Deco era. Unfortunately, few details are known about the firm's production, as the factory was severely damaged during World War II and most records were destroyed. Those works signed or stamped with Charles Catteau's signature, especially when decorated with sleek deer and other animals, are the most sought-after in today's market.

Dealers such as Morton Abromson in Brookline, Massachusetts, have specialized in Boch Frères for a number of years. However, the collecting base is still relatively small, and good and very good examples are still affordable, although the best pieces have started to climb quite high.

In Paris, another retailer, Robj, is best known on the market for its humorous decanters representing people from all walks of life. Robj also produced bibelots, or "knickknacks": statuettes, lamps, bookends, ashtrays, and candy dishes. Even the tradition-loving Quimper pottery produced a line called "Odetta" in an Art Deco style to compete with the times.

GERMAN AND AUSTRIAN

The German company Rosenthal produced porcelain figures, vases, covered boxes, and other decorative items for the department store trade, often painted with stylized natural and geometric patterns. Their figures are often modeled as Pierrots, women in modern dress, and animals. Rosenthal pieces were often designed by Ferdinand Lieberman, and are almost always identified by the factory stamp.

German tablewares in the late 1920s and early 1930s were inspired by the functional aesthetic of the Bauhaus, sometimes with abstract geometric decorations. One of the major manufacturers of tablewares in this style was Villeroy & Boch.

In Austria, the firm of Goldscheider, which was well-known for bronze and bronze and ivory statues, also created porcelain and ceramic decorative figures. Often the same artists, such as Lorenzl, were commissioned to create models for both bronze and ceramic production. Figures include dancers, nude maidens, sleek animals, and women in modern dress. These figures today can command high prices.

Another firm, Augarten, also produced figural porcelains in the Art Deco style starting in about 1922, and commissioned artists such as Wiener Werkstätte ceramist Valerie (Vally) Wieselthier to produce models.

SWEDISH

Gustavsberg pottery began producing Modernist ceramics in 1917, under the artistic direction of Wilhelm Kåge. In tablewares, Kåge introduced his decorative "Worker's Service" in 1917, and his functional "Praktika Service" in 1933.

Best known on the Art Deco market is his "Argenta" stoneware, introduced in the late 1920s, usually of a green mottled glaze with designs in overlaid silver of fish, mermaids, and other motifs. In just the past few years, "Argenta" has appeared more and more frequently on the Art Deco market, but its collecting base is not yet firmly established. (See "Today's Market" for more information.)

After World War II, Kåge and his successor Stig Linberg experimented with biomorphic shapes. Kåge created his "Soft Forms" dinnerware in 1940, and the same year introduced "Surrea," which is more Cubist than Surreal in inspiration.

ENGLISH

Bernard Leach (1887–1979) is perhaps the best-known potter from England of the period. Other collected English studio ceramists include Michael Cardew and William Staite Murray (1881–1961). Their work is becoming better known to Art Deco collectors.

However, in the world of Art Deco English ceramics, Clarice Cliff leads the market, along with a more recent but tremendous upsurge in interest in the ceramics of Susie Cooper. (See "Special Focus: Susie Cooper.")

Cliff attended Burslem School of Art, as did several of the best-known ceramists. She signed on with A. J. Wilkinson, and from 1916 to 1920 began experimenting in decorating old stock at the nearby Newport Pottery Company, which was later bought by Wilkinson.

In all, she directed the creation of about 250 shapes and over 200 different paint designs for vases, jugs, tableware, coffee sets, and more. She commissioned other artists such as Laura Knight, Vanessa Bell, Graham Sutherland, Milner Grey, and Eva Crofts.

Her pottery was first exhibited in this country at the Minneapolis Institute of the Arts groundbreaking revival exhibition in 1971. It occupied a good portion of the ceramics section, awakening new interest in her. It has bold designs, with brilliant color in motifs often borrowed from Cubism, and brightly painted fantastic scenes with blobby trees perhaps inspired by Matisse and the Fauves.

The market for Clarice Cliff in the United States was initially driven by dealers Susan and Louis Meisel. Their book on Cliff, co-authored with Leonard Griffin and entitled *A Bizarre Affair: The Life and Work of Clarice Cliff*, published in 1988, caused a surge of interest, and the collecting field has been expanding ever since.

Today, individual pieces of Cliff's pottery can bring very high prices, and dealers such as Carole Berk in Maryland have strong specialties in her work. The market here is firmly established, although most auctions of her work still take place in England.

In 1929, her "Bizarre" ware, designed for Wilkinson, was growing in popularity, and the company devoted the entire production of Newport Pottery Company to its manufacture. "Bizarre" has several painted patterns, such as "Tennis," "Delicia Citrus," "Lugano," "Autumn," and many others. Although collectors of Cliff today ask for it by pattern name and even model numbers, generally you'll hear the entire line referred to simply as "Bizarre." Another Cliff line which has several pattern names is called "Fantasque."

The vivid colors that were the source of her popularity were also the tragic cause of her death. (Bright red in both ceramics and cameo-glass production is created from uranium oxide, which was largely halted when uranium came under the control of the military in World War II). The bright orange and red colors used in many of her pieces, such as her important Deco pattern "Sunray" with its geometric design, probably helped cause her death by emphysema.

Other English ceramic designers working in modern idioms were Keith Murray and Eric Slater. Keith Murray, an architect who also created glass designs for Stevens & Williams, was hired by Wedgwood in 1932. Wedgwood needed a competitive edge in the 1930s market, and Murray provided it with simple shapes and solid light-colored glazes, often with horizontal banding, as well as designs in deep brown and black basalt.

Eric Slater took over the position of art director at Shelley in 1928, a position once held by his father. He produced some of the best modern designs for that company throughout the 1930s, including porcelain tea sets with geometric decorations and angular handles. In 1937–1938, he was also commissioned to produce tableware for Imperial Airways.

In addition, the Art Deco designs of Charlotte Rhead for Burgess & Leigh, Poole Pottery, and Wiltshaw & Robinson's "Carlton Ware" are gaining a share of the English collecting market, but haven't yet made inroads in the United States. These companies, along with Clarice Cliff and Susie Cooper, are represented frequently in auctions at Christie's South Kensington in England. (*See the chapter "Today's Market" for more information.*)

AMERICAN

Rookwood, Van Briggle, Greuby, and Newcomb were some of the ceramic producers represented at the 1900 Exposition Universelle in Paris, and won many prizes. These makers are highly prized today in the Arts and Crafts market.

Of then, only Rookwood went on to create some Art Deco designs by artists such as William Henschel, Elizabeth Barrett, and Harriet Wilcox. These are difficult to find, but usually cost less than Rookwood's Arts and Crafts production.

Fulper Pottery also sometimes exhibits the simplified lines of Art Deco, and later, around 1930, did produce some striking modern pieces. Overbeck Pottery was founded in Cambridge City, Indiana, in 1911 by four sisters, and created some outstanding Art Deco designs. However, production was small, and for the most part these are never seen on the market.

While the academic foundations for a modern ceramics movement were strong in America, the arrival of World War I slowed down ceramic development. Between the two wars, American ceramics underwent dramatic changes, especially in Cleveland.

Students at the Cleveland Institute of Arts came under the influence of a Viennese teacher, Julius Mihalik, who exposed them to the thinking of the Wiener Werkstätte.

Outstanding students from the school included Thelma Frazier Winter (1904–1977), Paul Bogatay, and Edris Eckhardt, all of whom would later design for Cowan Pottery Company, located in a suburb of Cleveland. Many other young ceramists from the Midwest, including Russell Aitken and Viktor Schreckengost, traveled to study in Vienna.

These Cleveland artists started a renaissance in American ceramics. Even though many won prizes, and annual exhibitions were held starting in 1919, their work was largely ignored. In 1926, the Metropolitan's show largely consisted of French ceramics. In 1928, when the Metropolitan hosted the International Exhibition of Ceramic Art, the work of the Wiener Werkstätte and many Americans finally came to the fore.

The artists recognized in this exhibit are also those most popular on today's market: Henry Varnum Poor, William Zorach, Carl Walters, William Hunt Diederich (1884–1953), and Viktor Schreckengost. Another important ceramist was Maija Grotell, who was associated with the Cranbrook Academy of Art.

Susi Singer and Vally Wieselthier, notable Austrian Wiener Werkstätte ceramists, emigrated to this country in 1932. Singer settled on the West Coast, and Wieselthier received commissions from Contempora and General Ceramics in New York and Sebring Pottery in Ohio.

It is interesting to note that neither of the two most important Art Deco revival exhibitions in this country, "Art Deco," at the Finch College Museum of Art, and "The World of Art Deco," at the Minneapolis Institute of Arts in 1971, included American potters and ceramists. At Minneapolis, German, English, and even Japanese stood side by side with the French, but the only identifiably American company represented, and only by a single piece, was the American Art Clay Company.

Many of the American artists mentioned eventually became part of what would be America's most successful Art Deco ceramic enterprise: Cowan Pottery Studios in Ohio. Founded in 1921 by Reginald Guy Cowan, a successful studio ceramist whose work had won awards as early as 1917, it drew together talented young artists such as Russel B. Aitken, Arthur E. Baggs, Alexander Blazys (1894–1963), Waylande DeSantis Gregory, Paul Manship, A. Drexel Jacobson, Margaret Postgate, and Viktor Schreckengost.

Cowan produced both limited editions and larger series of decorative and functional ceramics that have become prized in the Art Deco collecting world. The firm lasted about twelve years. At its largest, it had about fourteen hundred dealer outlets nationally, including Marshall Field of Chicago, Wanamaker's of Philadelphia, and Halle's of Cleveland. Commercial production increased, but smaller editions of ceramic sculptures continued to be made. Then financial difficulties caused the company's failure during the Depression. Interestingly, many stylish pieces were created in 1930 and 1931, when the company was in receivership and the artists were finally free from the pressures of commercial production.

R. Guy Cowan's most popular creation was the figural "flower frog." These are ceramic stylized women and animals rising from lily pads and grasses, set in a shallow bowl of water. Loops in the drapery or holes in the base make it possible to arrange flowers in the piece. He designed numerous other pieces for Cowan Pottery Studio, but most are not signed as his designs.

Almost as prolific as Cowan himself was Waylande Gregory, who joined the firm in 1928. When it closed, Gregory continued producing ceramics under his own name from his studio at the Cranbrook Academy of Art. Gregory often took subjects from mythology and history, such as "Persephone" and "Salome." He even depicted "Radio" as a woman in white ceramic, hair blowing at right angles in the wind, and the famous Deco zigzag bolt emanating from her fingertips. During Prohibition, the favorite Gregory designs were "King and Queen" decanters, inspired by *Alice Through the Looking-Glass*, and disguised as bookends. (*See description and photo in the "Ceramics Price Listings."*)

Gregory also designed the *Fountain of Atoms*, a monumental ceramic sculpture for the New York World's Fair, with twelve figures, each weighing over a ton. The work was commissioned by the WPA under its Welfare Arts Program. The Ceramics Division for this program was set up in Cleveland.

Viktor Schreckengost joined the firm in 1930, and is perhaps best known for his punch bowl called the "Jazz Bowl." The "Jazz Bowl" has black "Jazz Age" designs of New York on New Year's Eve: skyscrapers, neon signs, cocktail glasses, records, and streetlamps. It was created in the "sgraffito" or drypoint technique, which Schreckengost perfected, and glazed in "Egyptian Blue," a glaze developed by Arthur Eugene Baggs, chief chemist for Cowan. Only about fifty of the bowls were made, and several were purchased by Eleanor Roosevelt. (*See color section.*)

Roseville Pottery Company of Ohio annually produced lines of ceramics, often with flowered patterns. While many of its designs show some Art Deco influence, its "Futura" line, introduced in 1928, is the most distinctive and most sought-after on the Art Deco market. The line experimented with form as well as glaze, creating odd-angled and geometric vases with angular handles, stepped-back skyscraper forms on necks and bodies, and glaze combinations such as green and orange, and green and pink.

Other American ceramics firms which produced decorative work in the Art Deco style include American Art Clay Company of Indianapolis, or AMACO, as its pieces are often signed. Not frequently found on the market, its best pieces can command several hundred dollars, and are notable for the quality of their glazes, which are often finely crazed.

Frankoma Pottery, which started in the mid-1930s in Oklahoma and is still in operation today, created some Modernist designs in their single-handled, lidless water pitchers. Decorative glazing techniques included a brushed glaze in green and copper-color sometimes called "Prairie Green," and high-luster black glazes with metallic tones. It is difficult to date Frankoma, as its most popular glazes are still being used today.

In New Jersey, Lenox, which was founded under another name in 1889 in Trenton, produced interesting figural and functional Art Deco ceramics, as did Trenton Art Pottery, which operated in the 1930s and into the 1940s. Generally, Trenton pieces are geometric spheres and circles, unadorned, with pastel glazes in yellows, blues, greens, and pinks. As previously mentioned, General Ceramics of New York also produced decorative wares, notably those designed by Vally Wieselthier.

Mass-produced ceramic tablewares and kitchenwares were the final outcome of the transition from early Art Deco to industrialized production. In 1937, Russel Wright was commissioned by Steubenville Pottery Company to create a line of tableware which he called "American Modern." This style reflects the "Streamline" design of late 1930s.

In 1904, Robert T. Hall became the president of the family company, Hall China in East Liverpool, Ohio. He developed a single-step glaze which would withstand kiln-firing at high temperatures, and brought the price of functional ceramics down dramatically. Durable and practical, it was first sold to the restaurant and hotel trade, and later retailed in department stores.

Among the most collectible Hall items are the late 1930s "Refrigerator Ware" left-over dishes and water pitchers designed for appliance manufacturers such as Westinghouse and Hotpoint. These were given away as premiums with the purchase of a new refrigerator, and are colorful and stylish. Also popular are streamlined teapots such as "Aladdin," "Surfside," "Airflow," and rare works with novelty forms such as "Automobile," "Basketball," "Doughnut," and "Football."

Hall withdrew from the retail market in the 1950s, due to low sales caused mostly by cheaper Japanese ceramics, and returned to producing for the restaurant trade. However, in 1984, it reintroduced many of its Art Deco styles to the public, and even included a new line of plates and platters for microwave ovens. All of the molds for the eleven-hundred-plus pieces Hall ever made were still in storage, and many are being reissued—in over a hundred colors—so buyer beware.

Homer Laughlin introduced Frederick H. Rhead's "Fiesta" dinnerware in 1936, and their "Harlequin" pattern in 1938. "Fiesta" was produced continuously from 1936 through 1972, and reintroduced again in 1986. Pre–World War II colors were red, blue, yellow, green, and ivory, with turquoise added in 1938. Red was discontinued in 1943 because of the war and the unavailability of uranium oxide used to produce it, but was reintroduced in 1959. New colors are pastel shades of apricot, rose, and sea-mist, plus a cobalt-blue, black, and white. Again, it is up to the collector to know which colors are the original line.

Cheaper and cheaper ceramics with Deco stylings were produced, including the swarms of pink flamingos that flew home from Florida in tourists' baggage. Much of this production can still be found in flea markets and fairs, and some of it is interesting, decorative, and functional. However, the further dissolution of the style in cheap ceramics helped sound the death knell for Art Deco. As a final blow, Russel Wright's "American Modern" tableware was ultimately produced in plastic.

CERAMICS PRICE LISTINGS
(Alphabetically by designer or manufacturer)

JACQUES ADNET (French, 1900–1984)

Figural group, "Jockeys," c. 1930, 18" long. Molded as three streamlined jockeys steeple-chasing, in crazed cream and salmon glaze, signed "Adnet." A fine example of figural Art Deco ceramics, in excellent condition.   **$2,500–$3,000**

"Jockeys" by
Jacques Adnet.
*Courtesy of
Christie's East,
New York.*

GABRIEL BEAUVAIS (French, work: 1910–1930)

Bookends, penguins, c. 1935, 8½" high. Bookends modeled as penguins, each leaning on an L-shaped base, glossy glaze accented in black on a cream ground, marked "Editions Kaza" and signed "G. Beauvais." In good condition, but with minor chips.

$275 (Auction)

BOCH FRÈRES (Belgian)

The factory was severely damaged during World War II, and most production documentation was destroyed. Several marks were used and pieces will be found marked "B.F.K. La Louvrière," "Grès Keramis," "Keramis," "Boch Frères," and "Boch Frères Keramis," often accompanied by a model number beginning with "D" or "WD."

Lamp, 11" high. Elongated hexagonal form on angular base, in crackled ivory glaze, with geometricized flowers and leaves in sapphire blue and deep green on a raised hexagonal plaque. Stamped "Boch Frères La Louvrière" and "D.1249." A good example in fine condition. $750–$800

Lamp, 12" high. Ovoid shape, in a crackled ivory glaze, with stylized fruits and leaves in pale green, orange, and terra cotta, and decorated with pale blue ribbons hanging from a sapphire-blue neck. Stamped "Boch Frères La Louvrière" and "D.745." In fine condition.

$750–$850

Lamp, 12" high, plus stepped wooden base. In a crackled ivory glaze with nine full-length parading penguins in black and pale green. A very good example of a Boch Frères lamp in very good condition. $1,200–$1,500

Vase, c. 1920, 7" high. Ovoid, in matte glazes, with brown and green stylized leaves and flowers in a band against a mottled gray and green ground. Hand painted "Grès Keramis" and "D.669." An early example of Boch Frères. $550–$650

Boch Frères lamp.
Author's collection. Courtesy of
Skinner, Inc., Massachusetts.

Vase, 9" high. Cylindrical with stepped openings, glazed with stepped motif in yellow and black on a cream crazed ground, stamped "D.1283" and "Keramis Made in Belgium."
$600–$750

Vase, c. 1935, 9" high. Ovoid, painted with stylized clouds in ivory, yellow, and aqua against a dark brown ground. Stamped with firm's circular mark, and painted "D.2505."
$800–$850

Vase, c. 1925, 9" high. Ovoid form with everted rim, in crackled ivory glaze, with stylized leaves and spiraling patterns of ferns and flowers in sapphire-blue, green, and yellow contained in triangle forms alternately hanging from the rim or rising from the base. Stamped "Boch Frères La Louvrière" and "D.1101." A good example in fine condition. (*See photo in section "Motifs," page 14.*) $700–$800

Vase, c. 1920, 9¼" high. Ovoid, with six panels, each with a floral medallion in black and white on tan, against a cream crazed ground. Stamped "Grès Keramis" and "D.914."
$600 (Auction)

Vase, 10¼" high. Ovoid with everted rim, glazed in yellow, blue, and turquoise with stylized rosettes, on a crazed cream ground, with firm's mark and "D.1175."
$425 (Auction)

Vase, c. 1930, 10¼" high. Ovoid with everted rim, on a crazed cream ground, with an abstract design of lines, triangles, and circles in orange, yellow, gray and black. Stamped with firm's mark and "D.1210." A very good example of a more geometricized design.
$800–$850

Vase, c. 1925, 11" high. Baluster form, the ivory ground with stylized flowers in the so-called Opera Colors of orange and blue. Stamped "Boch Frères Keramis" and impressed "806." A good example in fine condition. (*See photo in section on "Motifs," page 14.*) $600–$650

Vase, c. 1925, 11" high. Cylindrical shape, tapering to a small mouth, in crackled ivory glaze, with stylized leaves and spiraling patterns of ferns and flowers in sapphire-blue, green, and yellow contained in triangle forms alternately hanging from the rim or rising from the base. Stamped "Boch Frères La Louvrière" and "D.1101." A good example in fine condition. $750–$800

Vase, 12" high. Ovoid, painted with stylized pendant vines in brown and black with yellow blossoms on a gray ground, stamped with firm's circular mark, painted "D.1089 D MB."
$850 (Auction)

Vase, 13½" high. Large ovoid, with a continuous frieze of birds in deep red, gray, black, and yellow, perched on branches with leaves in sapphire and lighter blue. Stamped "Keramis Made in Belgium" and "D.1322." A fine example in excellent condition. (*See color section.*) $1,500–$2,000

Vase, 20" high. Large ovoid, with everted rim, with stylized deer leaping through a forest in black and gold, trees rising from base, their leaves clustered at the neck, against azure and pale blue glazes and flowering branches. With firm's stamp, printed "D.2928" and impressed "961 K." Probably designed by Raymond Chevalier. A fine example.

$3,800 (Auction)

Vase, 20" high. Ovoid, with everted rim, a white ground with large polychrome birds perched on branches amid jungle foliage. Stamped with the firm's circular mark and "WD1130." Probably designed by Jan Windt for Boch Frères. $1,200 (Auction)

Charles Catteau (b. 1880)

€ Charles Catteau was chief designer for Boch Frères from 1907 through the mid-1930s, and many works are stamped with a facsimile signature "Ch. Catteau." However, some designs known to be by him do not carry this mark.

Vase, c. 1925, 19½" high. Ovoid body with short cylindrical neck, a white crackled ground, with a frieze of antelope grazing borders filled with geometric designs in sapphire-blue, turquoise, blue-green, and black. Stamped "Boch Frères," "Ch. Catteau," and "D943." One of the most sought-after designs by Catteau, examples of it were exhibited at the 1925 Paris Exposition. A fine example in excellent condition, and rare in this size. $3,500–$4,000

Jardiniere, 8" high, same design and marks as above, but without geometric borders.
$1,000 (Auction)

Lamp, 11½" high, plus base, same design and marks as above, but without geometric borders. $1,400–$1,600

Vase, 6¾" high. Bulbous form, wax glaze stylized leaf pattern on a pale celadon ground, stamped "Boch Frères" and "Charles Catteau." $550–$650

Vase, 9½" high. Ovoid, painted with stylized clustered blossoms in tan, yellow, and orange against a background of swags on ivory ground, stamped with firm's circular mark and "Ch. Catteau," and painted "WD 963." $900 (Auction)

Vase, 11" high. Pear-shaped, painted with stylized blossoms of orange and yellow scrolling foliage in turquoise and blue on an ivory ground, stamped with firm's mark and "Ch. Catteau," and painted "D1109/L." $750 (Auction)

Vase, 11⅜" high. Ovoid with folded back rim, decorated in five vertical panels enclosing pattern of birds in flight, in dark brown semi-matte glaze over tan body, stamped with firm's mark, incised "Grès Keramis," painted "Ch. Catteau" and "D. 1009."
$1,100 (Auction)

Boch Frères vase by Charles Catteau.
Courtesy of Moderne, Pennsylvania.

Vase, 12¼" high. Baluster form, decorated in chocolate-brown glaze with a central band of stylized birds against an unglazed tan ground, printed with firm's marks, "Ch. Catteau," and "D.1086A."   **$900 (Auction)**

Vase, 13⅜" high. Ovoid shape with everted rim, painted with geometricized clustered blossoms in white, yellow, orange, blue, and red, against a vertical striped background of blue and ochre, stamped with firm's mark and "Ch. Catteau," and painted "WD962." A very good example, in fine condition.   **$1,900 (Auction)**
$2,500–$2,800

Vase, 13½" high, same design and marks as above.   **$1,600–$2,000**

Vase, 9" high, same design and marks as above. (*See color section.*)   **$1,200–$1,500**

RENÉ BUTHAUD (French, 1886–1986)

> ℂ   **Works by René Buthaud are rare on the open market. His hand-painted vases of stylized women can bring $15,000 and more.**

Vase, 9" high. The bulbous vessel painted in sienna, black, and green with a stylized leaf and blossom pattern, painted signature "R. Buthaud."   **$7,000 (Auction)**

Vase, 12½" high. Oviform with everted rim, painted with Islamic-inspired figures in a landscape in bronze, light gray, and beige, painted initials "RB."   **$4,200 (Auction)**

EDOUARD CAZAUX (French, 1889–1974)

> ℂ   **Cazaux also designed Lalique-like decorative glass for the firm of Gueron.**

Vase, c. 1925, 9" high. Moonflask form, on flared foot; glazed in pink and gold and molded on one side with a stylized seated figure; signed "Cazaux." Very good quality and fine condition.   **$1,800–$2,000**

CLARICE CLIFF (English, 1899–1972)

Ashtray, 4½" diameter. A "Bizarre" ashtray in the "Delicia Citrus" pattern, painted with an orange and a lemon in bright colors. Printed factory marks. $150–$175

Breakfast set, c. 1930, pitcher: 6⅛" high. In the "Autumn Crocus" pattern with pitcher, teapot, creamer, sugar bowl, two cups, two saucers, two egg cups, two octagonal bowls, one small and one large plate, all decorated with orange, blue, and purple crocuses. Marked "Clarice Cliff, Wilkinson Ltd." $1,500–$1,800

Candlestick, 3¼" high. A "Fantasque Bizarre" candlestick, modeled as three stepped-back squares, in the "Trees and House" pattern, painted in a scenic design in several colors. A fine example of a Clarice Cliff candlestick. $700–$750

Candlesticks, 2" high. A pair of "Fantasque" candlesticks, in the "Melon" pattern, with orange banding. With rubber stamp marks. Pair. $550–$600

Cigarette box and ashtray, 3¼" high. A "Fantasque" cigarette box and ashtray in the "Melon" pattern, the open cigarette holder and incorporated ashtray painted in blue, orange, and yellow. $400–$450

Cup and saucer. An "Applique Bizarre" coffee cup and saucer in the "Lugano" pattern, painted with a red-roofed house and pine trees, with blue and orange banding. Printed and painted factory marks. $600–$650

Cup and saucer. A "Bizarre" coffee cup and saucer in the "Blue Autumn" pattern, with trees with blue balloonlike leaves, painted in colors with red, green, and yellow banding. With rubber stamp marks. $400–$450

Cup and saucer. A "Bizarre" coffee cup and saucer in the "Orange Chintz" pattern, with a design of bright sliced oranges, painted in colors with orange banding. With printed factory marks. $350–$400

Demitasse set, coffee pot: 8" high. A "Fantasque Bizarre" set in the "Windbells" pattern, comprising coffee pot, six demitasse cups and saucers, creamer and sugar bowl, painted with a stylized tree on one side and stylized hollyhocks on the other. $2,500 (Auction)

"Fantasque Bizarre" demitasse set in the "Windbells" pattern by Clarice Cliff. *Courtesy of Wolf's Fine Arts Auctioneers, Ohio.*

Ceramics by Clarice Cliff, including "Laughing Cat"; double-handled lotus jug in the "Carpet" pattern; single-handled lotus jug and tea set in the "Tennis" pattern; "Blue W" octagonal plate; and "Age of Jazz" figures. *Courtesy of Christie's South Kensington, England.*

Figure, "*Laughing Cat,*" 6" high. A "Bizarre" model of a laughing cat, after a design by Louis Wain, the orange body with black spots, and green bow tie. With rubber stamp mark.
$1,500 (Auction)

Lotus jug, double-handled, 11½" high. A "Bizarre" lotus jug in the "Carpet" pattern, painted in red, gray, and black, between red and gray borders. With rubber stamp mark. In fine condition. (*See photo, above.*)
$5,000 (Auction)

Lotus jug, double-handled, as above, but in the "Inspiration Bizarre" pattern, with a swirling blue pattern.
$2,800 (Auction)

Lotus jug, double-handled, as above, but "Fantasque" in the "Sunray" pattern, with its strong geometric design and stylized sun in red, purple, blue, and yellow, with orange and yellow banding. An outstanding example of a Clarice Cliff pattern.
$7,500–$8,000

Lotus jug, single-handled, 11½" high. A "Bizarre" lotus jug in the "Tennis" pattern, painted in gray, blue, red, yellow, purple, and black. With rubber stamp mark. In fine condition. (*See photo, above.*)
$3,200 (Auction)

Lotus jug, single-handled, as above, but in the "Delicia Citrus" pattern, with bright oranges and wide yellow banding.
$560 (Auction)

Lotus jug, single-handled, as above, but "Fantasque Bizarre" in the "Solitude" pattern, with a scenic landscape design. A fine example of a Clarice Cliff design.
$5,000–$6,000

Plate, 7" diameter. A "Bizarre" plate in the "Farmhouse" pattern, painted in colors with contrasting band.
$500–$550

Plate, 9" diameter. A "Bizarre" octagonal plate in the "Blue W" pattern, painted in red, yellow, purple, and deep blue, with yellow and blue banding. (*See photo, above.*)
$1,100 (Auction)

Plate, 9" diameter. A "Bizarre" plate in the "Orange Roof Cottage" pattern, painted with a scene of the cottage in colors, with orange, yellow, and black banding. Painted factory marks. A very good example, in fine condition.
$800–$1,000

Sardine box and cover, 5" long. A "Bizarre" sardine box and cover in the "Crocus" pattern, painted with crocuses in blue, red, and purple, banded in yellow. $600–$650

Sugar bowl, 3" diameter. A "Bizarre" sugar bowl in the "Sunrise" pattern, shaped as small cauldron with angular handles and three feet, painted in orange and red. With rubber stamp mark. $200–$250

Sugar sifters, 5½" high. Pointed, conical sugar sifters, painted in various "Bizarre" patterns. This clever "dunce cap" form lends itself to a variety of banding, vertical decorations, and scenic designs. Depending on the pattern, each: $300–$600

Table decoration, "Age of Jazz," 6" high. A "Bizarre" table decoration modeled as two musicians in evening dress, one playing the drums and the other a trumpet. In red, yellow, white, and black. With rubber stamp mark. An outstanding example, and very sought-after. (*See photo, opposite.*) $4,400 (Auction)

Tea set, teapot: 4½" high. A "Bizarre" Stamford trio in the "Tennis" pattern, painted in red, blue, orange, green, and black on white, comprising a teapot and cover, milk jug, and sugar bowl. In fine condition with one chip to teapot cover. (*See photo, opposite.*) $4,400 (Auction)

Vase, 5½" high. A "Fantasque Bizarre" mushroom-shaped vase (shape #341), in the "Summerhouse" pattern, painted in colors above red banding. With rubber stamp mark. $700 (Auction)

Vase, 8" high. A "Fantasque Bizarre" vase, with sharply canted sides (shape #365) in the "Orange Roof Cottage" pattern, painted with a scene of the cottage above and below orange banding. A very good example of a smaller vase. $1,500–$2,000

Vase, 7¾" high. A "Fantasque Bizarre" vase, swelling cylindrical form (shape #266), in the "Autumn" pattern, with stylized trees with balloonlike leaves in many colors, above and below blue banding. $1,300–$1,600

Vase, 8" high. In the "Delicia Pansy" pattern, shaped like the base of a bomb or torpedo standing on its fins (shape #452), painted with pansies in red and yellow. $750 (Auction)

Vase, 14½" high. A "Bizarre" vase in the "Inspiration" pattern, in baluster form, with turquoise-blue, tan, and purple underglaze decoration of an imaginary landscape, printed mark. $2,400 (Auction)
$3,000–$3,500

COWAN POTTERY (American, Ohio 1921–1931)
Reginald Guy Cowan (1884–1957)

> Cowan employed many outstanding artists to create models for its lines, and the most sought-after today are figural pieces. (See "Ceramics" for additional background.)

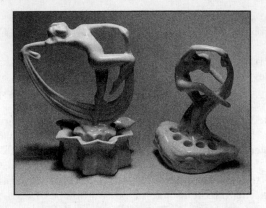

**Flower frogs by
R. Guy Cowan.**
*Author's collection.
Photo by Robert Four.*

Centerpiece, c. 1925, 2½" high, 7" wide. Seven-sided bowl, on incorporated seven-sided pedestal base, in ivory glaze, with pale green glaze in the bowl. Impressed with circular "R G Cowan" mark. In fine condition.   **$150–$225**

Flower frog, "*Nymph*," c. 1925, 7½" high. Designed by R. Guy Cowan. In ivory glaze, a nude maiden with one knee raised, scarf draped from hand to hand, rising from stylized lotus flower, with holes in the base for holding flowers. Impressed circular "R G Cowan" mark. A good example of a Cowan flower frog, in fine condition.   **$200–$225**

Flower frog, "*Nymph*," c. 1925, 6" high. Designed by R. Guy Cowan. In ivory glaze, a nude maiden, her scarf hanging from her arched hand to the stylized wave base on which she stands, with nine holes in the base for holding flowers. Impressed circular "R G Cowan" mark. In fine condition.   **$125–$175**

Lamp, table, c. 1925, 19½" high. Metal shade of square flaring form, simulating mica, on standard fitting into a bulbous pottery base, predominate rust-colored matte glaze, impressed circular "Cowan" mark. In very good condition.   **$1,000 (Auction)**

Vase, c. 1925, 5¾" high. Ovoid form, in a rose high-luster porcelain glaze. With impressed circular Cowan mark, and also impressed "Cowan." In fine condition.
                                                                          $75–$125

Vase, c. 1920, 7" high. Baluster form with elongated neck, in an orange-gold high-luster porcelain glaze. Ink-stamped "Cowan Pottery." In fine condition.   **$150–$175**

Alexander Blazys (1894–1963)

Figure, "*Bird on a Wave*," c. 1929, 15" high. In deep turquoise-blue glaze, stylized double wave echoes the shape of a peacocklike bird which appears to be riding the wave. A very good example in fine condition.   **$2,500–$3,500**

Waylande DeSantis Gregory (1905–1971)

Bookend/decanters, "*King and Queen*," 1930, each 8½" high. Inspired by Lewis Carroll's *Alice Through the Looking-Glass*, in an ivory glaze, seated King and Queen figures double

Lacquered wood and metal "Skyscraper" bookcases, by Paul Frankl, c. 1930. Courtesy of Christie's, NY.

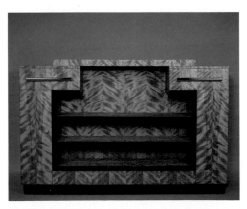

Bookcase/cabinet by Michel Dufet for Au Bucheron, 1930. Courtesy of Calderwood Gallery, PA.

Acajou bergères by Süe et Mare, c. 1920. Courtesy of Christie's, NY.

Chandelier in nickel-plated bronze and frosted glass by Muller Frères. Courtesy of Moderne, PA.

Table lamp in aluminum and frosted glass by Pattyn Products, c. 1935. Courtesy of Christie's, NY.

Chrome-plated bronze and marble clock by Jean Puiforcat, c. 1932. Courtesy of Christie's, NY.

Console and side tables in Formica and aluminum by Donald Deskey, c. 1932. Courtesy of Christie's, NY.

A selection of bronze and ivory figures by
Demetre Chiparus. Courtesy of Christie's, NY.

Russian Dancers, a bronze and
ivory sculpture by Demetre
Chiparus, depicting Vaslav
Nijinsky and Ida Rubenstein of
Les Ballets Russes. Courtesy of
Christie's, NY.

Suzanne by René Lalique, c. 1932, in molded opalescent glass. Courtesy of Christie's, NY.

"Ruba Rhombic" vase in smokey-topaz, 1928. Courtesy of Moderne, PA.

Schneider "Le Verre Française" vase in a rare geometric pattern. Courtesy of Antiquers III, MA.

Photo by Gene Ritvo

An acid-etched table lamp by Daum Frères Courtesy of Christie's, NY.

"Jazz Bowl," 1931, by Viktor Schreckengost for Cowan pottery. Courtesy of the Cowan Pottery Museum. *Photo by Larry L. Peltz*

Enameled pottery vases by Boch Frères, Belgium. Author's collection.

Photo by Robert Four

Enameled pottery vanity set by Longwy. Courtesy of As Time Goes By, CA.

Photo by Laurie Gordon

A selection of Gustavsberg "Argenta" pottery. Courtesy of Moderne, PA.

A selection of pottery by Susie Cooper. Courtesy of Christie's South Kensington, England.

"Dresser Ensemble." Courtesy of Glad Rags, VT. *Photo by After Image Photography*

Whiting & Davis enameled mesh bag. Courtesy of Mike and Sherry Miller, IL.

Whiting & Davis enameled mesh bags. Courtesy of Mike and Sherry Miller, IL.

Nord Express, 1927, by A.M. Cassandre. Private collection.

L'Eventail D'Or, (The Golden Fan), 1920, *pochoir* illustration by Georges Lepape for *La Gazette du Bon Ton*. Private collection.

Photo by Robert Four

Asia magazine cover, 1932, by Frank McIntosh. Author's collection.

Photo by Robert Four

Fine book bindings (left to right): *The Girl with the Golden Eyes*, 1928; *Exposé des Travaux*, 1937; and *Epitaph*, 1929. Courtesy o Thomas G. Boss Fine Books, MA.   *Photo by Robert Four*

Emerson "Cathedral" model radio, 1937, in rare tomato red Catalin plastic. Courtesy of John Sideli Art & Antiques, NY.

Photo by Michael Fredericks

Distinctive designs for book dust jackets. Courtesy of Thomas G Boss Fine Books, MA.   *Photo by Robert Four*

"King and Queen"
bookend decanters
by Waylande Gregory
for Cowan Pottery.
Author's collection.
Photo by Robert Four.

as bookends and decanters, with removable cork-based crowns as stoppers. Created during Prohibition when it was prudent to disguise one's liquor supplies. Queen impressed "Cowan," both inscribed in large block letters "Waylande Gregory." A fine example of Gregory's work for Cowan, in excellent condition. Pair.   **$2,000–$2,500**

Bust of a Woman, c. 1930, 15¼" high. The head and base cast as one piece in metallic charcoal and bronze glazes; inscribed "W. Gregory" and with impressed Cowan mark. In fine condition.   **$1,600 (Auction)**

Flower frog, "Fan Dancer," c. 1928, 13½" high. Stylized woman with long pleated hair, standing on one foot, one arm arched above her head, a large feather fan partially covering her nude torso, her draped dress falling to the base, designed with twelve holes for flowers. A very good example of Gregory's work for flower frogs, with impressed circular "R G Cowan" mark, in fine condition.   **$750–$900**

Drexel Jacobson

Bookends, c. 1925, 5¼" high, 4½" long. In black glaze, modeled as comical pelicans with large beaks. Pair.   **$2,000–$2,500**

Margaret Postgate

Bookends, "Elephants," 1929, each 4½" high, 5½" long. In ivory glaze, modeled as angular elephants. Each impressed with circular "Cowan" mark. A very good example of Postgate's work for Cowan, in fine condition. Pair.   **$800–$900**

Elephant bookends
by Magaret Postgate
for Cowan.
Author's collection.
Photo by Robert Four.

Figure, "*Madonna,*" 1929, 7⅛" high. Stylized kneeling woman cradling her child, cast as a single piece with a stepped rectangular base, in a crazed burnt-orange glaze, impressed with Cowan mark and paper label. Created in an edition of 150. A very good example in fine condition. $600–$700

Viktor Schreckengost (b. 1906)

Vase, 1931, 6¼" high. In mossy-green with yellow sgraffito design of fish, bubbles, and scrolling seaweed; with impressed "Cowan" mark. A good example of drypoint design, illustrated in the Cowan catalogue for 1931.   **$350 (Auction)**
$700–$900

Punch bowl, "*Jazz Bowl,*" 1931, 16½" wide. Decorated by Schreckengost on a form designed by Guy Cowan. In sgraffito, etched through the black glaze to the white body underneath and then glazed in "Egyptian Blue," a color developed by Cowan's chief chemist, Arthur Eugene Baggs. A limited number of punch bowls were created, each with slightly different urban, "jazzy" designs reflecting New Year's Eve in New York City—a last hurrah for Cowan Pottery, which closed the same year due to the Depression. Impressed with the "Cowan" mark and signed by the artist. The most sought-after of all Cowan designs. (*See color section.*)   **$15,000–$20,000**

JOSEPH DESCOMPS (French, 1869–1950)

Figure, a female nude, c. 1930, 15¾" high, 23" long. Female figure, seated, nude except for draped shawl, stylized birds on base. Signed "E. Joe Descomps."   **$1,500 (Auction)**

ANDRÉ FAU (French, work: 1920s–1940s)

Figural group, "*The Initiation,*" c. 1925, 14" high. In cream, pale brown, and pastel lavender. The famous vampire scene in an elegant Art Deco style.   **$1,200–$1,400**

Stylized ceramic figure by Joseph Descomps.
Courtesy of Christie's East, New York.

"The Initiation" by André Fau.
Courtesy of Moderne, Pennsylvania.

GOLDSCHEIDER (Austrian, 1885–1953)

€ Goldscheider was one of the largest producers of decorative bronzes during the Art Deco period, and also produced figural porcelain and ceramics for the department store trade, using some of the same artists to model their figures.

Figure, "Butterfly Girl," 9¾" high. Designed by Lorenzl. Seated figure, her dress flared and painted in brown, blue, and yellow to resemble wings of a butterfly. Stamped "Hand-Decorated Made in Austria Goldscheider Wien," and signed "Lorenzl."
$1,600 (Auction)

Figure, clown, c. 1930, 13½" high. Designed by Thamasch. Porcelain lady clown seated and holding a mandolin, in a high-gloss glaze in white, black, light green, gray, and ecru, marked with logo, incised signature "Thamasch" and numbers "5030/70/65."   **$800–$1,000**

Figure, dancer, c. 1925, 19¾" high. Designed by Lorenzl. Polychrome figure of an exotic dancer with flowing veil on oval base. Signed "Laurenzl" [sic] and "Made in Austria." A very good example, in fine condition.   **$2,900 (Auction)**

GUSTAVSBERG (Swedish, 1825–present)

€ Wilhelm Kåge was artistic director from 1917 to 1949, and created many Modernist styles including "Worker's Service" (1917) and "Praktika Service" (1933). Most sought-after by Art Deco collectors today is his "Argenta" line (late 1920s–early 1940s), usually a green pottery with silver overlay designs, for which the listings below are given. (*See color section.*) After the war, Kåge and his successor, Stig Linberg, experimented with biomorphic shapes.

Bowl, 4½" high. In green pottery with overlay silver design of a lion motif, stamped with firm's marks.   **$150–$175**

Centerpiece, 11" diameter. Scalloped footed bowl in green pottery, decorated with the figure of Diana on the interior. Stamped with the firm's mark and "Kåge." A very good example of "Argenta."   **$950 (Auction)**

Charger, 1937, 11½" diameter. A rare example in red pottery, with central stylized silver overlay design of plants and flowers, and additional silver overlay designs of flowers scattered around the plate. A fine and rare example of Gustavsberg.   **$1,500–$2,000**

Charger, 13" diameter. Shallow bowl in green pottery, centering a stylized seashore in silver overlay, the wide rim with repeating clusters of silver overlay bubbles on mottled green ground, stamped "Gustavsberg. Kåge, 909." In fine condition.   **$500 (Auction)**

Charger, 13½" diameter. Circular in green pottery, decorated with radiating bands and a nude female holding a flimsy drape in the center, stamped with firm's marks and "Kåge." In fine condition.   **$800–$850**

Dish, 5" long. Rectangular dish in green pottery with silver overlay design of a steamship. A good example of "Argenta," with firm's marks.   **$275–$350**

Vase, 5½" high. Bulbous form in green pottery with silver lily of the valley design overlay. Stamped with firm's marks.   **$175–$225**

Vase, c. 1935, 6" high. Cylindrical, in green glaze with horizontal bands of silver overlay. Stamped with the firm's marks and "A27."   **$225–$250**

Vase, 6½" high. Ovoid shape with short neck, in green pottery, with overlay silver design of a fish trailing bubbles and vertical ribbing. A good example of "Argenta."
$350–$400

Vase, 8" high. Cylindrical, raised on three rectangular feet, in green pottery overlaid with silver design of a man under water, surrounded by seaweed and sea grasses. A very good example of an "Argenta" design.   **$600–$650**

Vase, 10¼" high. Tapering cylindrical body on a short flared foot, in green pottery with silver overlay of a reclining mermaid and scrolling vine, silver lip band and line band at the foot rim, firm's mark with "Argenta/978/III," and "Made in Sweden." A fine example of "Argenta." (*See photo, below.*)   **$900 (Auction)**

Vase, 12⅝" high. Cylindrical in green pottery overlaid in silver with a nude male among seaweed and vertical bands and squares, with firm's marks. A fine example.
$1,200–$1,300

Vase, 13¾" high. Cylindrical with conical flaring neck, in green pottery, overlaid in silver with a nude figure swimming astride a sea monster. With firm's marks, a fine example of an "Argenta" vase.   **$1,800–$2,000**

Gustavsberg "Argenta" vase.
Courtesy of Butterfield & Butterfield, California.

Vase, 1943, 14½" high. Decorated by Oskar Sillen. Bulbous circular shape, sharply shouldered, in green pottery, with a silver overlay of a mermaid bearing a basket of blossoms on her head. With firm's marks and signed "Oskar Sillen 29–11 1943." An outstanding example of "Argenta."   **$2,600 (Auction)**

ROBERT LALLEMANT (French, 1902–1954)

Vase, 6" high. Spherical vessel decorated as a terrestrial globe including animals, boats, pyramids, tents in a desert, and mountains, in turquoise and black on a cream ground, the relief-molded, diagonally tilted meridian calibrated in black, with short ring neck and foot.   **$450 (Auction)**

LEMANCEAU (French, work: 1920s–1930s)

Figural group, stag and doe, c. 1930, 17¾" long, amid stylized grasses, in cream glaze, molded "Lemanceau."   **$400–$600**

LONGWY (French, 1789–present)

> Longwy is known primarily for cloisonné enameled ceramics inspired by Far and Near Eastern motifs, but during the 1920s and 1930s, Longwy produced pieces in Art Deco style, which sold through the Printemps department store workshop Primavera, the Au Bon Marché department store workshop Pomone, and others. Marks will often reflect the name of the store as well as Longwy.

Bowl, 14¾" diameter. Flaring vessel in a white crackled glaze decorated with Cubist stylized vines, in blue, green, yellow, and gray, the exterior glazed in blue. Stamped "Primavera Longwy France."   **$480 (Auction)**

Box, covered, 4" diameter. Circular, lid designed in yellow, orange, blue, and green, depicting a stylized nude beneath exotic trees with yellow fruit. Stamped "Longwy" and "Pomone." A fine example of a Longwy covered box.   **$700–$750**

Box, covered, 5½" diameter. Circular, decorated in orange, green, and yellow in an abstract floral design, on a pale pink crazed ground, stamped "Longwy" and "Bon Marché." A good example of a Longwy covered box.   **$300 (Auction)**

Box, covered, 7" diameter, 2" high. Circular, in a white crazed glaze, decorated with overlapping flowers in orange and red on a deep blue ground, stamped "Longwy" and "Atelier Primavera." A very good example of a Longwy covered box.   **$450–$500**

Charger, 14¾" diameter. Decorated by R. Rizzi, circular, painted with a white stork surrounded by yellow, pink, and salmon blossoms against a blue and green ground, stamped with firm's mark and marked "Decor de R. Rizzi," numbered "33/60." Stylized design, but more Asian in influence than Art Deco.   **$600 (Auction)**

Charger, 14¾" diameter. Circular, design with a native riding on an elephant, with a smaller elephant leading the way, surrounded by tropical foliage in bright polychrome glazes. With the firm's printed marks and "Atelier d'Art Bon Marché." A fine example of a Longwy charger, in excellent condition.   **$1,900 (Auction)**
                                                                          $2,800–$3,200

Vanity set, plate: 10" wide. Comprising a hexagonal underdish, covered jar, handleless cup, and small matching dish, the three smaller pieces all fitting on the underdish. Decorated with stylized flowers in yellow, orange, blue, and green, and the three smaller pieces with a checkerboard pattern in cranberry red. A fine example of Longwy's Art Deco style, in excellent condition. (*See color section.*)   **$2,000–$2,200**

Vase, 7" high. Hexagonal flattened form with flaring mouth, decorated with stylized blossoms in blue, white, and orange. Stamped "Longwy."   **$300–$350**

Vase, 7½" high. Baluster form with red vertical stripes and central polychrome floral band. Stamped "Longwy."   **$325–$375**

Vase, 8" high. Bulbous form with elongated neck, with an abstract design of overlapping circles in deep red, purple, and deep green. A good example of a Longwy Art Deco vase.
                                                                          $400–$450

Vase, 9½" high. Bell shape, in a crackled ivory glaze, with a band of red and orange stylized flowers at the shoulder, the neck in curved hexagonal form tapering to a circular mouth, ribbed vertically. Stamped "Société Des Faienceries Longwy France." A good example of this shape which Longwy produced in several sizes and decorations.
                                                                          $1,200–$1,400

Vase, 10⅞" high. Footed cylinder with everted rim, decorated with a Cubist-influenced landscape in rust, gray, and moss over a crackled glaze, enhanced with black. Stamped "Atelier Primavera" and "Longwy France." In good condition, but with some restoration at rim.   **$550 (Auction)**

Vase, 11½" high. Moon-flask form, celadon glaze decoration of a suspended mask and similar stylized band around the neck against a cream crackled ground, stamped "Atelier Primavera Longwy."   **$280 (Auction)**

Vase, 11¾" high. Moon-flask form, with a central stylized mask in black on a crazed aqua ground, signed "Primavera Longwy." A good example of a Longwy moon-flask form.   **$450–$500**

Vase, 12" high. Bulbous shape tapering to slender neck, decorated in blue, black, green, and magenta stylized nude maidens and plants, including cactus plants. Marked "Atelier Primavera/Longwy France." Other examples of this vase in the past have brought as much as $3,750 at auction. A fine example of Longwy's Art Deco style. (*See photo, opposite.*)   **$2,400 (Auction)**
                                                                          $5,000–$6,000

**Longwy
Primavera 12"
enameled vase.**
*Courtesy of
William Doyle
Galleries,
New York.*

Quimper "Odetta" series pieces.
Courtesy of Skinner, Inc., Massachusetts.

Vase, 13" high. Bell shape, crackled cream ground, with stylized floral border in turquoise, blue, and cinnamon, with blue and turquoise vertical stripes, stamped with Longwy marks, painted "CMC D.5134."   **$1,000 (Auction)**

Vase, 13⅜" high. Bell shape, with a low band of stylized flowers and fruits in mustard and cherry, the octagonal upper portion with defined ribbing ascending to rim, over crackled glaze, stamped "Société Des Faienceries Longwy France" with firm's logo. A fine example of the Longwy bell-shaped vase.   **$1,800–$2,000**

QUIMPER (French, late 1600s–present)
Vase and covered box, vase: 7¼" high; covered box: 3¾" high, 6" diameter. "Odetta" series, bulbous vase with stoneware gray-blue glaze and three black sgraffito decorative portrait repetitions; covered box of eight-pointed star design with portrait in cover. Each signed on base "Quimper Odetta" and numbered.   **$550 (Auction)**

ROBJ (French, 1920–early 1930s)
Decanter, figural, 9¾" high. Porcelain figure of a rosy-cheeked maiden in a blue dress and yellow apron holding a basket of fruit, the stopper modeled as her bonnet. Figures of women in Robj decanters are rarer than those of men.   **$550–$600**

Decanter, figural, 10½" high. Porcelain figure of a country preacher in long robes and circular stopper hat. In fine condition. Impressed "Robj."   **$275–$300**

Decanter/music box, figural, 12" high. Porcelain musical decanter, designed as a Russian man in traditional costume, his hat forming the stopper, on music-box base. Impressed "Robj." In good condition, but music box not working.   **$250 (Auction)**

Figure of a woman, 11¼" high. Seated figure in stylized draped robes on a rectangular base in a pale gray glaze. A very good example of a Robj figurine, impressed "Robj."   **$550–$600**

Inkwell, figural, 6¼" high. Porcelain, modeled as a seated Indian servant, in turban and full robes, holding a covered pot for ink, in white with black face and gilt details, with firm's marks.   **$600 (Auction)**

ROSEVILLE POTTERY (American, Ohio, 1898–1954)

> ℂ Roseville produced numerous styles of art pottery, and several show some Art Deco influences. Most sought-after by Art Deco collectors is "Futura" (1928), and all listings below are for "Futura." "Futura" was unmarked, identified only by a paper label, which in most cases has not survived. Model numbers below refer to Roseville's catalogue. About seventy-five different models were made.

Jardiniere, 6" high. Two-handled jardiniere, as originally designed without pedestal, in an angular, flaring form, with stylized pink leaves and blue triangles against a tan ground.   **$450–$500**

Vase, 5" high, model #81, called "Pillow Vase." Rectangular form, on a stepped rectangular base, in two tones of blue glaze painted as sunrays descending from one corner of the face. A good example of the style.   **$450–$500**

Vase, 6" high, model #82, called "Fan Vase." In a brown and blue speckled matte glaze, the squared fan design flaring to 9" wide at the top with green leaf design, rectangular opening, and stepped base. A good example of the style. In fine condition.

                                                                                       $275 (Auction)

Vase, 7½" high. Large open oviform, four open buttress supports on square base, green spots streaking into pale terra cotta glaze with a wash of blue at the base.

                                                                                       $375 (Auction)

Vase, 7¾" high, model #387. Square, wedge-shaped base supporting spherical vessel with narrow neck, designed with long, curved triangles rising from the base in creamy brown on pale yellow ground speckled with blue and green. A very good example of the style.   **$800–$850**

"Futura" vases by Roseville *(left to right):* model #404, model #432, model #383, and another model #432. *Photo by Robert Four.*

Vase, 8" high, model #386. Upright rectangular form with stepped rectangular neck and two long angular handles descending to the base, glazed in diamonds and triangles of blue and rose. A very good example of the style. $650–$750

Vase, 8" high, model #427. Open oviform on a circular base with stylized thistles in relief in deep blue-lavender on a pink and green ground. A good example. $400–$450

Vase, 8" high, model #383. Slightly flaring triangular form on triangular stepped-back base, with inverted triangular design in soft tints of tan and green. A good example of the style. $425–$500

Vase, 8" high, model #404. In a deep green crystalline glaze with colorful pattern of overlapping "balloons," the spherical form with short flaring neck, with three supporting vertical buttresses descending to each corner of its pyramidal triangular base. A very good example of "Futura." (Also produced in a deep blue glaze.) In fine condition.
$950 (Auction)
$1,500–$1,750

Vase, 9" high. Circular base, flaring to a broad shoulder, surmounted by a long, circular stepped-back neck with two angular handles, glazed in blue, green, and brown within an intersecting diamond-shaped pattern. A fine example of "Futura."   **$1,800–$2,000**

Vase, 10" high, model #432. The bulbous body in a darker blue glaze, surmounted by a short flaring circular neck in a lighter blue, the neck with an incorporated raised "collar" and four buttress supports. A very good example of the style. $850–$1,000

Vase, 10" high, model #433. Blue and green matte background with abstracted pinecone decoration, ovoid body with two openwork handles under flared top. A good example of the style.   **$600 (Auction)**

Vase, 12" high, model #393. A square, stepped base supporting four semispherical lobes, in turn supporting a squared, flaring vessel, in blue, with an inverted triangle design on each side in a light tan. A fine example of the style.   **$550 (Auction)**
$900–$1,200

Vase, 15" high, model #438. Tall modified cylindrical form, with stylized thistles in relief in honey and cream with green glaze. A very good example of the style, in fine condition.   **$1,100 (Auction)**
$1,500–$1,800

WEDGWOOD (English, 1759–present)

> In 1932, architect Keith Murray was retained to design a line of Modernist wares which have become popular with Art Deco collectors. Most pieces were produced in white, yellow, and green glazes, as well as in a dark brown and black basalt.

Coffee set, c. 1938. Comprising a covered coffee pot, covered sugar bowl, creamer, and six cups and saucers, all in a cream-white "Moonstone" glaze with horizontal ribbed banding. Coffee pot stamped "Keith Murray, Wedgwood, Made in England," other pieces marked "KM, Wedgwood." **$1,200–$1,500**

Vase, c. 1935, 6" high. Ribbed spherical form with short cylindrical neck, in a pale yellow glaze. Stamped "Keith Murray, Wedgwood." In fine condition. **$250–$300**

Vase, c. 1935, 7¼" high. Ribbed trumpet form in a cream-white "Moonstone" glaze, stamped "Keith Murray Wedgwood." In fine condition. **$500–$600**

Vase, 7¼" high. Brown basalt vase, tapering cylindrical form, cut with five sets of horizontal bands. A fine example of Murray's designs for Wedgwood. **$1,800–$2,000**

Vase, 7¾" high. Black basalt vase, fluted form on a circular foot, cut with horizontal banding beneath the rim. A fine example of Murray's designs for Wedgwood.
$1,200 (Auction)

VALLY WIESELTHIER (Austrian/American, 1895–1945)

> **Valerie (Vally) Wieselthier was one of the leading ceramists of the Wiener Werkstätte, and also designed for the Austrian firm Augarten. After emigrating to the United States, she modeled works for several ceramic producers, including General Ceramics, New York.**

Candelabra, c. 1930. Probably designed for Augarten. Seated nude supporting two candle bobeches with her hands and head, in white, blue, and green glazes, impressed artist's monogram and "Made in Austria." **$700–$900**

Figural group by Vally Wieselthier for Augarten. *Courtesy of Christie's East, New York.*

Vally Wieselthier designs for General Ceramics.
Author's collection. Photo by Robert Four.

Figural group, c. 1925, 12¼" high. Designed for Augarten. Blanc de chine porcelain figural group of a fashionable lady in plumed hat being admired by two small boys. Stamped with the initials "VW" and Augarten mark. A very good example of the artist's work for Augarten, in fine condition. $1,200–$1,300

Paperweight, c. 1930, 6" long. Designed for General Ceramics. Stylized drooping design, with dripped gray glaze, hollow figure weighted with sand held by small cork on bottom. Ink-stamped "VW" and "General Ceramics" on base. A very good example of Wieselthier's designs for General Ceramics, in excellent condition. $600–$700

Vase, figural, c. 1930, 9" high. Designed for General Ceramics. Stylized bust of a woman wearing a very wide-brimmed hat, open at top, in a white crackled porcelain glaze. Stamped "VW" with chalice logo and "By General Ceramics" on base. (*Fakes Alert!* Poorly executed reproductions of this piece are on the market.) $200–$225

Vase, figural, c. 1930, 10" high. Designed for General Ceramics. Stylized bust of a woman with elongated neck and almond-shaped eyes, her shoulders draped, wearing a small hat, open at top, in a very pale gray smooth porcelain glaze. Stamped "VW" with chalice logo, and "By General Ceramics" on base. A very good example of the artist's designs for General Ceramics, in fine condition. $400–$450

AMERICAN MASS-PRODUCED TABLEWARES

HALL CHINA COMPANY (American, 1903–present)

> While Hall has reintroduced many shapes in new colors, 1930s production can be distinguished by changes in the company's mark on the bottom. Early colors include "Cadet," "Delphinium," "Marine," and "Cobalt" blues, "Chinese" and "Indian Red" reds, "Emerald" and "Lettuce" greens, and "Canary" yellow. Rare novelty shapes such as the "Automobile," "Football," and "Basketball," all introduced in 1938, can easily bring hundreds of dollars.

"Airflow," teapot, 1940, canary.	$80–$100
"Aladdin," teapot, 1939, cobalt.	$75–$100
"Aladdin," teapot, 1939, emerald green.	$60–$75
"Aristocrat," water server, 1940, cobalt.	$125–$150
"Ball Jug," water jug, 1938, various colors.	$30–$60
"Doughnut," water jug, 1938, Indian red.	$80–$100

"Doughnut" water jug by Hall China. *Author's collection. Photo by Robert Four.*

"Fiesta" water pitcher by Homer Laughlin. *Author's collection. Photo by Robert Four.*

"Moderne," teapot, 1935, delphinium. $60–$80

"Nautilus," teapot, 1939, canary. $60–$80

"Patrician," water server, 1938, lettuce. $80–$100

"Rhythm," teapot, 1939, Chinese red. $150–$200

HOMER LAUGHLIN COMPANY—"FIESTA" WARE

> Homer Laughlin introduced "Fiesta" in 1936, and it was made through 1972, and reintroduced again in 1986. Pre–World War II colors were red, blue, yellow, green, and ivory, with turquoise added in 1938. Red was discontinued in 1943, but was reintroduced in 1959. New colors are pastel shades of apricot, rose, and sea-mist, plus a cobalt-blue, black, and white.

Coffee mug, red. $65–$70

Coffee pot, red. $225–$250

Compote, 12", red. $165–$175

Covered casserole, red. $150–$160

Demitasse pot, red. $300–$325

Demitasse pot, yellow. $250–$275

Fruit bowl, 5½", red.	$30–$35
Fruit bowl, 5½", yellow.	$18–$20
Gravyboat, yellow or ivory.	$35–$40
Plate, 10", red.	$35–$40
Plate, 10", yellow.	$20–$25
Plate, 7", red.	$15–$18
Plate, 7", yellow.	$8–$10
Platter, 12" oval, yellow.	$25–$30
Teacup, turquoise or yellow.	$20–$25
Vase, 8", red.	$425–$450

SPECIAL FOCUS
SUSIE COOPER
An Interview With Linda Cheverton

Linda Cheverton is the owner of Linda Cheverton Art & Antiques, a dealership that specializes in a variety of areas including the ceramics of Susie Cooper. You can contact her at Box 53, Colebrook, CT 06021, or call (203) 379-5345.

In November 1991, the auction house Christie's South Kensington in England hosted a groundbreaking sale of 150 lots of ceramics by Susie Cooper (b. 1902), an innovative English designer who started her career with A. E. Gray & Company in 1923, and whose work represents a wide range of tableware, figural pieces, and unique studio pieces. In November 1992, marking the artist's ninetieth birthday, the same auction house hosted yet another large sale of her work.

It seems as if, overnight, Susie Cooper's name is everywhere in the Art Deco collecting field. In fact, her "renaissance" didn't happen that fast. Cooper's work has been sought-after by collectors in England since the late 1970s, and bought up by a handful of collectors and dealers in the United States over the past ten years or so. Today, her name is fast become a Deco household word.

"There seem to be more collectors of Susie Cooper in Florida and California than anywhere else in this country, and her work is not easy to find in the United States," comments Linda Cheverton. "A few collectors here have been hoarding it for years, and it has taken off like a shot in England."

Cheverton, for whom dealing in antiques is a second career, has been a stylist in New York City for many years. In the advertising and publishing fields, a stylist is someone who designs the setting for a photographer. Cheverton has worked as the stylist for over thirty cookbooks, and for most of the cover photos for *Food and Wine* magazine—thus her fascination with tablewares and her attraction to Susie Cooper ceramics.

Susie Cooper attended Burslem School of Art, where one of her teachers introduced her to "Gloria Lustre" a new line of pottery being produced by A. E. Gray & Company. Cooper joined Gray as a designer, and shortly thereafter, by October 1923, her name began to appear on the pottery she designed. This was a distinct honor, as no other designers in the factory were permitted to sign their work.

Though successful and one of the highest-priced Cooper collectibles on the market today, "Lustreware" is really more of a transitional style than it is Art Deco, even though Cooper broke new ground in terms of color and decoration.

Starting in around 1928, she began to create "Cubist" tableware with an uninhibited range of strident colors. The design was a success, but the pottery itself is easily chipped, meaning that collectors today will pay a premium for pieces in perfect condition.

Once Cooper left A. E. Gray and began operating her own factory, Crown Works, in 1931, she was at last in total control of both the design and the finished product. She operated Crown Works until 1961, and today her designs are produced by Wedgwood.

"The 'Cubist' pattern is perhaps the most easily appreciated by collectors," comments Cheverton. "I think that's because the design and colors resemble those of designs of Clarice Cliff, with whom the market is already familiar."

Many collectors still prefer the bright colors and patterns of Clarice Cliff, whose prices today can range much higher than Cooper's on the market. However, Cheverton feels that "Susie Cooper was in many ways a much more unique artist in terms of revolutionizing shape. Cliff was a painter whose talent was in decoration."

Perhaps it was the astronomical rise of Cliff's popularity in the United States in the second half of the 1980s that delayed Cooper's full introduction to the American Deco market. At the same time, many collectors began looking more closely at English Art Deco ceramics because of the success of Cliff's work on the market.

With her "Cubist" line, Cooper began to experiment with unique shapes as well as with decoration, forming her shapes by hand. After she set up her own factory, her individual style truly emerged, and she created new forms. "Fitness for Purpose" was her slogan as she created new sophisticated but simple forms and began to use a more delicate, more restrained palette.

For example, "Kestrel," a style she trademarked in 1931, combines fairly traditional body shapes with subtly aerodynamic spouts and finials and gracefully looping handles. The "Kestrel" style appeared with a variety of glazes and decorations, including wonderful delicate patterns of crosses, dots, or squiggles. Collectors should note, however, that sometimes her "Kestrel" shape is decorated with a more traditional design, just as some Hall China teapots in modern form were gilt or painted in traditional patterns.

Over the years, Cooper also experimented with a range of color palettes, carved wares, lithographic transfers, and sgraffito, a method of incising the outer glaze on a ceramic to create a design on a different ground of color. As her production grew and she began exporting her tablewares after World War II, the use of lithographic transfer instead of hand decoration enabled her to produce larger quantities.

The market for Cooper is still expanding, and therefore prices are still climbing. As with many other Deco collecting fields, publicity surrounding auctions and dealer exhibitions of her work, along with recent books cataloguing her work, have advanced the Susie Cooper collecting market.

Exposure of this kind both broadens the collecting base and allows for more detailed documentation and comparison of her designs. It is only a matter of time before her patterns "Scarlet Runner Bean," "Nosegay," "Patricia Rose," "Orchids," and even the cute cartoony animals of her "Nursery Ware" lines are better known.

The most rapid price increases will probably be for Cooper's most striking Art Deco designs: her "Cubist" line for Gray's, as well as some of the designs on her "Kestrel" shapes. Other Cooper Art Deco styles that seem to be in favor are designs using stylized gazelles, foxes, squirrels, and other animals, including figurals of animals. While sometimes incised with very good Art Deco line drawings of animals, her "Carved Ware" is, overall, less outstanding.

Not all of Cooper's design can be called Art Deco, but then there are those people who don't collect "Art Deco," they collect "Cooper"—period.

FIVE SUSIE COOPER SHOPPING TIPS

1. Learn more about Susie Cooper's overall output by reading, visiting specialized dealers, attending auctions, or subscribing to auction catalogues.
2. As in all ceramic collecting, condition is important in determining value. Inspect pieces for chips, cracks, and overpainting or alterations. Collectors should note that Cooper's designs for Gray's were made of a less durable pottery, so small chips in her "Cubist" pattern are more common and pieces in excellent to mint condition will be more expensive.
3. To build a more valuable collection, try to acquire full sets of her tableware in a particular pattern or style, whether purchased as a set or piece by piece, in the best condition you can find them. Another way to help ensure the value of your collection is to focus it on one aspect of her work: studio pieces, "Carved Ware," animals, "Nursery Ware", etc.
4. In terms of quality and quantity, her post–World War II lithographic transfer production is the least whimsical, the most available, and the least desirable on the collecting market today. Designs that carry the Cooper monogram in the shape of a gazelle are worth more than unmarked pieces on the collecting market.
5. Cooper ceramics are not easily found in the United States. To date, the important auctions of her work have been centered at Christie's South Kensington in England, and England is also the best place to shop for her work at antique dealerships.

SUSIE COOPER PRICE LISTINGS
(In approximate chronological order)

A. E. GRAY & COMPANY (1923–1929)

"Gloria Lustre"

Jar, 8" high. Depicting stylized rams beneath slender fruit trees, and painted in gilt, yellow, and green. In excellent condition, with factory mark.   **$500 (Auction)**

Vase, 7½" high. Overall pear shape with scrolling flowers and foliage in gold, on a banded green and purple ground. In excellent condition, with printed factory mark, and painted Susie Cooper monogram.   **$700–$900**

"Cubist"

Beakers, approximately 4½" high. Painted in vivid colors, with overlapping rectangles and other decoration. In fine condition, with the Susie Cooper mark. Each.

$325–$375

Coffee set for six, coffee pot: 7½" high. A striking set, painted in red, yellow, blue, green, and black. The set includes coffee pot and cover, five cups and six saucers, cream jug, and sugar bowl.   **$1,800–$2,400**

Coffee set for four, coffee pot: 7½" high. Painted in red, yellow, blue, green, and black. The set includes coffee pot and cover, milk jug and sugar bowl, and four cups and saucers, each with printed factory marks. In fine condition except for damage to the coffee pot lid.   **$1,400 (Auction)**

Dish, 12" diameter. Circular dish painted in red, yellow, blue, green, and black, with factory marks. In fine condition.   **$1,500 (Auction)**

Jug, 4" high. Handled jug painted in blue, red, yellow, green, and black. In good condition, with some overpainting, and with factory marks.   **$400–$500**

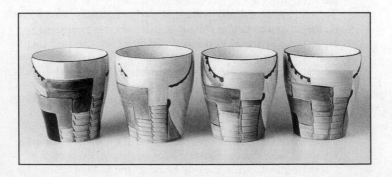

Susie Cooper "Cubist" beakers for Gray.
Courtesy of Linda Cheverton Art & Antiques, Connecticut.

**Susie Cooper
cup and saucer
for Gray.**
*Courtesy of Linda
Cheverton Art &
Antiques,
Connecticut.*

Jug, 4" high. Handled jug, painted with geometric pattern of overlapping circles and zigzags, painted in red, blue, green, yellow, and black. In excellent condition, and with factory marks.   **$600–$800**

Jug, 4¾" high. Handled jug, painted in red, blue, yellow, green, and black. In good condition, with some overpainting, and with factory mark.   **$500 (Auction)**

Tea set for six. Painted with a geometric rectilinear pattern in green, blue, brown, black, and silver luster. Set comprises six cups and saucers, six small tea plates, six larger plates, milk jug, sugar bowl, cake plate, and fruit bowl. In fine condition with some wear to sugar bowl.   **$2,300 (Auction)**

Other Patterns for Gray's

Cup and saucer, decorated with circular wavy pattern in red, yellow, orange, blue, purple, green, and black. In fine condition. Signed "Susie Cooper for Gray's." (*See photo, above.*)
$525–$575

Pitcher, as above. (*See photo, above.*)   **$325–$375**

Hors d'oeuvres set for six. Decorated in stylized flowers painted in red, yellow, green, and black. Comprises rectangular handled serving dish and six canape plates. Signed "Susie Cooper for Gray's."   **$1,200–$1,300**

**Susie Cooper
hors d'oeuvres set.**
*Courtesy of
Linda Cheverton
Art & Antiques,
Connecticut.*

CROWN WORKS (starting 1931)

"Carved Ware"

Bowl, 9½" diameter. Overall flaring form, incised with a stylized design of squirrels, with a pink glaze. In fine condition, with incised signature. $250–$300

Bowl, footed, c. 1932, 8¼" diameter. Shallow bowl on four grooved feet, the interior incised with a floral spray, covered in a matte green glaze, incised signature. $130 (Auction)

Jug, 4¾" high. Oviform with handle, incised with sprays of flowers, covered in a pale green glaze, with incised signature. (*See color section.*) $200–$225

Jug, 8¼" high. Oviform with leaping rams, covered in a matte cream glaze, incised signature. $325 (Auction)

Vase, 9¼" high. Baluster form, with a continuous incised frieze of stylized leaves, covered in a matte ochre glaze, incised signature and "592." $200 (Auction)

Vase, 10¾" high. Ovoid form, incised with squirrels on foliage, and covered in a pale green glaze, incised factory mark. $275 (Auction)

Vase, 11¼" high. Swollen cylindrical form, incised with squirrels, covered in a matte blue glaze, incised signature. An excellent example of the artist's Art Deco style in incised pottery, and a large size. $400–$450

Other Patterns for Crown Works

Biscuit barrel and cover, "Seagull" pattern, 5¼" high. Cylindrical shape, a stylized gull above blue and green waves, painted in colors, printed facsimile signature. (*See color section.*)
                                                                         $800 (Auction)

Bowl, 7⁄12" diameter. The interior decorated with a band of leaf motifs and the exterior with dots in pink and green, with printed factory mark. $150–$175

Cocoa pot and cover, "Skier" pattern, 5" high. A "Nursery Ware" Kestrel cocoa pot and cover, printed and painted with the figure of a skier in orange, black, and blue, gazelle "SCP" mark. (*See color section.*) $1,200 (Auction)

Coffee set for six, "Kestrel." Decorated with star motif on a blue ground, comprising coffee pot and cover, six cups and saucers, cream jug, sugar bowl, six side plates, six entree plates and six dinner plates, six dessert plates, two oval platters, gravy boat, tureen and cover, with printed factory marks. $550 (Auction)

Cup and saucer. Each printed with the whimsical cartoon of a golfer in a yellow spotted sweater and black plaid plus-fours, with green and yellow banding, printed factory marks. $250 (Auction)

Demitasse set, "Kestrel." Comprising a covered coffee pot, creamer and sugar bowl, and cup and saucer. Each in a cream glaze with brown bands and decorated with tiny

Susie Cooper "Kestrel" demitasse set.
Courtesy of Linda Cheverton Art & Antiques, Connecticut.

crosses. An excellent example of Cooper's talent for form and restrained decoration, in excellent condition. Signed. $950–$1,100

Dish, 8¼" wide. Oval form, painted in orange, black, yellow, gray, and green with overlapping rectangles and wavy lines, with sgraffito chevrons and spots, triangular "SCP" mark. (*See color section.*)   **$425 (Auction)**

Figure, 5" long. Earthenware figure of a fox, on curved base, naturalistically painted, incised signature. (*See color section.*)   **$700 (Auction)**

Jug, "Orchids" pattern, 5¼" high. Oviform, painted in pastel shades on a cream ground. In fine condition, with painted signature.   **$300–$400**

Jug and five tankards, jug: 5" high. Each tapering cylindrical form variously painted in colors with stripes, chevrons, and spots, with gazelle "SCP" mark. In good condition, chip to jug spout, one tankard cracked.   **$600 (Auction)**

Lamp base, 5¾" high. Triangular, the front with a galleon and the sides and back with stylized clouds, water, and leaping fish, painted in sepia, black, and brown, gazelle "SCP" mark. In very good condition, with minor flaking to base. (*See color section.*)
                                    $450 (Auction)

Plate, 8¾" diameter. Matte glazed, painted with pale green and black spirals and green crayon crescents on a cream ground, printed factory mark and facsimile signature.
                                    $225–$250

Plate, 11" diameter. Sgraffito, the bloodred center with a goat among foliage, the pink border with looped band, and another from the same series depicting a squirrel, gazelle "SCP" mark.   **$1,000 (Auction)**

Plate, 11" diameter. Painted with a fox in shades of brown and yellow, with a turquoise border with sgraffito scrolls between bands of silver luster, with printed factory marks.
                                    $900 (Auction)

Tea set, "*Kestrel,*" "*Bachelor.*" Glazed blue with crescent sgraffito decoration, comprising teapot and cover, milk jug, sugar bowl, cup, saucer, and plate, with gazelle "SCP" mark.   **$700–$800**

Tea set, "*Kestrel,*" "*Cactus*" *pattern,* teapot: 4½" high. Printed in shades of green and rust, comprising teapot and cover, coffee cup and saucer, and milk jug, with gazelle "SCP" mark.   **$300–$400**

Tea set for twelve, "*Rex*" *pattern.* Decorated with leaping deer motif, printed in pink, yellow, and gray, comprising teapot and cover, hot water pot and cover, milk jug, sugar bowl, seven cups, twelve saucers, twelve side plates, two larger plates, rectangular dish, and six square plates, with printed factory marks.   **$1,000 (Auction)**

Tea set, "*Cube*" *pattern,* teapot: 5" high. Painted with panels of overlapping rectangles and wavy lines, in black, yellow, green, gray, ochre, and brown, comprising teapot and cover, two cups and saucers, side plate, milk jug, and sugar bowl, printed triangular "SCP" mark. (*See color section.*)   **$2,700 (Auction)**

Vase, 1932, 9" high. A cylindrical earthenware vase covered in a matte buff glaze and painted in pastel shades of lavender, peach, and green with sprays of stylized tulips, painted signature, and dated 1932. (*See color section.*)   **$250 (Auction)**

4

FASHION
AND JEWELRY

FASHION, ACCESSORIES, AND COSTUME JEWELRY

It is a curious historical fact that the first of the grand couturiers in Paris was an Englishman, Charles Frederick Worth. Before Worth, women's clothing was essentially made by seamstresses. Worth's customers dressed in yards of fabric with lace trim and beadwork. Hats were large and covered by then-plentiful ostrich feathers. The style was designed to suit an elegant, rich society where the women were inactive enough to not need to worry about flowing trains on their dresses.

Paul Poiret challenged the Worth empire with his new style of fashion. Of course, Worth thought Poiret's designs were wicked and vulgar, but his styles were popular with women. Many women wore clothes that were risqué, which at the time did not mean "salacious" as much as "daring." The new clothes were symbolic of women's newly liberated attitudes.

Poiret, who had been an employee of Worth, opened his first shop in 1903. He, in turn, influenced younger designers, such as Paul Iribe, and built an interior decorating empire through his firm Martine.

At the beginning of his career, Poiret promoted an Orientalism in fashion, no doubt influenced by Les Ballets Russes, which was the *dernier cri*, or "the latest rage." Although the rage died out, it did establish his reputation.

Over the years, his design changed to a more vertical, slim style with bright Fauve colors. The song "Anything Goes" could easily be about his designs: it was he who introduced transparent colored stockings. His short skirts were designed to show off the knee-high Moroccan boots that he suggested be worn with them. As if all that was not shocking enough, he also abolished corsets and invented the bra.

Poiret was a truly "modern" fashion designer as we understand the term today. He was one of the first to create his own perfume. In addition, because he also designed interiors, it was possible for someone to become totally absorbed in his style. He made no secret of the fact that he wanted to "fashion" his clients' lives in every way.

World War I had a strong effect on fashion. It speeded up the development of man-made materials and ready-to-wear clothing. It also accelerated the emancipation of women, whose active role in society now required a new kind of clothing. Two million Frenchmen died in the war, and many women found themselves still working for a living even after the war was over.

The department stores were filled with a diversity of fashion never before seen. Supple, lightweight materials were used for straight, free-flowing dresses, and their long lines were not broken up by defined waistlines. Hemlines went up and down, reaching their shortest length in 1926. New fabrics were invented for sportswear. Elegant pajamas were acceptable attire for lounging around the house.

The world was full of trains and cars and other speeding vehicles, and clothes, too, took on a faster look, with geometric patterns, lines, and angular cuts. Hairstyles were shingled or "bobbed." Women smoked in public, and even drew attention to their new freedom with long jeweled cigarette holders and Deco-designed cigarette cases.

For evening wear, dresses were styled with low-cut V-shaped backs. Accessories came to include silk scarves and veils, with designs in gold and silver lamé thread. Hats were still de rigueur, but now cloche hats, a close-fitting variety, made their appearance, in a wide variety of shapes and colors. In the United States, mesh bags decorated with enameled patterns surged in popularity. (*See "Special Focus: Mesh Purses."*)

In all, no fewer than twenty new fashion houses were opened in Paris in the first quarter of the century, but primarily four other designers had the major impact on fashion in the 1920s: Madeleine Vionnet, Jeanne Lanvin, Coco Chanel, and Jean Patou.

Fashion became one of France's biggest exports, not only because it was appealing, but also because many of these designers were skilled at promoting their work and dealing with the press and magazines. They often visited showrooms around the world where their work was sold, and always took advantage of "photo opportunities" by being seen in the right places.

Vionnet is credited with the invention of the "bias cut" in fashion, which is the slanting or diagonal cut of clothing that was to become a hallmark of 1920s fashion. So many designers borrowed ideas from one another, claiming them as their own, that Vionnet went to the trouble of documenting her designs by photography to deter them.

Coco Chanel is perhaps the best-known name in fashion design from the era, and her work commands high prices at auction. As a celebrity of the era, she was extensively written about, and all of her many love affairs were followed in the gossip magazines. She worked for a very established clientele and was the first to introduce costume jewelry.

Her name would become well-known in the United States, especially after she had the idea to create paper patterns of her dresses for sale to homemakers who couldn't afford her original designs. In 1925, the year of the Paris Exposition, she introduced her famous Chanel No. 5 perfume. The four previous attempts had not been successful.

Jeanne Lanvin was really the first to introduce an internationally successful perfume—Arpege, in 1923. Also well-known in the United States, she opened the first ready-to-wear boutique for high fashion in Paris in 1929. The same year, Jean Patou opened a ready-to-wear boutique. Patou's name may not be as recognized today, but he was an important male designer in a women's world. His sportsclothes and white satin evening gowns established him as the designer for the "Café Society" in the 1920s. He also had a number of celebrities, such as Gloria Swanson, as clients.

He is perhaps best known for the *garçonne* style, a world created from the French word for "boy" with a feminine ending. When he introduced the look at Wimbledon in 1922 on a famous tennis player of the day, it was an immediate success. Women immediately took to the casual "tomboy" look.

The Depression had a devastating effect on the fashion world, which really did not recover until the mid-1930s. By then, many of the 1920s fashion designers had lost their appeal or had been forced to change their designs to meet new tastes.

However, these and other designers of the 1920s had such an impact that hardly an area of fashion or accessories does not reflect their style. Many makers of lesser quality created imitations of Chanel, Lanvin, Patou, and Vionnet-inspired dresses, handbags, scarves, shoes, hats, and more.

The most finely made fashions of the day are still worn. However, if the clothes are damaged, the restoration process requires special skills and specially re-created materials. The clothing is fragile and easily destroyed unless properly stored in an environment that is climate-controlled and protected from ultraviolet light. However, many still collect and wear the ready-to-wear and commercially produced fashions of the day.

Mention luggage, and the name Gaston Vuitton springs to mind. Everyone traveled—by motorcar, by airplane, by luxury ocean liner. No traveling ensemble was complete without a matching set of Vuitton luggage. Vuitton went beyond clothing trunks to create specialized cases for fishing gear, typewriters, shoes, and more. Like the works of many famous designers, Vuitton suitcases, handbags, and other creations have been imitated or counterfeited from the start.

Oskgosh suitcases and steamer trunks are popular collector pieces, as are both Vuitton and Oskgosh men's and women's fitted cases or "traveling" cases for toiletries and the like. Men's cases were designed in heavy cowhide, and often have squared-off toiletry bottles in enameled glass. More expensive cases have ivory components, while less expensive models used ivorine, a type of plastic.

The innumerable accessories and boudoir "decorations" of the day are also popular. For example, the eggshell lacquer technique which Jean Dunand perfected was also used by goldsmiths and silversmiths, and for small objects such as belt buckles, hair clips, and vanity cases. Newer, faster-drying enamels were developed, and accessories such as compact cases, cigarette cases, buttons, and cufflinks began to be produced in bright-colored or black and eggshell enamel. Makeup cases and lipstick batons came in a variety of shapes and sizes, and are now some of the most easily collectible items of the era.

In addition, cigarette cases and smoking accessories, lacquered boxes and silverplated coffers, jewelry boxes, and other boudoir items are popular, and many are still affordably priced. Other items often found in antique fashion stores include desk sets, manicure sets, humidors, boudoir lamps and nightlights, powder boxes, bookends, mirrors, letter openers, and letter seals—the list seems endless.

As fashion accessories and decorations such as these proliferated, cheap imitations of expensive materials became the norm. Silver was replaced by silverplate, nickelplate, and chrome. Enameling was replaced by transfer printing. And plastic came to look like ivory, tortoise shell, coral, and jade. What saved this production from being thrown away, and what makes it collectible today, is that although it was cheap, it was fashionable.

All of these categories of collectibles can vary widely in quality, design, and execution. After all, some were made of semiprecious materials, and others were made of Bakelite. It is up to you to develop an eye for quality workmanship and for what fits your budget and pleases you.

The influence of Paris as the epicenter of fashion began to wane as new magazines, geared to American women, saw rapidly rising circulations—*Harper's Bazaar* and *Vogue* seized the imaginations of young urban American women while continuing to promote an essentially French style of fashion.

However, by the end of the 1920s, there was a reaction against the style of fashion which had been carried on since the war, and long hair and flowing gowns once again returned to the scene. By 1930, hemlines had dropped all the way down, and skullcaps had replaced cloche hats. In the early 1930s, elegant evening and cocktail gowns had a reappearance. Elbow-length gloves, padding, and oversized coats were added.

As the world trudged through the Great Depression and headed again toward war, a plainer, more serious style of everyday clothing reclaimed dominance. In fact, fashion was looked upon as one of the more frivolous aspects of urban society in a world where Hitler had raised the flag of the Third Reich. Toward the end of this era, it was the gold diggers, the collaborators, and even the hookers who were depicted as hanging on to the more dramatic aspects of Deco style in fashion, like the ubiquitous exaggerated cigarette holders of the era.

BAKELITE AND OTHER COSTUME JEWELRY

As jewelry became more associated with "fashion" than with "investment," its styles came in and out of vogue more frequently. No longer did jewelry require the use of diamonds, gold, and other highly precious materials.

The use of silver and semiprecious materials by talented artists created a higher demand for popular fashion jewelry than ever before. In Mexico, William Spratling and others led the way in silver jewelry design. (See "Special Focus: Mexican Silver Jewelry.")

In the 1930s, Coco Chanel took the vogue for trendy jewelry to its logical conclusion and began producing elegant "costume" jewelry, intended to be worn only as long as it was in fashion.

The Depression brought new styles of costume jewelry, such as marcasite, which is a name given to crystallized iron pyrite when it is set in silver. When marcasite jewelry was introduced in France in the late 1920s, the American manufacturers soon followed their lead.

From a distance, a brooch set with hundreds of small marcasites appears to be shimmering with diamonds. Marcasite was even mounted on plastic jewelry of the era. Many marcasite designs have been re-created, and reproductions are widely available. On much of the new production, however, marcasites are glued in, rather than set in mounts. Older, elaborate pieces are less available, and unique pieces command strong prices.

However, the most accessible and collectible costume jewelry today is made of Bakelite and other plastics. This is the ultimate in costume jewelry. It is worn completely for effect, to enhance the costume, and in the spirit of colorful fun in which it was intended. One can find some examples of great design work in the harder-to-find pieces that have made their way up the price ladder.

In the 1920s, most plastic jewelry and plastic boudoir items like powder-puff boxes were made from celluloid. Sometimes celluloid was colored and carved to look like jade.

In the 1930s, jewelry made of Bakelite was introduced. Bakelite is the trade name for a synthetic plastic, made from formaldehyde and phenol, first discovered by Belgian chemist Leo H. Baekland in 1909. Numerous plastics with other trade names were also used to make jewelry, but collectors tend to refer to all of them as Bakelite.

Bakelite and other plastics could be produced in a number of different colors—yellow, black, brown, blue, red, and maroon. Later, colors such as ivory and tortoise shell were added. Plastics were baked to harden, and sliced into blanks that could then be carved into individual pieces of jewelry by machine. Translucent Bakelite was introduced in the late 1930s. There was also an "end of the day" color, created by mixing all the colors together, and colors could be laminated into one another, creating polka dots when the piece was sliced. Some of these colors and combinations are very rare and bring high prices.

Today, as prices on Bakelite jewelry continue to rise, an increasing number of fakes are on the market. Because Bakelite was processed in rods or sheets that were cut into blanks, there should be no "seam."

As we mentioned in the chapter "Fakes Alert!" another test that dealers and collectors use to determine if the piece is really Bakelite is to rub the piece between the thumb and forefinger, which might release the musty odor of the formaldehyde. In addition, a hot pin will not melt or burn into Bakelite as it will with celluloid or new plastic.

Since these tests can be embarrassing or impossible to perform in a dealer's shop, here are some other tips from Marsha Evaskus, owner of the shop Zig Zag in Chicago. Buy only from reputable dealers, and don't be afraid to ask questions. Also, be wary of too many rare pieces of Bakelite in one place, and of dealers who claim they've made a "warehouse find."

In pricing Bakelite, Evaskus offers the following general guidelines. Harder-to-find colors include red and black, and blue is extremely rare. The size of a piece or width of a bracelet can impact its value, but size isn't the sole determining factor, as some less interesting pieces can also be large. Carved bracelets and other pieces are more valuable than smooth ones, and the depth of the carving increases the value. Reverse carved pieces are hard to find, as are very good examples of the translucent Bakelite. With laminated pieces, the number of colors will have an impact on value. Figural pins are highly sought-after, especially dangling pins of fruit and vegetables.

FASHION, ACCESSORIES, AND COSTUME JEWELRY PRICE LISTINGS

A SELECTION OF FASHION AND ACCESSORY ENSEMBLES

Courtesy of Ruth Smiler

> Ruth Smiler is the owner of Glad Rags Fine Vintage Clothing and Antiques, which specializes in vintage fashions and accessories, fine and costume jewelry, dresser sets, bedspreads, linens, lace and more. You can contact her at Glad Rags, 6 State Street, Montpelier, VT 05602, (802) 223-1451.

"Evening Ensemble"

Evening Gown, c. 1925–1930. Size small. White silk satin, bias-cut. Sleeveless bodice with asymmetrical dropped waist, right hip accented with multiple parallel darts; two-tiered skirt. In fine condition. **$150–$175**

Evening jacket, c. 1925–1930. Size small. Red silk-wood velvet, lined in white silk charmeuse. Convertible stand-up shawl collar with deeply ruched detail. In fine condition. **$165–$190**

Cap, c. 1930. Crocheted rayon cord with oversized gathered rosette. **$14–$18**

Necklace, 1920s. Alternating red and black glass tubular beads strung on chain, with large pear-shaped red glass drop. **$35–$45**

"Evening Ensemble." *Courtesy of Glad Rags, Vermont. Photo by After Image Photography.*

"Fashion Ensemble." *Courtesy of Glad Rags, Vermont. Photo by After Image Photography.*

"Fashion Ensemble"

Three-piece ensemble, c. 1925–1930. Size small. Yellow silk chiffon dress with dropped waist, sleeveless, ivory linen handmade needle-lace shawl collar. Matching silk under-dress. Matching coat of watered silk, narrow shawl collar, oversized carved mother-of-pearl button forming asymmetrical closing accented by large self-fabric bow. Fine condition. $195–$225

Shawl/table cover, French, c. 1917–1920, approximately 45" square. Multicolor silk and gold lamé center with wide black chiffon bands and lamé corners. A very good example of the post–World War I luxury textiles whose development and marketing was subsidized by the French government to regain export-trade market after the war. In fine condition. $175–$200

Necklace, 1920s. Black faceted glass bead sautoir. $40–$50

Hat, c. 1930. Glazed straw, lucite ornament. In fine condition. $25–$35

"Wedding Ensemble"

Wedding dress, c. 1926, size extra-small. Silk velvet with asymmetrical, weighted, short hemline. Seed pearl embroidered detail at left hip accenting side drapery. V-neckline and wrists trimmed with extremely fine handmade Venice lace; wrists closed with tiny crocheted silk buttons. Underdress with scalloped hem, weights. Long train from shoulders, lined with ivory silk chiffon, ending in two tapered-point corners. Excellent condition.
                                                                                 $400–$500

"Wedding Ensemble."
*Courtesy of Glad Rags,
Vermont. Photo by
After Image Photography.*

Necklace, c. 1930s. Double-strand choker of faux pearls with green blown-glass ornament embellished with gilt brass filigree and pearl, rhinestones, ending in gilt chain
fringe pendant pearls. $50–$60

"Dresser Ensemble" (*See color section.*)

Dresser set, c. 1920s, tray size: 11½" long, 7½" wide. Three pieces: tray, hand mirror,
hairbrush. "La Futuriste" black Bakelite, accented with engraved and painted gold and
silver geometric motifs. Mirror has beveled glass; natural boar bristles in brush. Tray has
Bakelite frame and small feet surrounding a double layer of glass enclosing a geometric
patterned lace in ivory, gold, and black. In fine condition. $250–$300

Figurine, Czechoslovakian, c. 1925, 11" high. No mark, in very good condition with
minor restoration. $225–$250

Scarf, c. 1920s, 70" long, 8½" wide. Black silk and gold lamé in stylized pomegranate
pattern; fringed ends. In fine condition. $45–$65

Purse, c. 1925, 9" long, 6" wide. Snakeskin waltz bag with marcasite clasp with aqua-
marine glass cabochon star. Excellent condition. $175–$200

Hat, c. 1918–1920, 17" diameter. Cartwheel horsehair with egret feather pinwheel trim
surrounding crown. A fine example of the wide-brimmed hat that was soon superseded
by the famous cloche of the 1920s and 1930s, in fine condition. $200–$225

Curtain panels, each panel 46" long, 22" wide. Machine-lace in geometric pattern of
Mackintosh influence; handmade Battenburg lace borders. $18–$25

**"Accessories
Ensemble."**
*Courtesy of
Glad Rags,
Vermont.
Photo by
After Image
Photography.*

"Accessories Ensemble"

Curtain panels, see listing in previous ensemble.

Shoes/purse, c. 1925. Shoes are red leather with glass seed beads. Cuban heels. Beaded purse to match, velvet-lined. Excellent condition. Set.   **$350–$400**

Dresser tray and hairbrush, 1920s. Tray with glass center enclosing ivory lace with embroidered rosebud center. Brush has natural boar bristles. In very good condition.

Tray	**$45–$50**
Brush	**$30–$35**

Corsage, 1930s, from a gown. Silk geranium with velvet leaves.   **$20–$30**

Waxed silk leaves, c. 1915–1920. Millinery trim leaves.   **$12–$15**

OTHER ACCESSORIES

ANONYMOUS

Cigarette case, American, c. 1930, 6" long. Rectangular, in silver with geometric design in red, black and white eggshell lacquer, impressed marks.   **$400–$500**

Purse, beaded, American, c. 1926, 16" long. Gilt-metal and "jewel" mounted, worked with the pattern of a Persian rug in tones of red, gray, green, and gold suspending a long fringe; foliate-cast frame mounted with multicolored stones and white enameled foliate scrolls and suspending a similarly decorated ring; oval clasp mounted with a large red enameled "cabochon," and enameled flowers; frame inscribed "Bessie M. Grossman, December 31, 1926."   **$1,000 (Auction)**

Traveling toiletries case, Austria, c. 1920. Fitted with nine cut-glass bottles and sterling silver engraved covers, an alarm clock, three brushes with ivorine handles, manicure set, sewing kit, shoehorn, glove stretcher, sterling silver frame, mirror, desk blotter, comb, and three jewelry boxes, lined in taupe leather and cordovan-color leather case, keys included, with canvas and felt leather trim outer case (one glass chipped), hallmarked.

$800 (Auction)

DOMINIQUE ALONZO (French, work: 1912–1926)

Desk set, inkwell, 15¼" long. A gilt bronze desk set, cast from a model by D. Alonzo, comprising a double inkwell, rocker blotter, seal, and letter opener, all cast with thistles, each signed with maker's name.

$500 (Auction)

CARTIER (French, founded 1847)

Vanity case, rectangular with black enamel borders, jade corners, central panel of carved and pierced jade, pavé diamond thumbpiece, the interior with fitted mirror, lipstick and powder compartments, signed "Cartier, Paris, Londres, New York, Made in France, 0772."

$8,500 (Auction)

HAGENAUER (Austrian, 1920s–1930s)

Mirror, 24½" high. In chrome, the rectangular mirror held in the arms of a stylized woman resting her chin on her hands, raised on a bracket base, impressed with Hagenauer/Wiener Werkstätte mark, "Franz Hagenauer Wien Made in France."

$400 (Auction)

Mirror, 13⅜" high. In a nickel finish, the circular mirror supported by a stylized giraffe, impressed "wHw."

$1,600 (Auction)

HERMES (French)

Desk set, letterfile: 7½" high. Crocodile desk set, comprising an inkstand with clock, cigarette box, pair of bookends, letterfile, pad holder, writing pad monogrammed "ESW," seal with same monogram, letter opener and scissors, pen holder, blotter and candlestick, all covered with crocodile skin, stamped "Hermes-Paris Deposé."

$4,200 (Auction)

PAUL FRANKL (American, 1878–1962)

Vanity set, mirror: 11" long. Celluloid vanity set, designed for the Celluloid Corporation of America, produced by Rond Amerith. Comprising a brush, mirror, powder box, nail buffer, and shoehorn, the pale green celluloid with aluminum and black plastic inlays, with dark semicircular appliques, impressed with firm's mark.

$300 (Auction)

VAN CLEEF & ARPELS (French, founded 1904)

Lighter, c. 1940s. Engine-turned metal case with gold accents and navette-shaped blue stones, stamped "Styptor, VCA no. 39088."

$275 (Auction)

WINTZ (French)

Box, cinnabar and black lacquer box, with eighteen-karat gold and coral details, coral bead feet on gray agate platform, with carved jade animal pulls, French hallmark, retailed by Blums Inc., Chicago, in original fitted leather case. $5,000 (Auction)

OTHER CLOTHING

ANONYMOUS

Day dress, c. 1925–1930, size small. Natural silk pongee. Long sleeves, dropped waist, knee-length skirt with pleated front panel. Embroidered with pale blue and lavender silk rosebuds on bodice front and cuffs. Simple turned-back pointed collar. Shoulders and sleeves smocked with blue silk. Very good condition.   **$60–$80**

Dress, c. 1920s, size 12–14. Black beaded chiffon, neck and hip detail in pink, blue, and purple floral bands, overall black and gold beaded detail, minor wear.   **$375 (Auction)**

Dress, c. 1918–1920, size large. Violet blue silk cut-velvet "flapper," sleeveless; drapery neckline; asymmetrical hem skirt falling from a low dropped waistline. Matching underdress with cut-velvet panel at bottom. Cut-velvet pattern resembles tumbled pitted olives—very unusual. Repaired neckline on underdress.   **$160–$180**

Evening gown, c. mid-1930s, size extra-small. Silk and gold lamé; bias-cut full-length. Sleeveless bodice with raised waist, shawl collar. Bubble pattern fabric in bronze, beige, and gold. In fine condition.   **$125–$150**

Linen suit, c. 1930, size medium. Ivory color, tailored, straight long jacket, mid-thigh length, unlined; patch pockets, square pilgrim collar; hook closure at throat. Skirt slightly A-line with deep reverse pleats at center front and back. In fine condition.   **$125–$150**

Man's suit, c. 1920, size small. Double-breasted off-white "Palm Beach," mohair-linen blend fabric. Oversized mother-of-pearl buttons. Trousers with pleats, cuffs, button fly. In fine condition.   **$125–$150**

Opera coat, c. 1920, size medium. White silk and gold lamé brocade. Knee-length with single-button closure at throat. White ermine collar; loose-fitting with full bishop sleeves; lined in cream-colored silk velvet. Good condition, two large pale stains.   **$75–$100**
                                    If in fine condition   **$200–$250**

Shift, c. 1920s, size 8. Black beaded chiffon accented with pink, blue, green, and orange floral sprays, some minor bead loss. (*See photo, below.*)   **$400 (Auction)**

Dress and shift in beaded chiffon.
Courtesy of Skinner, Inc.,
Massachusetts.

BAKELITE JEWELRY

Bracelet, striped. 1½–2" wide. Using various colors in four- or six-color combinations, depending on the width and the number of colors. $450–$575

Bracelet, "bow-tie" pattern. 1" wide and wider. Using multicolored plastic, depending on the width and the number of colors. $425–$700

Bracelet, "polka dot" pattern. 1" wide and wider. Depending on the color, width, and number of polka dots. $175–$275

Bracelet, carved. 1" wide and wider. Various colors, depending on the quality, depth, and complexity of the carving.

Fine and rare examples	$300–$650
Very good examples	$150–$250
Good examples, smaller widths	$75–$150

Bracelet, plain. Various colors, depending on the color and width. $30–$75

Necklace, designed as a row of cherries (simple red balls). $125–$175

Necklace, German, combination of chrome and Bakelite in geometric designs, rare.
$175–$375

Pin, "Bananas," designed as a hanging pin. $300–$400

Pin, "Banana," designed as single banana. $175–$275

Pin, "Cherry," designed as a hanging pin, depending on whether there is a stem and/or a notched leaf. $175–$275

Pin, "Cherry," designed as hanging from a log. $125–$175

Pin, "Hat," approximately 2–3" diameter, with dangling cherries, bananas, or pineapples. A fine example of a Bakelite hatpin. $375–$450

Pin, "Hat," approximately 2–3" diameter, plain color, depending on the color and styling.
$150–$300

Pin, "Horse," approximately 2½" long. Side profile of a full figure of a horse with a metal bridle. A fine example of a Bakelite figural pin. $275–$350

Pin, "Horse," designed as just the horse's head. $175–$250

Pin, "Strawberry," designed as a clip pin. $175–$200

SPECIAL FOCUS
MESH PURSES
by Mike and Sherry Miller

Mike and Sherry Miller have been collectors of mesh purses for over twenty years. Their collection numbers close to six hundred different designs, including many Art Deco designs of Whiting & Davis. You can contact them at 303 Holiday Drive, Tuscola, IL 61953, (217) 253-4991.

When you think of graphic designers in the American Art Deco period, names like John Vassos, Ruth Reeves, and Joseph Binder may come to mind. These are names that are familiar to Deco enthusiasts. Although his work never graced the cover of *The New Yorker*, and while he is not generally thought of in the same vein as the designers mentioned, Charles Whiting also deserves recognition as an important Deco designer.

Through his company, Whiting & Davis, Charles Whiting became one of the most prolific graphic designers of the Deco period. Hundreds of his original designs dangled from the wrists of fashion-conscious women of the 1920s in the form of that "moderne" necessity, the metal mesh purse.

The firm was originally founded in 1876 in Plainville, Massachusetts, by Edward P. Davis and William H. Wade. The company manufactured jewelry and was known as Wade, Davis Company. In 1880, Charles Whiting joined the company and worked his way up from office boy to partner in 1890. In 1896, he bought out Wade, and the company was renamed Whiting & Davis Company. In 1907, Whiting bought out Davis but made no change in the company's name out of respect and friendship for his former partner. The company remains in business today as Whiting & Davis Company, Inc., and continues to manufacture mesh purses and other items.

Metal mesh had literally been around since the Dark Ages when it was rediscovered in the late 1800s as a fabric for women's purses. The same sort of metal ring mesh used to make chain mail worn by medieval knights was used to make the first mesh purses. Later another type of mesh, alternatively called fish-scale mesh, armor mesh, or flat mesh, was used. Flat mesh consists of series of cruciform links or "spiders," joined with small rings to create a metal fabric.

At first, mesh purses were expensive and difficult to produce, as each was made by hand. Whiting saw the opportunity to reach a mass market with this product, and invested in the research and development of machinery to manufacture mesh. In 1910, the first practical machine to make mesh fabric was patented. Lower retail prices resulted, and Whiting launched an extensive advertising campaign for the purses which used Broadway and Hollywood celebrities to promote the bags as an important part of a woman's evening attire. The moderately priced (around $5–$20) bags were distributed through jewelry and better department stores. Sears and Montgomery Ward also offered Whiting & Davis mesh bags through their catalogues. Some of these bags were offered at lower prices, and sometimes were not marked "Whiting & Davis."

The flat metal surface of armor mesh presented an ideal medium for both geometric and curvilinear designs in bold enamel paints. When daring flapper fashions demanded equally flamboyant accessories, mesh purses were "the cat's pajamas." Mesh bags were the perfect complement to costumes of well-dressed women of the era. Even the painted ring mesh purses, reminiscent of Impressionist paintings, were given a new Deco look with the addition of frames with striking geometric shapes. Mesh bags became haute couture among the fashion elite and a must for the wardrobe of the smartly dressed woman.

Mesh bags grew so popular that by 1928, Whiting & Davis was operating five hundred mesh machines to stay abreast of the demand. In 1929, Whiting & Davis commissioned the well-known French fashion designer Paul Poiret to create bag designs and Deco-styled frames as well.

The Mandalian Manufacturing Company was Whiting & Davis's only major competitor for mesh purposes. Although quite attractive in their own right, Mandalian designs tended more toward Victorian florals and Oriental rug patterns than Deco. Other mesh purse manufacturers include Napier-Bliss, R&G Company, and Evans. Only Evans produced some Deco-design pieces among the relatively few bags it made. Evans purchased their mesh from Mandalian or Whiting & Davis, but the designs of their Deco bags lacked diversity and flair and they were generally not marked. A small number of ring mesh purses also found their way to the United States from France and Germany, and some of these reflect Deco influence in their design.

Many of the mesh bags made by Whiting & Davis have survived in mint condition due in part to their popularity and to the large number that were made. Also, mesh bags were touted as gifts for special occasions and consequently were saved as treasured heirlooms or prized remembrances. And, although they appear to be somewhat fragile because of the delicate-looking enameling, they are very durable. After all, mesh bags were made entirely of metal and the enamel paints were furnace-fired. Occasionally, original silk linings and small beveled glass mirrors are still inside the bags. You might even find a bag with the maker's celluloid or paper tag still attached.

Mesh bags can be found at general-line antique shops, estate sales, and auctions, as well as at flea markets and antiques shows. Some collectors even find Goodwill stores, secondhand clothing stores, and vintage clothing shops worthwhile sources. However, since Deco-design bags comprise only a small portion of the mesh bags produced, dealers who specialize in purses are the best sources for such pieces. Typically, purse dealers buy through a network of other general-line dealers. It is not unusual for purse dealers to purchase for their own inventory all of the better mesh bags at a show or at all the shops in an area.

Today, Art Deco mesh bags are enjoying a strong revival of interest by collectors. Some people buy them to complement their vintage clothing for an Art Deco ball, while others hang them on the wall or display their collection as a colorful and "jazzy" reminder of an era gone by. Either way, they make an attractive, fascinating Art Deco collectible whose value is bound to continue rising in the years ahead.

SEVEN MESH PURSE SHOPPING TIPS

1. When purchasing from a purse dealer, you can expect to pay generally $100–$250 for an Art Deco mesh bag in mint or near-mint condition. Rare or outstanding purses may command $300–$400 or more in today's market. Prices do vary from one part of the country to another, with the East and West coasts and the Southwest tending to be the highest-priced areas, and the Midwest and South more moderate.

2. The value of a mesh bag depends on many of the factors noted below. However, higher-priced mesh bags may have one or more of these special features: elaborate or painted frames; frames set with stones in paste, marcasite, coral, carnelian, or other semiprecious stones; complex or stunning painted patterns, or even rarer figural Deco designs. Some collectors are willing to pay a little more if the bag has its original silk lining, although not all bags were lined originally. The size of the bag is a factor as well, with larger sizes bringing slightly more than smaller ones.

3. The condition of Art Deco mesh bags has an important impact on their value. The most critical aspect of condition is the enameling, which may have suffered from fading by sunlight or wear from handling. Check the top of the mesh where it joins the frame, and also under the hinges. Look closely at the mesh overall, since the exposed metal may have darkened and the wear might be "hidden" in the painted pattern. A novice collector might not be able to tell if the bag has faded uniformly overall. Look closely at the edges of the individual links to see if the paint is worn.

4. Other aspects of condition to note: Does the hinge close properly? Is the original chain handle present? In some cases another type of chain has been substituted for the original chain handle. Have the links pulled away from one another? Again, check under the hinges especially. Pulled links can be replaced, but missing links are hard to replace.

5. Try to buy mesh bags in the best condition you can find them. If they are more common styles, don't settle for less than near-mint. However, if it is an unusual or especially eye-catching design, you can relax your standards a bit and buy it, because you probably won't see it again. Some collectors buy purses in bad condition for the parts, but unless you are ready to learn the difficult art of purse repair, we don't recommend this practice.

6. To identify the origin of a mesh bag, you should note that the vast majority of Art Deco mesh bags were produced by Whiting & Davis, and most of their bags are marked (you may find some that have lost their little tag). Foreign-made bags are marked inside the frame with the country of origin ("Germany," "France," etc.), while the domestically made bags are marked with the maker's name.

7. Here are some guidelines for determining the approximate date of an Art Deco mesh purse. The first evidence of enamel-painted mesh bags appeared in Whiting & Davis advertisements in 1924. These first designs were very plain, but Deco designs soon followed within the next few years. Whiting & Davis attached a

small metal tag with their trademark inside the purse and later stamped the trademark inside the frame. Purses from the 1920s and early 1930s are longer than they are wide. In 1929, Paul Poiret designed "pouch style" purses for Whiting & Davis, which are wider than they are long, and which may also have attractive Art Deco designs.

To help in establishing values for mesh bags, consider the following illustrations (*See also color section*):

More common Art Deco mesh bag designs are often symmetrical patterns with a simple gold or silver frame. *Courtesy of Mike and Sherry Miller, Illinois.*

An unusual design, using a swirling painted motif. This mesh bag also has an elaborately painted angular frame. *Courtesy of Mike and Sherry Miller, Illinois.*

Finer, higher-priced Art Deco mesh bags may include some of the features shown here:

Another unusual and rare asymmetrical design composed of elongated diamonds and triangles in several colors. The rigid handle is original and rare. *Courtesy of Mike and Sherry Miller, Illinois.*

A rare figural design, depicting a dragon. This frame is also set with a swinging, carved ornament. *Courtesy of Mike and Sherry Miller, Illinois.*

Note: *With special thanks to the Chicago Art Deco Society for the portions of this article, which originally appeared in their newsletter CADS News.*

SPECIAL FOCUS
MEXICAN SILVER JEWELRY
by Carole A. Berk and Penny Morrill

Carole A. Berk, Ltd., is a dealership in 20th-century decorative arts, offering a wide variety of furniture, ceramics, metalwork, glass, and jewelry, with specializations in several areas, including Mexican silvery jewelry. Contact Carole Berk or Penny Morrill at Carole A. Berk, Ltd., 8020 Norfolk Avenue, Bethesda, MD 20814, (301) 656-0355, fax: (301) 986-8776. Special photos for this section were provided by Luisa DiPietro of Shadowfax Studio, Silver Spring, Maryland, specializing in antiques and jewelry, (301) 589-9111.

In the early years of the 20th century in Mexico, the scene was set for a social and artistic revolution. Conditions that resulted in widespread dissatisfaction and unrest culminated in the overthrow of Porfirio Diaz in 1911, and then were exacerbated by the murder of Francisco Madero by Victoriano Huerta in 1913. The heroes of the revolution were Pancho Villa, Emiliano Zapata, and, later, the much-loved American ambassador to Mexico, Dwight Morrow. A new constitution was written in 1917, and Mexico began the process of democratization.

The revolution brought about an extraordinary burst of creativity and excitement. This Mexican Renaissance focused world attention on the great muralists Diego Rivera, José Orozco, and David Alfaro-Siquieros, and on the artists Frida Kahlo, Miguel Covarrubias, Rufino Tamayo, and Carlos Merida. It is no wonder that artists from Europe and the United States were drawn to Mexico in this time of cross-fertilization and inspiration. Silver artists were no exception.

FREDERICK DAVIS

In the 1920s, Frederick Davis, an American, was manager of the Sonora News Company's store in the Palacio Iturbide in Mexico City. Davis's appreciation for Mexican folk art and for the work of the extraordinarily gifted Mexican painters was reflected in what he chose to display. Davis was the first to employ silversmiths to carry out designs for silver jewelry based on pre-Columbian motifs, and his work was received with acclaim.

The silver jewelry that was designed by Davis and produced by native artisans was technically well-made. The necklaces and bracelets have a recognizable elegance of line, reflecting the designer's hand. There is a naiveté and liveliness that indicates Davis's willingness to give the artisans the freedom to participate in the creative process.

Today, Davis is one of the most admired artists of Mexican silver, along with William Spratling, Hector Aguilar, and Antonio Pineda, and with strong interest in the work of Los Castillo, Matilde Poulat, and Margot de Taxco. While there were literally hundreds of other silver artists in Mexico from 1930 to 1960, and a growing number of collectors for Mexican silver in general, these are the ones most sought after by collectors today.

WILLIAM SPRATLING

William Spratling had come to Mexico from Tulane University's School of Architecture to write and teach. In 1929, he bought a house in the old silver mining town of Taxco and began writing *Little Mexico*, a book that is now considered a classic study of that country. On a visit, Dwight Morrow recommended to Spratling that he open a silver workshop in Taxco. In establishing his atelier, Las Delicias, Spratling became the catalyst for a reaffirmation of an ancient cultural tradition.

In the beginning, Spratling rented a three-story building as a workshop. The jewelry he made was heavy, all done by hand in almost pure silver and signed simply with a "WS." From its modest beginning, Las Delicias grew in less than ten years to include almost a hundred silversmiths and a number of other artisans who produced hand-loomed rugs and blankets, articles made of tin, and hand-carved wooden furniture. During the first half of the 1940s, there were almost four hundred silversmiths employed in the workshop, which was then called Spratling y Artesanos.

The earliest pieces Spratling designed reflected the influence of international trends that ultimately shaped his creative vision. The vocabulary of the Bauhaus and Art Deco movements are expressed in the flowering line, perfect proportions, and simple, refined elegance of each of his designs, which are works of art in silver. They are simple, direct, and powerful.

He only used the traditional materials of the region, but in new creative ways: rosewood handles for salad sets, amethyst quartz, tortoise shell, and obsidian combined with silver for earrings and brooches. Although many of the pieces were influenced by pre-Columbian art, there is a definite Spratling style which some have described as a refined simplicity—a restraint of decoration and unnecessary detail.

During World War II, Spratling silver was in tremendous demand. A contract was signed with Montgomery Ward to provide jewelry, flatware, and hollowware; and these designs appeared in the Ward catalogues.

His sun and moon earrings, necklaces of amethysts held in silver hands, and pins that depict Aztec gods are wearable art. However, his work is collected not only for its design impact, but for what he accomplished—the establishment of the silver industry in Taxco. Both Spratling and Davis discovered and admired the artistry of the Mexican people, and today, they are revered for having provided a livelihood for hundreds of artisans.

Spratling fostered the work of the really gifted designers. He had a profound appreciation for the Mexican aesthetic and inspired the artists in his workshop to use their own imaginations in the production of silver jewelry. By 1940, as a result of their training and with Spratling's blessing, many of his silversmiths went on to form their own ateliers, including Hector Aguilar, members of the Castillo family whose hallmark is Los Castillo, Salvador Teran, and Enrique Ledesma.

HECTOR AGUILAR

Hector Aguilar worked closely with William Spratling as manager of Taller de las Delicias. He went out on his own in the late 1930s, establishing his Taller Borda in the Borda Palace on the Zocalo. His early work, however, was quite reminiscent of Spratling's.

Simplicity and strength of design characterize his work. His powerful designs are much closer to the heart of Mexico, inspired primarily by pre-Columbian and colonial Mexican models. His silver jewelry, hollowware, and tableware are heavy, and until after World War II, mostly in .980 or .940 silver.

The bracelets by Hector Aguilar take the shape of repeating two-dimensional motifs, either alternating balls and rectangular units or alternating units derived from pre-Columbian clay seals. His brooches represent strong Aztec images, and with these cast pieces, he used oxidized line to provide texture. The handles of knives and forks are very heavy and the design is simple and direct, obviously Aztec in derivation. His mark can also be found on copper candlesticks, wall sconces, large faceted mirrors, and curio cabinets.

ANTONIO PINEDA

What is intriguing about Antonio Pineda is that he was an artist first, having attended art school in Taxco and studied with David Alfaro Siquieros before working with Spratling. In fact, at one time, he produced a number of sculptures in silver. Antonio opened his shop in 1941.

Pineda's approach reflects a more international vision and remarkable technique. His settings for stones in bracelets and necklaces are technically so complex that at times the stones seem to float in the silver setting.

Another aspect of Pineda's work which is remarkable is its variety. Inspiration came from many sources. He has created large centerpieces which are abstract sculptures in silver or in silver combined with copper or tin. He articulated pre-Columbian forms, and other bracelets and necklaces with smooth, planar, and highly polished surfaces. His jewelry which is cast and is often hollow has mass, but is not heavy either in weight or appearance. Stones are incorporated into the design, but the overall composition remains the most important element.

LOS CASTILLO

The Castillo brothers, Antonio, Miguel, Justo, and Jorge, were teenagers when they started their apprenticeship with William Spratling. Their own atelier, Los Castillo, was characterized by experimentation from the beginning.

They have produced jewelry which combines metals as well as stone and shell, and their decorative pieces can be spectacular. Los Castillo earrings and pins of turquoise, conch, and particularly feather inlay were made according to Indian methods. Enamel on silver was first done at Los Castillo, as was the jewelry made of onyx encrusted with silver.

One of the most innovative techniques inherited from the past was the *metales casados*, or "married metals." Metals as diverse as nickel and bronze, silver and steel, or silver and gold were fused with little or no soldering. Los Castillo continues up to the present to innovate with new materials and design motifs.

MARGOT DE TAXCO

Margot Carr Banburges arrived in Mexico from San Francisco in the 1920s. She married Antonio Castillo and worked closely with him as a designer for Los Castillo from the late 1930s and into the 1940s.

Margot established her own atelier in the late 1940s with a number of silversmiths who had trained with Spratling and at Los Castillo. Among them were Arturo Sorio, Manuel Robles, and Miguel Melendez. According to Melendez, Margot did all the design work. However, Margot owes much to the men who worked under her, for they did provide her with jewelry that is unsurpassed in mastery of technique.

She drew on a number of sources as influences in her work with silver. Her jewelry reflects an understanding of the simple elegance of Oriental art and Art Deco's pattern, color, and movement. Margot de Taxco produced jewelry which was distinctive and technically perfect. Her work is destined to become more respected and collectible.

MATILDE POULAT

"MATL"—the unusual signature of Matilde Poulat—is indicative of a unique approach to silver jewelry. In a 1955 article on contemporary Mexican silver, William Spratling described how Matilde Poulat had combined her own creativity with the whimsy of Mexican folk art to produce works of art in silver: "She has continued to produce some of the most charming native jewelry in Mexico, intensely Mexican and intensely her own. Her jewelry has the same charm and delight, surface and colorful quality as the old lacquer work from Uruapan."

Matilde Poulat was trained as an artist and began working in silver in 1934. With her nephew, Ricardo Salas, she opened a shop in Mexico City in 1950. After her death in 1960, Ricardo Salas continued the tradition, and the signature pieces are still being produced today.

What characterizes the work of Matilde Poulat is the use of a vocabulary of motifs taken from the Mexican tradition. The silver necklaces, bracelets, earrings, and small religious figures are formed in repoussé, then encrusted with bits of turquoise and coral, square-cut amethyst quartz, and curling silver wire in an all-over pattern. This approach is derived from an early 18th-century Rococo style, Churrigueresque, based on the work of a Catalan architect and enthusiastically taken up by Mexican architects and artisans. Examples of this style can be found on church façades in Taxco, Ocotlan, and Tepozotlan.

Matilde found inspiration in the cache of pre-Columbian gold jewelry unearthed at Monte Alban in the 1930s. Roses and doves, shells and cascableles (tiny bells) are found often in her jewelry and impart a sense of gaiety and naiveté, although the overall effect of one of her multi-tiered necklaces can be spectacular.

Today, the excitement of collecting Mexican silver jewelry is based in part on the unique talents of designers such as these. The principal artists approached the medium in unique ways so that the work of a particular artist in silver can be identified, compared, appreciated, and collected.

While the most serious collectors are primarily interested in signed pieces by major artists, many collectors today find pleasure in collecting lesser-known artists and even well-made anonymous pieces. It is such a fascinating field that even a casual collector often will want to learn even more about Mexican silver.

For years, the American market was flooded with cheap imitations of Spratling designs, and so there was a stigma of poor craftsmanship, design, and low silver content attached to "Mexican silver." This stigma is being removed as a result of a growing appreciation for the high quality and design of the better silver artists. Collectors are learning to distinguish between the commonplace and the innovative work of the best artists. Mexican silver is now considered on a par with other silver that has always been collectible, such as the work of the Scandinavians.

Although not all of the designs can be called "Art Deco," the 1930s and early 1940s saw a rich and varied production of work in the international style of the day. Even the silver with more traditional Mexican motifs can have a modern feeling, especially because many Mexican motifs were adopted by European artists of the Art Deco period.

The market for Mexican silver is becoming more and more established every day. The work of William Spratling, Hector Aguilar, and Antonio Pineda will continue to be highly prized, and the less-well-known artists will begin to rise in popularity and price. Until recently, jewelry has been the most popular, but collectors are now seeking objects in silver as well—hollowware and flatware. Another important sign to watch for in the collecting field as its popularity grows is the more frequent appearance of Mexican silver at auction.

FIVE MEXICAN SILVER SHOPPING TIPS

1. Don't be in a hurry to buy. Educate yourself by looking at a lot of Mexican silver. Feel it, touch it, and examine it. Buy from a reputable source that will stand behind each piece. Most importantly, ask questions.

2. To identify Mexican silver, become familiar with each of the distinctive hallmarks the silversmiths in Taxco used. Spratling used several different marks over the years, either a simple "WS," "Spratling Silver," or his initials inscribed inside a circle. Hector Aguilar's signature, an "H" and "A" that are linked, changed slightly to become more stylized. The Castillo brothers always signed their work "Los Castillo," but the marks varied. Antonio Pineda and Margot de Taxco made no changes to their signature marks over the years. These last three artisans also numbered each of their designs. Most of this silver is marked "Taxco."

3. In terms of condition, a collector of Mexican silver should look for small indications that a piece has been tampered with in some way. For instance, a necklace may have the look of a Margot enamel but not the hallmark because the previous owner may have shortened the necklace, removing the link with the mark on the back. There might be a dramatic element in a necklace which you recognize from other pieces by that artist, but the attached chain does not seem compatible in any way. This change implies that a single piece was broken up to make more than one. To avoid being duped, study by looking at as many pieces by a favorite artist as possible.

4. Beware of replicas, reproductions, and "lookalikes." There are innumerable replicas of Spratling designs made by other artisans who had worked in his atelier, down to the appearance and their hallmarks. One artisan actually had the initials "SM," and he made his signature so much like Spratling's that his "SM" looks exactly like "WS" upside down.

Fred Davis was at Sanborn's for a number of years, but if a piece is marked "Sanborn's," do not assume that it was made under his supervision.

There have been replicas of Spratling's designs made recently by the "Sucedores de William Spratling, S.A.," but these are specifically marked "TS-24." Margot de Taxco's enamel serpent necklace has also been replicated in the last several years.

Los Castillo is the only atelier still operating according to the model initiated by Spratling, a workshop with a master silversmith who supervises and teaches artisans. Therefore, the new work by the Castillos is as fine as pieces produced fifty years ago.

5. Overall, the best advice is to buy what you like. Designs by Mexican silversmiths are varied enough to offer something for everyone—from jewelry and objects inspired by pre-Columbian manuscripts to more international styles and trends such as Art Deco and "1950s Modern."

MEXICAN SILVER JEWELRY PRICE LISTINGS
(Alphabetically by designer)

HECTOR AGUILAR (Mexican, work: 1930s–1960s)

Belt, c. 1950. Simple buckle, but remarkable five large silver X's on belt, with slightly curved lines and enhanced with asymmetrical incising. Mark on buckle "Taller Borda, 940, HA, Taxco, Mexico" with eagle stamp.   **$1,100–$1,200**

Pin, c. 1940. Traditional, elegant orchid with undulating form and incised lines. Marked "Made in Mexico, HA, Sterling."   **$400–$450**

Pin, c. 1940. Handsome and unusual pyramidal shape, with forms that are like large leaves of a cactus plant. Marked "Made in Mexico, HA, Sterling."   **$600–$650**

Pin, c. 1945. Large stylized flower in repoussé. Marked "Made in Mexico, Sterling, HA."   **$350–$400**

Pin, c. 1945. Unusual design for Aguilar: branch with four silver leaves and five round onyx flower buds. Marked "Made in Mexico, Sterling," around "HA."   **$650–$700**

FREDERICK DAVIS (American, d. 1961)

Box, c. 1930–1935, 3⅝" long, 2⅛" wide, 1⅜" deep. In silver, with carved obsidian face mask in the center of the top. Marked "FD." (*See photo, page 258.*)   **$750–$800**

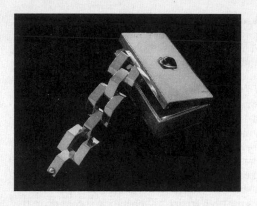

Silver box and bracelet by Frederick Davis.
Courtesy of Carole A. Berk, Ltd., Maryland. Photo by Shadowfax Studio.

Bracelet, c. 1935. Composed of three-dimensional hinged triangular silver shapes, alternating one, then two. When worn, edges of triangles sit out away from the wrist in a very dramatic and sculptural effect. In the original Sanborn's box. Marked "Sterling, Mexico, FD." (*See photo, above.*)   **$950–$1,000**

Pin, c. 1932. Small circular pin decorated with silhouetted forms of a Mexican man seated next to a cactus.   **$375–$400**

Pin, c. 1935. Very large rectangular-cut amethyst surrounded by silver shapes that resemble fleurs-de-lis. Marked "FD Silver Mexico."   **$1,100–$1,200**

LOS CASTILLO (Mexican brothers, work: 1930s–present)

Bracelet, c. 1940. Beautifully hinged bracelet, comprising small silver leaves. Marked "Los Castillo, Taxco, Sterling, Mexico, #329."   **$475–$525**

Bracelet, c. 1940. Heavy bracelet of hinged leaf shapes. Marked "Sterling, Made in Mexico, Los Castillo, Taxco, #560."   **$1,200–$1,300**

Clip pin, c. 1942. Designed as a large flower with three large leaves, and stamens extending beyond the flower. Fine, undulating lines. Marked "Los Castillo, Taxco, Sterling, Made in Mexico, #460."   **$250–$300**

Necklace, c. 1940. Heavy silver necklace of repeating stylized rectangular forms, a pre-Columbian motif. Marked "Los Castillo, Taxco, Sterling, Made in Mexico, #480."
                    $800–$900

Necklace, c. 1950. Heavy necklace, ornate baroque forms ornamented with balls of silver. Medallion is hinged in the center. Marked "Sterling, Made in Mexico, Los Castillo, Taxco," eagle stamp, "#395."   **$1,100–$1,200**
                    With matching cuff   **$1,800–$2,000**

Pin, c. 1940. Designed as two fish with heavily incised scales surrounded by waves. Probably designed by Margot de Taxco at the Castillo workshop. Marked "Los Castillo, Taxco, Sterling, Mexico, #106." An early piece.   **$300–$350**

Pin, c. 1940. Curved baroque setting for three large amethyst cabochons. Marked "Los Castillo Taxco Sterling Made in Mexico, #385." $350–$400

MARGOT DE TAXCO (American, work: 1930s–1960s)

Bracelet, c. 1948. Designed as large circular shapes in four colors of enamel with dots of silver. Marked "Margot de Taxco, Sterling, Made in Mexico." $400–$450

Necklace, c. 1948. Designed as hinged double rectangles of black enamel on silver. Marked "Margot de Taxco, #5897, Made in Mexico, Sterling," with eagle stamp.
$300–$350

Necklace, 1950s. Vermeil necklace of tiny paired rose blossoms. Marked "Margot de Taxco, Sterling, Made in Mexico, #5194." $450–$500

Pin, c. 1940s. A rose—very formal and traditional. Marked "Margot de Taxco, #5352, Hecho en Mexico," around eagle stamp. $125–$150

Zodiac pendant, c. 1950. Pendant with swinging scales for "Libra," with star and zodiac symbol as others in this series. Marked "#5226, Margot de Taxco, Sterling, Made in Mexico" around eagle stamp. $400–$425

ANTONIO PINEDA (Mexican, work: 1940s–1960s)

Bracelet, c. 1950. Beautiful and heavy, composed of horseshoe shapes. Marked with Antonio crown mark, "Taxco," eagle stamp, and "970." A technically perfect piece.
$675–$700

Bracelet, c. 1950. Design as six egg-shaped cut amethysts in sterling setting of thin silver outlines. Stones seem to be wrapped in silver frame. Marked with Antonio crown signature, "925, Taxco, Sterling," eagle stamp. $875–$925

Bracelet, c. 1950. Designed as pear-shaped amethysts, set in X's of hollow silver. Marked "Silver, 970, ZZ, #700, Sterling, Mexico" with Antonio crown mark and eagle stamp. A beautiful combination of exacting design and technique. $1,600–$1,800

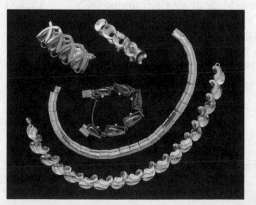

Silver necklaces
and bracelets by
Antonio Pineda.
Courtesy of
Carole A. Berk, Ltd.,
Maryland. Photo by
Shadowfax Studio.

Necklace, c. 1948. Composed of trapezoid shapes. Marked "Antonio, Taxco" (in crown-shaped mark), "Hecho en Mexico," eagle stamp, and "970." A beautiful, almost pure silver necklace.   **$1,200–$1,300**

Necklace, c. 1955. Designed as linked heavy leaf forms with incised lines ending in small cabochons of Chilean lapis. Marked "Silver, 970 Hecho en Mexico," and Antonio crown mark and eagle stamp.   **$1,200–$1,300**

MATILDE POULAT ("MATL," Mexican, d. 1960)
Bracelet, c. 1940–1945. Large motif in center of bracelet with dove surrounded with turquoise; on either side, small curling forms linked and each decorated with coral. Marked "Matl, 0.925."   **$775–$825**

Bracelet, c. 1950. Four panels, two with doves set in coral. Marked "MATL, 925, Hecho en Mexico, D.F. Old Matl."   **$650–$750**

Pin, c. 1940. Square-shaped with a rectangular-cut amethyst in the center. Also has a typical ornamentation of small pieces of coral and turquoise, three dangles. Marked "Mexico, 925, Matl."   **$400–$450**

WILLIAM SPRATLING (American, 1900–1967)
Bracelet, c. 1959, 7½" long, ⅞" wide. Sterling silver bangle, formed as three silver bands joined together by circular silver motif at alternating heights.   **$2,000–$2,250**

Bracelet, c. 1940. Very unusual sterling bracelet; wedges of green and blue stone set in silver. Abstract forms with incised lines down the center. Marked "Made in Mexico" around "WS."   **$1,800–$1,900**

Cuff, c. 1937. Early design by Spratling, with incised lines and with the waves of the lines interrupted by half-spheres. Marked "WS, Mexico, 980."   **$1,200–$1,300**

Earrings and necklace, c. 1942. Earrings formed as a silver hand with an amethyst drop. Necklace designed as series of hand-made silver balls from large to small, centering on a large amethyst cabochon held by silver hands which are each surmounted by a smaller amethyst. All marked "Spratling, Made in Mexico" around "WS."   **$2,800–$3,000**

Earrings, c. 1938. Swirling shape in silver with incised line down the center. Edge is ornamented with a thin silver wire and tiny silver balls. One marked "Spratling, Made in Mexico" around "WS," and other marked "Sterling."   **$275–$325**

Earrings, c. 1950. Designed as six circles of silver on raised silver wires, shaped like a crown. One marked with the eagle stamp and the other "William Spratling, Taxco" around "WS 925."   **$150–$200**

Earrings, c. 1955. Designed in simple, elegant shape made up of opposing swirls of silver. One marked with the eagle stamp and the other "William Spratling, Taxco" around "925" and script "WS."   **$400–$450**

Silver pin in the shape of a
clown by William Spratling.
*Courtesy of Rosebud Gallery,
California.*

Pin, c. 1938, 4⅜" long, 2⅝" wide. Sterling with copper overlay, in the shape of a clown in full costume.   **$1,200–$1,300**

Pin, c. 1942. Circular, with raised depiction of the traditional feathered serpent intertwined around an arrow. This early design was made again years after the original design was conceived. Marked "Spratling, Made in Mexico" around "WS."   **$300–$350**

Pin, c. 1940. Formed as a banner of silver, incised and ornamented with curls of incised silver around a raised square. Marked "Spratling, Made in Mexico" around "WS."
$575–$625

Pin, c. 1942. Rectangular with incised wavy lines surrounded by thin line with little balls of silver. Pre-Columbian inspiration, abstract forms. Marked "Spratling, Made in Mexico" around "WS." Also with the Montgomery Ward mark.   **$525–$600**

Pin/pendant, c. 1940. Circular sterling pin composed of triangles filled with jadeite alternating with triangles of silver, all ending in little balls of silver. Marked "Spratling, Made in Mexico" around "WS."   **$1,600–$1,800**

Silver pins by
William Spratling.
*Courtesy of
Carole A. Berk, Ltd.,
Maryland. Photo by
Shadowfax Studio.*

Silver pins by William Spratling.
Courtesy of Carole A. Berk, Ltd., Maryland.
Photo by Shadowfax Studio.

Pin, c. 1942. Owl with large onyx dome eyes. Marked "Spratling, Made in Mexico" around "WS." Also with the Montgomery Ward mark. A humorous, strong design.
$950–$1,000

Pin, c. 1942. Butterfly with two small amethyst cabochons. Marked "Spratling, Made in Mexico" around "WS." Shown in the Montgomery Ward catalogue. $850–$900

Pin, c. 1950. Dragonfly made of silver and tortoise shell. Marked "William Spratling, Taxco, Mexico" around "925" and script "WS." $600–$650

Ring, c. 1932. Shaped as a cartouche made up of a central large dome on either side of which are two tiny balls and then two smaller domes. Wide band with incised line down the center. Very old mark: "WS, Taxco." $375–$400

5

ART DECO
ON PAPER

POSTERS AND GRAPHICS

Graphic design changed to attract wider markets to the host of new products being offered. In Europe, posters were an effective way of reaching mass audiences; however, Art Nouveau posters were too leisurely in delivering their message. Modern posters had to be strong enough to be read from passing cars, capturing attention with typography, the image of the product, bold lines and colors, short messages, and interesting angles. The poster's job was to sell a product in a competitive way.

The magazine publishing world was transformed by technical advances such as the rotary press, the linotype machine, and cheaper paper. Some early French fashion magazines used *pochoir* printing, a stenciling method, to render color plates of fashion designs. In America, magazines were a more formidable advertising vehicle than posters, and cover graphics became an important means of selling a magazine at the newsstand.

It has also been argued that, were it not for advertising art and magazines, many of the new artistic movements would not have gained acceptance so rapidly. Each school of art or design had its "journal." More importantly, many fine artists were asked to illustrate both posters and magazines, bringing new design styles to the attention of a wider public.

POSTER PRINTING TECHNIQUES

Early color lithography was a cumbersome process of applying grease pencil on heavy slabs of Bavarian limestone. One stone for each color was needed to achieve the desired effect. In the 1870s, Jules Chéret, called "The Father of the Pictorial Poster," greatly advanced color lithography.

The finest posters of the Art Deco era were also color lithographs, usually rendered on zinc plates. Commercial printing soon became a photographic plate process, and offset printing became popular. Some posters were "photo-montage" designs, incorporating both photographs and lithography with startling, eye-catching effects. The photographic image finally overcame the illustrated image as the dominant design.

Early lithographic posters will generally be more valuable than photo-offset posters, no matter who the artist. When in doubt about the printing technique used, look at the poster under a jeweler's lens. Photographic printing is really achieved by a series of straight lines and dots that can be discerned on close inspection. (*See* "Fakes Alert!" *for more information.*)

TYPOGRAPHY

The German Bauhaus did as much to revolutionize typography as they did architecture. Often elongated and condensed, the new typography lent itself to the new sense of speed that dominated graphic design. Many of the new typefaces were sans serif, that is, the letters did not have little feet. Popular new styles included Paul Renner's "Futura" (1928), Koch's "Kabel" (1927), Eric Gill's "Gill Sans" (1928), and others such as "Bifur," "Bauhaus," and "Broadway," a decidedly American Art Deco type style. In looking at Art Deco posters, notice how much the typography can impact the overall visual appeal.

POSTER DESIGN INFLUENCES

Posters, as other decorative arts, were influenced by many earlier design movements, such as the Vienna Secession. From the first Vienna Secessionist exhibition poster, by Gustav Klimt (1862–1918), it was clear that the poster would be used both to advertise and to make known the Secession's artistic values. Koloman Moser (1868–1918), Egon Schiele (1890–1919), Berthold Löffler (1874–1960), and other artists introduced bold geometric shapes and patterns and radical use of typography to achieve graphic effects.

Dutch De Stijl posters made incredibly clever use of typography to achieve geometric and abstract designs. The most sought-after example of the style was by H. Th. Wijdeveld, publisher of the De Stijl magazine *Wendingen*. Produced in 1931 for the first Frank Lloyd Wright exhibition in Holland, it is comprised entirely of type, in red and black.

These and other artistic movements, such as Cubism and Futurism, had profound impact on advertising design.

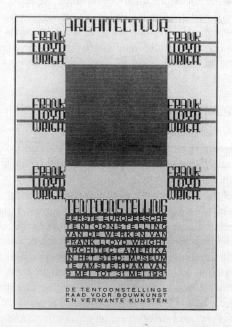

"Architectuur—Frank Lloyd Wright," by H. Th. Wijdeveld.
Courtesy of Bernice Jackson Fine Arts, Massachusetts.

French

The best-known and highest-priced French Art Deco posterist is A. M. Cassandre. Cassandre's first poster "Le Boucheron" (1923) set the tone for a whole new style. He influenced an entire generation of graphic designers, both in France and abroad. Though he won the Grand Prix for poster design at the 1925 Paris Exposition and had a prolific career, it was not until 1951 that the Musée des Arts Décoratifs held a retrospective of his work.

By subject, travel posters are the most highly realized Art Deco designs, and Cassandre was the master of these. His posters include many for ocean liners and trains: "Etoile du Nord" (1927), "Nord Express" (1927), "L.M.S. Bestway" (1928), "L'Oiseau Bleu" (1929), "Chemin de Fer du Nord" (1931), "L'Atlantique" (1931), "Wagon Bar" (1932), and "Normandie" (1935). Other artists who designed for trains and ocean liners are inevitably compared to Cassandre.

Cassandre also designed posters for a wide range of companies and products, including cigarettes, radios, liquors, magazines, newspapers, light bulbs, shoes, and more. It is no wonder that the first "advertising agencies" were founded by poster artists, such as Cassandre's agency Alliance Graphique. After 1930, Alliance Graphique published most of his posters.

He also produced magazine covers and illustrations for *Harper's Bazaar*, *Fortune*, and others; handbills; and smaller graphics. His fame today means these are snatched up quickly.

Other French posterists worth finding are Robert Bonfils, Roger Broders, Jean Carlu, Paul Colin, Jean-Gabriel Domergue, Jean Dupas, Maurice Dufrène, Pierre Fix-Masseau, Charles Gesmar, Georges Lepape, Daniel de Losques, and Charles Loupot.

Fix-Masseau, whose style is similar to Cassandre's, is best known for his train posters. Broders is known for his highly stylized destination posters for the French railways. Bonfils was a fashion illustrator who created a poster for the 1925 Paris Exposition, with its leaping gazelle and stylized flowers. (*See photo in the chapter "The Paris Exposition of 1925."*)

Loupot was a fashion designer, and also designed a poster for the 1925 Exposition. With its smokestacks, it makes environmentalists today cringe, but it represented the marriage of industry and art which was the overall exposition theme.

Another fashion designer, Georges Lepape, is best known for his fashion illustrations for *La Gazette du Bon Ton* and *Vogue* magazine, but also created several posters for clients such as entertainers, the department store Galeries Lafayette, and the Théâtre des Champs Elysées.

Many great posters were created for stage performers such as Josephine Baker, Mistinguett, and others. Paul Colin's 1925 poster for Josephine Baker's Revue Nègre introduced a new style of poster design influenced by the rhythms of jazz. Josephine Baker posters and memorabilia have skyrocketed. The very rare Revue Nègre poster was recently sold by a dealer for $45,000.

Colin created posters for Loie Fuller, the Casino de Paris, Tabarin, other performers, and theaters; for exhibitions and businesses; and even for the war effort. He had a very productive career, creating poster designs into the 1950s.

An artist called Zig (Louis Gaudin) also created posters for Josephine Baker and Mistinguett. Charles Gesmar, who designed about fifty posters in his short lifetime, created almost half of them for Mistinguett!

Jean Carlu was inspired by the Cubists. He was the creator of neon tube posters, both in three dimensions and as graphic designs. He did neon-inspired designs for the cover of *Vanity Fair*. He designed the poster for the 1937 Paris Exposition, as well as for everyday items such as toothpaste. During World War II, he created effective wartime Art Deco posters.

Jean Dupas was a fine artist who was drawn into the world of advertising through commissions by department stores. His distinctive, recognizable style carried over into his advertising graphics. Among others, his posters for the Salon des Artistes Décorateurs, the influential circle of artists who controlled the world of French design until the 1925 Exposition, for the English train lines and the department store Arnold Constable are very desirable.

Many other talented though lesser-known French designers created appealing Art Deco posters, which tend to be more affordable to collectors that those by the artists named.

Belgian

The best "Belgian" Art Deco posterist came from Switzerland: Léo Marfurt (1894–1977), who moved to Belgium in 1927 and created an advertising agency, Les Créations Publicitaires, which he ran until 1957. Like Cassandre's agency, Marfurt created posters for many clients, such as Belga Cigarettes, Chrysler and Minerva automobiles, the English LNER, resorts, and a host of others.

In addition to Marfurt, some good poster designs of the period came from Francis Delamare, who also founded an advertising agency; Auguste Mambour (1896–1968); Milo Martinet; Lucien de Roeck (b. 1915); and others, including the country's leading Surrealist painter, René Magritte (1898–1967).

From the 1930s until now, many of the best Belgian posters are for travel, fairs, and festivals. The Art Deco style continued to be used in Belgium through the 1950s, and posters from this period are now increasingly seen at shows.

Dutch

The best Dutch Art Deco posters were for products and travel. One notable designer is Wim ten Broek (b. 1905), whose posters for Holland-America Line ocean liners are reminiscent of A. M. Cassandre. Small wonder—Cassandre also designed posters for Holland-America and other Dutch companies.

Other Dutch designers include Jan Wijga; notably his posters for KLM (Royal Dutch Airlines); Johann von Stein for Lloyd Lines; Nicolaas Petrus "N.P." de Koo (1881–1960); and Agnes Canta (1888–1964). Photo-montage posters appeared earlier in Holland than in many other countries, and one fine example in the Deco style is Willhem Gispen's (1890–1981) poster for Giso Lamps.

Swiss

Switzerland is a vacationer's playground, and travel posters in a Modern style appeared early. Emile Cardinaux and Otto Morach (1877–1973) were the first to make notable contributions in this field.

Swiss artist Herbert Matter, a pioneer in the photo-montage posters, is well-known for his designs for the men's clothing store PKZ. Another recognized Swiss artist is Otto Baumberger, in whose posters the product takes center stage, and who also designed posters for PKZ.

Other Swiss artists to look for are Donald Brun, Hans Erni (b. 1909), Herbert Leupin (b. 1916), and Nicklaus Stoecklin (1896–1982).

In keeping with their national character of tidiness, in 1914, the Swiss established a standard format for posters, which is roughly 35" wide by 50" high, and with the exception of very few, all Swiss posters are this size.

English

In England, the finest poster artist was an American, Edward McKnight Kauffer, known for his posters for the London Underground, English Rail, and Shell Oil, the three most important poster "patrons" in England. Perhaps his best-known poster is "Power, The Nerve Center of the London Underground" (1930), depicting a man's fist emanating from a factory and train wheel, punctuated by zigzag lightning bolts.

Shell Oil produced a series of posters using variations of the slogan "Motorists Prefer Shell," and along with both London Transport, and English Rail, commissioned numerous artists. Although some collectors of English posters specialize by artist, more often they seem to collect the advertiser.

Many of the best artists worked for more than one of the clients mentioned: Austin Cooper (1890–1964), who emigrated to England from Canada; Charles Pears (1873–1958); Frank Newbould; Tom Purvis; Fred Taylor (1875–1963); J. S. Anderson; John Armstrong; and Paul Nash.

Almost all British Rail posters were produced in two standard sizes, a vertical one-sheet 25" wide by 40" high (sometimes called a "double royal"), and a large horizontal format 50" wide by 40" high (sometimes called a "quad royal").

German

Ludwig Hohlwein was the master of modern design in German posters, creating literally thousands of posters in his dramatic style and striking color combinations. His posters of animals, especially for the Munich Zoo, are prized, and he was also skilled at film, travel, and advertising posters.

Lucien Bernhard (1883–1972) is notable because of his typography, and was the creator of the Bernhard type styles. He was the innovator of something he called the "Sach Plakat" or "Object Poster" as early as 1906, where the product being advertised occupied the main field of the illustrated design. He moved to the United States in 1923 and taught design at the Art Students' League in New York City.

Hans Rudi Erdt (1883–1917) produced an enormous number of posters for the theater, cars, and cigarettes, often using a theme of horseriding, race driving, or tennis playing. Walter Schnackenberg (1880–1961) created posters with a darker "cabaret" feel, and is noted also for magazine covers.

Other German artists who are collected today are Edmund Edel (1863–1934); Julius Klinger (1876–1950); Ernst Deutsch (1883–1938); Fritz Rehm (1876–1950); Jupp Wiertz, known for his posters for German travel and cinema; and Hans Koch (1899–1977), who designed with a Hohlwein style. The rise of Hitler in Germany put an end to the inventiveness of posters of the era, turning them into little more than propaganda.

Italian

Italian Art Deco posters have been increasing in popularity recently. Many of the best Italian posters were designed for the opera and music publisher Ricordi, including works by Leopoldo Metlicovitz and Marcello Dudovitch, both of whom also created posters for other clients as well.

Another outstanding Italian artist, Severo Pozzati, signed his works "Sepo." His product posters have been compared to those by Cassandre, and in fact he worked in France after 1920. Other Italian artists worth finding are Marcello Nizzoli (1887–1960), who created some stunning posters for Olivetti; Giorgio Muggiani (1887–1938); Erberto Carboni (1899–1984); Gino Boccasile (1901–1952); Plinio Codognato (1878–1940); Fortunato Depero (1892–1960); Mario Sironi (1895–1961); and Federico Seneca (1891–1976).

American

One might assume that the Modern style in the United States would yield a wealth of fine posters. However, in America, posters were a less effective advertising vehicle than magazines. In addition, American advertising used photographic images much earlier, and when illustrations were used, often European designers were commissioned to execute them.

One "American" posterist we proudly claim is Joseph Binder, an Austrian who worked extensively in Germany before coming to the United States. Binder won the competition for poster design for the New York World's Fair of 1939. Ironically, another great collectible Art Deco American poster for the 1939 World's Fair is by Englishman John Atherton. (*See "World's Fair Memorabilia" for descriptions of these.*)

Binder did numerous posters before emigrating to the United States, including a now well-known ski travel poster for Austria, published in several editions for global distribution, with the headline "Austria" in several languages. He also created covers for magazines such as *Fortune*.

American train posters from the 1920s and 1930s are hard to find, but some of the best are by Leslie Ragan for the New York Central Railroad; Sascha Maurer for the New Haven Railroad; and Gustav Krollman for Northern Pacific Railways.

SOME NOTES ON POSTER COLLECTING

The value of a poster depends on many things, including artistic achievement and scarcity, although with most "vintage" posters (pre–World War II) nobody really knows how many were printed, let alone how many were saved. When a poster is rarely seen on the market, it will attract more attention and command a higher price.

The appeal of the subject can also play a role in determining value. Broadly speaking, Art Deco posters for entertainers and for ocean liners and trains bring higher prices than those for products. As mentioned, lithographic posters are generally more valuable than photo-offset posters.

Condition also greatly affects value. (*See the chapter "A Key to Collectible Value" for more information.*) Collectors will pay premium prices for posters in fine condition. The same poster in only average condition might bring only 50 percent of the price. Inspect posters carefully, as many posters on the market have been repaired, restored, and touched up. Unless it is an extremely rare poster, collectors would do best to avoid any poster with large amounts of restoration.

The vast majority of posters on the market are mounted on linen or cotton canvas, which makes the poster easier to handle, and diminishes creases and folds. However, linen mounting has not proven to be the most effective means of preservation, and collectors should try to acquire posters mounted on Japan paper or unmounted posters whenever possible.

GRAPHICS

The two most popular areas of collecting in Art Deco graphics are *pochoir* plates from portfolios and *pochoir* illustrations from French fashion magazines, and illustrated covers from American magazines of the period. Many people also collect the advertising designs from magazines, especially advertisements for cars, or those created by famous artists such as Erté.

Pochoir Illustrations

Many graphic artists began as fashion illustrators, rendering the fashion designs of Parisian couturiers such as Paul Poiret, Doeuillet, Paquin, Lanvin, and Worth. The illustrations were usually in gouache, an opaque paint mixed with water and applied like watercolors. The growth of fashion magazines allowed designers to reach new audiences, and the development of *pochoir*, or "stencil" printing, in fashion magazines became popular.

These illustrations were published in numerous French magazines such as *Gazette du Bon Ton, Modes et Manières d'Aujourd'hui, Art, Goût et Beauté, Journal des Dames et des Modes, Falbalas et Fanfreluches, La Guirlande des Mois, Les Idées Nouvelles de la Mode*, and *Les Feuillets d'Art*. Some German magazines also used *pochoir* printing.

Within a few years, however, most magazines turned to photomechanical printing. By the 1930s, *Art, Goût et Beauté* was the only fashion magazine still using *pochoir* hand-colored illustrations, and it stopped publication in 1932.

Both the complete publication and individual plates from these fashion magazines are good collectibles of the period. Because often the plates were hand-painted, they were more likely to be saved than later magazine illustration. This may sound laborious, but it produced a high-quality illustration which suited the deluxe marketing of fashion.

Gazette du Bon Ton publisher Lucien Vogel brought the *pochoir* method to perfection, and *pochoir* illustrations from its 1912–1925 life are the most valuable. However, *pochoirs* from many magazines can still be found at moderate prices.

Artists who created *pochoir* illustrations include George Barbier, Edouardo Benito, Paul Iribe, Georges Lepape, Charles Martin, Leon Bakst, André Marty, and Pierre Brissaud.

In many ways, Paul Iribe set the standard for such illustration with his 1908 album of designs *Les Robes de Paul Poiret*. He was followed by another album for Poiret by Georges Lepape in 1911.

Collecting fashion *pochoirs* is often a double treat: an illustration of a Cinderella gown by Doucet, executed by the well-known illustrator André Marty, or a Rodier "afternoon" dress illustrated by Georges Lepape, are twice as interesting for the collector.

Many of these same designers were also gifted book and portfolio illustrators. Several portfolios of *pochoirs* were designed during the early Art Deco period to illustrate legends and biographies of artists such as Nijinsky, or as fashion portfolios that designers would show or offer to their clients.

Plates by Edouard Benedictus from the portfolios *Variations, Nouvelles Variations*, and *Relais* (1930), which were created as designs for textiles, are also often found as individual pieces. Their strong design and color combinations make them decorative favorites.

Magazine Covers

Illustrated magazine covers are also a popular collecting area. Originally rendered by the artist in watercolor, gouache, pen and ink, and other mediums, magazine covers were usually photographically reproduced. The original works of art are much higher-priced than the covers themselves.

Magazines which featured notable Art Deco covers include *Harper's Bazaar* (spelled "Bazar" until 1929); *Vanity Fair; Vogue; Woman's Home Companion*, especially covers by William Welsh; and *Fortune*. Some of the best covers are from a lesser-known magazine, *Asia*, which employed artist Frank McIntosh as art director from 1924 to about 1933.

Lepape designed *Femina, Modes et Manières d'Aujourd'hui, Art et Décoration* and Lucien Vogel's *Gazette du Bon Ton*. He also designed for *Vanity Fair* starting in 1915 and for *Vogue* starting in 1916, both Condé Nast publications. His 114 covers for *Vogue*, created from 1916 to 1939, are highly prized. He had an eye for lettering, and changed the magazine's logo with each design. Today it is unthinkable that a magazine could compete on the stands if it changed its logo with every issue.

From 1915 to 1936, Erté designed a total of 240 covers for the Hearst publication *Harper's Bazaar*, which was the direct competitor of *Vogue* on the newsstands. His illustrations, including numerous fashion layouts for various Hearst publications, number close to 2,500. *Harper's Bazaar* covers by Cassandre are also highly collectible.

Vanity Fair employed a number of outstanding artists to design its covers, including Benito, Carlu, and George Bolin, whose 1920s Jazz Age themes reflect the impact of Cubism. Miguel Covarrubias's most famous cover for *Vanity Fair* is the February 1932 issue featuring Greta Garbo, whose pointed shoulders match her pointed eyebrows. In the 1930s, *Vanity Fair* commissioned Frederick Chance and Paolo Garetto, and covers started depicting the political realities of the day. One of the many outstanding Garetto covers, for November 1932, is a bold red, white, and black graphic in which the German swastika forms the body of a very Cubist-faced Hitler.

News magazines, such as *Fortune*, which started one month after the stock market crash of 1929, also featured Modern idiom graphics and covers. Cover artists for *Fortune* include Cassandre, Joseph Binder, Antonio Petrucelli, Garetto, Fernand Leger, Ernest Hamlin Baker, Covarrubias, and others. *Fortune* magazine is a good source for covers in mint condition, because it came with a slipcase for storage.

With relatively low prices, magazine covers are a popular collectible, and often one can still find them in garage sales. However, the best Art Deco magazine covers in excellent condition are becoming harder to find, especially in urban markets, and dealers are more aware of their value than before.

POSTER PRICE LISTINGS
(Alphabetically by designer)

OTTO BAUMBERGER (Swiss, 1889–1961)

"Hotel St. Gotthard," 1925, 50" high, 35" wide, lithograph. Depicting a lobster, a bottle of wine, and an elegant bowl, in black, red, and green. In fine condition, linen-mounted.
$1,400–$1,600

"PKZ," 1923, 50" high, 35" wide, lithograph. Extremely finely executed close-up of a coat with the PKZ label, so exact that many wrongly assume it to be a photograph. In

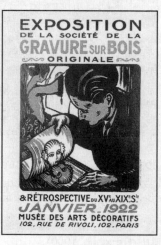

"Autriche" by Joseph Binder. *Author's collection. Photo by Robert Four.*

"Société des Graveurs en Bois" by Robert Bonfils. *Author's collection. Photo by Robert Four.*

fine condition, linen-mounted. An important example of Swiss poster art.

$4,500–$5,000

JOSEPH BINDER (Austrian/American, 1898–1972)

"*Autriche,*" c. 1930, 37½" high, 24½" wide, lithograph. Stunning ski poster, which was printed with the word "Austria" in several languages. In mint condition.

$1,600–$1,800

ROBERT BONFILS (French, 1886–1972)

"*Exposition Internationale des Arts Décoratifs,*" 1925, 23½" high, 15¼" wide, woodcut. A very good example of early French Art Deco style, in fine condition. (*For photo see chapter "The Paris Exposition of 1925.*")

$2,500–$3,000

"*Société des Graveurs en Bois,*" 1922, 23¼" high, 14¾" wide, woodcut in two colors, for the Society of Wood Engravers. In fine condition.

$600–$700

ROGER BRODERS (French, 1883–1953)

"*Antibes,*" c. 1927, 42" high, 30" wide, lithograph. Travel poster in bold colors. In very good condition, linen-mounted.

$2,000–$2,200

"*Chamonix Mt. Blanc—Tous les Sports d'Hiver,*" c. 1930, 40" high, 25" wide, lithograph. Hockey game with bright, contrasting colors, in very good condition, linen-mounted.

$1,200–$1,400

"Challenge Round de la Coupe Davis" by A. M. Cassandre. *Courtesy of Christie's, New York.*

EMILE CARDINAUX (Swiss, 1877–1936)

"*Bally*," 1935, 50" high, 35" wide, lithograph. A mountain climber holding on to a rope that trails below; in white, red, brown, and blue. In very good condition, linen-mounted.
$1,500–$2,000

JEAN CARLU (French, b. 1900)

"*Exposition Internationale Paris 1937*," 15" high, 10½" wide, lithograph. Profile of a woman's face against a background of international flags. In fine condition.
$600–$800

"*Give 'Em Both Barrels*," 1941, 30" high, 40" wide, lithograph. War poster showing a G.I. firing his machine gun and a worker using a rivet gun. An excellent example of an Art Deco war poster, in very good condition.
$1,200–$1,300

A. M. CASSANDRE (French, 1901–1968)

(Fakes Alert! Collectors should note that Cassandre's posters are favorites for photo-offset reproduction.)

"*Challenge Round de la Coupe Davis*," 1932, 62" high, 45" wide, lithograph. Davis Cup tennis poster with strong composition. In very good condition, linen-mounted.
$8,000–$10,000

"*Etoile du Nord*," 1927, 41" high, 30" wide, lithograph. Cassandre's well-known image of train lines disappearing at the horizon where they converge at the North Star. A fine example of the artist's style. In very good condition, linen-mounted.
$13,000–$16,000

"*Nord Express*," 1927, 41" high, 30" wide, lithograph. The locomotive and power lines disappear into the horizon. Recognized as one of Cassandre's very best designs, though not as rare as some of his images. In very good condition, linen-mounted. *(See color section.)*
$12,000–$15,000

**"Paris/1937/Exposition
Internationale" by Paul Colin.**
Private collection.
Photo by Robert Four.

"Normandie," 1935, 39½" high, 25" wide, lithograph. Cassandre's famous image for the great ocean liner. This poster was produced in several versions for different sailings of the ocean liner. In very good condition, linen-mounted.   **$9,000–$12,000**

"L'Oiseau Bleu," 1929, 39" high, 25" wide, lithograph. For the Chemin de Fer du Nord, with a close-up of a stylized bluebird flying alongside the speeding train. In very good condition, linen-mounted.   **$7,000–$9,000**

PAUL COLIN (French, 1892–1985)
"Falconetti . . . Théâtre de L'Avenue," 1930, 62" high, 47" wide, lithograph. Wispy woman in pink, floating in a cloud. In good condition, linen-mounted.

$2,000–$3,000

"Marguerite Valmond," 1928, 63" high, 47" wide, lithograph. Wonderfully soft portrait of the French singer. In very good condition, linen-mounted.   **$1,200–$1,500**

"Paris/1937/Exposition Internationale," 1937, 23" high, 16" wide. Nicely stylized design in dark blue, red, yellow, light blue, gray, brown, and black. In good condition, linen-mounted.   **$900–$1,000**

"Tabarin," 1928, 24" high, 15" wide, lithograph. Cubist influence evident in the juxtaposition of the three different images of the same female dancer. Smaller version, in very good condition, linen-mounted. A fine example of the artist's work.   **$2,000–$2,500**

JEAN-GABRIEL DOMERGUE (French, 1889–1962)
"Alice Soulie," 1926, 63" high, 46¼" wide, lithograph. A portrait of the entertainer with her bare breasts hidden behind a fan of ostrich feathers. In very good condition, linen-mounted.   **$1,800–$2,000**

"Galeries Lafayette," 1920, 63" high, 42" wide, lithograph. Elegant woman in striped coat with fur collar and cuffs, buying French savings bonds at the department store. In fine condition, linen-mounted.   **$2,000–$2,500**

MARCELLO DUDOVICH (Italian, 1878–1962)

"Distillerie del l'Aurum/Pineta di Pescara," c. 1935, 55" high, 39½" wide, lithograph. A close-up of a woman in white wearing a conical hat and holding an Aurum liquor bottle, blue background. In good condition, linen-mounted.   **$2,100–$2,300**

"Esposizione Rhodia Albene Alla Rinascente," 1936, 77⅛" high, 54¾" wide, lithograph. Fashion poster for the department store La Rinascente, one woman wearing a red, green, yellow, orange, and black plaid dress, the other a red and white polka dot dress. In good condition, linen-mounted. A fine example of the artist's style.   **$5,000–$6,000**

MAURICE DUFRÈNE (French, 1876–1955)

"Rayon des Soieries" ("The Silk Department"), 1930, 46" high, 31" wide, lithograph. For an operetta which takes place in a department store. Stylized woman with arm out-stretched, draped with bolts of silk. (*Fakes Alert!* Lithographic forgeries of this poster are on the market. Original has only one fold of green cloth, forgeries have more than one fold in green.) In very good condition, linen-mounted.   **$1,400 (Auction)**
$1,400–$1,800

JEAN DUPAS (French, 1882–1964)

"Arnold Constable," 1928, 46" high, 30" wide, lithograph. Text in English, with three women, each wearing a different fashionable ensemble. In very good condition, linen-mounted.   **$2,500–$3,000**

"XVme Salon des Artistes Décorateurs," 1924, 23¼" high, 15" wide, lithograph. In gray and red, two women, one in profile, one full face. In fine condition, linen-mounted. A very good example of the artist's style.   **$1,100 (Auction)**
$1,800–$2,000

"Rayon des Soieries"
by Maurice Dufrène.
Courtesy of Bernice Jackson
Fine Arts, Massachusetts.

"XVme Salon des
Artistes Décorateurs" by
Jean Dupas. *Courtesy of*
Christie's East, New York.

"Exactitude" by Pierre Fix-Masseau.
Courtesy of Christie's, New York.

"Giso Lampen" by Willem Gispen.
Courtesy of Bernice Jackson Fine Arts,
Massachusetts.

PIERRE FIX-MASSEAU (French, b. 1905)

"Côte d'Azur," 1929, 39" high, 24" wide, lithograph. Advertising the "Pullman Express" cars for the French Railways, with text around the margins in the style of Cassandre. In very good condition, linen-mounted.   **$6,000–$7,000**

"Exactitude," 1932, 39½" high, 25" wide, lithograph. Strong image of the train traveling directly toward the viewer. (*Fakes Alert!* This poster is a favorite for photo-offset reproduction.) In very good condition, linen-mounted.   **$10,000–$12,000**

CHARLES GESMAR (French, 1900–1928)

"Mistinguett," 1925, 63" high, 44" wide, lithograph. A close-up of the chanteuse with mammoth jewels on her fingers. In very good condition, linen-mounted.
                    $2,500–$3,000

"Mistinguett/Casino de Paris," 1922, 47" high, 30" wide, lithograph. The performer sitting on a three-legged stool, with a cockatoo perched on her bejeweled fingers. In very good condition, linen-mounted.   **$3,000–$4,000**

WILLEM H. GISPEN (Dutch, 1890–1981)

"Giso Lampen," 1928, 39½" high, 27½" wide, photo-montage and lithograph. For Giso Lamps, rendered in eye-catching red, black, and white. In fine condition, linen-mounted. An excellent example of photo-montage.   **$9,000–$10,000**

"Wilhelm Mozer" by Ludwig
Hohlwein. *Courtesy of Christie's
East, New York.*

LUDWIG HOHLWEIN (German, 1874–1949)

"Passau," 1929, 26" high, 34" wide, lithograph. Travel poster with bold, flat, sometimes stippled color planes: in brown, green, yellow, and tan. In good condition, linen-mounted.
$800–$1,000

"Wilhelm Mozer," 1909, 44" high, 31" wide, lithograph. For the Munich delicatessen, features brightly colored foods and wines, with a large lobster in the foreground. An early example of modern poster design. In very good condition, linen-mounted. (*Fakes Alert!* This poster is a favorite for photo-offset reproduction.) $1,800–$2,300

EDWARD MCKNIGHT KAUFFER (American/English, 1890–1954)

"Actors Prefer Shell," 1933, 30" high, 45" wide, lithograph. An actor holds a rectangular mask in front of his face. A good example of the artist's posters for Shell Oil. (Others in the series of those who "prefer Shell" by Kauffer include explorers, magicians, and merchants.) In fine condition, linen-mounted. $2,200–$2,800

"Aeroshell Lubricating Oil," 1932, 30" high, 45" wide, lithograph. A yellow race car against a dark blue field, subtitled "The Aristocrat of Lubricants." In fine condition, linen-mounted. The most sought-after excellent example of both the artist and Shell Oil posters. $10,000–$12,000

"Power, The Nerve Center of London Underground," 1930, 39½" high, 25" wide, lithograph. Avant-garde design of a factory and a train wheel from which a fist protrudes, emanating zigzag lightning bolts. In good condition, linen-mounted. $8,000–$10,000

GEORGES LEPAPE (French, 1887–1971)

"Spinelly," 1914, 45" high, 33" wide, lithograph. The singer smiling behind her lace fan. A very good example of Lepape's style. In very good condition, linen-mounted.
$1,400–$2,000

"Exposition Internationale
des Arts Décoratifs—Paris 1925"
by Charles Loupot.
Private collection.

CHARLES LOUPOT (French, 1892–1962)

"Exposition Internationale des Arts Décoratifs—Paris 1925," 23" high, 15" wide, lithograph. The other official poster for the 1925 Exposition, reflecting the marriage of art and industry that was the theme of the fair. In very good condition, linen-mounted.

$2,500–$3,000

LÉO MARFURT (Belgian, 1894–1977)

"Bruxelles Exposition Universelle," 1935, 62" high, 46" wide, lithograph. Belgian national colors—black, red, and aqua—as the backdrop for Atlas carrying the world, designed for the 1935 World's Fair. In good condition, linen-mounted. $800–$1,200

HERBERT MATTER (Swiss, 1907–1984)

"PKZ," 1928, 50" high, 35" wide, lithograph. A valet showing men's coats. In very good condition, linen-mounted. An excellent example of the artist's early style.

$9,000–$12,000

"PKZ" by Herbert Matter.
*Courtesy of Bernice Jackson Fine Arts,
Massachusetts.*

"Ski/The New Haven R.R." by Sascha Maurer. *Private collection.*

"North Berwick" by Frank Newbould. *Courtesy of Nancy Steinbock Fine Posters and Prints, New York.*

"Suisse," 1935, 40" high, 25" wide, photo-montage. A skier's head with sun visor, multiple photos of downhillers and Swiss crosses in the background; in white, red, and green. In fine condition, linen-mounted.   **$2,000–$2,500**

SASCHA MAURER (American, work: 1930s–1940s)

"Ski/The New Haven R.R.," c. 1940, 42" high, 25" wide, lithograph. A smiling man with skis thrown over his shoulder, in blue, green, red, orange, and brown. In very good condition, linen-mounted.   **$800–$1,000**

LEOPOLDO METLICOVITZ (Italian, 1868–1944)

"Copertoni Impermeabili," 1933, 77¾" high, 55" wide, lithograph. A horse-drawn cart, in a Cubist style, carries a load covered by a tarpaulin made by Ettore Moretti Company. In fine condition, linen-mounted.   **$1,200–$1,400**

"Impermeabili Moretti," c. 1930, 56" high, 36" wide, lithograph. A man in a coat and hat stands on top of an open umbrella, with rain pelting down all around. In fine condition, linen-mounted.   **$550–$700**

FRANK NEWBOULD (English, 1887–1950)

"North Berwick," c. 1935, 40" high, 50" wide, lithograph. Beautiful, bright beach scene, a man with golf clubs and two women, one in a bathing suit, seated for a picnic. In very good condition, linen-mounted. A fine example of both the artist's style and the English Rail posters of the period.   **$3,000–$3,500**

TOM PURVIS (English, 1888–1959)

"Getting Ready on the East Coast," c. 1935, 40" high, 50" wide, lithograph. Old salt sits on a box of kippers as his mate watches him paint the new name on the bow of his dory. In very good condition. A very good example of Purvis's style.   **$1,800 (Auction)**

"New York—The Upper Bay From Lower Manhattan" by Leslie Ragan. *Courtesy of Nancy Steinbock Fine Posters and Prints, New York.*

LESLIE RAGAN (American, work: 1930s–1940s)

"New York—The Upper Bay From Lower Manhattan," c. 1935, 40" high, 25" wide, photo-offset. Manhattan and Battery Park, with the bay and the Statue of Liberty in the background. In very good condition, linen-mounted. A fine example of both the artist's style and American train posters of the period.   **$1,800–$2,200**

SEPO (aka SEVERO POZZATI, Italian, 1895–1983)

"Noveltex," 1928, 56½" high, 36⅝" wide, lithograph. A strong geometric design advertising Noveltex collars for men. A fine example of the artist's style. In very good condition, linen-mounted.   **$4,000–$4,500**

"Noveltex" by Sepo. *Courtesy of Bernice Jackson Fine Arts, Massachusetts.*

JOHANN VON STEIN (Dutch, 1896–1965)

"Rotterdamsche Lloyd," c. 1930, 28½" high, 18" wide, lithograph. Ocean liner poster advertising Sumatra and Java. White steamship with long reflection in water echoes elongated typeface. In very good condition, linen-mounted. **$3,500–$4,000**

FRED TAYLOR (English, 1875–1963)

"Ipswich," c. 1925, 40" high, 50" wide, lithograph. For English Rail, a scene from Dickens in browns and greens: Mr. Pickwick riding past "The Ancient House" in Ipswich. In fine condition, linen-mounted. **$1,500–$1,800**

JUPP WIERTZ (German, 1881–1939)

"Bayreuth. Festival du Theatre," 1938, 40" high, 25" wide, lithograph. With the orchestra silhouetted in foreground, Wagner's bust like a medallion glowing above. In very good condition, linen-mounted. **$450–$500**

JAN WIJGA (Dutch, 1902–1978)

"Royal Dutch Airlines," 1933, 39" high, 24¾" wide, lithograph. Cleverly subtitled "The Flying Dutchman—Fiction Becomes Fact," with a four-propeller plane flying over the Dutch countryside while in the background a ghostly galleon sails; in purples, blues, and greens. In very good condition, linen-mounted. **$1,600–$1,800**

GRAPHICS PRICE LISTINGS

POCHOIR PLATES

EDOUARD BENEDICTUS (French, 1878–1932)

> **€** Benedictus created three portfolios of *pochoir* plates for textiles designs in the late 1920s: *Variations, Nouvelles Variations,* and *Relais,* with the last being published in 1930.

General market range, each plate **$100–$150**

Plates with either outstanding Art Deco designs and/or with metallic ink **$150–$250**

POCHOIR FASHION PLATES

> **€** *Pochoir* prints of fashion designs appeared until about 1932 in French magazines of the era, such as *Modes et Manières d'Aujourd'hui, Art, Goût et Beauté, Journal des Dames et des Modes, Les Idées Nouvelles de la Mode,* and *Les Feuillets d'Art.*

General price range **$50–$100**

Selected designers or well-known artists **$75–$150**

"Relais 3" by Edouard Benedictus. *Author's collection. Photo by Robert Four.*

LA GAZETTE DU BON TON (1912–1925)

> Publisher Lucien Vogel brought the *pochoir* method to perfection, and *pochoir* illustrations from this publication are the most valuable, with certain artists bringing high prices, especially when designs incorporate metallic ink and/or are for well-known couturiers. Plates are approximately 8½" high, 6½" wide.

General market range for designs by less well-known artists or for less finely executed designs   **$50–$100**

Plates by George Barbier (1882–1932)   **$150–$200**

Plates by Barbier with metallic ink   **$150–$250**

Plates by Edouardo Benito (b. 1891)   **$125–$175**

Plates by Georges Lepape (1887–1971)   **$125–$175**

Plates by Lepape with metallic ink (*see color section*)   **$150–$200**

Plates by Charles Martin (1884–1934)   **$125–$175**

Plates by André Marty (1882–1974)   **$125–$175**

Plates by Marty notably for designs by Paul Poiret (1879–1944) with metallic ink
                                                                                        $150–$200

L'HEURE DU THÉ
Manteau de fourrure, de Jeanne Lanvin

Pochoir by Benito for Jeanne Lanvin. *Author's collection.*
Photo by Robert Four.

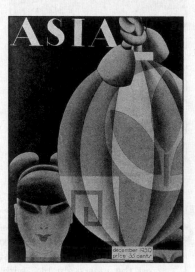

december 1930
price 35 cents

Asia magazine cover by Frank McIntosh. *Author's collection.*
Photo by Robert Four.

MAGAZINE COVERS

Many collectors prefer to try to find complete magazines rather than covers only. However, on the market today, one is more likely to find covers that have been removed and matted for framing. Many fine Art Deco cover designs can still be found for $25–$50, although prices for the best covers and designers when found in fine condition can be significantly higher.

ASIA MAGAZINE (1924–1933)

Almost all of the covers for this short-lived news magazine were designed by its art director, Frank McIntosh (American, b. 1901), and are usually signed with his name or "FM" somewhere in the design.

Covers with good to very good designs $35–$50

Fine cover designs, with more complex images and bold Art Deco colors (*see color section*)
$50–$100

Fortune magazine cover by Antonio Petrucelli. *Author's collection. Photo by Robert Four.*

FORTUNE MAGAZINE (started 1929)

> From its start until the 1940s when photography began to replace illustration, *Fortune* commissioned many artists for its covers, which are among the easiest to find in excellent condition because subscribers received a slipcase box to house their issues. Many *Fortune* magazines can be found for under $25, but the best designers will bring considerably higher prices.

Covers by Ernest Hamlin Baker	$40–$80
Covers by Joseph Binder (1898–1972)	$80–$150
Cover by A. M. Cassandre (1901–1968)	$100–$150
Cover by Miguel Covarrubias (1904–1957)	$100–$150
Covers by Paolo Garetto (b. 1903)	$50–$150
Cover by Fernand Leger (1881–1955)	$150–$200
Covers by Antonio Petrucelli (b. 1907)	$60–$100

HARPER'S BAZAAR (Covers 1915–1930s)

> Hearst Publications revamped the existing *Harper's Bazaar* to compete with *Vogue,* and *Vanity Fair.* In 1915, it signed Erté to a ten-year contract which he renewed for another ten years, designing some 240 covers in all. In 1934, Hearst again revamped the magazine, hiring the avant-garde Alexey Brodovitch (1900–1971) as art director, who commissioned new artists including Cassandre.

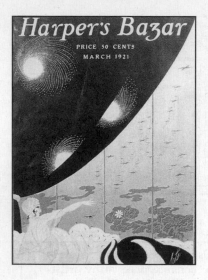

Harper's Bazar **magazine cover by Erté.**
Author's collection. Photo by Robert Four.

Vanity Fair **magazine cover
by George Bolin.**
*Author's collection.
Photo by Robert Four.*

Covers by Erté (Romain de Tirtoff, 1892–1990)	$125–$175
Covers by A. M. Cassandre (1901–1968)	$125–$175

VANITY FAIR (Covers 1913–1930s)

> Publisher Condé Nast revamped this 19th-century publication in 1913 to feature illustrations. Georges Lepape started designing covers for the publication in about 1915, and many other artists were also commissioned.

Covers by Eduardo Benito (b. 1891)	$50–$125
Covers by George Bolin (American)	$75–$100
Cover by Jean Carlu (1900–1983)	$100–$150
Covers by Miguel Covarrubias (1904–1957)	$40–$100
Covers by Paolo Garetto (b. 1903)	$40–$100
Covers by Georges Lepape (1887–1971)	$100–$150

VOGUE (Covers 1913–1930s)

€ Also revamped by publisher Condé Nast in 1913 to feature illustrations. An American, George Plank, started designing covers for the publication in about 1912, and Georges Lepape began designing covers in 1916.

Covers by Georges Lepape (1887–1971) $100–$150

Covers by George W. Plank (American) $100–$125

WOMAN'S HOME COMPANION (Covers 1920s–1930s)

€ Many covers for this magazine can still be found inexpensively. Some of its best Art Deco covers were designed by William Welsh.

General market range $15–$25

Covers by William Welsh (b. 1889) $50–$75

Woman's Home Companion magazine cover by William Welsh. *Author's collection. Photo by Robert Four.*

SPECIAL FOCUS
VINTAGE BOOKS AND PUBLICATIONS
by Thomas G. Boss

Thomas Boss is the owner of Thomas G. Boss Fine Books, which specializes in visually striking books, publications, and printed materials which reflect or document design movements such as Arts and Crafts, Art Nouveau, the Vienna Secession, and Art Deco. You can contact him at 355 Boylston Street, Boston, MA 02116, (617) 421-1880.

The Art Deco period was a time of artistic experimentation and change in every field, and book design was no exception.

Today, collectors of Art Deco furnishings, glass, fashion, industrial design, posters, and other objects of the period are also rediscovering the world of Art Deco books.

Some Art Deco books are treasured for their bindings, striking illustrations, covers, dust jackets, typography, and other decorations by the leading artists, graphic designers, and illustrators of the day. New advances in printing, papermaking, and color reproduction technology were put to the service of their talents, often with remarkable results.

Other Art Deco period books, magazines, exhibition catalogues, and specialty publications are sought by collectors, dealers, and institutions because they document the creative work, innovations, and thinking of the era's preeminent designers.

FINE BINDINGS

In the rare book field, many collectors are attracted to the craftsmanship and hand work that go into fine bindings. Wealthy connoisseurs and collectors during the early Art Deco period commissioned leading artists to create bindings for their personal libraries. In France, where books were usually published with relatively plain and somewhat flimsy paper covers, serious collectors wanted protective and decorative bindings in which to clothe them. Publishers also commissioned artists to create binding designs for small, deluxe editions often printed on unusual handmade papers, signed by the artist and/or author, and marketed to the wealthy collectors.

Today, Art Deco tooled-leather fine bindings with geometric Art Deco designs by artists such as René Kieffer, Louis Gilbert, or Pierre Legrain can bring $5,000 and more on the market. Rarer still are bindings by artists of such stature as Jean Dunand, recognized as the preeminent lacquer artist of the period.

Swiss/French artist François-Louis Schmied commissioned Dunand to execute his designs for lacquered bookbindings. Schmied was one of the leading figures in artistic bookmaking during the Art Deco period, and very successful until his excessive spending caught up with him and he was ruined by the Depression. He died in virtually penniless in 1941.

One extremely rare Dunand-Schmied collaboration in a Dunand binding, created in 1924 for the book *Daphné* by Alfred de Vigny, sold for $70,000 at the Paris auction of the collection of Alain Lesieutre. The binding was baked with a night-blue, triple-layered lacquer. The design, which evoked a swirling mass of stars and galaxies, was created with *coquille d'oeuf*, or eggshell, and metallic elements for sparkle. Commissioned by the French Society of the Contemporary Book, only 140 copies of *Daphné* were printed. The binding was, of course, unique. The auction price no doubt also reflected the fact that the book contained two gouache illustrations and forty-eight color wood engravings created by Schmied, each hand-signed by him.

However, Art Deco bindings are not entirely out of the reach of average collectors, as many can still be purchased in fine condition for under $1,000, while still others command under $500.

Condition is of course important, but value in fine books or books with fine bindings depends on many factors, which might include the designer of the binding (or cover, or dust jacket), the author of the book itself, whether the book is a small or limited edition or a first edition, or if it is signed by the author or the designer. The quality of the paper, the presence of the original slipcase, and other factors play a role as well.

BOOKS AND PUBLICATIONS WITH ILLUSTRATIONS OR PLATES

Schmied was obsessive about controlling every aspect of the design and production of his books, and they are masterworks of Art Deco in every sense. Some of his books were, in effect, portfolios of Modern art: in addition to the in-text illustrations, there is a separate suite of just the illustrations, so they can be enjoyed without any distraction.

For example, *Le Livre de la Verité de Parole (The Book of the Truth of the Word)*, was created and published by Schmied in 1929. The book is a symphony of design surrounding transcriptions of ancient Egyptian texts that tell the story of the twelve doors of life. For the first plate of each of the twelve chapters, Schmied created a bold color wood engraving, with abstracted designs influenced by Egyptian motifs. The text pages display striking designs combining geometric shapes and lines. Only 150 copies of the book were printed by the artist, and each book and each of the twelve wood engravings was signed by him. The whole was printed as an unbound portfolio, with illustrated wrappers, a slipcase, which the French call an *étui* (literally "sheath"), and an inside second cover called a *chemise* (literally "shirt"), to hold the pages. Today, this book sells for as much as $6,000.

However, a wide range of wonderfully illustrated Art Deco books and publications can still be found at extremely affordable prices—under $100 in many instances, making it a rapidly growing collecting field for both book collectors and those interested in the design of the period.

Many different kinds of Art Deco books and publications contain fine illustrations, decorations, or stylized printing.

Nonesuch Press in Britain and the Limited Editions Club in America published numerous books with fine Art Deco illustrations. American artist W. A. Dwiggins designed hundreds of books with Art Deco decorative motifs for the publisher Alfred A. Knopf.

In France, numerous outstanding illustrators left their mark on the art of the book, including French designers Jean-Emile Laboureur, André Marty, Jean Dupas, Charles Martin, George Barbier, and Georges Lepape. The most popular illustrated books and publications of the early French Art Deco period are those which incorporate *pochoir* illustrations.

Pochoir, or stencil printing, was a favorite method of producing fashion illustration plates in small-edition, high-quality publications such as *La Gazette du Bon Ton*, the "Gazette of Good Taste." Under the direction of Lucien Vogel, this publication, which lasted from 1912 to 1925, featured the leading fashion designs illustrated by Barbier, Lepape, Charles Martin, André Marty, and numerous other talents. A complete "number" or full volume of *La Gazette* is rare on the market today, as the fashion plates have been removed and sold singly over the years.

The same is true for the dynamic textile designs in *pochoir* produced by French artist Edouard Benedictus. Starting in the late 1920s and ending in 1930, he produced three superb portfolios of plates: *Variations*, *Nouvelle Variations*, and *Relais*. While meant to gain him commissions as a textile and wallpaper designer, the portfolios were immediately seized upon as art, making it much easier today to find individual plates than complete portfolios.

Several other French artists turned to the creation of portfolios or "albums" of illustrations. In 1929, artist Paul Colin produced perhaps the best known album, *Le Tumulte Noir*, or "The Black Rage," which chronicled Paris's fascination with Josephine Baker and black jazz musicians. It contained forty-four color lithographic plates printed on Japan vellum, a high-quality lustrous paper, and only five hundred copies were published. The complete portfolio has rarely appeared on the contemporary market, but today would easily command $15,000–$20,000 or more.

In the United States, there were also several notable book illustrators and designers, including John Vassos, Rockwell Kent, and Lynd Ward.

John Vassos's bookbindings and illustrations for both his own and his wife Ruth's books such as *Contempo* (1929), *Ultimo* (1930), and *Phobia* (1931) are fine examples of American Art Deco design, and the books themselves are commentaries on modern life. The reissues of works by Oscar Wilde he designed and illustrated for the New York publisher E. P. Dutton are also sought-after: *Salomé* (1927), *The Ballad of Reading Gaol* (1928), and *The Harlot's House* (1929).

Rockwell Kent was one of the leading artists of the 1920s and 1930s, though he fell out of favor for many years because of his highly publicized communist/socialist politics. In the world of books, he is best known for his wood engraved illustrations. Books he illustrated for authors other than himself included Melville's *Moby Dick* (1930), Shakespeare's *Venus and Adonis* (1931), and numerous others. As author and illustrator, he produced the bold adventure *N. by E.* (1930), *Salamina* (1935), and others.

Lynd Ward's achievement was "writing" several novels without using any words, with only page after page of woodcuts to tell the book's story. His woodcut novels *God's Man* (1929), *Madman's Drum* (1930), and *Wild Pilgrimage* (1932) are highly sought-after.

The first "trade" editions of many of these books, for general bookstore distribution, were printed in relatively large quantities. However, there were often special or signed editions of these books as well. These limited issues are more valuable to collectors.

For example, a special edition of *God's Man* prior to the first trade edition was limited to 409 slipcased copies signed and numbered by the artist. This edition today can sell for $250 or more, while the first trade edition can still be found on the market for about $100 to $125, and second and subsequent printings can often be purchased for about $50.

A special edition of *N. by E.* by Rockwell Kent, bound in blue linen with silver decorative stamping and slipcase, was limited to nine hundred copies signed and numbered by the author and can sell today for $300 or more. The first trade edition, in a smaller format with fewer illustrations, was printed in such large quantities that it can often be found for about $50.

ART DECO COVERS AND DUST JACKETS

Like everything else in the 1930s, book publishing as an industry became increasingly geared toward mass-marketing. Both novels and nonfiction books were printed in quantities previously unheard of in publishing. Colorful Art Deco designs were often printed directly on the covers of hardbound books. A major book design development of the Art Deco period was the development and popularization of the pictorial paper dust jacket.

Dust jackets, like posters, were designed to catch the eye of the consumer who was walking past a bookstore window or glancing along a shelf. Dust jackets existed prior to the Art Deco period, but most were relatively plain, at least compared to the extravagant designs of the 1920s and 1930s.

The identity of many of the artists who designed dust jackets in the Art Deco style for thousands of novels and other books may never be known. Many were staff graphic artists at the large publishing houses, and others were freelancers who didn't sign (or whose contract didn't allow them to sign) their work. Since designing for dust jackets was relatively low paying, few of the best-known artists of the day received commissions.

However, there are some well-known names who did design dust jackets: Rockwell Kent, Boris Artzybasheff, W. A. Dwiggins, and Louis Lozowick are a sampling of the more famous.

Today, very little is known about many of the artists whose names appear frequently on outstanding dust jacket designs, such as Cosimini, Kubinyi, and the English artist Lee-Elliott.

Collectors who trust their taste will not be put off by the fact that these artists are "unknown." First, the price of such books hasn't climbed into the stratosphere based on the name or reputation of the artist alone. Secondly, a decade ago, in many Art Deco collecting fields, very little was "known" about designers who are today widely recognized. As the Art Deco period continues to be increasingly documented, no doubt new light will be shed on dust jacket artists. The quality of the designs and the talent of the artists is apparent, and the price is right—for now. Many exciting and unusual designs in fine condition can still be purchased from under $50 to $100.

DESIGN HISTORY REFERENCES

First editions of books written by the leading design theorists of the period are also sought by collectors, such as Norman Bel Geddes's *Horizons* (1932), and Paul Frankl's *New Dimensions* (1928) and *Form and Re-Form* (1930).

In addition, many collectors are now actively seeking other books, periodicals, and publications that help them document or better understand the history of their collections of other Art Deco materials.

For example, periodicals such as the French *Art et Décoration*, the English and American *Art and Industry*, and others documented the leading edge of design in the 1920s and 1930s. Auction houses and dealers often turn to these publications when trying to authenticate a desk by Ruhlmann, a table by Leleu, or a lacquered screen by Jean Dunand. Is it really a Leleu? When was it made? Who commissioned it? Questions like these may be answered in a simple photo caption.

Likewise, American and foreign consumer and trade periodicals of the day were the first to showcase new ideas by leading designers, prize-winning advertising posters, industrial designs, prototypes, and more. Collectors pore through the layouts, advertisements, and articles in publications such as the French *Arts et Métiers Graphiques* and the English *Modern Publicity*. In the American publication *Advertising Arts*, one finds articles written by the leading exponents of modern design: Norman Bel Geddes, Raymond Loewy, Lucian Bernhard, and others. Opening one of these publications is like opening a door on the past.

Other trade publications for the design field, such as paper manufacturer's sample books, suppliers' directories and catalogues, and printing brochures often have great Art Deco designs, as well as offering collectors a picture of the technological and artistic advances in advertising, printing, packaging, and other fields.

Happily, many of these periodicals and publications can still be found at very moderate prices, with single issues of most of them bringing retail prices of under $100. Sometimes they can still be found in miscellaneous bins at book fairs, garage sales, flea markets, and secondhand bookstores.

SPECIALTY PUBLICATIONS

Today, with the growing appreciation of Art Deco design in all fields, specialty publications of all kinds have become collectible. By specialty publications, we mean the widest possible variety of books, magazines, bound sheet music, advertising booklets, and more.

Some of these may be very high-priced, depending on the reputation of the artist. For example, a small promotional portfolio, entitled *Toi* (*You*), for the deluxe Parisian furrier Max carries seven full-page illustrations by Jean Dupas of women wearing furs. The cover of the portfolio is printed with stylized flowers and intersecting lines in red and silver ink on a black ground. This tiny advertising portfolio can bring $2,500 or more on the market today.

Numerous other specialty publications are much more moderately priced, bringing under $100, and in many instances under $25.

A WORD ABOUT FAKES AND MISREPRESENTATIONS

Luckily, forgeries are not a widespread problem in the book collecting field, except in the case of a few very expensive books, or forged signatures of well-known artists or writers in books. When in doubt, it is best to seek the advice of a specialist, especially for signatures. Elaborate hand-tooled bindings are so difficult to produce that they discourage forgers, and in my eighteen years in the book business, I can recall having only one forged binding.

Another way in which beginning collectors are sometimes fooled is by so-called association copies of books. Generally speaking, an association copy is one that is inscribed by someone involved in the production of the book: a publisher, illustrator, editor, or the author to a relative, a famous friend, the printer, a business partner or employee, or someone else closely associated with the inscriber. Books with these kinds of association inscriptions can bring higher prices than uninscribed copies. Sometimes beginners pay a high price for an "association," only to find that it is inscribed to a total stranger or to someone who is not important.

Another pitfall for buyers is buying a first or fine edition for a high price, only to find that the important original slipcase or dust jacket is not present. The presence of the slipcase or dust jacket can often increase the value of the book greatly.

No matter what your particular interest in Art Deco books—fine bindings, artists and illustrators, dust jackets, vintage periodicals and references, or even specialty publications—it is a field that remains accessible to a growing number of beginners, while also continuing to fascinate and attract advanced collectors.

SIX VINTAGE BOOK SHOPPING TIPS

1. Seek out the best available books within the price range you can afford. If you can only spend about $100, then buy a book where $100 gets you the best example of a book in good condition, rather than spending $100 on a terrible copy of a $1,000 book. That way you ensure the resale value of your collection. Many books of the Art Deco period are still available in almost mint condition, while older books might only be found in good condition. If you care about your investment, buy books in the best condition you can find them.
2. As in many other fields, the best advice for collectors is to learn about the field. Start by visiting the rare book room of your local library or by attending book fairs or visiting dealers. Book fairs are great places to see many books at different levels of condition and price and to do some comparison shopping on the more widely available books. If you are serious about book collecting, you should also build a reference library of "books about books." The price of a reference work can often be returned by a single use of its information!
3. By focusing on a particular subject, type of book or publication, artist, or some aspect of book collecting such as dust jackets or fine bindings, you can build a collection that is more valuable because its elements are related. In addition, specialist collectors can easily know more about a particular field than generalist book dealers, leading to better buys and more rewarding book hunting.
4. The book field has not universally adopted a standard guide for grading condition, and the possible defects are myriad. In buying from a catalogue at a distance, collectors need to be especially

cautious. You can usually rely on the word of a reputable dealer, but don't be afraid to ask questions or to double-check condition.

5.   Members of the Antiquarian Booksellers Association of America (ABAA) subscribe to a code of ethics, and any legitimate dealer will have a money-back return policy within reasonable time limits. If a dealer says purchases are nonreturnable, then forget it.

6.   Novice collectors might want to start with a popular or established area for which historical records, auction results, or multiple catalogue listings are available for research and comparison.

VINTAGE BOOKS AND PUBLICATIONS PRICE LISTINGS

BOOKS WITH FINE BINDINGS

Epitaph, 1929, by Theodore Dreiser, with decorations by Robert Fawcett. New York: Heron Press. Printed by August Gauthier. The striking binding in black tooled leather with the shape of a skyscraper composed from silver gilt rules and the title of the book in gold gilt. Limited to eleven hundred copies numbered and signed by the author. (*See color section.*)

    Numbers 1–200, printed on handmade Dutch Van Gelder paper   **$150–$225**

    Numbers 201–400, printed on handmade Kiejyokami, bound in silk   **$125–$175**

    Numbers 401–1,100, printed as above, but cloth bound   **$100–$125**

Exposé des Travaux, 1937, by P. Lecomte Du Nouy. Paris: Hermann & Cie. Quarto. 218 pages. Full red morocco leather binding by Charles Pagnier, tooled in gilt with diagonal and zigzag lines. Fine condition, with original slipcase. (*See color section.*) **$550–$600**

La Rapsode Foraine, 1929, by Tristan Corbière, with binding and designs by Louis Gilbert. Lithographs by Maurice Asselin. A fine tooled-leather binding with geometric

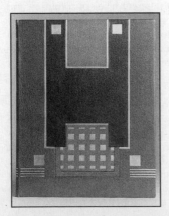

La Rapsode Foraine, 1929,
by Tristan Corbière.
Courtesy of Thomas G. Boss
Fine Books, Massachusetts.
Photo by Robert Four.

designs in gold, silver, black, and red, on both covers and inside covers. With its original *étui* and *chemise* (slipcase and second inside leather cover). One of only five printed on Japon Nacré paper, with original drawings. A stunning example of Art Deco fine binding by one of its leading artists.   **$4,500–$5,000**

BOOKS WITH ILLUSTRATIONS OR PLATES

Feuillets d'Art, No. III, 1922, edited by Lucien Vogel and André Marty. Paris and New York: Condé Nast. Large octavo. Eight unbound signatures. Pictorial wrappers and containing illustrations by Foujita and André Marty, as well as plates showing Egyptian sculpture and other subjects. In fine condition.   **$100–$125**

The Girl With the Golden Eyes, 1928, by Honoré de Balzac, translated by Ernest Dowson and illustrated by Donald Denton. Chicago: Peacock Press. Small quarto, 145 pages. Black cloth-backed gold foil boards with patterns of fans printed in black, with eight plates by Denton. In fine condition. (*See color section.*)   **$150–$200**

Le Livre de la Verité de Parole, 1929. Transcriptions of ancient Egyptian texts by Dr. J. C. Madrus, with twelve full-color wood engravings and other designs by François-Louis Schmied (1873–1941). Paris: Schmeid. Quarto. 64 folios, unbound as issued. Laid into illustrated wrappers and housed in a cloth-backed board *chemise* and *étui*. Each of the twelve chapters or *portes* ("doors") of the ancient Egyptian teachings is illustrated by a full-page abstract color wood engraving by Schmied. Each chapter has an impressive geometric opening and the text is set with dozens of abstract designs combining shapes and rules. Limited to 150 copies signed by the artist. This copy also has a personal inscription from Schmied in ink. One of Schmied's masterworks and a landmark in Art Deco bookmaking.   **$5,500–$6,000**

Motifs Japonais, c. 1920. Paris: Charles Moreau, with *pochoir* designs executed by L'Atelier Ferrariello. Octavo. Title page and forty plates, unbound as issued. Housed in a cloth-backed board portfolio with ribbon ties. A brightly colored selection of Japanese inspired designs colored by *pochoir*.   **$450–$500**

Feuillets d'Art, No. III.
Courtesy of Thomas G. Boss
Fine Books, Massachusetts.
Photo by Robert Four.

Nowel (Noel), 1926, illustrated by Walter Dorwin Teague. Currier & Hartford. A book of Elizabethan verses. Inscribed by the printer. With original wrappers.   **$60–$75**

Thais, 1931, by Norman Levy, with illustrations and cover design by Abner Epstein. A stunning cover design of overlapping geometric patterns in vivid colors and gold foil. One of only 250 copies on Mabuki paper.   **$100–$150**

The Time Machine, 1931, by H. G. Wells, and with designs by W. A. Dwiggins (1880–1956). New York: Random House. Octavo. 86 pages. Wonderful illustrations in color and black and white. Limited to twelve hundred copies printed at the Abbey Press. In near fine condition in slipcase.   **$100–$125**

Traité d'Enluminaire d'Art au Pochoir (Treatise on the Art of the Pochoir), 1925, by Jean Saudé. Paris: Editions de l'Ibis. 75 pages and twenty *pochoir* plates (in thirty states), plus illustrations, some color, in the text. Unsewn as issues in folder with cover *pochoir* by Benedictus, *pochoir* endpapers by Chapius and original *pochoir* slipcase. Plates include work by Lepape, Rodin, Albert Besnard, and others. One of 475 copies signed by Saudé. A stunning work.   **$4,500–$5,000**

BOOKS WITH ART DECO COVER DESIGNS

Blackfeet Indians, 1935, story by Frank B. Lindeman, illustrated by Winold Reiss, and signed by the artist. Published "May 11, 1935, the 25th Anniversary of the establishment of National Glacier Park by the Congress." Stunning zigzag cover design, repeated on the dust jacket. Inside full-page color illustrations of Blackfeet chiefs. Octavo. In fine condition, with dust jacket.   **$250–$300**

Chicago, the World's Youngest Great City, 1929. Presented by Marshall Field & Company. Chicago: American Publishers Corporation. 196 pages. Chamber of commerce–type publication touting the City of Chicago prior to the World's Fair. Numerous

**Chicago, 1929, cover
by William Welsh.**
*Courtesy of Thomas G. Boss
Fine Books, Massachusetts.
Photo by Robert Four.*

Art Deco dust jackets:
The Red Dancer of Moscow, Rings on Her Fingers and *The Knife.*
Courtesy of Thomas G. Boss Fine Books, Massachusetts. Photo by Robert Four.

photos of Chicago when the Art Deco buildings were the highest on the skyline. Stunning cover design of a stylized male head with wavy hair in yellow, brown, and gold by William Welsh (American, b. 1889). $100–$125

BOOKS WITH ART DECO DUST JACKETS

Artemis Weds, 1932, by Cicely Farmer, with a dust jacket design by Wgnck of a woman in profile. New York: Morrow. First American edition, cloth, fine condition, in dust jacket. (*See color section.*) $50–$60

Looking Backward, 1930, by Edward Bellamy, with a dust jacket design by Cosimini of an urban scene of fantastic skyscrapers in deep blue and black. Boston: Houghton-Mifflin. First edition, cloth, fine condition, in dust jacket. (*See color section.*) $50–$60

Gallows Orchard, 1930, by Claire Spencer, with an outstanding dust jacket design. New York: Jonathan Cape & Harrison Smith. First edition, cloth, fine condition, in dust jacket. (*See color section.*) $70–$85

The Knife, 1930, by Peadar O'Donnell, with a cover design by Lee-Elliott. London: Jonathan Cape. First edition, cloth, in very good condition. Strong graphic dust jacket in green, lavender, and black. $85–$110

Machinery, 1929, poems by MacKnight Black, with a cover design by Jacks. New York: Horace Liverwright. Interesting Deco dust jacket incorporating a motif of gear wheels. In very good condition, with small tears in dust jacket. $50–$70

The Red Dancer of Moscow, 1928, by H. L. Gates, with an outstanding dust jacket design by V. Kubinyi. New York: Grosset & Dunlap. This novel was the basis for the movie *The Red Dance* starring Dolores Del Rio. First edition, cloth, in very good condition, with small tears in dust jacket. $75–$100

Rings on Her Fingers, 1930, by Ryes Davies, with dust jacket design by Bissitt. London: Harold Shaylor. First edition, cloth, signed by the author, in good condition. Strong graphic dust jacket in black and white.   **$70–$85**

The Z Ray, 1932, by Edmund Snell. New York: J. P. Lippincott. Fine Deco design with a large "Z" along the top and bottom of which a streamlined car and airplane race in opposite directions. First edition, cloth, in good condition, dust jacket chipped.
                                                                                   $100–$125

DESIGN HISTORY REFERENCE WORKS

The Architect and the Industrial Arts, 1929, New York: Metropolitan Museum of Art. Catalogue of the exhibition. Cloth cover with an abstract Modern pattern in black and green.   **$100–$125**

Art and the Machine, 1936, by Sheldon and Martha Cheney. New York: McGraw-Hill. An interesting and informative work on industrial design of the early 1930s. **$65–$85**

L'Art Dans la Vie Moderne (Art in Modern Life), 1937, by P. Duckerman. Paris: Flammarion. 143 pages. Green wrappers, decorated on front and back covers. Text and three hundred illustrations on all areas of art from architecture to bookbinding representing ironwork by Subes; glass by Lalique; lacquer by Dunand; furniture by Leleu, Adnet, and Royere; and artists Matisse, Picasso, Rouault, and many others. In fine condition.
                                                                                   $150–$200

Horizons: A Glimpse Into the Not Far Distant Future, 1932, by Norman Bel Geddes. Boston: Little, Brown & Company. An important theoretical work on Modern design. In Chapter 1, "Towards Design," Bel Geddes presages, "In the perspective of fifty years

Advertising Arts, November 1934, cover by Joseph Binder. *Courtesy of Thomas G. Boss Fine Books, Massachusetts. Photo by Robert Four.*

Horizons, 1932, by Norman Bel Geddes. *Courtesy of Stephen Visakay, New Jersey.*

hence, the historian will detect in the decade of 1930–1940 a period of tremendous significance." $100–$150

New Dimensions, 1928, by Paul Frankl. "The Decorative Arts of Today in Words and Pictures." New York: Payson & Clarke. This work is dedicated to Frank Lloyd Wright and begins with a chapter entitled "What Is Modern?" An important design reference. Collectors should note that this book was reprinted in 1975. For the first edition, 1928, with dust jacket designed with overlapping color rectangles. $250–$300

DESIGN/ADVERTISING TRADE PUBLICATIONS

Advertising Arts, late 1920s–1930s. Trade publication, issued as a special section of *Advertising and Selling* magazine, New York City. Later issues are spiral bound. Each issue with outstanding covers, loaded with photos of modern design and illustrations by leading designers, as well as fascinating articles and advertisements for many of the leading industrial and advertising designers of the day.

April 1930 issue, cover by type style designer Lucien Bernhard, containing an article by Walter Dorwin Teague entitled "Designing for Machines," a profile of poster artist McKnight-Kauffer, layout illustrating the new Bernhard type style "Fashion." $55–$70

September 1932 issue, cover design by Boris Artzybasheff, with special articles and layouts on advertising photography and a profile of French artist/illustrator Jean Dupas. $45–$55

March 1934 issue, cover photograph of a hydroelectric plant by Margaret Bourke-White, containing an article by Walter P. Chrysler entitled "I Believe in Design"; photo spreads on new industrial designs by Vassos, Dreyfuss, Deskey, Guild and others; an article by Raymond Loewy entitled "The Evolution of the Motor Car." A fantastic issue! $85–$100

November 1934 issue, cover design by Joseph Binder, and containing a five-page photo layout of his graphic designs for posters and advertising; an article entitled "Design for the Electrical Appliance Field," with photos of industrial designs by Guild for Westinghouse and Chase, Dreyfuss for General Electric and Seth Thomas, and others. $50–$60

Advertising Arts and Crafts, 1930s. An address directory of designers, illustrators, and other design specialists in the advertising industry in New York. Illustrated with ads from the professional designers which show samples of their work, such as "Shoe Illustration." $100–$125

Metropolis, 1930s. Frankfurt: D. Stempel, A.G. German publication for graphic designers showing the latest in typography and design. $40–$60

Modern Advertising and the Paper Demonstrator, Volume 6. Published by the Paper Demonstrator, Chicago. Spiral bound notebook with tabs showing the latest paper samples, sizes, and printing techniques. $75–$85

Packaging Catalog, 1937. New York: Breskin & Charlton. Plastic-backed cover with embossed design of stylized people showing aspects of "Design," "Production," and "Merchandising." Catalogue for advertising agencies showing latest trends in printing, design, and production of product packaging. Enormous number of tipped-in samples. An elaborate production.   **$375–$450**

Paper Specimens, 1930s. Thomas N. Fairbanks Company. A paper sample book for graphic designers. 24 pages. Demonstrating the use of six colors of "Fiume Rubicone" Italian-made paper, with striking design illustrations.   **$50–$60**

The Rumford Imprint, 1930s, Concord, NH: Rumford Press. Printer's paper and design sample book with a striking cover design.   **$50–$60**

Sixth Annual Advertising and Publishing Production Yearbook, 1940, New York: Colton Press. Burlap-backed boards with a sculptural raised cover in a composite material showing artists and illustrators at work. Used as a reference book in advertising agencies for paper selection, typography, specialty printing processes, and the like.   **$75–$100**

Westvaco Inspirations for Printers, Series of 1936–1937, published by Westvaco Corporation. A catalogue of papers, inks, and printing techniques, illustrated with fine designs by the country's leading artists such as Rockwell Kent, Thomas Hart Benton, and others.   **$60–$80**

SPECIALTY PUBLICATIONS

Balanced Recipes, 1933, by Pillsbury Flour Company, Minneapolis. The cover of this spiral-bound recipe book is an aluminum box with "speed lines" and a circle embossed in black on the cover. An unusual item.   **$50–$75**

Cincinnatian, 1932, yearbook of the University of Cincinnati. Embossed cover in silver and black with a geometricized design of a student reading a book. Strong black and white geometricized designs throughout, and including the poster for the annual play, *When Tarts Are Trumps*. A hoot!   **$300–$350**

Harvard-Yale, November 22, 1930. Official program for the Harvard-Yale football game of 1930, with an eye-catching cover design by Robert Foster with two stylized helmeted faces of football players and a young woman.   **$35–$45**

Metal Progress Magazine, 1930s. New York. Trade publication devoted to the latest technologies in metal. Technical contents but stunning Art Deco cover designs showing factories, ocean liners, trains, building façades, and other metal applications.

October 1936 issue, Cover design illustration of a factory.   **$20–$30**

February 1936 issue, Cover design photograph of Art Deco metal grillwork on the entrance to an office building.   **$20–$30**

June 1937 issue, Cover design illustration showing a streamlined train next to a Cassandre-style ocean liner.   **$30–$50**

Toi, c. 1925, with designs by Jean Dupas. *Courtesy of Thomas G. Boss Fine Books, Massachusetts. Photo by Robert Four.*

Vesper George School of Art, 1930–1931 catalogue. *Courtesy of Thomas G. Boss Fine Books, Massachusetts. Photo by Robert Four.*

Music, 1931 by Paramount Publix. A bound portfolio of musical song scores from the late 1920s and early 1930s, including "Falling in Love Again," the song made famous by Marlene Dietrich in the movie *The Blue Angel*. Stylized, geometric design on cover.
$40–$50

Saving the Pieces, 1930, by Sidney Skolsky, with a cover design by R. Floethe. Reprints of articles which appeared in the writer's column "Behind the News" in the *New York Daily News*. Elongated "pocket" size, with a jazzy cover design of Rockettes-type dancers and saxophone players.
$75–$85

Toi (You), c. 1925. For Max Fourrures (Max Furriers), and illustrated by Jean Dupas (1882–1964). A small promotional portfolio of designs on paper. Unbound. The cover printed with a design of intersecting lines and stylized flowers in red and silver ink on a black ground. Inside, seven full-page illustrations by Jean Dupas of women wearing furs. A postcard of the furrier's shop at 19 Avenue Matignon in Paris slips into a die-cut on the back inside cover. A stunning portfolio of Dupas's work.
$2,500–$3,500

Vesper George School of Art, 1930–1931, Boston. Catalogue for this well-known art school of the period. A stunning cover design incorporating geometric patterns, a stylized winged Pegasus, and a background of stars.
$25–$40

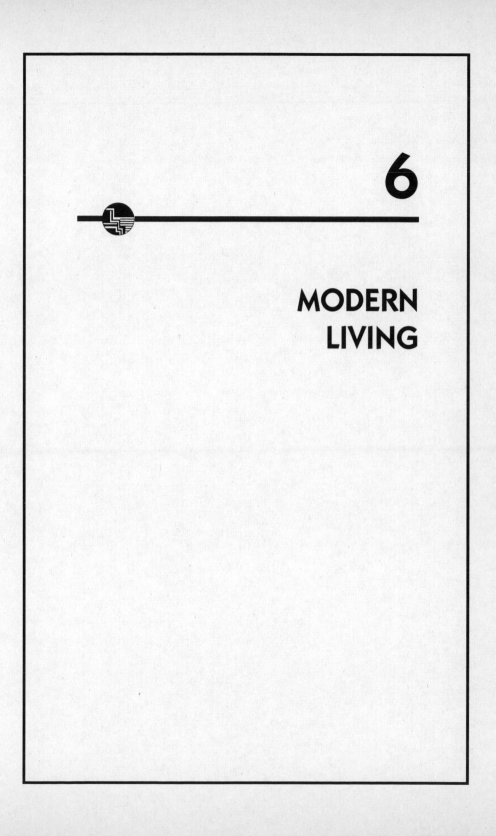

6

MODERN
LIVING

OCEAN LINER MEMORABILIA

Ocean cruising is enjoying a resurgence of popularity. *Time* magazine reported that a record four million Americans took cruises in 1991, in spite of the recession. Classic companies, such as Cunard, which is over 150 years old, are still known for the high-quality personalized service that has been their reputation. Other cruise ships today are more like floating Las Vegas hotels, complete with headline entertainment and crowded casinos.

In 1992, there was a resurgence of interest in ocean liner memorabilia as well, as the world remembered the eightieth anniversary of the sinking of the *Titanic* on April 14, 1912. In June 1992, the oldest survivor of the *Titanic*, Marjorie Robb, died at age 103. The Titanic Historical Society today has almost five thousand members.

The rare souvenirs and memorabilia of the luxurious 46,328-ton liner which went down on its maiden voyage are bringing record prices today. Postcards can easily bring $300 and more, books and newspaper accounts of the disaster can bring $200 and more, and a rare carpet fragment from a first-class stateroom was recently offered for $5,000.

While many people collect the memorabilia of both older and newer ocean liners, Art Deco collectors will find a rich treasure of memorabilia and souvenirs from the 1920s and 1930s.

Collectors turn to two different sources for finding items for their collections: attics and specialized dealers in the field, such as Ken Schultz of Hoboken, New Jersey. Schultz's catalogues of ocean liner memorabilia are loaded with fine examples of collectibles from the Art Deco period from a variety of different countries.

The 1920s and 1930s were the heyday of the great luxury *paquebots*, or ocean liners. Many of the French liners were floating museums of the finest in Art Deco design. Perhaps they were inspired by the French, or perhaps it was something inherent in the modern, streamlined design of the vessels themselves, but many other nations, too, designed and furnished their liners in the sleek new style.

Then again, perhaps it was because the liner companies had to appeal to a sophisticated clientele—a clientele which had already developed a taste for the new design as part of their up-to-date lifestyle. Later, ocean liners would have to fulfill tourists' dreams of romance and style as epitomized in Hollywood films.

The opulence and good taste of the *Normandie* decor included French coffee service by Christofle, with circular coffee pot and creamers, and semicircular sugar bowls, set on triangular bases. Still considered stylish today, the set was reproduced in a numbered edition for Bloomingdale's by Christofle in silverplate with semicircular ebony handles.

The leading early French Art Deco designers were commissioned by the government to design the interiors and furnishings of the *Normandie* and other ocean liners as a sort of official patronage.

Besides the *Normandie*, other French Line ocean liners which are favorites with Art Deco collectors are the *Ile de France*, *L'Atlantique*, and *Paris*. Several vessels of the Dutch Holland-America Line, the English Cunard Line, the Canadian Pacific Line, the Italian Line, the German Lloyd Bremen Line, and others have prized Art Deco furnishings, decorative arts, functional objects, and ephemera.

It would take more than a whole book to describe both the fine furnishings which are now sold at major auction houses, and the low-end collectibles such as postcards, which can be found at ephemera fairs. The range of what is collected is phenomenal—almost the same range represented in this book for the entire field of Art Deco: furnishings, silver, glass, ceramics, books, posters, graphics, and fashion accessories.

Many collectors of ocean liner memorabilia start their collection with a few souvenirs of an ocean crossing made by a parent or grandparent, and try to collect as much as they can about a certain liner. Other collectors focus on a whole line, such as Cunard, and their collecting spans much more than just the Art Deco period. Some collectors specialize in the colorful lithographic pre–World War II posters for the famous liners, designed by outstanding graphic artists such as A. M. Cassandre. (*See "Posters and Graphics" for additional examples of Art Deco ocean liner posters.*)

Below is just a small sampling of the treasures from a few of the well-known liners which extensively used Art Deco design.

OCEAN LINER MEMORABILIA PRICE LISTINGS
(Alphabetically by name of the ocean liner or line)

L'ATLANTIQUE
Booklet, 1930s. Color interior/exterior renderings from pre–maiden voyage of *L'Atlantique*. 34 pages. Foil cover with ship's portrait against the tricolors of the French flag.
$550–$600

Booklet from *L'Atlantique*.
Courtesy of Ken Schultz,
New Jersey.

Postcard. Depicting lobby of the ship with a car in glass showcase. Printed in the top left corner, "C. De Navigation Sud-Atlantique," and in lower right corner "Paquebot 'L'Atlantique'—Vitrines de la Rue Centrale." Very rare.   **$40–$45**

BLUE STAR LINE
Baggage label. For their South American Service—unused.   **$15–$20**

Booklet, 1930s, first-class, 24 pages. Excellent booklet of photo interiors/exteriors for the *Arandora Star*—a tear at spine, otherwise fine.   **$75–$85**

Deck plan. With photo interiors/exteriors for the *Arandora Star*—excellent condition.
                                    $65–$75

Handbook, 1930s, 216 pages. The *Arandora Star* cruise handbook, photo interiors/ exteriors, passenger information, and places to be visited.   **$65–$75**

Menu, 6/1/31. Colorful menu for the *Arandora Star*.   **$15–$20**

Postcard. Great postcard for the *Arandora Star*—unused.   **$15–$20**

CANADIAN PACIFIC LINE
Booklet, 24 pages. "Cabin Service to Europe," with photo interiors/exteriors for their cabin class vessels, including the *Monts*, *Melita*, *Metagama*, *Marburn*, *Marloch*, and *Montreal*—excellent condition.   **$75–$85**

Booklet, 1931–1932. "7 West Indies Cruises," with photo interiors/exteriors, rates, sailings, places visited, etc., for the *Empress of Australia* and *Duchess of Bedford*. Together with the original mailing envelope.   **$65–$75**

Calendar, 3" high. Rare silverplated perpetual calendar with a beautifully enameled crest with C.P. house flag over the name of the *Melita*—all pieces present. Excellent condition.   **$100–$125**

Clock, 4" diameter. Handsome standing chrome clock in the shape of a ship's wheel with the name of the *Duchess of York* engraved on it. In working order, and excellent condition.   **$125–$150**

Deck plan, February 1930. Rare color-coded tissue deck plan with photo interiors/ exteriors for the *Melita*. Excellent condition.   **$100–$125**

Egg cup, 3" high. Unusual silverplated egg cup with filigreed sides and a beautifully enameled crest with the C.P. house flag and the name of the *Duchess of Richmond* on it and a place on the base to hold a spoon. Excellent condition.   **$75–$85**

Folder, January 1929. Folder of photo interiors/exteriors for the tourist/third cabin on the *Montclare*—text in Swedish. Great full color cover. Excellent condition.
                                    $65–$75

· CONTE DI SAVOIA ·

Postcard of a veranda apartment on the *Conte di Savoia*. *Courtesy of Ken Schultz, New Jersey.*

Napkin ring. Silverplated with a beautifully enameled crest with the C.P. house flag and the name of the *Duchess of York* on it. Excellent condition.   **$65–$75**

Postcard. Excellent postcard of the *Duchess of Bedford* at Liverpool–unused.   **$25–$30**

CONTE DI SAVOIA

Ashtray, 6½" long, 4½" wide, 1" deep. Much sought-after china ashtray by Ginori used aboard both the *Conte di Savoia* and the *Rex.* Triangular shaped, white with gold trim and house logo. Excellent condition.   **$250–$300**

Deck plan, October 1932. Most important color-coded pre–maiden voyage tissue deck plan—first class. A small seam tear, otherwise in excellent condition.   **$350–$400**

Launch booklet, October 1931, 26 pages. Photos of her construction from cradle till on the stocks just before the launch. Great Art Deco covers with much gold leaf. Excellent condition.   **$500–$600**

Menu, 2/24/33. Menu for a private dinner aboard—unusual cover. Excellent condition.   **$20–$25**

Postcard. Rare oversized postcard for a veranda apartment. Unused.   **$25–$30**

CUNARD LINE

Baggage label, 1930s. Red, white, and green—unused.   **$15–$20**

Baggage label. Highly graphic with full-color portraits of the *Britannic* and *Lancastria.* Unused.   **$25–$30**

Booklet, 1920s, first class, 20 pages. Excellent booklet of photo interiors/exteriors for the *Caronia, Carmania, Lancastria, Tuscania, Laconia, Scythia, Samaria,* and *California.* Excellent condition.   **$75–$85**

Charger, 24" diameter, 2" deep. Lithograph on tin with the Cunard logo filling the entire center and between the caption "Cunard Line tickets and drafts for sale here." Dazzling color and excellent condition.   **$2,500–$2,750**

Display unit, 36" high, 33" wide, 6" deep. Standing display unit with the stylized bows of the *Aquitania, Mauretania*, and *Berengaria* literally reaching for the sky over the black letters "Cunard" and the caption, "The shortest bridge to Europe," and beside the caption, "The Big 3 to France and England." An attached plaque states: "Designed and executed by Kay of Austria—New York Sales Office Chanin Building." This piece was exhibited at *Forbes* magazine in New York during the Cunard Sesquicentennial Exhibition a few years ago. Excellent condition.   **$3,500–$3,750**

Folder, 1920s, 16 pages. Great folder of photo interiors/exteriors for most of the Cunard and Anchor Line fleets. Many rare shots of areas like mailrooms, etc. Great shot of Pearl White (*Perils of Pauline*) being photographed aboard the *Aquitania*.   **$75–$85**

Magazine, June 1923, 36 pages. Copy of the *Cunard Magazine*, house organ of Cunard, great articles on the new *Franconia* and shopping at sea.   **$65–$75**

Muffiner, 7½" high. Silverplated, by Elkington—marked with the Cunard White Star logo. Excellent condition.   **$125–$150**

Pie stand and trays, pie stand: 7" high; trays 9" diameter. Silverplated pie stand by BSL with three trays, all four pieces marked with the Cunard name and lion. Excellent condition.   **$350–$400**

Postcard. Rare color postcard of the *Campania* by Odin Rosenvinge—unused.   **$35–$40**

Postcard. With an exceptionally fine image of the *Lucania*—unused.   **$25–$30**

Stationery. Rare piece of crested stationery for the *Bothnia* with companion envelope. Unused.   **$35–$40**

Tureen, 5" high. Silverplated tureen with lid and ladle by Embassy and all bearing the Cunard White Star logo and stamped kosher for meat. Excellent condition.   **$350–$400**

EMPRESS OF BRITAIN II

Baggage tag. For the anniversary crossing—original string.   **$15–$20**

Deck plan, c. 1931–1932. Color-coded deck plan with full-color interior/exterior renderings by Kenneth Shoesmith and F. Geffin for her first world cruise. Excellent condition.   **$125–$150**

Folder, c. 1936. Color folder for 1/20/36 crossing from Barcelona and Monaco—spectacular color cover opens to a 36" by 12" photo of the *Empress*—rates on reverse. French text. Folded.   **$65–$75**

Menu, c. 1933. Spectacular menu for celebrating one hundred years of steamship travel between Quebec and Europe commencing with the sailing of the *Royal William*, August 17, 1833. Special color and silver leaf cover. $75–$85

Postcard. A great postcard of the *Empress* possibly leaving her builders—unused.
$35–$40

Postcard. Depicting the *Empress* in the Suez Canal—unused. $35–$40

EUROPA
Ashtray, 1930s. In china, triangular-shaped with ship's full-color portrait in the center.
$75–$85

Deck plan, 1936. Color-coded, done in page form. $50–$60

Menus from *Europa*. Each. $10–$12

FRENCH LINE
Baggage label, c. 1920s. Green and white, first class, original string. Mint. $20–$25

Booklet, 18 pages. Photo interiors/exteriors for the *Rochambeau*. Excellent condition.
$85–$95

Booklet, 20 pages. Photo interiors/exteriors for the tourist class on the *Ile de France*, *Paris*, *Champlain*, and *Lafayette*. Excellent condition. $65–$75

Folder. Rare full-color interior renderings for first class on the *Colombie* and *Cuba* by Odin Rosenvinge. Excellent condition. $125–$150

Lapel pin, 1½" long. Enameled, in the form of a crest with anchor and the company name in both French and English—excellent condition. $65–$75

Thermos, c. 1930s, 13½" high. Silverplated with large house logo on the side. Liner intact and still usable. Some dents and wear, but on the whole quite presentable. $600–$700

HOLLAND-AMERICA LINE
Ashtray, 1930s–1940s. Silverplated, with raised house logo in the center. $40–$50

Playing cards, 1930s. In original box, red with full-color house flag. $60–$65

ILE DE FRANCE
Color postcards, 1930s. A series of postcards by John Frey which have become well-known. Unused. Each. $20–$25

Silk scarf, c. 1939. A portrait of the vessel, with the crest and name surrounded by the company's, and in each corner a French Line sailor and house flag. Done in tones of greens, reds, and blues on a cream background. $75–$90

Wine list, c. 1926, 10 pages. Beautifully engraved cover of the *Ile de France*'s dining saloon and an equally fine engraving inside. Excellent condition.   **$75–$85**

ITALIAN LINE

Book, 40 pages. Much sought-after hardcover book *The Mild Southern Route to Europe*, photo interiors/exteriors along with magnificent full-color renderings for the *Rex, Conte di Savoia, Augustus, Conte Grande, Roma, Saturnia*, and *Vulcania*—all first class. The famous full-color double-page center section of "The Royal Family of the Seven Seas." Repaired spine.   **$350–$400**

Deck plan, c. 1933. Utterly spectacular color-coded deck plan for the 1933 world cruise of the *Augustus* with photo interiors/exteriors. The design of this plan is remarkable— literally presented as a cutaway, yet a deck plan.   **$100–$125**

Folder, c. 1933. Rare folder announcing the 1933 world cruise, giving the sailing schedule and rates.   **$45–$50**

Poster, c. 1927, 27½" high, 19½" wide. Extremely rare broadside poster with a dazzling color portrait of the *Esperia* over the sailing schedule for May-June 1927. Excellent condition.   **$500–$600**

Poster, c. 1934, 39" high, 26½" wide. Extremely rare, by Kodic for the *Francesco Morosini*, much use of silver leaf. Excellent condition. A vessel for which little if anything is seen.   **$500–$600**

(See also the chapter "Posters and Graphics" for additional information and price listings on posters depicting ocean liners.)

NORMANDIE

Ashtray, 7" long, 3½" wide. Octagon shaped with the *Normandie* raised in the bowl. Two-tone coloring on the metal gives a lovely effect. Excellent condition.   **$200–$225**

Baggage tag. Color portrait baggage tag—unused. Original string.   **$25–$30**

Booklet, 22 pages. Rare pre–maiden voyage booklet of first-class color interior/exterior renderings. Excellent condition.   **$250–$300**

Chairs, c. 1934, 34½" high, 22½" wide, 20½" deep. A pair of mahogany dining chairs from the first-class dining room. The cantilevered seat with the fluted shirt, supported on four tapering, curved legs ending in brass feet, the arms as a continuous band, the rolled seat backs with flutes at either side, the entire chair weighted for stability, the modern needlepoint upholstery a faithful reproduction of the original.   **$11,000 (Auction)**

Cordial glass, 3½" high. Created by Lalique for the deluxe suites—mint condition.   **$500–$600**

Cream pitcher, 4" high. Silverplated, by Christofle—a small dent on rim, otherwise excellent condition.   **$400–$450**

Deck chair from the *Normandie*.
Courtesy of Ken Schultz, New Jersey.

Normandie silver medallion, by Jules Vernon, 1935. *Courtesy of Skinner, Inc., Massachusetts.*

Ashtray from the *Paris*.
Courtesy of Ken Schultz, New Jersey.

Deck chair, c. 1934, 36" high, 56" long, 22½" wide. A teak deck chair and cushion. Designed to collapse for storage, with a pressed cane seat and back, the footrest with eight slats, with the original cushion and rust-colored cover with buff piping and CGT logo.

$1,600 (Auction)
$2,500–$3,000

Folder, c. 1935. Pre–maiden voyage folder of first-class interiors/exteriors—excellent condition. $200–$225

Fork, 7" long, silverplated. $125–$150

Matches, book of her portrait matches—unused. $35–$40

Medallion, 2½" diameter. Designed by Jules Vernon for her maiden voyage and executed by the French Mint in sterling silver in a very small edition. $1,500–$1,750

Menu, 13½" high, 10½" wide. Large first-class dinner menu. Excellent condition.
$45–$50

Nut dish, 1½" high. Excellent condition. $350–$400

Pin, 2" wide, 1½" long. Extremely rare blue Bakelite pin in the form of a blue riband with the *Normandie*'s name in silver on it. $400–$450

Plates, 9" diameter, set of five. Designed by Haviland Limoges. In porcelain, each circular plate with double gilt ring banding concave center, the rim with gilt "Compagnie Generale Transatlantique" logo, printed firm's mark.   **$300–$350**

Postcard. Excellent postcard for her maiden entry into New York—unused.   **$35–$40**

Postcard. Color photo of the first-class dining saloon—unused.   **$20–$25**

Soup spoon, 7½" long. Silverplated soup spoon—on the whole in excellent condition.   **$125–$150**

Teapot, 5½" high. Silverplated, by Christofle—on the whole in excellent condition.   **$800–$900**

Tray, 10" long, 8" wide, ¼" deep. Silverplated octagonal shape with house logo in the center. Excellent condition.   **$600–$700**

Water glass, 5" high. Cut crystal with house logo on the side. Mint condition. **$250–$300**

NORTH GERMAN LLOYD

Baggage label. Rare die cut baggage label for the *Bremen* and *Europa* "Where Society Meet"—unused. Excellent condition.   **$25–$30**

Booklet, c. 1931, 11½" long, 10½" wide, 20 pages. Photo interiors/exteriors for the *Bremen*, *Europa*, and *Columbus*—first class. German text. Excellent condition.   **$200–$225**

Booklet, c. 1930, 16 pages. Full color tipped in interiors/exteriors for the *Bremen* and *Europa* in the height of Art Deco styling by Felix Schwarmstadt. Gold leaf, covers are rough, contents good, renderings are perfect.   **$200–$225**

Booklet, c. 1936, 12 pages. Rare booklet for their Panama Canal Service with photo interiors/exteriors for the *Werrer*, *Elbe*, *Tacoma*, *Este*, and *Schwaben*.   **$125–$150**

Postcard. Super color, oversized postcard—unused.   **$65–$75**

PARIS

Ashtray, 1930s, 5" diameter. Cut crystal, in the style of Lalique. Frosted in the center, with the ship's three funnels and the French Line name.   **$275–$300**

Booklet, April 1937, 16 pages. With photos of interiors/exteriors.   **$80–$90**

Deck plan, 1938. Color-coded, for West Indies cruises. Stylized graphic Art Deco cover.   **$75–$85**

Postcards, showing various rooms on the *Paris*, including the dance floor, the grand staircase entrance to the smoking room, the dining salon, the playroom, the promenade deck, and other exteriors. Each.   **$10–$15**

WORLD'S FAIR MEMORABILIA

World's Fair memorabilia collecting got a tremendous boost in 1989, the fiftieth anniversary of both the 1939 New York World's Fair and the 1939 Golden Gate International Exposition on Treasure Island in San Francisco Bay. Numerous magazine stories, newspaper articles, and new books recalled the magnificent pavilions and wonders of the fairs. Across the country, exhibitions, television specials, and commemorative events celebrated the anniversary.

Even Steuben, the American glass company, hosted at its posh Fifth Avenue store in New York an exhibition called "Steuben and the '39 World's Fair." The exhibit included major works which had been designed for presentation at their pavilion in 1939, such as American sculptor Sydney Waugh's 39", three-hundred-pound mermaid "Atlantica," one of the largest clear crystal sculptures ever cast.

All 1939 World's Fair memorabilia—from salt and pepper shakers to posters to fine glassware—rose in price on the collecting market in response to the publicity. Suddenly, the cheapest toothpick holder commemorating the 1939 New York World's Fair took on the patina of a fifty-year-old collectible.

For the Art Deco collector, the most popular fairs are the 1933 Chicago World's Fair, called "Century of Progress," and the 1939 New York World's Fair, called "The World of Tomorrow."

"It was actually the Chicago World's Fair of 1933 that had a true European Art Deco look," states Herbert Rolfes, owner of Yesterday's World in New Jersey, which specializes in World's Fair memorabilia, and co-author of *The World of Tomorrow*, published by Harper & Row in 1988. "By the time the New York World's Fair happened, the style was really more 'Streamline.'"

The Chicago "Century of Progress," held in 1933, at the height of the Depression, was intended to be an uplifting fair, one that would set America back on track. It was a showcase for modern materials, modes of transportation, and glimpses of what the future looked like in 1933. Though the effort had to be scaled down from its original plans due to economic constraints, the fair was popular enough to attract over thirty-five million visitors. You can just imagine how many souvenirs that means, even though people did not have a lot of money to spend!

The 1939 New York World's Fair, "The World of Tomorrow," was even more optimistic, given that it was presented just before World War II, and over fifty million people turned out for it. The vision of a technological future was even more evident at this fair.

Incredible exhibits captivated the thoughts of Americans, such as the spacious automated freeways of the General Motors "Futurama" designed by Norman Bel Geddes. Other stunning examples of modern exhibition architecture were created by Walter Dorwin Teague, who designed Con Edison's "City of Light," Ford's "Road of Tomorrow" and the giant National Cash Register.

It is estimated that there were over twenty-five thousand different souvenirs produced for the 1939 World's Fair, some "officially" licensed, some not. The vast majority of them, including photographs, postcards, ashtrays, spoons, matchboxes, and so much more, can be collected for under $100. However, some of the best or rarest examples of Fair memorabilia can bring $2,000, $3,000, or more.

For example, an advance publicity poster for the Fair, designed in 1937 by Nembhard N. Culin, and published by the New York World's Fair 1939 Corporation, can sell today for as much as $4,000, depending on condition. This stunning color lithographic poster is a captivating serial view illustration of the Trylon and Perisphere, with fireworks overhead. (*See photo and description in "World's Fair Memorabilia Price Listings."*)

Perhaps the best-known poster of the fair to Art Deco collectors is Austrian/American graphic artist Joseph Binder's prize-winning design. More graphic than illustrative in style, it shows the searchlights of the fair above the Trylon and Perisphere and planes flying overhead.

Comments Rolfes, "It's a fine design, and can sell for a thousand dollars or more. But it's not as great as the Culin poster, or, for that matter, John Atherton's poster for the fair, which is very rare and can bring as much as $3,000."

Besides being a dealer in World's Fair memorabilia, Rolfes has an enormous personal collection, including a wide variety of memorabilia from the 1933 Chicago and 1939 New York fairs.

He comments that one of the most popular souvenirs of the New York World's Fair were commemorative plates. These were usually not meant to be used as dinner plates, but to be displayed in china closets back home after the folks returned from the "Big Fair." They range from undistinguished designs that can be purchased today for under $25, to the intricate and refined decoration on Homer Laughlin Company commemorative plates for 1939 and 1940, which can sell for $350 each. (*See photo and description in the "World's Fair Memorabilia Price Listings."*)

"These plates were designed by Charles Murphy, who also designed Fiesta ware for Homer Laughlin," notes Rolfes. "Actually, I think the 1940 plate should sell for more than the 1939 plate because perhaps one-third fewer were made."

The New York World's Fair, like others before it, made a comeback in 1940, and while millions of people attended, the fair was just a ghost of its original self. In 1939, some of the major pavilion sponsors, such as foreign governments, packed up and went home in the shadow of the ominous war that was to come. The fairgrounds took on the aspect of a carnival, complete with carnival-type sideshows. This is one reason that, today, 1940 Fair souvenirs are generally much less desirable.

At the time, advances in transfer printing in ceramics, both in England and in the United States, allowed for elaborate colors and patterns to be mass-produced for these plates.

"You'll find that 99 percent of them have flaws," notes Rolfes. "Especially on the gold rim. I'm not talking about chips in the ceramic, but just where the gold transfer on the rim has rubbed off. After all, a transfer is nothing but a decal. Sometimes you'll find the decals were applied crookedly, too."

New York World's Fair souvenirs weren't sold just at the fairgrounds. Department stores like Tiffany and Abraham & Straus commissioned ceramics and glass companies

One of the murals by Carlo Alberto Ciamaglia at Fair Park in Dallas.
Courtesy of The Friends of Fair Park.

to create World's Fair pieces especially for their customers. Eastman Kodak issued "special editions" of their "Baby Brownie" and "Bullet" cameras with new applied fair logos to sell at their own pavilion. Collectibles today include posters from European ocean liner companies advertising the fair as a destination. Companies both here and abroad manufactured an incredible range of World's Fair items.

This was the case with another popular collectible, women's compacts, which usually came with powder puffs and a small mirror. Many of these were produced for export in England and other countries as well as in the United States.

"I have about two hundred of them in my private collection," Rolfes comments. "They come in a wide variety of colors and shapes, and most are enameled metal. Today they sell for $50 to about $125, and seem to be almost as popular as they were then."

World's Fair memorabilia collecting encompasses both the staggering array of cheaply mass-produced items and much more expensive materials, such as finely sculpted bronze medallions from famous expositions. Each fair seems to have something unique to offer collectors. It is a field unto itself, with its own publications, clubs, and networks of collectors, such as World's Fair Collectors Society, which is headquartered in Florida. For information on their activities, write to Mike Pender, World's Fair Collectors Society, P.O. Box 20806, Sarasota, FL 34276–3806.

Other than New York and Chicago, there were numerous great fairs held during the 1930s Depression years. Many of these also produced desirable souvenirs in the Art Deco style: the 1935 Universal Exposition in Brussels, the Great Lakes Exposition in Cleveland in 1937, the International Exposition in Paris in 1937, and San Francisco's Golden Gate International Exposition in 1939.

Another 1930s fair was the Dallas Centenary Exposition in 1936. Today, Dallas's Fair Park has the largest existing collection of Art Deco fair buildings in the world, and they are the focus of a massive preservation and restoration project under the auspices of the Friends of Fair Park. (*See "Resource Guide" listing for contact information.*)

Unfortunately, fairs and their pavilions were considered temporal. Constructed to remain in place for a few months or a year, the pavilions are generally left to fall apart, or be torn down for new development or new fairs. Occasionally, a monumental structure is left standing as a permanent recollection of the fair: the "Space Needle" in Seattle, or the Eiffel Tower in Paris.

The New York World's Fair was certainly the ultimate playground for great architects and "industrial designers" such as Raymond Hood, Lee Lawrie, Joseph Urban, and Walter Dorwin Teague. General Motors "Futurama," designed by Norman Bel Geddes, was considered by many as the highlight of the fair. Leaving this pavilion with its exhibit of how America might look in the future—in 1960—the visitor could buy a souvenir lapel pin reading, "I have seen the future."

Westinghouse looked even further into the future. Its pavilion contained a time capsule which was sealed at the end of the fair, not to be reopened until the year 6939. One can only imagine what its contents will bring on the World's Fair memorabilia market 4,950 or so years from now!

WORLD'S FAIR MEMORABILIA PRICE LISTINGS

1933 CHICAGO "CENTURY OF PROGRESS"

Book, 1933 Chicago and the World's Fair, 1933. Chicago: F. Humson Publishing. A comprehensive overview of the fair. A good reference work with a great cover design showing searchlights over stylized buildings and throngs of people.   **$75–$85**

Bookends, 6" high. Chrome greyhounds on marble base, with "Century of Progress" seal in metal affixed to base, excellent condition. Pair.   **$400–$450**

Cocktail shaker, 11" high. In light aluminum, with a tapering cylindrical form. Stamped with the symbol of the fair and with cocktail recipes.   **$45–$65**

1933 Chicago and the World's Fair book. Courtesy of Thomas G. Boss Fine Books, Massachusetts. Photo by Robert Four.

1933 World's Fair aluminum cocktail shaker. *Courtesy of Stephen Visakay, New Jersey.*

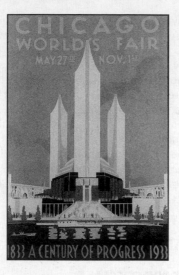

1933 World's Fair poster by **Weimar Purcell.** *Courtesy of Yesterday's World, New Jersey.*

Glasses, 5½" high. Set of four drinking glasses with transfer design of "Century of Progress" seal in blue and white. Some flaking to transfer, otherwise excellent condition.
$200–$250

Medallion, 2½" diameter. Bronze medallion for the "1933 Century of Progress International Exposition, Chicago, 1833–1933," awarded for "Industry and Research"; artist signed "Zettler." Very good souvenir of the fair.
$150–$200

Photo booklet, 10" high, 7" wide. "Official Pictures," published by Reuben H. Donnelly Corporation, Chicago, 1933. With dozens of black and white photos of buildings, exhibits, and monuments. In excellent condition.
$85–$95

Poster, designed by Weimar Purcell for the Neely Printing Company. A striking design in bright colors. Collectors should note that this poster has been reproduced. The original poster is printed on thin paper, similar to movie poster paper, and the reproduction is printed on a heavier stock. In excellent condition.
$850–$1,000

1939 NEW YORK WORLD'S FAIR

Ashtray, 4" diameter. In hammered brass with Trylon and Perisphere applied medallion in the center.
$15–$20

Beaded drawstring bag, 4¾" high. Composed of glass satin tube and seed beads, depicting Trylon and Perisphere, interior with small mirror. A good-quality souvenir.
$100–$125

Cameras. Eastman Kodak "Baby Brownie" and "Bullet" special-edition cameras, which added "The New York World's Fair" and an applied Trylon and Perisphere to existing models. (The "Baby Brownie" was designed by Walter Dorwin Teague, and produced

Kodak's "Baby Brownie" *(left)* and "Bullet"
(right) special-edition cameras. *Courtesy of
Yesterday's World, New Jersey.*

Combination cane and fold-down seat.
Courtesy of Yesterday's World, New Jersey.

from 1934 to 1941 without the World's Fair logo in a total of over three and a half million.) A desirable collectible of the fair. In working condition. $500–$550
With original camera box $600–$650

Cane/seats. Combination cane and fold-down seat for waiting in the long lines at pavilions. Made of solid wood, usually found with a single cane handle, decorated with a fair decal on the seat. "Kan-O-Seat," marked on the bottom of the seat, "Kan-O-Seat/ Pat. May 21 1935/ Stafford-Johnson Corp./ Iona/ Mich." Depending on condition $25–$75
With rarely-found T-handle on cane $150–$200

Compacts. Complete with powder puff and small mirror. Produced in a wide variety of colors and shapes, most in enameled metal; some with applied metal decoration to leather cases or needlepoint applied to metal. Makers' names on compacts include Girex, Zell, and the English company Gwenda. Each, depending on quality of design and condition. $50–$125

Cup and saucer. In ivory glazed ceramic, with transfer of Trylon and Perisphere in orange and blue. $75–$80

Guide book, 8" high, 5" wide. The "Official Guidebook" to the World's Fair, with dramatic cover in red, yellow, black, and lavender. 256 pages, with fold-out map of the fairgrounds. First edition, in excellent condition $60–$80
Third edition, in excellent condition $40–$50

Lamp, 6⅞" high, 4" wide. Circular glass shield of frosted glass, depicting Trylon and Perisphere, fitting into stepped rectangular base. Mint condition. $220 **(Auction)**
$300–$400

Map, pictorial. "The Official World's Fair Pictorial Map," created by Tony Sarg, a popular artist of the 1930s who had his own exhibit at the fair. Great fold-out map with an Art Deco flair. $35–$40

**Plates designed
by Charles Murphy for
Homer Laughlin.**
*Courtesy of Yesterday's
World, New Jersey.*

Plates, c. 1937. Set of six plates produced in England by Copeland for Abraham & Straus department store. With a fairly traditional dinner plate border design. Produced early; unfortunately, three of the six buildings had changed their official names by fair time. In blue transfer on white ground. When purchased individually   **$50–$125**
Complete set of six   **$600–$650**

Plate, 1939. Commemorative plate designed by Adams, England for Tiffany & Company. Jazzy transfer design in blue or coral color. Verso marked "Made especially for/ Tiffany & Co./ New York World's Fair/ 1939," and set in a circle enclosing the above information: "Modern New York • Old New York • Transportation • City Hall • Bridge • Liberty • Tunnels • Construction • Transportation," perhaps referencing the border design. An excellent fair collectible.   **$150–$200**

Plates, 1939 and 1940. Designed by Charles Murphy for Homer Laughlin. Murphy also designed the "Fiesta" ware line for Homer Laughlin. Subtly pastel-colored border design showing the Marine Transportation Building, the United States Building, and the Communications Building. Verso on 1939 plate is marked: "Decoration by Charles Murphy/ 105th Anniversary/ Inauguration/ of/ George Washington/ First President/ of/ the United States/ 1789–1939." 1940 mark is identical, except the dates are omitted. In good condition, with some flaking to the gold transfer rim. Each.   **$350–$400**

Postcard folder. "Greetings From the New York World's Fair," pictorial postcard folder which unfolds to show eighteen colorful scenes of the fair, in excellent condition.
$20–$25

Poster, 1937, 39¾" high, 28" wide. Advance publicity poster for the fair, designed by Nembhard N. Culin, and published by the New York World's Fair 1939 Corporation. Color lithograph signed "Culin" in the image. Aerial view, entering the Perisphere from the Trylon, and exiting via the semicircular ramp called the Hellicline. A stunning image. Depending on condition.   **$3,000–$4,000**

Poster, approximately 20" high, 16" wide. Designed by John Atherton, depicting "Mithrana," an allegorical representation of the fair, carrying the globe, showing a giant Trylon and Perisphere toward which a line of people are traveling. A scarce poster and a great design.   **$2,000–$3,000**

1939 World's Fair poster by
Nembhard N. Culin. *Courtesy of
Yesterday's World, New Jersey.*

1939 World's Fair poster by
John Atherton. *Courtesy of
Yesterday's World, New Jersey.*

Poster, approximately 32" high, 23" wide. Designed by Albert Staehle, and depicting a woman fair guide lifting her arm to wave fairgoers into the Fair. Also produced in several smaller sizes down to approximately 8" by 10".

Larger size, in fine condition   **$1,000–$1,200**
Smaller poster   **$150–$175**

Poster, approximately 32" high, 23" wide. Designed by Joseph Binder, this poster won first prize in the New York World's Fair competition of 1938. Strong graphic design, showing a New York skyline, Trylon, and Perisphere as searchlights flash across the sky and a small squadron of red planes zooms vertically skyward. In excellent condition.   **$1,000–$1,500**

Radio. RCA Victor special model table radio, with outlines of several exhibition buildings on the thermosetting plastic case. The RCA Building is featured prominently to

**RCA Victor special
model table radio.**
*Courtesy of Yesterday's World,
New Jersey.*

the right of the dial. Sought-after by radio and World's Fair collectors alike. In good to very good condition. $2,000–$2,200

Silverware service. Service for twelve, produced by Rogers Brothers, in plated silver, including twelve salad forks, twelve dinner forks, twelve teaspoons (without design of pavilions in the bowl of the spoon), twelve soup spoons, twelve knives, twelve individual butter knives, master butter knife, and serving pieces. Complete set $2,000–$2,200
Original cedar-lined box with trays $200–$250
Iced tea spoons (not included in set), each $50–$75

Teaspoon, matching above silver set, except with design of pavilions in the bowl of the spoon. Individual, loose spoon $5–$10
Spoon in original cardboard box, with certificate of authenticity, each $15–$20
Set of twelve spoons, in boxes $200–$225

Tray, 17½" long, 12¾" wide. Rectangular tin tray with rounded rim, red with cream, maroon, and aqua decoration and repetitive Trylon and Perisphere logos. $150–$200

Trivet, 10¼" long. In tin, octagonal in shape and impressed with a view of the Fair showing the Trylon and Perisphere. $100–$125

INDUSTRIAL DESIGN

The term "industrial designer" was coined by Norman Bel Geddes, who opened the first industrial design studio in America in 1927. From the late 1920s through the 1930s, several outstanding talents distinguished themselves as designers for industry: Walter Dorwin Teague, Raymond Loewy, Donald Deskey, Kem Weber, Gilbert Rohde, Walter von Nessen, Russel Wright, and others.

The early recognition of industrial design as a true "art" form came in 1934, when the New York Metropolitan Museum of Art hosted the "Contemporary American Industrial Art" exhibition, and the Museum of Modern Art hosted its "Machine Art" exhibition.

The term "industrial design" can be used to describe a vast range of objects, if one defines it as "design for machine production." Much of the furniture, lighting, clocks, kitchenware, and even mesh purses and Bakelite jewelry discussed elsewhere in this volume are industrial design by this definition.

Some people use the term most often to apply to large-scale design for airplanes, ocean liners, dams, trains, and cars. Major appliances, which do not yet figure greatly into the collecting market, also underwent industrial design changes in the 1920s and 1930s: refrigerators, stoves, washing machines, and oil burners.

Today, however, collectors of industrial design tend to focus their attention on household appliances and equipment: tools, radios, telephones, irons, toasters, cameras, barware and chrome, smoking accessories, office machines, phonographs, and the like, all of which were redesigned to spur consumption during the Depression. (*See also the chapter "From Artiste Décorateur to Industrial Designer" for more background on the rise of industrial design.*)

Streamlining was the overriding principle of industrial design. Speed, machine efficiency, and progress were the buzzwords of the day. Streamlining, which started with the new aerodynamic shapes of transportation vehicles to reduce resistance, is identified by its smooth, rounded surfaces and parabolic curves. One of the most frequent design motifs on Streamline consumer products are three horizontal or diagonal parallel lines that represented speed. When looking at industrial products, you'll notice that the logos of many corporations were "modernized" and applied to surfaces, becoming part of the overall design of the object.

The rediscovery of industrial design came much later than the resurgence of interest in Art Deco furnishings, decorative objects, or posters. It really wasn't until the ground-breaking 1986 exhibition "The Machine Age in America: 1914–1941" at the Brooklyn

Museum that dealers and collectors started avidly seeking the best examples of the leading industrial designers of the period.

Even though it has matured rapidly in the years since that 1986 exhibition, it is still relatively young as a collecting field. This means that while certain industrial designs are already "established" as the "best," there are still many discoveries to be made, and the market will continue to have broad fluctuations.

In the late 1980s, it was one of the hottest, trendiest areas for collecting. Prices on designs which could be attributed to leading designers shot up rapidly. At that time, the leading New York dealer in the field was Jacques-Pierre Caussin, owner of the First 1/2, who has since moved his dealership to Detroit.

"I'm not the only one interested in industrial design any more by any means," Caussin says, laughing heartily through his French accent. "I would say that overall, because of the recession, the market for industrial design has softened somewhat, but many pieces have held their own. The rarer, outstanding designs still easily find collectors who are willing to pay top dollar."

For Caussin, many of those collectors are now European rather than American. "European industrial design collectors seem ready to pay more than Americans, and they are buying American industrial design of the period," Caussin notes. "However, I have found that Detroit, with its automobile history and appreciation of design because of institutions such as the Cranbrook Academy, is an excellent market for industrial design."

A favorite area for collectors is early electric appliances and equipment of all kinds designed in Modern and Streamline idioms. While many of these today may seem old-fashioned or even rudimentary, they were the technological "modern living" breakthroughs of their day.

The first AC plug-in radio was not manufactured until 1927, and by 1933 millions were tuning in to FDR's "Fireside Chats." In 1929, over six hundred thousand refrigerators were sold in this country, but that number jumped to over one million the following year. The goal of the industrial designer of the day was not to just make easier-to-produce, better-looking appliances, but to improve the product itself.

The November 1934 issue of *Advertising Arts* magazine carried an article by Arthur Hirose entitled "Design in the Electrical Appliance Field," which underscored this point:

> Manufacturers, jobbers and retailers are looking for something that will make genuinely obsolete the appliances that long ago should have been retired. In many American homes today are toasters, percolators, vacuum cleaners, washers, waffle irons, heating pads, fans, lighting fixtures and portable lamps that should be scrapped. Most of them still do the jobs poorly when contrasted with the newer developments of electrical appliance factories. Working together, electrical appliance makers and industrial designers can develop electrical appliances that will be profitable not only because these household devices look better but are better appliances.

The household appliances field was also an important arena to develop public acceptance of the new industrial materials. Prior to 1930, only very cheaply made clocks were fashioned from metal, and higher-priced clocks were generally encased in wood. Just as the French had recoiled in shock when Bauhaus designer Marcel Breuer developed tubular steel furniture in 1925, many middle-class Americans were horrified at the thought of a metal mantel clock until the new design made them desirable.

New materials, treatments, finishes, and colors speeded the acceptance of household objects fashioned from plastics, chrome, and aluminum. The economic distress of the Depression was not enough to purchase a cocktail set in chrome instead of silver—it had to look good, too.

Talented industrial designers were behind every successful consumer product corporation of the day, recommending new materials and design innovations which both made for greater attractiveness, and offered improved salability and cheaper production costs.

Manufacturers soon realized that a design- and fashion-conscious public would more readily buy an object if the designer's name was touted in product brochures, catalogues, and magazine advertisements: "the new washing machine designed by Lurelle Guild for General Electric Company," "the new clock designed by Henry Dreyfuss for Seth Thomas"—the list is almost endless. Soon the products themselves carried the designer's name, thus Henry Dreyfuss's facsimile signature is stamped into the bottom of his thermos design.

Dreyfuss's early career was in the theater, and he worked as an apprentice to Bel Geddes. He was only twenty-five in 1929 when he established his own industrial design firm in New York. Over the years, he designed alarm clocks, pens and pencils, typewriters, telephones (*see "Special Focus: Telephones" for more information*), and even farm equipment. He collaborated with designer Wallace Harrison, to create "Democracity," the model city contained in the Perisphere at the 1939 World's Fair. He completely redesigned the New York Central Railroad's Mercury and the 20th Century Limited trains in 1936 and 1938 respectively.

Raymond Loewy, who emigrated from France after World War I, worked in the world of store window display at Saks Fifth Avenue and fashion illustration for *Vogue*, *Vanity Fair*, and other magazines. Like Dreyfuss, he opened his industrial design studio in 1929, and he, too, eventually designed for a railroad: Pennsylvania Railroad. His swivel chair for the train line's observation cars is an excellent example of "form meeting function." (*See description and photo in "Industrial Design Price Listings."*) Loewy designed the Hupmobile car and packaging for companies like Lucky Strike and Coca-Cola.

Dreyfuss and Loewy, along with Norman Bel Geddes and Walter Dorwin Teague, are considered the "Big Four" in industrial design of the period. Teague's "conversion" to industrial design and streamlining came suddenly in 1926 when he visited Europe and studied the work of Le Corbusier. Of those named, he is the best known for design of household and everyday objects: cameras, lamps, radios, pens, and much more.

Many industrial designers, including Lurelle Guild and Russel Wright, were commissioned by Chase Brass and Copper Company for its housewares line. (*See chapter "Chase Chrome."*) The most prolific Chase designer was Walter von Nessen, who actually made his reputation as a lighting designer. (*See descriptions in "Lighting and Lamps Price Listings."*) Nessen Lighting is still a major resource for interior designers, and continues to produce some of his most successful and popular designs.

Many industrial objects are hard to find in excellent condition: they were used every day, got banged or dented, and were taken on journeys. In addition, when something "nice" owned by an aunt—a vase, a Chanel dress, a table, a lamp—went out of fashion, she wasn't likely to throw it away. Instead, she packed it away in the attic, or gave it to a child setting up an apartment. The situation was different with most industrial design. When a clothing iron had outlived its usefulness, or an advanced model appeared, it wasn't enshrined with the family photos—it was thrown on the junk heap.

Thus the rarity and high prices for some of the collectibles in this field. However, some prices have come down quite a bit from the heights they reached in the late 1980s, or have stabilized.

"Some designs which we thought at the time were hard to find started appearing in great numbers in the collecting field," explains Caussin. "Such as the streamlined Victor adding machine. You can find them quite frequently now at lower prices. I think that everyone who wanted one got one."

The same sentiment was expressed by Jim Meehan of Radioart in Connecticut. "Teague's mirrored Sparton radios turned out to be plentiful. Perhaps because they were so attractive with the blue glass mirror, people didn't throw them out, so there has been a dip in the market. Those who wanted one have bought one, and it seems there were enough out there to satisfy the market for the time being."

In general the same is true of typical household appliances such as juicers, toasters, and irons. Though many are well-designed, they were not design breakthroughs for the most part. They remain good examples of industrial design of the period, but they are less desirable today because such huge numbers of them have surfaced. In each category, though, a few outstanding designs exist which can command higher prices.

Other industrial design items, such as Dreyfuss's thermos, Teague's Kodak Gift Camera, Vassos's "RCA Victor Special" portable phonograph, have become almost "icons" of the era, and will no doubt continue to appreciate in the years ahead. Industrial design objects of this quality will undoubtedly find their way into American and foreign museums at an increasing rate as we approach the year 2000.

INDUSTRIAL DESIGN PRICE LISTINGS
(Alphabetically by manufacturer or designer)

ANONYMOUS/VARIOUS

Desk lamp, c. 1935, approximately 15" high, 13" wide. In chrome, aluminum, wood, and plastic. Lamp fixture supported by U-shaped chrome bar, resting on banded base. A strong overall design and a good example of industrial design in a desk lamp. Unmarked. (*See photo, page 330.*) In very good, working condition.   **$650–$700**

"Gyroscopic" rack, c. 1935, 80" long, 8½" diameter. In chrome, designed to hold eight cocktail glasses. Can stand vertically or horizontally. Sold in department stores such as Abercrombie & Fitch and Ovington's. In fine condition.   **$200–$225**

"Gyroscopic" serving table, c. 1935, inner circle: 21" diameter; outer circle: 24" diameter. Designed to hold cocktail shaker and eight cocktail glasses, the inner circle swings down to form cocktail table top, or up for storage. In excellent condition.   **$500–$750**

Irons, clothes, 1930s, produced by various American companies, such as the "American Beauty" by American Electric Heater Company, American, with see-through red plastic handle; "General Mills" by General Mills, with black Bakelite V-shaped handle; and "Lady Dover" by Knaff-Monarch. Most desirable are those with accentuated Streamline design. Price range depends on condition, design, and working order.   **$40–$100**

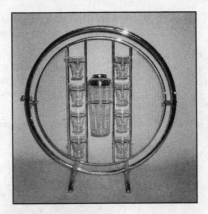

"Gyroscopic" serving table.
Courtesy of Stephen Visakay, New Jersey.

Juicers, 1930s, approximately 8–11" high. Produced by various American companies, usually in painted steel, some with chrome or Bakelite trim. Most desirable are those which have accentuated Streamline design. Price range depends on condition, design, and working order. $35–$75

Toasters, 1930s, produced by various American companies, usually in polished stainless steel, some with Bakelite handles or bases. Most desirable are later toasters which have accentuated Streamline design. Price range depends on condition, design, and working order. $55–$125

Tray, called "Jazz Modern," American, after 1930, 18" long, 12" wide. Rectangular chrome, with open rail gallery and pivoting black handles; abstract geometric designs in black, red, and cream silk-screened on the reverse of the glass. Value depends strongly on condition of the silk-screened colors. In good condition. $500 (Auction)
$600–$800

"Jazz Modern" tray.
Courtesy of Savoia's Auction, Inc., New York.

"Soda King" seltzer bottle by Norman Bel Geddes. *Courtesy of Stephen Visakay, New Jersey.*

A General Electric **"streamlined" phonograph.** *Courtesy of Of Rare Vintage, New Jersey.*

ALLEN MANUFACTURING COMPANY (American)

Lawn sprinkler, after 1930, 9¾" high. Designed in the form of a rocket ship by the Allen Manufacturing Company, Chicago; composed of cast metal in red paint with adjustable chrome nozzle. **$300 (Auction)**

NORMAN BEL GEDDES (American, 1893–1958)

Syphon bottle, "*Soda King*" (seltzer dispenser), c. 1935, 10" high, 4½" diameter. Designed by Bel Geddes for Walter Kidde Sales Company. In chrome-plated and enameled metal with rubber fittings. Stamped "Soda Syphon King pat #20536 Walter Kidde. Bloomfield N.J. Designer Norman Bel Geddes." **$150–$200**

HENRY DREYFUSS (American, 1904–1972)

Thermos bottle and tray, 1935, 7¼" high, 5¼" diameter base. Designed by Dreyfuss for American Thermos Bottle Company, Norwich, Connecticut. Manufactured from 1935 until after 1946. Composed of aluminum, steel, glass, and rubber with enamel paint. This example enameled brown, but also produced in gray-blue, green, and white; with an arched slim handle. Stamped with Dreyfuss's facsimile signature, Thermos company mark, and "Pat. Office No. 549." With matching tray. **$800 (Auction)**
$600–$900

FAIRFAX CORPORATION (American)

Vacuum cleaner, c. 1930, 15" diameter, 19" high. One of the earliest wet and dry vacuum cleaners designed for home use. Shaped like a torpedo, in red painted steel and chrome, complete with attachments, very good condition. **$250–$300**

GENERAL ELECTRIC COMPANY (American, Bridgeport, CT)

Phonograph, 1930s. Streamlined, teardrop shape in brown Bakelite, locomotive-shaped arm, #30770. **$225–$250**

Stapler for Hotchkiss Sales Company. *Courtesy of Moderne, Pennsylvania.*

Swivel chair by Raymond Loewy for the Pennsylvania Railroad. *Courtesy of The Discerning Eye, New York.*

HOTCHKISS SALES COMPANY (American)

Stapler, c. 1930. A stunning geometric design on a rarely seen item, with original box.
$450–$550

RAYMOND LOEWY (French/American, 1893–1986)

Chair, swivel, 1940, 41" high. Designed for the observation car for the Pennsylvania Railroad. An excellent example of "form meeting function" by one of the foremost American industrial designers of the period. This streamlined chair with aluminum sides and steel base and original tuscan red fabric both swivels and reclines. In very good condition.
$1,800–$2,200

MANNING BOWMAN COMPANY (American, Meriden, CT)

"Twin-o-Matic Waffle Iron," 1937. Designed by Karl Ratliff for Manning Bowman and exhibited at the 1939 New York World's Fair.
$300–$400

ISAMU NOGUCHI (Japanese/American, 1904–1988)

Radio intercom, "Radio Nurse," 1938, 8" high. Designed by Noguchi for Zenith Radio Corporation, with molded Bakelite plastic case, used residentially and in hospitals to monitor patients or babies. On end, front appears to have a shape like the face of a nurse. In excellent condition.
$1,500 (Auction)
$2,000–$2,200

"Radio Nurse" by Isamu Noguchi.
Courtesy of Savoia's Auction, Inc., New York.

Polaroid "Executive" desk lamp and another
industrial design lamp. *Courtesy of*
The Discerning Eye, New York.

Ronson cigarette lighter.
Courtesy of Butterfield & Butterfield, California.

POLAROID CORPORATION (American)

Desk lamp, "Executive," 1939, model #114, 13" high, 10" wide, 9" deep. Designed by Clarence Kennedy and Charles Baratelli for Polaroid Corporation. In black Bakelite and aluminum, with company marks. Sometimes mistakenly identified as being designed by Walter Dorwin Teague. In very good, working condition. **$750–$800**

RONSON CORPORATION (American)

Cigarette dispenser, after 1930, 5" high. A "Penguin" cigarette dispenser manufactured by Ronson, in black, white, and green-painted metal; base impressed "Ronson Pick-a-Cig, Mfd. by Art Metal Works, Newark, NJ." **$900 (Auction)**

Cigarette lighter, c. 1935, 5" high. Cast as a bartender mixing a cocktail behind a fully stocked bar, the side compartments opening to hold cigarettes centered by a panel fitted with a lighter, the front enameled in striated brown and black, raised on a black painted base, minor scratches, one shaker replaced. **$1,200 (Auction)**
$1,100–$1,400

SPARTON (Spark Withington Company, Jackson, Michigan)

Radio, after 1930, 7¾" high. Executed in wood-grained metal with stylish chrome band; designed in a sweeping style similar to Kem Weber's "Zephyr" clock. Face marked "Sparton." **$150 (Auction)**
$200–$300

WALTER DORWIN TEAGUE (American, 1883–1960)

Camera, "Banta M Special," 1936, 4¾" long. Designed by Teague for Kodak. The black-enameled body divided by horizontal chrome-metal bands, hinged lens, cover molded "Kodak Banta M Special Made in USA by Eastman Kodak Co. Rochester, NY." Price range depends on condition and working order. **$320 (Auction)**
$600–$800

Camera and box, "*No. 1A Gift Kodak,*" 1930, 8¾" long, 4⅜" wide. Designed by Teague for Kodak. The camera in brown leather case with metal hinged lid set with chromed-metal geometric design of rectangles and circles, enameled in red, silver, and brown. Fitted black-lacquered box, the lid with chromed metal and same enamel design, impressed metal tag "No. 1A Gift Kodak Made in USA by Eastman Kodak Co. Rochester, NY." $1,500–$2,000

Camera box, as above but sold separately. $280 (Auction)
$350–$400

Camera, "*Baby Brownie.*" Designed by Teague for Kodak. (*See* "*World's Fair Memorabilia Price Listings*" *for description and photo.*)

Radio, "*Bluebird,*" 1936, face: 14½" diameter. Designed by Teague for Sparton (Spark Withington Company, Jackson, Michigan). Circular face of blue mirrored glass, with dial slightly lower than center of circle, surrounded by two smaller chrome rings with three chrome horizontal lines running through to the edge of mirrored circle, three chrome knobs resting on outer chrome circle, blue lettering on marbelized Bakelite dial background. *Fakes Alert!* A reproduction of this radio has appeared on the market in recent years. In average condition $1,700 (Auction)
As above, but in very good condition $2,400 (Auction)
In excellent condition, a fine example of industrial design of the period $2,500–$3,000

"*Stormoguide,*" 1931, 5" square. Designed by Teague for Taylor Instrument Company. Chrome and black plastic with dial readings for rain, snow, and even tornadoes. Face stamped "Taylor Stormoguide." $150–$200

JOHN VASSOS (American, 1898–1985)
Phonograph, portable, "*RCA Victor Special,*" 1935, 8" high, 17¼" wide, 15½" deep. Designed by Vassos for RCA, New York, in aluminum and various other metals. An excellent example of American industrial design of the period. $3,100 (Auction)
$3,000–$5,000

"Stormoguide" by Walter Dorwin Teague. *Photo by Robert Four.*

"RCA Victor Special" phonograph by John Vassos. *Courtesy of Skinner, Inc., Massachusetts.*

VICTOR CORPORATION (American)

Adding machine, 1920, 7" high, 12½" deep. Streamlined design in brown Bakelite with green keys and nameplate; in working condition with original cover.   **$100–$150**

In excellent condition   **$150–$200**

WAVERLY TOOL COMPANY (American, Sandusky, Ohio)

Clothes iron, "Petipoint," 1941, 10" long, 5" wide. Designed by Clifford Brooks Stevens and Edward P. Schreyer for the Waverly Tool Company, Ohio. In metal and black plastic with streamlined oval shape and stepped-back, protruding wings. Stamped "Waverly Tool Co., Sandusky, Ohio" with patent number. (*See photo in section "Motifs," page 15.*)

$195 (Auction)

$250–$350

WESTINGHOUSE ELECTRIC COMPANY (American)

Tray, c. 1935, 15" diameter. Design attributed to Donald Dohner; in micarta, the Westinghouse brand of Formica; burgundy, silver, and turquoise; with three horizontal bands and another two bands and quarter circles set at right angles.   **$250–$300**

SPECIAL FOCUS

CATALIN RADIOS

First things first: Catalin is not Bakelite. Although both are nearly identical in chemical composition, Bakelite was molded as a powder, and is usually found in only black, brown, and maroon, and was later manufactured in white and ivory. It has a dense, heavy appearance that rarely has any luster. Catalin, which is translucent, was cast as a liquid with a resin that could be clear, tinted to almost any color, or produced with eye-catching "marbleized" effects by mixing colors.

Both names are actually trademark names: Bakelite is a trademark of the Union Carbide Corporation, and Catalin was produced by the American Catalin Company. Not so long ago, people were referring to all plastic radios as "Bakelite," but the more exact use of the name became de rigueur when the Catalin models skyrocketed in price at the end of the 1980s, leaving their less-illustrious and more common cousins behind.

In the same way that "Kleenex" became the name for any facial tissue, and, more recently, "Xerox" for any photocopy, the Bakelite Corporation so dominated the plastics industry in the 1930s that you'll also hear the name "Bakelite" applied universally to other plastic collectibles of the period, such as jewelry. However, the most colorful, sought-after jewelry is actually Catalin as well.

Not to confuse you further, but there were many other trade plastics that looked like "Bakelite": Beetle, Durez, and others, as well as those that looked like "Catalin": Marblette, Joanite, and Fiberlon. In addition, other plastics of different chemical composition were also widely in use. One example, celluloid, the oldest of all plastics, was first produced around 1870 and was used into the 1920s for household and boudoir items.

Before plastic radios stole the scene, most home radio sets were contained in fairly traditional wood furniture. At first, there was a real need for the considerable size of the radios, as the technology had not advanced to a point where the radio components could be held in anything resembling a "portable." Yet, even after the components had shrunk, the cabinets continued to be manufactured in wood because it looked better in the home. In other areas of design as well, the "modern" age was somewhat hidden behind traditional façades. As technological advances became more acceptable, the machine became a national symbol, and technology was beautiful enough to show itself. Table-model radios began being produced in plastic in vast numbers.

Today, very well-designed Bakelite radios in very good condition can bring $300 or more, but most Bakelite radios are found at prices under $200, and many still cheaper. Some very rare Catalin radios, on the other hand, sell for over $10,000, and even those considered less scarce have climbed above the $1,000 range.

Although these prices reflect to some degree the appeal of the Catalin colors and the radios' strongly Modernistic designs, the real reason for such high prices is rarity. Even the "less scarce" models and colors could really be called rare.

There are numerous reasons that so few Catalin radios survived, even though they were manufactured by about twenty American companies such as General Electric Company, Emerson, Fada, Motorola, Bendix, and lesser-known firms.

First, although "AC plug-in" table radios were introduced in about 1927, the first Catalin model did not appear until around 1935–1936. Just as they were gaining some real market popularity in 1939–1940, the war broke out, and production was suspended. Even though new models appeared after the war, many prewar brands and models were never produced again.

"In addition, there were problems with the design of the radios," comments Jim Meehan, owner of Radioart in Centerbrook, Connecticut, one of only a handful of dealerships which specialize in Catalin radios. "There was a lot of breakage, cracking of the cases in shipment to the buyer or in the home."

Other radios were damaged by a tube burning through the plastic case, or by warping and fading if left in sunlight. Once a plastic radio got damaged or old and dirty, or broke down beyond repair, it was thrown out with the trash.

How rare, then, are the Catalin models?

"Take the Symphony model for example," comments Meehan. "I have only seen three others like this in the last ten years." (*See photo on page 338.*) Other very rare models include the tomato-red Emerson "Cathedral" radio, which can sell for over $10,000. (*See color section.*)

"I don't think that the market for these radios has at all peaked," says New York dealer and author John Sideli. "In fact, I think that many have a long way to go. We're going to yawn at $10,000 for a Catalin radio a few years from now."

The collecting field got a boost with Sideli's *Classic Plastic Radios of the 1930s and 1940s* (E. P. Dutton, 1990), reinforcing the already high prices being paid for radios made of Catalin plastic. Of the fifty-four models listed in his book, at the time he considered twenty-four of them rare or very rare, twenty-one scarce, and only eleven common.

"To keep things in perspective, though, even the ones I call 'common' I don't think I've seen more than one hundred examples of," Sideli states.

While the recession which followed the publication of Sideli's book affected the Catalin radio market to some degree, prices have since stabilized, and will no doubt resume their climb as the economy recovers.

Notes Meehan, "The interest and the demand is there from collectors who are looking for really fine pieces to add to their collections."

Generally speaking, models with color cases, such as red, blue, or green, are rarer. Relatively more common, although they may have rare colors in their trim, are those with yellow, amber, orange, or orange-brown cases. It is hard to believe at first glance, but these radios were actually originally white, ivory, or pale pastel-colored radios which have completely yellowed over the years. All of the colors have darkened with age to some degree, and the dark blue and dark green radios of today were actually brilliant blue, green, or even turquoise.

Some collectors and dealers are painstakingly sanding and buffing the radios back to their original colors, but the vast majority of collectors and dealers prefer to buy and sell their Catalin radios as they are.

The condition of the radios greatly affects the value on the market, and collectors should be discouraged from buying radios that are cracked, discolored from hot tubes, warped, or badly faded. This is particularly true with the more available models, which should only be purchased in excellent condition. However, working condition isn't necessarily part of the value.

"The design is the thing," explains Meehan. "High-end collectors aren't concerned if a radio is working. When you pay $5,000 or more for a radio, chances are you aren't going to use it anyway, for fear of damaging it."

The designs of the radios were widely varied, even though many look alike. Some have handles, some were designed like mini-skyscrapers, and still others have rounded sides or intersecting bases. The treatment of the grillwork that covered cloth speakers on the faces of the radios is sometimes reminiscent of car radiators, or vertical or horizontal bands of plastic. Knobs, dials, and numbers were all stylized. The zigzag or bolt of electricity was a common motif.

Meehan describes the collecting base for Catalin radios as "primarily men, although women are also attracted because of the colors and shapes. I find a lot of my clients actually work in radio—as broadcasters or on-air personalities."

Collectors should beware that there are now reproductions on the market. "They are poor reproductions when you compare them to the originals, but a novice can get taken," comments Meehan. "Some people are making decent repairs on the cases, and you'll find on some that parts have been replaced. I personally don't get involved with that, and most dealers will inform you if they've made repairs or replacements, but don't be afraid to ask.

"You will have a hard time finding a Catalin radio in a flea market today," Meehan continues. "Most dealers have heard enough about them to know what they have. There was a lot of buying in the 1980s, and there isn't much fresh material coming on the market anymore."

This means that even though dealers in the Catalin models keep running "wanted" classified ads, few of these models are coming out of attics or closets.

Once a market begins to consist mainly of collectors and dealers "exchanging" a known or more or less finite inventory, prices tend to stabilize and then climb steadily. In the years ahead, you can also expect to see Catalin radios appear more frequently at better auctions, as well as more record-breaking auction prices.

CATALIN RADIOS PRICE LISTINGS
(Alphabetically by manufacturer)

Note: *Price ranges collected for the following radios are for the specific color described, and can vary widely for other colors.*

ADDISON INDUSTRIES (Toronto, Canada)

Model 2, 1940, 10¼" high, 6" wide, 5" deep. Maroon with yellow trim, the large ridged grille covers nearly half of the top of the radio and plunges down over the front like a waterfall and terminates in a 180-degree arc. $1,500–$1,750

Model 2, as above, but yellow with red trim. $4,200–$4,400

BELLETONE

Model 126, c. 1940, 10½" high, 7" wide, 6" deep. Maroon with yellow trim, the grille designed with interlocking circles and peaked roof cabinet. This same design was produced as the 1940 model 126 by Garod, and has also been found with an "AMC decal" on the front instead of the Garod name. $7,500–$8,000

Addison model 2, 1940.
Courtesy of Radioart, Connecticut.

Belletone model 126, c. 1940.
Courtesy of Radioart, Connecticut.

EMERSON RADIO AND PHONOGRAPH CORPORATION (New York)

Model "Cathedral," 1937, 7⅜" high, 10" wide, 5⅛" deep. In very rare tomato-red. One of the earliest Catalin radios made, a very beautiful and almost elegant design with a well-designed and sensitively used grille cloth woven in herringbone pattern. (*See color section.*)

$8,500 (Auction)
$10,000–$13,000

Model AX235, "Little Miracle," 1938, 8⅞" high, 5¼" wide, 3¾" deep. Red with cream trim, a charming little radio of very simple design, rare and much sought-after in any color other than yellow and black.   **$2,800–$3,500**

Model 400, "Patriot," 1940, 10⅞" high, 7¼" wide, 5⅜" deep. Designed by Norman Bel Geddes. Red with blue and white trim, two-toned grille with contrasting colored handle and star knobs.   **$2,200–$2,600**

Model EP 375, c. 1941, 9½" high, 5¾" wide, 4⅞" deep. Yellow with brown trim, unique separate grille bar at the right.   **$2,500–$2,750**

FADA RADIO AND ELECTRIC COMPANY (Long Island City, NY)

Model L-56, 1939, 5½" high, 9" long. In rare emerald-green Catalin plastic, with yellow wraparound grille and colorful patterned dial. Fine condition and a very good example of Catalin radios of the period.   **$3,800–$4,000**

Emerson "Patriot," model 400, 1940 by Norman Bel Geddes.
Courtesy of John Sideli, New York.
Photo by Michael Fredericks.

Emerson model EP 375, c. 1941.
Courtesy of Radioart, Connecticut.

Fada model L-56, 1939.
Courtesy of John Sideli, New York.
Photo by Michael Fredericks.

Fada model 1000, 1945.
Courtesy of Radioart, Connecticut.

General Electric model L570, 1941. *Courtesy of Radioart, Connecticut.*

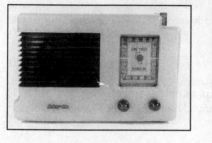

Lafayette model 62, 1939.
Courtesy of Radioart, Connecticut.

Model 1000, 1945, 6¾" high, 10½" wide. "Bullet" shape rectangular with one rounded side, in green marbleized Catalin with an orange handle, knobs, and bezel.

$1,350 (Auction)

Model 1000, as above, but yellow with red trim.

$900 (Auction)
$1,250–$1,500

GENERAL ELECTRIC COMPANY (Bridgeport, CT)

Model L570, 1941, 9½" high, 6¼" wide, 6" deep. The only Catalin set put out by G.E. Rarely found in marbleized black with yellow trim or in maroon with yellow trim. Shown here in yellow with maroon trim. $1,500–$1,750

GENERAL TELEVISION AND RADIO CORPORATION (Bridgeport, CT)

Model 591, 1940, 8⅞" high, 6" wide, 4⅞" deep. Red with white trim, very boxy, but nice-looking, quite scarce. $2,500–$3,000

LAFAYETTE RADIO COMPANY (New York)

Model 62, "Push Button," 1939, 10¼" high, 6¾" wide, 5" deep. Yellow with amber trim, one of the only Catalin radios ever produced with a push-button feature.

$2,500–$2,750

Motorola model 50XC, 1940.
Courtesy of John Sideli, New York.
Photo by Michael Fredericks.

MOTOROLA: GALVIN MANUFACTURING CORPORATION (Chicago)

Model 52, 1939, 9⅜" high, 5¾" wide, 4⅜" deep. Yellow with amber trim, the first in a series of three Catalin models, with a vertically louvered grille that feathers out to the left and right from the center.   **$2,000–$2,250**

Model 52, as above, but green with yellow trim.   **$3,000–$3,500**

Model 50XC, 1940, 9⅝" wide, 5¾" wide, 5⅛" deep. Marbleized green and yellow, beautifully designed with a round speaker bezel, odd-shaped handle, and hexagonal knobs and horizontal ribs going around the cabinet.   **$4,500–$5,500**

SENTINEL RADIO CORPORATION (Evanston, IL)

Model 284 NI, 1945, 11" high, 7½" wide, 6⅛" deep. Marbleized red with yellow trim. The grille looks like that on a car, with knobs in the place of headlights.
$2,500–$2,750

SYMPHONY

Model (unknown), c. 1939, 9⅜" high, 5¾" wide, 3¾" deep. Marbleized yellow with marbleized green trim.   **$8,500–$9,000**

Sentinel model 284 NI, 1945.
Courtesy of Radioart, Connecticut.

Symphony, model unknown, c. 1939.
Courtesy of Radioart, Connecticut.

TELEPHONES
An Interview With Dan Golden

Dan Golden has been collecting vintage telephones for twenty-five years. His collection numbers over five hundred, including forty Art Deco phones, and he specializes in their history and restoration, and in tracking current market values. You can contact him c/o Golden Telecom, 5751-F Palmer Way, Carlsbad, CA 92008, (619) 929-9099.

When people think of antique telephones, perhaps the first thing that comes to mind is the rural exchange wooden wall-crank telephones. However, Art Deco style telephones from 1925 to 1955, in both black and a variety of colors, are becoming increasingly popular with collectors, and prices in some cases are rivaling those brought by much older phones.

"There are two reasons for this phenomenon," comments Dan Golden, a collector, historian, and restorer of antique phones. "First, the color sets are more difficult to acquire at this time than the older wooden sets. Secondly, they can be easily hooked up and used on today's modern telephone system without replacing their original parts."

However, whether you collect telephones, or are looking to acquire one just to add another touch of authenticity to your Deco decor, there are many pitfalls to avoid. This is largely due to the great numbers of refurbished, altered, and replica Art Deco phones that are on the market.

"Collectors have to be very wary about replicas in this field," Golden cautions. "I see Korean-made replicas all the time being sold at antique malls for $400 and more. I use the word 'replica' rather than 'reproduction.' It would be great if they were true reproductions with the original quality. A 'replica' just looks like an original, they aren't engineered with the quality that the original Bell System phones had.

"The replicas will last perhaps a few years before causing static and before their plastic parts begin falling apart," he notes. "The originals were built to last over a hundred years."

The problem with replicas began in the 1970s, when shiny brass reproductions of both candlestick and round-bottom sets began to be sold as "originals." Korean factories began stamping 1920s dates into the Bell System copied moldings.

While smaller companies such as Kellogg, Leich, Stromberg, Carlson, and foreign companies made a few Deco styles, the major American manufacturers of Art Deco phones were Western Electric, part of the Bell System, and the Automatic Electric Company, part of General Telephone.

One reason that original Art Deco telephones are so hard to find today is that until the deregulation of the Bell System in 1984, it was illegal to own rental equipment marked "Bell System Property—Not for Sale."

"Within just a short period after deregulation, these items went from an 'illegal' category to a 'difficult to acquire' collectible," notes Golden. "The great lengths the Bell System went through to identify company property inadvertently resulted in a passion to collect these items."

Another reason these phones are so rare, as with many areas of industrial design, is that once they broke down they were often consigned to the scrap heap. In addition, many people believe that the old rotary dial sets won't work on modern phone lines, lessening the market for them.

"Certain phones require a separate bell box, or ringer box. People tried to hook up these phones without use of the bell box which also has the amplifier in it," Golden comments. "This results in a tunnel sounding effect, and people believe that the phone isn't working right. The truth is that if these sets are properly hooked up, they should sound better and last many times longer than modern-day telephones. Rotary dial phones will work just fine on touch tone lines."

Today, one of the most collectible Art Deco phones is the A/E (Automatic Electric) Type 34 and 40 "Monophone," which was made of Bakelite or thermo plastic in a variety of colors.

The most common color is a very high-luster ebony-black. Those which could be called "scarce" are a dark jade-green; a high-luster red-mahogany; a brown-walnut; and a translucent cream color called "Old Ivory." There was also a deep red-maroon color which today could be classified as "rare," and a translucent lime-colored Nile-green and a dark royal-blue which could be called "very rare." Unless an even rarer color is yet to be identified, today the most difficult color to find is a very pale lavender called "Orchid."

"There were also some special-order colors," says Golden, who has a puce-colored example in his collection. "These phones are extremely rare, and have become the most highly sought-after."

He explains that during the era, you could commission a telephone to be made in a particular color, say, to match your wallpaper. The phone company would often subcontract the work to the Bakelite Corporation. If you couldn't afford the $5 charge—a week's salary for some people during the Depression—they would custom-paint a black phone for you.

"Red phones were so much in vogue at the time that Woolworth's sold red plastic 'shells' that you could fit over your black phone," he says, laughing.

In addition to the colors, variety in the collecting field is offered by the fact that these Automatic Electric sets were trimmed in various metals that could be ordered: highly polished heavy chromium plate, ebony over brass, or a stunning twenty-four-karat satin gold plate over brass-trim finish.

"One common mistake beginning collectors make is buying a shiny brass phone as an original," cautions Golden. "No phones were made in shiny brass prior to 1950, and most of the fakes on the market are shiny brass phones from Korea."

In the market, phones are often referred to by their model numbers, such as "A/E 40," described above. The wall version of this set was called "A/E 50." In the late 1920s and early 1930s, there were round-based sets with separate bell boxes called the "1A Monophone." Since the bell box on the "1A Monophone" was separate from the set, sometimes twenty feet away, it is critical for a collector to have it if the phone is going to work properly. This style A/E phone is known as a "Shirley Temple."

Dealers and collectors have taken to nicknaming the phones with the names of movie stars or heroes. "I nicknamed the 1A Monophone 'Oliver Hardy,'" Golden says, "because I have a movie still which shows Oliver Hardy talking on this style 1A Monophone. Ollie, of course, has a pretty lady on his knee."

Golden explains that collectors enjoy finding movie stills or newspaper articles about Hollywood stars which show certain phones being used. The phones then get nicknames such as "Lucy," "Twilight Zone," "Bowery Boys," and "Bogart," among others.

The Bell System mid-1930s desk sets with two buttons in the top were called "Type 302," and the companion wall phone was called a "Type 354." Again, the most common color is black—an ebony baked enamel over cast aluminum. Phones were offered in ivory, dark blue, old rose, a dark gold, an old brass, and other colors and metallic finishes. This "302" phone is called a "Perry Mason" phone by collectors today.

The "Perry Mason" was created by leading industrial designer Henry Dreyfuss. Bell Telephone was one of Dreyfuss's most important clients. His "Model 300" desk phone was extremely successful, and stayed in production from 1937 until 1949. Dreyfuss continued to design phones well after the Art Deco period had passed; in 1964, he introduced the "Trimline" phone with which many readers are no doubt familiar.

The candlestick telephones that were popular in the early 1920s are called "Elliott Ness" sets by many, and were black over brass or steel. Roycroft made a hammered copper candlestick telephone, apparently with the blessing of the Bell System.

European phones are not as sought-after by collectors as American-made phones, but even smaller American companies produced some great Art Deco styles. For example, the Kellogg "Redbar," which came in white and a mahogany color, with a bright red switch hook, and the "Beehive" phone produced by Leich Corporation of Genoa, Wisconsin, are collectible.

As in many Art Deco collecting fields, some people do buy replicas or altered originals knowingly, and some prefer to have their Deco-style phone refitted with a touch tone pad. The deception only comes when someone tries to sell a replica, or a phone that has been refurbished or repainted, as an original. Real telephone collectors will go after completely original phones with their original finish. These are the sets which will continue to increase in value in the years ahead.

FIVE TELEPHONE SHOPPING TIPS

1. Perhaps the best source today for buying original Art Deco telephones is a hobbyist/dealer, a collector who is committed to buying and trading originals. Antique malls and gift shops are loaded with replica telephones, and many general antique dealers can't tell an original from a replica.

2. Just because a phone is marked "Made in U.S." or has a patent number stamped on it does not guarantee its originality. "People think that manufacturers of replicas wouldn't be allowed to mark phones this way," says Golden. "But there is no law against it. The Bell System no longer exists and nobody is regulating it, so beware."

3. As mentioned, many original Art Deco phones need a separate ringer box or bell box to work properly. Watch out for shiny brass phones sold as originals. "On many of the replicas, the parts don't fit well either, whereas the originals fit perfectly," Golden notes. "Another tipoff that a phone is a reproduction are Phillips-head screws—they just weren't used before 1940."

4. Try to buy phones that have their original finish. Beware of plastic phones that have cracks, are discolored, or are warped. Don't repaint phones or buy phones that have been repainted. "For Bakelite phones, the best method of restoring the original luster is a little Turtle Wax paste," advises Golden.

5. Perhaps the best advice, as in many fields, is to learn as much as you can before you buy. Go to specialized shows; look at and handle original phones. "Better yet," Golden adds with a laugh, "take a gadget collector with you."

TELEPHONES PRICE LISTINGS

AUTOMATIC ELECTRIC (General Telephone)
"A/E 40," "Shirley Temple," 1930s, desk set.

In black, the most common color, when purchased retail in excellent, working condition
$125–$150

In black, average condition, with the working condition unknown $50–$75

In dark jade-green, high-luster red-mahogany, brown-walnut, or a translucent "Old Ivory," colors that are considered scarce $450–$550

In deep red-maroon, considered rare $550–$650

In a translucent lime-colored Nile-green, or dark royal-blue, considered very rare
$1,500–$1,600

"A/E 40," "Shirley Temple" telephone.
Courtesy of Golden Telecom, California.

"A/E 50," "Shirley Temple"
wall model. *Courtesy of Golden*
Telecom, California.

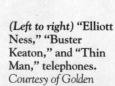

In a pale lavender "Orchid," of which only two are known to exist   **$2,000–$2,500**

"A/E 50," "Shirley Temple," 1930s, wall model set.

In black with brass dial and brass bands on the speaker and receiver, in excellent working condition   **$200–$250**

WESTERN ELECTRIC (Bell System)

"50" and "141" series candlestick, "Elliott Ness" or "Gangster," approximately 1922–1926,
with dial feature. Collectors should note that this phone needs a metal, wood, or
Bakelite bell box.

In black with brass base metal, in excellent, working condition   **$175–$200**

In nickel, in excellent working condition   **$500–$600**

AA1 Type, "Buster Keaton," manufactured 1922–1926. An early model, with the
appearance of a chopped-down candlestick phone. This was Western Electric's first cradle dial set. Collectors should note that this phone needs a bell box.

In black, in excellent, working condition   **$200–$225**

(Left to right) "Elliott
Ness," "Buster
Keaton," and "Thin
Man," telephones.
Courtesy of Golden
Telecom, California.

In gold or silver metallic finish, in excellent working condition $500–$550

B1 Type, Model 201, "Thin Man," and Model 102, "Garbo," manufactured 1927–1930. Similar in design to the AA1, but somewhat more streamlined stem and greater tilt to the dial. Collectors should note that this phone needs a bell box.

In black, in excellent working condition $100–$150

In colors, in excellent working condition $300–$350

202 series, "Lucy" or "Twilight Zone," manufactured 1930–1937, remanufactured 1957, an oval-bottom desk telephone with dial, including the "Lucy" phone (with F-1 handset), and the "Twilight Zone" (with E-1 handset).

In black, in excellent working condition $150–$200

In colors, in excellent working condition $250–$350

In metallic finish colors, in excellent working condition $300–$400

Type 302, "Perry Mason," manufactured 1937–1949, designed by Henry Dreyfuss for Bell. Desk set with two buttons in the top.

In black baked enamel over cast aluminum, in excellent working condition $145–$160

In ivory, dark blue, or old-rose colors, in excellent working condition $350–$400

In a dark gold or old-brass metallic finish, in excellent working condition $400–$500

NORTHERN ELECTRIC
"H6," "Bogart," 1939–1951, so nicknamed because it appears in a well-known movie still of Bogart as Sam Spade in *The Maltese Falcon.*

In black, in excellent working condition $135–$165

In mahogany, in excellent working condition $350–$400

Type 302, "Perry Mason" telephones, designed by Henry Dreyfuss.
Courtesy of Golden Telecom, California.

CHASE CHROME
AND OTHER MANUFACTURERS

Although Chase's actual name is the "Chase Brass and Copper Company," the products of this Waterbury, Connecticut, firm are almost always referred to as "Chase Chrome" in the collecting field. Chase Chrome is by far the most popular of chromium housewares in today's Art Deco market, and was produced from 1930 until 1941, when World War II forced the company to retool as a manufacturing plant for war materials. After the war, its housewares line was not revived.

A few years ago, the Connecticut Historical Society acquired a collection of Chase Chrome, underscoring both its increasing emphasis on documenting the state's 20th-century manufacturing heritage, and its recognition of the Chase family's tremendous impact on the city of Waterbury, Connecticut. Chase was the city's major employer during the Depression. At one time you might have joined the Chase Country Club, and you can still drive down Chase Avenue or go to Chase Park.

The collecting field got its first boost in 1978, when Gladys Koch Antiques of Stamford, Connecticut, published *Chase Chrome*, now out of print, a brief history of the company and the full Chase catalogue for 1936–1937 called "Chase Chromium, Copper and Brass Specialties for 1936–1937."

It is easy to understand by this catalogue why Chase housewares were so popular. There was a wide variety of inexpensive, good-looking "Buffet Service Articles," "Decorative Items," "Drinking Accessories," "Lamps," "Smoker's Articles," and more. Chase had targeted the average American who was spending much more time entertaining at home

Chase Chrome items including breakfast set by Ruth Gerth; canape plates by Lurelle Guild; "Comet" coffee and teas sets and "Taurex" candlesticks by Walter von Nessen; and pitcher for pancake set by **Russel Wright**. *Courtesy of The Discerning Eye, New York.*

during the Depression. Buffet-style parties suited America's informal lifestyle. Even Emily Post was enthusiastic about buffet gatherings, and heartily endorsed Chase's products.

However, it wasn't only the product line which made Chase so popular—it was the marketing of the line. Sprinkled with the names of a few nationally known industrial designers such as Walter von Nessen, Ruth Gerth, Russel Wright, Lurelle Guild, and even artist Rockwell Kent, the line dazzled with sophistication. The illusion of high style was completed by giving the products sophisticated names such as the "Diplomat" coffee set and the "Stratosphere" smoker stand.

The image of the product was then underscored by the "Chase Shops," complete boutiques of Chase housewares, which were installed in major department stores in several parts of the country. So successful was this style of marketing that some stores reportedly saw sales increase 400 percent after they were introduced. Chase advertised new designs frequently in well-read magazines such as *Good Housekeeping*.

It is really just in the last five years or so that Chase collecting has taken off like a shot. The next important book to appear was *Art Deco Chrome: The Chase Era*, by Richard Kilbride of Jo-D Books in Stamford, Connecticut, published in 1988. This book reprinted the Chase catalogue for 1941, with a more complete history of the company.

Kilbride then embarked on a more ambitious project, *Art Deco Chrome, Book 2*, setting out to identify as many of the designers of the Chase items as possible. He solicited the support of collectors and dealers across the country, some of whom are also contributors to this volume; interviewed former Chase employees; and ran a search of U.S. patent records.

Sadly, Richard Kilbride died before he could see his work published. Jo-D books carried on with the project, and the book finally appeared in 1992. The impact of his massive research will reverberate in the Chase collecting field for years to come, and we will miss him. His book is a must for anyone serious about collecting Chase Chrome.

Kilbride was successful in identifying the previously unheralded Chase staff designers, such as Harry Laylon, who worked at Chase from 1933 to 1939, was director of design from 1937 to 1939, and went on to a full career as an industrial designer and design consultant.

When there was resistance to the idea of work going to outside designers, Chase hit upon the progressive idea of inviting employees to submit designs for the company's products. Kilbride identified previously "anonymous" designs by Chase employee designers Edward J. Malvey, Randal L. Hale and others, including eighteen patents by Howard Reichenbach. In fact, Reichenbach designed the company's number one best-selling "Gaiety" cocktail shaker. (*See "Special Focus: Cocktail Shakers" for additional information.*)

Kilbride also identified over sixty Chase designs by Walter von Nessen; over twenty-five designs by Ruth Gerth, wife and partner with her husband, William, in the industrial design studio Gerth & Gerth; three designs by Rockwell Kent, which are described below and in the listings; over fifty designs by Lurelle Guild, including about thirty lamps; and over ten designs by Russel Wright. Several other designers were identified as well, including Dr. A. Reimann, a professor at the Reimann-Schuker School in Berlin. Chase used very few foreign designers, and Reimann sent his designs in from Germany. Today, they are extremely rare and can range up to $2,000 and more in the collecting field.

To many collectors, what is most "Deco" about Deco is reflected (pardon the pun) in chrome. World War I weapons research perfected the technique of chromium plating, and as early as the 1920s, chrome was being used with brass and other metals for furnishings and decorations.

People could not afford silver for their dining rooms and homes. Chrome, brass, and copper were solutions for filling the gap. By the mid-1930s, almost any houseware item you can think of was available in chrome with colorful ivory or black plastic handles: cocktail shakers, ashtrays, serving utensils, breakfast sets, trays, ice tongs, lamps, and cigarette boxes all sold widely. Most of these items originally sold for less than a dollar to about $3, but some sold for the then high price of $7.50. Today, they can bring $30, $50, $200, $500, $1,000, or more.

The value of a piece of Chase Chrome depends on the designer, the strength of the design, its rarity, and its condition. When Chase was still plentiful on the market, much of it was showing up in mint condition in the original box—wedding presents that had been packed away generations ago.

"Chase collectors today are more discriminating," comments Ken Berkowitz of The Discerning Eye at the Port Chester Antiques Mall in Port Chester, New York. "The common pieces aren't selling as fast as they used to, but the better designs are still finding buyers."

Rockwell Kent was one of the best-known artists of the 1930s. Kent designed only three items for Chase: a cigarette box, a wine cooler, and a wine bottle stand, all with a young Bacchus motif, and all considered rare today. When these designs made their way into the spotlight again in the late 1980s, the cigarette box and the wine cooler each brought $2,000 at major auctions. The interest level in Kent's designs took a cooling with the entire market in the early 1990s, and these prices seem to have come down quite a bit, although they are still among the highest-priced pieces of Chase. (*See descriptions in "Chase Chrome Price Listings."*)

Von Nessen's best contributions to the Chase line are also highly sought-after today, and include the "Diplomat" tea service. This is one of the "chestnuts" of the chrome collecting field, of which there are now several. With its elongated, fluted styling and side pouring handles, it was one of the most popular Chase items, and was in production from the 1920s through the mid-1930s. He also designed the "Lazy Boy" and "Stratosphere" smoker stands, service dishes, cheese knives, cake trowels, trays, and more.

The "Stratosphere" was a large ball 5¾" in diameter, mounted on a fluted, tubular post, and stood 26" high. The top half of the ball swings down in any direction, and closes to hide cigarette ashes. The "Lazy Boy" smoker stand had a compartment for cigars, pipes, or what-have-you under the pivoting top, which has a 14" diameter. It was promoted as a "manly" piece for the office, and was available in an English bronze finish, a combination of black and satin nickel, or chromium with a red or black top, and stood 22" high. Both of these pieces are hard to find today.

OTHER MAKERS

Chase's success created its own competition, and several other companies entered the market around the same time. Revere Copper and Brass Company entered the chrome housewares market in 1935 with seventeen designs by Norman Bel Geddes. Bel Geddes's design talents had already been recognized in furniture, graphics, and more. He was a household name after he designed the General Motors "Futurama" exhibit at the 1939 World's Fair. When Prohibition was repealed in 1933, the bar alternated with the buffet as the center of adult entertaining in the home. Many Bel Geddes chrome designs were bar accessories: trays, ice buckets, cocktail shakers, and more. (*See "Special Focus: Cocktail Shakers" for more on Bel Geddes's designs.*)

Revere also used evocative names, such as the "Manhattan" tray and cups with their "Skyscraper" cocktail shaker; the "Normandie" water pitcher; and other pieces called

"Penthouse," "Empire," "Aristocrat," and "Tuxedo." Revere also introduced its money-making line of copper-bottom saucepans with streamlined black handles, which are still favorites in the kitchen today.

Farber Brothers, a New York City company, used the trade name "Krome-Kraft" and sometimes "Silvercraft." A third brother, S. W. Farber, had his own company, and sold his chrome products under the trade name "Farberware." The Farber Brothers used many glass companies like the Cambridge Glass Company, Fostoria, Fenton, and even Corning-Pyrex to create the colorful ruby-red, cobalt-blue and other colored glass inserts for their chrome holders, rims, and bases.

Many of the designs that were produced under the trade name "Krome-Kraft" are more traditional in nature, but there are a few Art Deco designs which collectors seek.

Manning-Bowman was another chrome manufacturer, today best known for its highly prized chrome mantel clocks, tea sets, and other housewares. Manning-Bowman had some outstanding modern designs where tea set handles appear as black, angular wings on the pieces. In the late 1920s, they produced a type of chromium plate which was trademarked as Aranium. Their catalogue for 1934 celebrated the end of Prohibition with a cocktail service called "The Repealer." Their "Craftware" was a line of fluid, streamlined pieces.

Aluminum also came into use for housewares, but unlike chrome, it did not have the appearance of silver. Much of the popularity of chrome was based on the illusion of elegance that it maintained. Aluminum was lightweight, durable, and inexpensive, but it wasn't very "chic," and was really used only in industry until the late 1920s. However, toward the end of the 1930s, and into the 1940s when almost all metal was going to the war effort, chromium-plated housewares finally gave way to aluminum. One of the biggest makers of aluminum home products toward the end of the Deco era was West Bend Aluminum, which often used the popular Art Deco motif of a penguin to decorate its products.

Interest in the aluminum collecting field is growing, particularly in the pioneering aluminum designs of Russel Wright. Aluminum was also used by leading Modernist furniture designers such as Donald Deskey and Warren MacArthur Corporation. However, good Art Deco housewares are fewer in aluminum, and much of the hammered aluminum which has become popular recently is more traditional, and some of it downright "homey" in design.

When collecting chrome, try to buy only pieces in excellent to mint condition. The original box will have an added value to a collector. Make sure that the piece you are buying has its chrome plating intact. Chrome can be replated, but it is difficult and expensive, and dents are almost impossible to repair. Look also for cracks and chips to the plastic trim and handles, and inspect glass liners closely.

Caring for chrome is easy—in fact, that was one of its strongest selling points in its heyday. Just some mild soap and water and a soft drying cloth, and it looks as if you've been polishing silver all day. Displayed on a blue glass mirror tray, it still has the look of an elegant silver service, and, as in the 1930s, for a fraction of the cost.

We add that the prices on chrome can vary widely, especially with geographic differences, although pieces by well-known designers have established "going" market prices. This is the kind of collectible you can still sometimes find at a flea market or garage sale at real bargain prices. Usually, however, you'll find even flea market dealers are much more savvy about the chrome they are offering. As a collector, you should learn as much as you can about the field, especially by reading the fine books by Richard Kilbride we've referenced above and in the bibliography.

CHASE CHROME PRICE LISTINGS
(Alphabetically by designer)

CHASE BRASS AND COPPER COMPANY (American, Waterbury, CT 1876–1976)

> ₡ Chase had many employee designers, and commissioned several others to create their housewares. As the collecting market for Chase continues to grow, identifying the designers has added value for collectors. Easy to identify, almost all Chase products are stamped "Chase," with their centaur trademark. Catalogue numbers in the listings below are Chase catalogue numbers. Prices are given for items in excellent to near-mint condition.

Anonymous

Bookends, "Sentinel," 7¼" high; catalogue #17109. In brass with red or blue plastic body and black plastic hat, designed as soldiers, each stands next to an oversized brass cannon ball. Pair. $400–$450

Pitcher, "Sparta," 8" high; catalogue #90055, water pitcher, cylindrical chrome with a flared rim and spout, ribbing at the base, fitted with a cream geometric handle. This pitcher was part of a "Sunday Morning Waffle Set," which included a smaller syrup pitcher, sugar shaker, and small or large tray.

Pitcher alone	$100–$150
Full set with large tray	$175–$200

Relish and jam dish, tray: 12" diameter; jar: 4" high; catalogue #90053. A relish dish in chromium plate with a ribbed glass liner with four compartments, and a jar in the center with a chrome top and serving spoon. $35–$40

Charles Arcularius

Buffet warming oven, 1941, 7½" high, 12½" long, catalogue #90096. Cylindrical electric warming oven with white plastic ball feet and semicircular ribbed handles. $100–$125

Ruth Gerth (Wife and Partner of William Gerth)

Breakfast set, tray: 11¾" long; sugar bowl: 4¼" high; creamer: 3⅛" diameter; catalogue #26003 with tray, #26001 without tray. Three-piece set of semispherical design, in chrome with white or black plastic handles. $125–$175

Candy dish, 7" diameter, catalogue #90011. Satin-nickel, brass, or copper cover with plastic finial for a three-compartment glass liner, in a circular plastic holder. $35–$50

Lurelle Guild (b. 1898)

Canape plates, 6¼" diameter, catalogue #27001. Small trays with a rimmed circle to hold a glass or cocktail cup, and a quarter-sphere "wing" handle.

Set of four	$200–$225

Lamps, table and wall, in various sizes, including "The Ionic" (#502), "The Plato" (#505), "The Doric" (#506), "The Troy" (#523), and several others. Some of Guild's designs are more in the Modern style than others, and prices on the Chase lamps he designed can range as high as $500. However, many are available on the market in the general range shown.   **$200–$300**

Newspaper rack, 11⅜" high; catalogue #27027. A humorous tilted wire rack, with a rooster and the word "N-E-W-S," designed to hold up your newspaper for easy reading at breakfast. Originally available in silver, bronze, or combination brass/copper finish.
                                                                                    $80–$120

Pretzelman, 18" high; catalogue #90038. A humorous two-dimensional figure of a "pretzelman," one leg kicked up in the air, holding a tray on which a thin pole is centered to hold pretzels. Originally available in copper or chromium, and sometimes described as a donut or bagel holder.   **$225–$275**

Rockwell Kent (American, 1882–1971)

> Rockwell Kent designed only three items for Chase, all with the same young Bacchus motif, and all considered rare today.

Cigarette box, 6⅜" long, 5¼" wide, catalogue #847. In copper, a hinged rectangular box with wood interior, decorated with a young Bacchus striding nude figure carrying two large bunches of grapes, with two leaping goats in the background and mountains in the distance. Incised "R. K." Touted by Chase as "Mr. Kent's first design in metal," and originally sold for $7.50, a lot of money when other cigarette boxes from Chase were selling for $1 to $3. This box sold for $2,000 at auction in 1988, but prices haven't held.
                                                                        $1,200–$1,400

Wine cooler, 9⅛" high, catalogue #27015. Cylindrical, with handles, impressed with a plaque of a young Bacchus carrying grapes, with two leaping goats, as above. Incised "R.K." Originally available in polished chromium or combination polished brass and

Cigarette box by Rockwell Kent.
Courtesy of Wolf's Fine Arts Auctioneers, Ohio.

Wine cooler by Rockwell Kent.
Courtesy of Savoia's Auction, Inc.,
New York.

copper, and sold for $7.50. Only in production for a few years, as it was featured in the 1936 catalogue, but did not appear in the 1941 catalogue. This item, too, soared to $2,000 at auction in 1989. **$950 (Auction)**
$1,400–$1,800

Wine bottle stand, 2" high, 4½" diameter, catalogue #27016. The matching "wine coaster" which was available in polished chromium, or in a combination polished brass and copper, with a plaque design as above. **$800–$900**

Howard Reichenbach
Electric snack server, 6" high, 13" diameter, catalogue #90093. With three one-quart glass-lined compartments, this "Chase Table Electric" came in chrome or copper. The perfect "buffet dinner" item. Compartment covers have stepped-back design. White plastic handles, knobs, and feet. In working condition. **$150–$200**

A. Reimann (Germany)

> **C** Reimann, a professor in Berlin, created very few known designs for Chase, all considered extremely rare.

Candlepiece, catalogue #21005. A four-candle holder, in the shape of two perpendicular flat bars, each ending in simple, refined candle holders. **$480 (Auction)**
In satin copper or brass **$1,700–$2,000**

Walter von Nessen (1889–1943)
Candlesticks, "*Taurex*," 9¾" high, catalogue #24004. Designed to hold two candles in an uneven "J" shape. Produced in chrome, satin copper, and polished copper, and originally sold for $3 each. Sold as a pair. **$200 (Auction)**
$400–$450

Coffee maker service, "*Comet*," electric percolator: 8" high, catalogue #90120. Coffee pot of spherical form with banded bottom on flared cylindrical feet; large ivorine rounded ribbed handle and conical spout; open creamer and covered sugar; round tray with engraved banding. **$500–$550**

Coffee set, "*Diplomat,*" coffee pot: 8¼" high; tray: 10½" diameter, catalogue #17029. Coffee pot, sugar bowl with cover and creamer, each concave fluted oval, the pot and creamer with side black plastic handle, the pot with one flute convex forming spout, the detachable slightly raised cover topped by tapering black plastic finial, the circular tray with black plastic ground and chromium plating curled over border.   **$380 (Auction)**
$500–$600

Smoker stand, "*Lazy Boy,*" 22" long, 11" diameter, catalogue #17031. Pivoting tabletop revealing a recessed compartment on a cylindrical column housing a long ash receiver, the front supported by a scrolled-end band, in black enamel and polished nickel. Unidentified as a rarely seen von Nessen design, this smoker stand sold at auction recently for only $170—someone got a bargain!   **$650–$800**

Tea maker service, "*Comet,*" electric tea kettle: 8" high, catalogue #90119. Tea service, designed as above.   **$450–$475**

Russel Wright (American, 1904–1976)

Ice bowl with tongs, bowl: 7" diameter, catalogue #28002. A simple, chromium-finished bowl, with one arched handle that ends in a curl from which the striated ice tongs hang. This was a popular design for Chase.   **$150–$200**

Ice bowl with tongs, "*Antarctic,*" bowl: 7" diameter, catalogue #17108. Similar design, but bowl is ribbed at the top and has a white plastic handle which is attached at both sides. This item was available in chrome or copper.   **$125–$150**

Pancake and corn set, pitcher: 5¼" high; tray: 6" diameter; large sphere: 1¾" diameter; small sphere: 1⅛" diameter; catalogue #28003. In chrome, cobalt-blue glass lining on tray, described as "amusing" in the Chase catalogue, and created to work with syrup, butter, cream, or any pourable. Could be purchased with two "spheres" for salt and pepper or for powdered sugar, etc.

Pitcher and tray alone	**$400–$500**
Spheres alone	**$125–$150**
Full set	**$525–$650**

OTHER CHROME MANUFACTURERS PRICE LISTINGS
(Alphabetically by manufacturer)

(*See additional listings for other chrome manufacturers in Special Focus:* "*Cocktail Shakers.*")

ANONYMOUS

Creamer and sugar, English, 1930s, 4½" high. In chrome with white Bakelite side-pouring handle on creamer and white Bakelite feet. Marked "PBB" and "Made in England." Set.   **$25–$35**

Floor ashtray, American, 1930s, 24" high. Circular chrome base, with black enamel stem. Ashtray in chrome with lid that closes from either direction.   **$80–$100**

Pie rack, 1930s, 8½" high. Probably produced commercially for restaurants and diners.
$75–$80

Teapot, American, 1930s, 6" high. In chrome with overall dome shape and incised sky-scraper motif on side, red baked enamel handle, and red Bakelite whistling tea plug. A good example of Art Deco chrome, albeit anonymous. $125–$150

BELMET PRODUCTS (American, Brooklyn, NY)
Smoking stand, c. 1930, 20¾" high. Chrome and Bakelite smoking stand with mahogany colored Bakelite on top and base, chrome-topped ashtray and supports. Paper label: "Belmet Products, Brooklyn, New York." $200–$300

FARBERWARE (American)
Vase, 11" high. Chrome bud vase with a textured glass tall flute which inserts between a pair of Cubist nudes holding their faces in their hands. Impressed "Farberware."
$125–$150

FARBER BROTHERS (American)
Butter dish, late 1930s–early 1940s, 6¾" diameter. With a chrome cover and tray, clear glass liner, and white plastic knob. $25–$35

Compote, figural nude stem, manufactured 1932–1955, 7" high; glass insert: 5½" diameter. One of Krome-Kraft's most popular designs, issued with a wide variety of color glass inserts. Available in chrome or silverplate.

In chrome	$35–$50
In silverplate	$50–$75

Oil and vinegar set, early 1930s, cruets: 3¾" high. Stylized chrome holders and tray. Blue glass cruets with clear handles and stoppers. $50–$75

HAGENAUER (Austrian, 1920s–1930s)
Tray and cordials, tray: 22" long. In chrome, with two cordials. The tray formed as a stylized running horse, the bases of the cordials with openwork motif of dogs, all pieces with firm's impressed marks. (*See additional Hagenauer listings in other chapters.*) $900 (Auction)

MANNING BOWMAN (American, Meriden, CT)
Coffee making set, c. 1935, coffee pot: 11" high; tray: 18" long; sugar and creamer: 6" high. In chrome, with dramatic winglike handles and oval finials in Bakelite. The oval tray also lined in Bakelite. $750–$900

Coffee service, c. 1935, coffee server: 10½" high. In chrome with a squared design, including coffee server, creamer, sugar bowl, and tray. With brown Bakelite handles, bases, and spout cover. Stamped "Manning-Bowman." $500–$550

Thermos pitcher, "HotaKold," c. 1935, 12" high. Chrome in sleek design with wood-handled cork stopper, streamlined handle, and glass lining. Stamped "HotaKold" and "Manning Bowman." $50–$60

<u>**REVERE COPPER AND BRASS INC.**</u> **(American, founded in Canton, MA, in 1801 by Paul Revere)**

Ice bucket and tong set, 10" long, 6" diameter. An orange Bakelite wedge is set into the tongs and balances on the circular handle of the round bowl. Impressed mark. $75–$100

SPECIAL FOCUS
PHOTO FRAMES
An Interview With Steve Starr

Steve Starr is the owner of the Art Deco dealership Steve Starr Studios, which celebrated its twenty-fifth anniversary in 1992. He is also the author of *Picture Perfect—Art Deco Photo Frames 1926–1946* (New York: Rizzoli, 1991), and an avid collector. You can contact him at 2654 North Clark Street, Chicago, IL 60614, (312) 525-6530

Name your favorite Hollywood star from the 1920s and 1930s and it is quite possible you'll find his or her photo in a dazzling Art Deco glass and metal photo frame on the walls at Steve Starr Studios in Chicago. Starr's collecting passion, which started in 1976, has blossomed into a display of over six hundred photo frames which cover the walls of his shop.

"When I started collecting, I only paid $10 or $12 each for frames," he comments. "Today, prices are all over the map. I paid a lot for some of the frames, but I still find them from time to time at better prices."

Picture frames of the Art Deco period can be found in Bakelite, celluloid, marble, wood and other materials. Even René Lalique designed picture frames. However, Starr has focused his collecting on glass and metal easel-backed frames.

Originally, many of these photo frames were sold with stock photos of the great actors and actresses at Paramount, Universal, Metro-Goldwyn-Mayer, 20th Century Fox, and other studios. Some retailed at finer stores such as Tiffany & Company and Marshall Field, and thousands were sold through W. T. Grant, Kresge's, and Woolworth's, with original prices as low as ten cents.

"The stars probably weren't even paid for the use of their photo, as they would be today," says Starr. "But it was great publicity. And the more glamorous the star, the better the frame would sell."

Collectors can still sometimes find the frames with the movie star photos in them. "Some people kept the movie star photo and just slipped their own in on top, and sometimes the movie star photo was glued to the easel door," he explains. "But I've spent an enormous amount of time finding just the right photo to fit the style and size of each frame in my collection."

Starr's perseverance paid off, and the stunning array of frames and photos he assembled has become not only something of an Art Deco tourist attraction in Chicago, but also the subject of a book he wrote for Rizzoli International Publications in 1991.

In his book, Starr classifies the frames according to styles: "Romantic," embellished with floral themes, animal motifs, ribbons and bows, and other "pretty" elements; "Geometric," with angular and/or symmetrical patterns;

"Moderne," with simplified, line-based decorations; "Streamlined," with curved, almost aerodynamic line designs or curved corners to the window area; "Patriotic," which were popular during World War II; and small-sized "Greetings," with silk-screened messages such as "Remember Me."

"The frames are difficult to research because most of the makers were small firms and didn't mark the frames," Starr says. "Most of them were sold only with paper labels, which have fallen off. I've only found a few with their labels or price tags still attached."

In the 1920s and 1930s, the popularity of photo-taking soared with the introduction of mass-produced, lower-priced cameras from such companies as Kodak. Coinciding with the boom in family photos came the patenting of a new process to produce plate glass in 1928 by Pittsburgh Plate Glass Company. This new, faster process resulted in glass of better quality, without the "wavy" look of older glass. Put the two together, and you have a surge of popularity for photo frames.

Typically, a photo frame of the period had ⅛" to ¼" thick glass that was silk-screened in a variety of colors and Deco patterns. "Hand-painted frames are wonderful to find," comments Starr. "But they are pretty rare."

In other instances, the design on the glass was hand-engraved, hand-etched, or sandblasted, and some glass had scalloping or mirroring as well. "Tinted glass is rarer, especially cobalt-blue and peach-tinted glass. The designs done with tinted glass or strips of tinted glass can be very expensive and are highly sought-after by collectors," he says.

Usually, the easel back was made of cardboard, or very rarely of wood, and had turn buttons to keep the easel door closed. Sometimes the glass was mounted with rosette screws through drilled holes in the glass to the backing. Other times the entire piece might be surrounded with a thin frame of nickel- or chrome-plated brass or steel. These same metals were used in the most popular framing device: corner clips. These clips not only served to protect the corners of the glass but played a decorative function as well.

Corner clips, especially earlier ones, were embossed with Art Deco motifs: stepped-back, sunray patterns, speed lines, or other designs, adding a touch of elegance. The corner clips can be of some use in dating the frame. "Generally speaking, the fancier the corner clip, the older the frame," Starr notes.

Embossed turn buttons are an indication that the frame probably dates from the 1920s or early 1930s. On older frames, the easel back might have a pattern, especially a floral pattern, which was the preferred pattern on earlier easel backs of the 1920s and 1930s. Frames that are produced today generally do not use engraving or beveling on a curved edge. Colored glass trim or colored mirroring generally indicates the frame was made during the 1930s or 1940s.

Starr adds, "In some ways the easiest way to be sure a frame is original is the size of the window." He explains that window areas in the frames were geared to the popular sizes of photo prints of the day, just as today's frames are made for 3" by 5", 5" by 7", and 8" by 10" photos. From the 1920s to the 1940s, a popular film of the day, size 122, produced prints that were 3¼" by 5½". Kodak's Beau Brownie camera used 120 film and produced images measuring 2¼" by 3¼".

"But the real tipoff that they are old frames is that the window areas can be very odd sizes," he says. "Like 6^{15}/$_{16}$" by 4^{15}/$_{16}$". Today, the window areas are very standardized."

Sometimes a lucky collector will find photo frames that have been preserved in excellent condition, with no deterioration to the silk-screened design or silver mirroring. "However, I sometimes like to touch up the colors where bits of paint have flaked off," Starr says. "I just use a tiny brush and test the paint color on a piece of glass to make sure it's right. Black and ivory are easiest, but other colors may take some time to get the right match. And for polishing the corner clips, I use very fine steel wool or a dab of Wenol, a commercially available polish, or both. If you are a serious collector, you may also want to buy frames in less than good condition so you can salvage hardware, easel stands, clips, and other pieces to reuse."

Whether you are a serious collector or just an admirer of Art Deco seeking one or two nostalgic treasures, Art Deco photo frames can be stunning, attention-getting collectibles.

SIX PHOTO FRAME SHOPPING TIPS

1. For the more common Art Deco photo frames in terms of styles, colors, and materials, be prepared to pay between $50 and $100 when purchasing from a dealer. "For a really gorgeous one in A-plus condition, you might spend $150 to $200," says Starr. "I recently saw a military theme frame for $250, but that's really a lot at this time."

2. The most common colors are ivory, off-white, and black. More sought-after and harder to find are bright red or purples. "In my entire collection, I only have two in lavender and maybe three in turquoise," Starr notes.

3. The style of the frame will also affect value. "Romantic" style Deco frames are less sought-after by collectors than the "Stream-lined," "Geometric," or "Moderne" ones. "Patriotic" photo frames, which often had the Stars and Stripes in red, white, and blue, are more difficult to find. Also harder to find are the smaller-sized "Greetings" frames that carry sentimental messages such as "Think-ing of You," "Always Yours," or holiday greetings.

Marjorie Weaver in a "Romantic" style frame, c. 1938, size 11" by 13"; window 7^1/$_4$" by 9^1/$_4$". Silk-screened in black, ivory, and metallic gold on ^{1}/$_8$"-thick glass. Mounted to an easel back by chrome-plated steel corner clips. *Courtesy of Steve Starr, Illinois.*

Ronald Colman in a "Geometric" style frame, c. 1929, size 4½" by 5½"; window 3⁷⁄₁₆" by 2⅞". Silk-screened in beige, black, and metallic gold on ⅛"-thick glass. Mounted to an easel back by brass-plated steel corner clips.
Courtesy of Steve Starr, Illinois.

Corrine Griffith in a "Geometric" style frame, c. 1928, size 7½" by 9½"; window 6¹⁵⁄₁₆" by 4¹⁵⁄₁₆". Silk-screened in black, accented with silver mirroring and hand-engraved frosted lines, on ⅛"-thick glass. Mounted to an easel back by nickel-plated brass corner clips. *Courtesy of Steve Starr, Illinois.*

Gene Raymond in a "Streamlined" style frame, c. 1936, size 10" by 12"; window 6¾" by 8¹⁄₁₆". Silk-screened in black, accented with silver mirroring, on ⅛"-thick glass. Mounted to an easel back by chrome-plated steel rosettes. *Courtesy of Steve Starr, Illinois.*

Fred Astaire in a small-sized "Greetings" frame, c. 1934, size 2⅞" by 3½"; window 1⁵⁄₁₆" by 1⅝". Rope and anchor design and "Thinking of You" silk-screened in ivory, black, and metallic silver on ⅛"-thick glass. Mounted to an easel back with embossed steel bands. *Courtesy of Steve Starr, Illinois.*

4.   The condition of the photo frame will also have an impact on the price. Is the silk-screening or mirroring deteriorating? Are there chips or cracks in the glass? Are the corner clips damaged or dented? Some condition problems can be repaired or cleaned.

Backs, easels, turn buttons, rosette screws, and other hardware can be replaced. And full mirrored surfaces can be resilvered. Remember, however, that damage to a mirrored silver pattern or accenting integrated into the silk-screening can't be fixed because they were created by a special process.

5. The quality of materials used in the frame will also affect value. Some frames sold in higher-priced stores were velvet-backed. Cobalt-blue or peach glass are found less frequently. Look for unusual or higher quality materials.

6. Don't pass up a rare photo frame just because the condition isn't perfect, or even if the price seems just a little high to you. "I've done it, and I've always wound up regretting not paying that extra $10," says Starr, laughing. "If you are a real collector, you'll buy it—because you know you may never see it again."

SPECIAL FOCUS

COCKTAIL SHAKERS
by Stephen Visakay and Arlene Lederman

Stephen Visakay is a cocktail shaker collector whose extensive collection has been featured in numerous national magazines. Write to him at P.O. Box 1517, West Caldwell, NJ 07007. Arlene Lederman is the owner of Arlene Lederman Antiques, which has a strong specialization in cocktail shakers, and is located at 150 Main Street, Nyack, NY 10960, (914) 358-8616.

Gleaming with sophistication and style, vintage cocktail shakers are skyrocketing in value. These Art Deco gems have been waiting half a century to be recalled to service, rescued from grandmother's china closet, dusted off, and polished. They are swank and practical cultural artifacts—form and function never had a better mix.

On permanent display in the design section of the Museum of Modern Art in New York City are four cocktail shakers from the Art Deco era. And with people entertaining at home more frequently, as they did during the Depression, department stores report sales of cocktail shakers and martini glasses outweigh those of tea services as wedding gifts.

By the late 1800s, the bartender's shaker as we know it today had become a standard tool of the trade, invented by an innkeeper who was pouring a drink back and forth to mix. Finding that the smaller mouth of one container fit into another, he held the two together and shook "for a bit of show."

In the 1920s, martinis were served from sterling silver shakers by the very chic of the day, while the less affluent made do with glass or nickel-plated devices. Liberated flappers were not only smoking in public, but drinking cocktails with wild abandon. The Great War was over. A kind of euphoria marked by much partygoing and a frenzied quest for pleasure had seized the country. It was the Jazz Age, and the gin martini mixed in a cocktail shaker was the drink of choice.

But the real explosion of cocktail shakers occurred after the repeal of Prohibition in 1933. Now they were featured frequently on the silver screen. Movie fans watched William Powell instruct a bartender on the proper way to mix a martini in *The Thin Man*. He demonstrated the technique himself in *My Man Godfrey*.

To meet the popular demand for cocktail shakers, Machine Age factories, geared for mass production, began turning them out by the thousands. Fashioned from the high-tech materials of the day, chrome-plated brass shakers with Bakelite trim replaced those of sterling silver and were advertised as "non-tarnishing, no polishing needed." Many shakers themselves were fashioned after icons of the Machine Age, using skyscraper and streamlined forms.

Soon glass companies such as Cambridge, Heisey, and Imperial were also producing shakers and shaker sets. Stunning etched and silk-screened designs were applied to glass shakers in brilliant hues of ruby or cobalt.

Art Deco shakers were used to mix a wide array of trendsetting cocktails, including the "Singapore Sling" and "Pink Lady," as well as the traditional martini. By the end of the decade, shakers had become standard household objects, affordable to all. Every family had a shaker on the shelf.

To further increase sales, companies began to manufacture unusual shapes—roosters, penguins, barbells, bowling pins, golf bags, zeppelins, even ladies' legs!—but to no avail. Everyone had a shaker already. Few were sold, and production slowed. Today, collectors eagerly seek these whimsical shapes.

Many of these shapes were not entirely capricious. The rooster, or "Cock of the Walk," for example, had long served as a symbol for a tavern. The penguin, which appears again and again in Art Deco design, wears a natural "tuxedo" and symbolized the good life. The Graf Zeppelin had become the first commercial aircraft to cross the Atlantic, leaving Germany on October 11, 1928, flying over New York City, and landing in Lakehurst, New Jersey— an 111-hour flight that captured the attention of the world. The sports-related shapes reflected a new emphasis on leisure and the outdoors.

At the beginning of the 1940s, the Depression ended, but not in the way most had hoped. It ended on December 7, 1941. The "golden era" of the cocktail shaker was over and America's involvement in World War II began. All metal went to the war effort. Companies that once made cocktail shakers now made artillery shells. After the war, few thought of the shakers. We were in the Atomic Age, thinking of jet-propelled airplanes, a thing called television, and new cars with lots of chrome.

In the early 1950s, a brief renewal of interest in cocktail shakers occurred when new homes featuring finished basements, called "rec rooms," were equipped with bars. But the push-button age had taken the fun out of mixing drinks. Shakers came with battery-powered stirring devices. Worse yet, electric blenders became popular: drop in some ice, add the alcohol of your choice, a package of "redi-mix," flick a switch and . . . Gone were the rights and rituals, the showmanship, the reward for effort. Small wonder, then, that these elegant stars of the 1930s were forced into retirement.

And there they sat—in attics and closets nationwide—waiting to be recalled to life. Over fifty years have passed now, and one can faintly hear the clink of ice cubes as shakers are, once again, a symbol of historic elegance.

SEVEN COCKTAIL SHAKER SHOPPING TIPS

Cocktail shakers are hotter than ever. Not only are they great accent pieces, they're useful as well. They have all the earmarks of a classic collectible. They're easily found at auctions, antiques and secondhand shops, flea markets, and yard sales; they can be bought in all price ranges; they require little study to identify, and resources are readily available; and they're not easily reproduced.

1. Most valued by collectors of Art Deco are streamlined and skyscraper shapes from the mid-1930s, produced by companies such as Chase, Manning Bowman, and others, especially if the shaker can be identified as the work of well-known industrial designers of the age, such as Norman Bel Geddes, Water von Nessen, and Russel Wright. Remember, though, that thousands upon thousands of "anonymous" chrome cocktail shakers are out there, with values under $40. Others valued by collectors are of unusual shape: penguins, bowling pins, zeppelins.

2. One needs the tenacity and persistence of a bounty hunter. Get up the same time dealers do, and be at the flea market at set-up time, four or five A.M. Map out a plan of attack the night before and get there early. By nine or ten A.M., the best shakers have been picked up by the early birds. Also, ask! Just because you don't see a shaker doesn't always mean the dealer doesn't have one.

3. Who wants to buy a badly dented or scratched shaker? You do, as long as the price is low. You can use the top or spout cap on the next shaker you find that's missing one.

4. When buying glass shakers, run your fingers over the rim inside and out; likewise over the bottom edge—a small chip will reduce the value by 30 percent or more. Look for bright, clear colors in the glass. The more brilliant blue your cobalt shaker, the higher its value.

5. Inspect metal tops and chrome- or nickel-plated shakers for fractures or hairline cracks. Scratches and dents reduce value, as do chips or flakes in the plating. When buying a tarnished shaker, look for even color in the tarnish overall. Large spots of differing color may indicate missing or worn plating. With a good metal polish, even the blackest shaker will usually clean up beautifully. Use a sponge, never an abrasive. If your shaker is stamped "sterling" or ".925" on the bottom, congratulations! That garage sale find is worth a small fortune: $100–$600 or more, depending on size, weight, and workmanship.

6. Another word of advice: Buy! You'll only regret it if you don't go the extra dollar. Buy doubles and triples. You can sell or trade later.

7. Most of all, remember to have fun! The best part is the search—finding a shaker that's not in your collection. When the washing, cleaning, and polishing are over, we always like to mix a drink in that swell little thing as a celebration. Here are a few classic Art Deco cocktail recipes to try:

Between the Sheets
⅓ gin
⅓ Cointreau
⅓ Bacardi

Jersey Lightning
1 Applejack
2 drops Angostura
2 dashes sugar syrup
1 Maraschino cherry
1 dash lemon juice

New Yorker
¾ whiskey
1 spoon lemon
2 dashes Claret
1 spoon sugar syrup

Bronx
⅓ dry gin
⅓ dry vermouth
⅓ orange juice

Metropolitan
½ Cognac
2 drops Angostura
½ French vermouth
2 dashes sugar syrup

Palm Beach
⅔ dry gin
1 dash Italian vermouth
1 dash grapefruit juice

Note: With thanks to Helene Linne, editor of *Motif*, the newsletter of the Art Deco Society of Boston, in which this article originally appeared.

COCKTAIL SHAKERS PRICE LISTINGS
(Alphabetically by manufacturer)

ANONYMOUS (American)

No-name, No-nickname "generic" cocktail shakers, various sizes from approximately 10" to 14", in chrome, chrome-plated brass, or stainless steel, with Bakelite (or ivorine) plastic handles and/or tops. Mass-produced by the tens of thousands in the 1930s. May have short or long spouts, ribbed bodies, stepped-back bases, and angular or streamlined handles. These are unidentified, and stamped only "Chrome" or "Stainless" on the bottom.   **$25–$40**

"Bowling Pin" cocktail shaker, late 1930s, 15" high, 4⅜" diameter. With a chrome base and wooden top.   **$50–$75**

Generic cocktail shaker. *Courtesy of Stephen Visakay, New Jersey.*

"Clown" cocktail shaker, 1930s, 14" high. Consisting of three chrome balls, surmounted by a wooden handle, the top chrome ball has four "jingle bells" attached.

$200–$250

"Dumb-bell" cocktail shaker, 1930s–1940s, 13" high, 4" diameter. In chrome, with a red plastic screw-off top. Stands upright on circular base.

$75–$95

"Dumb-bell" cocktail shaker, c. 1935, 11¾" high, 3⅞" diameter. In chrome or silverplate, with a circular stand. Advertised by Wanamaker's department store in New York City in 1935 for $6.50.

$250–$350

"Dumb-bell" serving set, 1930s, shaker: 12" high, 3" diameter; tray: 16½" long, 10¾" wide. Shaker in glass with etched lines, chrome top, and chrome base, and tray in glass with chrome handles. With four glass cups.

$450–$500

"La Cucaracha" cocktail shaker, 1930s, 11⅛" high, 3½" diameter. Cylindrical body, with two circular red plastic handle knobs located at different heights on the body.

$175–$200

"Martini" cocktail shaker, 1930s, 9½" high. In ruby-red glass with chrome top, and with the word "Martini" in silver trim on the side.

$75–$85

"Penguin" cocktail shaker, some time after 1936, 11" high, 4" diameter. In chrome plate with screw-off knob on beak for pouring. Made some time after the 1936 Napier silverplate "Penguin" cocktail shaker (*See "Napier Company" listing "'Penguin' cocktail shaker."*)

$300–$350

"Rooster" cocktail shaker, mid-1920s. Rooster's head and breast in silverplate over brass, fitting on a clear glass bottom. The rooster, or "Cock of the Walk" adorned many tavern signs.

$500–$525

"Dumb-bell" cocktail shaker. *Courtesy of Stephen Visakay, New Jersey.*

"Rooster" cocktail serving set. *Courtesy of Stephen Visakay, New Jersey.*

"Rooster" cocktail serving set, 1920s, shaker: 14¼" high; cups: 4" high. Hand-hammered silverplate body surmounted by rooster head whose tongue unscrews to reveal spout. Tail feathers curl into handle. With eight silverplated metal cups with rooster head and tail and cut glass inserts. Stamped "W.B./U.S.A."   **$2,500–$3,000**

"Rooster" cocktail shaker alone, as above.   **$1,500–$1,600**

"Tam-o-Shanter" cocktail shaker, c. 1935, 12½" high. A cylindrical glass base, with a tilted chrome top surmounted by a round wooden handle to resemble a "tam" hat. In blue or red.   **$95–$110**

ANONYMOUS (German)

"Airplane" cocktail shaker, 1928, 12" long, 12" wingspan. Decanter wings, third decanter in body, four spoons in wheel well, four cups, juicer, and strainer. In chrome plate, stamped "Germany."   **$1,800–$2,200**

"Airplane" cocktail shaker, 1928, as above, except 17½" long, 17½" wingspan.
                    $4,000–$5,000

"Traveling Bar" set, c. 1929, shaker: 15" high. Self-contained set with two decanters, four cups, strainer, and juicer contained in the slightly flaring cylindrical body. Stamped "Germany."   **$250–$275**

"Zeppelin," c. 1928, 12" high, 3½" diameter. Made in chrome or silverplate, stamped "Germany." This unusual shaker has eighteen pieces in all. The gondola contains four spoons. The tail section sits on four fins and becomes a fruit cup with cover. The body contains a two-piece corkscrew, four cups, funnel, strainer, and juicer, and becomes the shaker.   **$3,000 (Auction)**
                    $1,500–$2,000

"Zeppelin," c. 1928, 9" high, 3" diameter. As above, but with ten pieces in all and with a gold wash interior.   **$750–$850**

"Airplane" cocktail shaker. *Courtesy of Stephen Visakay, New Jersey.*

"Zeppelin" cocktail shaker.
Courtesy of Stephen Visakay, New Jersey.

Cocktail shaker by Folke Arstrom.
Courtesy of Stephen Visakay,
New Jersey.

FOLKE ARSTROM (Swedish)

Cocktail shaker, 1935, 8⅝" high, 3⁹⁄₁₆" diameter. Arstrom was the leading industrial designer in Sweden in the 1930s. In nickel-plate, the shape composed of four parts of a circle, two concave and two larger parts convex. Black enameled "speed lines" at the bottom, complemented by horizontal banding on the black plastic top.   **$450–$550**

CHASE BRASS AND COPPER COMPANY (American, Waterbury, CT 1876–1976)

(See also chapter "Chase Chrome.")

"Blue Moon Cocktail Set," 1930s, shaker: 12½" high, 3½" diameter; tray: 12" diameter; cups, 3½" high; catalogue #90077. The cups are in cobalt-blue glass with stepped-back chrome feet.   **$200–$250**

"Doric Cocktail Set," 1937, shaker: 12¼" high, 3½" diameter; tray: 12" diameter; cups: 3" high; catalogue #90114. Consisting of the "Blue Moon" cocktail shaker, "Ring Tray," and "Doric Cocktail Cups" in chrome plate with white or blue plastic trim on cocktail shaker knob and cup bases. Sold in 1937 for $11 per set.   **$200–$225**

"Holiday Cocktail Set," 1930s, shaker: 11½" high, 3¾" diameter; tray: 15⅞" long, 5⅜" wide; cups: 2" high; catalogue #90064. The "Gaiety" cocktail shaker in chrome, with four bowl-shaped cups. Original cost $9 for the set.   **$100–$150**

"Holiday Cocktail Set"
with "Gaiety" shaker.
Courtesy of Stephen
Visakay, New Jersey.

Farber Brothers cocktail serving set #5468.
Courtesy of Stephen Visakay, New Jersey.

"Gaiety" cocktail shaker alone. Designed by Chase employee designer Howard Reichenbach, this was perhaps the most popular of all Art Deco cocktail shakers.

$45–$60

FARBER BROTHERS (American, New York City, 1915–1965)

The Farber Brothers company most often used the trade name "Krome-Kraft" and sometimes "Silvercraft." A third brother, S. W. Farber, had his own company and sold his products under the trade name "Farberware." The Farber Brothers used the Cambridge Glass Company, Fostoria, Fenton, and even Corning-Pyrex for casseroles, and other glass makers to create the inserts for their holders, rims, and bases.

"Bubble" cocktail serving set, late 1930s, shaker: 12¾" high; tray: 21" long, 18½" wide; cups: 4⅛" high. In chrome, with spout and pouring handle. The shaker and tray with red and black wood trim. Both the shaker and cups designed as three "bubbles," enlarging to the top.

$350–$400

Cocktail serving set #5468, mid-1930s–1939, shaker: 11" high; tray: 19½" long, 12" wide, or circular; glasses, in wine glass shape: 5⅞" high. The removable glass cups and cocktail shaker body in Cambridge Glass. Offered in six different colors, with amber, amethyst, green, and blue more common, and carmen and ebony rarer.

$200–$250

FORMAN BROTHERS (American, Brooklyn, NY)

Cocktail shaker, c. 1935, approximately 11" high. In chrome with an angular Bakelite handle. In case you've forgotten how to mix a "Side Car" or a "Pink Lady," there is a recipe stamped on the bottom.

$75–$80

"Golf Bag" cocktail shaker by
International Silver Company.
*Courtesy of Stephen Visakay,
New Jersey.*

INTERNATIONAL SILVER COMPANY (American, Meriden, CT)

Meriden, Connecticut was the center of American manufacture of silverwares and plated products. The International Silver Company was formed in 1898 by the merger of no fewer than twelve to fourteen silverware makers, and many of the products continued to be stamped with the names of the subsidiaries, such as "Derby S.P. Company," "Meriden Silver Plate Company," and "Rogers Bros."

"*Golf Bag*" cocktail shaker, 1926, 12½" high, 3" diameter. Designed by G. H. Berry. In silverplate, with pouring spout and golf ball top, and stamped on the bottom "Derby S. P. Co." **$1,200–$1,400**

"*Lighthouse*" cocktail shaker, c. 1924, 14" high, 5⅛" diameter. Designed to replicate the Boston Lighthouse, the country's first lighthouse, erected in 1716. Stamped "Meriden Silver Plate Co." or "International Silver Co." **$900–$1,000**

"*Rooster*" cocktail shaker, 1927, 13" high. In silverplate, not in the shape of a rooster, but with an engraved rooster enameled black and red on the side. Stamped "Meriden S. P. Co./International S. Co. 56 oz. patented Jan. 11 1927." **$100–$125**

MANNING BOWMAN (American, Meriden, CT)
Cocktail serving set, early 1930s, shaker: 13½" high; tray: 11¼" wide, 22½" long; footed cups: 3¼" high, 3" diameter. Chrome with Bakelite trim. Stamped "Manning Bowman." **$400–$500**

Manning Bowman cocktail serving set.
Courtesy of Stephen Visakay, New Jersey.

"Penguin" cocktail shaker by Napier.
Courtesy of Stephen Visakay, New Jersey.

Cocktail serving set, c. 1935, shaker: 9½" high, 4¾" diameter. Handleless shaker with spout, oval footed tray surfaced with black Bakelite, and six footed cups.   **$450–$550**

"Connoisseur" cocktail shaker, c. 1938, 12" high, 3⅝" diameter, catalogue #373. Skyscraper-inspired design in chrome with ivory "Arinite" (trade name of a Bakelite-type plastic) cover knob.   **$75–$95**

Cocktail shaker, 1930s, 11" high, 5½" upper diameter, 4¼" base diameter. With spout and serving handle, and with green and yellow marbled Catalin base and trim.

$200–$250

Cocktail shaker, late 1930s, 12½" high, 3⅝" diameter. In chrome with a walnut wood top and base. This shaker was advertised and sold by the John Wanamaker department store in 1939.   **$65–$75**

NAPIER COMPANY (American, Meriden, CT)

"Penguin" cocktail shaker, 1936, 12" high, 4¼" diameter. In silverplate, with 48-oz. capacity. The beak opens to reveal rubber stopper and pourer. Stamped "Napier—pat. pending" or "Napier pat D-101559." Advertised in December 1936 in the *New York Times* by Abercrombie & Finch for $12.50.   **$1,000–$1,200**

(See also the "Anonymous" listing "'Penguin' cocktail shaker.")

"Conical" cocktail shaker, 1930s, 9" high. In silverplate, the shaker tapering from a 3¾" diameter base to a 2¼" diameter top, with four cylindrical cups 2¾" high. Each piece with two red enameled horizontal bands at the bottom.   **$200–$250**

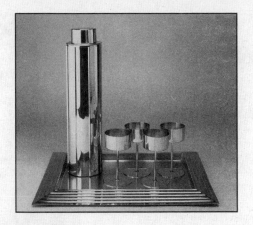

"Manhattan Serving Set" by Norman Bel Geddes.
Courtesy of Stephen Visakay, New Jersey.

REVERE COPPER AND BRASS COMPANY
Norman Bel Geddes   (American, 1893–1958)

"Manhattan Serving Set," sold 1937–1940, shaker: 12¾" high, 3½" diameter. Designed by Bel Geddes for Revere. This chrome "Skyscraper" shaker originally sold for $14.50 with six cups (set # 7046) and $16.50 with eight "Manhattan" cups (set #7048), each with its stepped back "Manhattan" tray. Today it is one of the most sought-after sets for cocktail shaker collectors. All pieces should be stamped "Revere, Rome, NY." While the shaker and tray may be found separately, it is extremely difficult to find the footed cocktail cups.

Tray alone	$150–$175
Shaker alone	$350–$450
Shaker, with two cups and tray	$1,200–$1,300
Shaker, with four cups and tray	$1,600–$1,750
Shaker, with six cups and tray	$2,500 (Auction)
	$2,500–$3,000
Shaker, with eight cups and tray	$3,200 (Auction)
	$3,000–$3,500

W. Archibald Welden   (Revere's Director of Design)

"Park Serving Set," sold 1937–1941 (set #7046). In chrome-plated brass, with the "Zephyr" cocktail shaker, circular tray, and four cups with Catalin bases. Stamped with the company name. Originally sold for $7.50.   **$250–$350**

"Sheridan Serving set," sold in the late 1930s (set #7030). In chromium-plated brass with Catalin trim, with the "Empire" cocktail shaker and six cups, and the circular "Hercules" tray. Stamped with the company name.   **$650–$700**

"Empire" shaker alone   **$250–$300**

STEVENS ELECTRIC COMPANY (American)

Electric cocktail mixer, 1933, 13" high. Chrome with maroon enameled cast-iron base. Stamped "Stevens Electric Co. Patented 4-19-33 #1300867."   **$200–$250**

"Lady's Leg" by West Virginia Specialty Glass Company. *Courtesy of Stephen Visakay, New Jersey.*

"Bottoms Up" cocktail set. *Courtesy of Stephen Visakay, New Jersey.*

WEST BEND ALUMINUM (American)

Cocktail shaker, 1934, approximately 11" high. Aluminum and plastic shaker with modern styling that looks as if it could be from the 1950s, but was designed by R. N. Kirchner and patented by West Bend in 1934. Black plastic base and top. Patent #93,928.

$45–$55

WEST VIRGINIA SPECIALTY GLASS COMPANY (American)

"Lady's Leg," 1937, 15½" high, 3½" diameter at calf. In ruby-red glass with sterling trim, chrome top, and removable high-heel chrome shoe, and with eight matching footed cups in ruby-red glass with applied sterling trim.

	$550–$650
Cocktail shaker alone	$450–$550
Cocktail shaker, cobalt-blue glass	$750–$800
Cocktail shaker, clear or frosted glass	$350–$375

Cocktail shaker, clear or frosted glass, as above but etched with the design of the Trylon and Perisphere of the 1939 New York World's Fair $950–$1,000

"Dumb-bell" cocktail serving set, c. 1935. Shaker and six cups in cobalt-blue glass, ribbed with silver trim. $550–$600

WHITE CLOUD FARMS (American, Rock Tavern, NY)

"Bottoms Up" cocktail shaker and tumblers, c. 1928–1930, shaker: 13" high; cups: 3¾" high. A pottery pitcher with a cork-bottomed bust of a nude woman as the stopper; the tumblers, which can stand only on their rims, have rounded bottoms over which is draped a nude woman, thus the name. Very rare, almost the "Holy Grail" of cocktail

**"The Cocktail Hour Set"
by Russel Wright.**
*Courtesy of Stephen Visakay,
New Jersey.*

shakers. Later, the maker was bought out by McKee Glass Company, which it had sued for copyright infringement over the manufacture of "Bottoms Up" tumblers in a variety of colors of glass.

Glass tumbler alone	$50–$60
Pottery tumbler	$100–$125
Pottery cocktail shaker	$2,000–$2,200

RUSSEL WRIGHT (American, 1904–1976)

"The Cocktail Hour Set," c. 1935, tray: 12½" diameter. In spun aluminum, the bulbous shaker with a long neck wrapped in cork, six cups with cork-wrapped feet, and a cork-surfaced circular tray.

$1,000 (Auction)
$1,200–$1,400

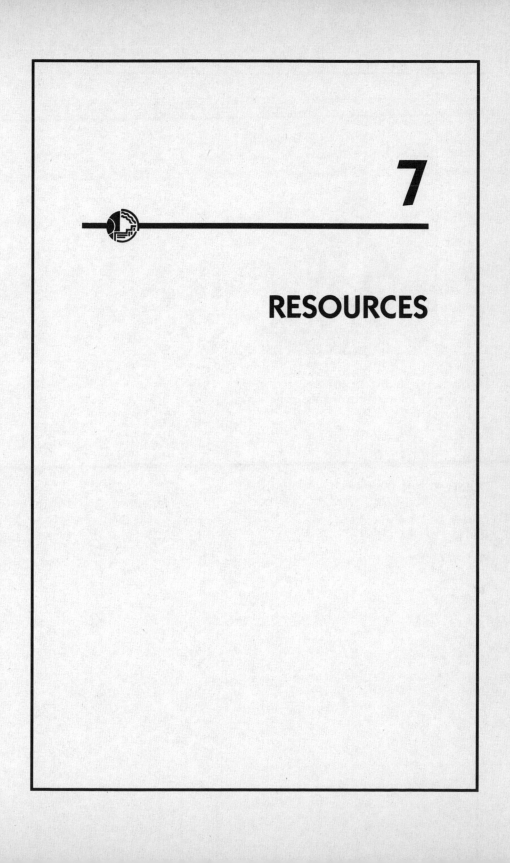

7

RESOURCES

RESOURCE GUIDE

AUCTION HOUSES

Butterfield & Butterfield, 220 San Bruno Avenue, San Francisco, CA 94103, (415) 861-7500, Cynthia Stern, director of public relations. The third largest auction house in the United States and fifth largest in the world. Art Deco specialty is specifically located at the Los Angeles gallery, (213) 850-7500, contact Jon King, ext. 217.

Christie's (Christie, Manson & Woods International, Inc.), 502 Park Avenue, New York, NY 10022, (212) 546-1000, Nancy McClelland, senior vice president and head, 20th Century Decorative Arts Department; Peggy Gilges, assistant vice president and specialist. Christie's has led the market in the area of 20th-century decorative arts at auction, with particular emphasis on high-level offerings from the Art Deco period. The firm is a significant factor also in offerings of Tiffany, Arts and Crafts, and architectural material such as that of Frank Lloyd Wright. Sales are distinguished by excellent exhibitions and catalogues.

Christie's East (Christie, Manson & Woods International, Inc.), 219 East 67th Street, New York, NY 10021, (212) 606-0530, fax: (212) 606-0530, Hélène Petrović, specialist, 20th Century Decorative Arts. Specialized sales in 20th-century decorative arts ranging from the Art Nouveau period up to contemporary ceramics and glass, with emphasis on Italian glass and furniture and design from the late 1930s up to the 1960s.

Christie's South Kensington, (Christie, Manson & Woods International, Inc.), 85 Old Brompton Road, London, SW7 3LD England, (71) 581-7611, contact Jane Haye or Mark Wilkinson in the Decorative Arts Department. The department holds twelve auctions a year, comprising a wide and varied selection of British and Continental decorative arts, 20th-century bronzes and sculpture, Moorcroft and Poole pottery, Doulton and Carlton Ware, Clarice Cliff and Susie Cooper ceramics.

William Doyle Galleries, 175 East 87th Street, New York, NY 10128, (212) 427-2730, fax: (212) 569-0892. Eric Silver, specialist, 19th and 20th Century Decorative Arts. William Doyle Galleries is one of America's leading auction houses and holds four annual Belle Epoque auctions every year which feature Art Nouveau, Art Deco, and Victorian furniture, decorations, and paintings.

Leslie Hindman Auctioneers, 215 West Ohio Street, Chicago, IL 60610, (312) 670-0010, fax: (312) 670-4248, Gary M. Piattoni, director, 20th Century Decorative

Arts. Monthly auctions of Old Master, 19th- and 20th-century paintings, drawings and prints; English, American, and Continental furniture and decorative arts; Oriental works of art, silver, porcelains, rugs, and jewelry.

Myers Antiques Auction Gallery, 1600 Fourth Street, Petersburg, FL 33704, (813) 823-3249, fax: (813) 823-3247, Michael Myers, owner/auctioneer. Florida's major specialty antiques auction gallery. Auctions held during the winter season include 20th-century decorative arts, Victorian, European, and Oriental, and Americana.

Savoia's Auction, Inc., Route 23, South Cairo, NY 12482, (518) 622-8000, fax: (518) 622-9452, Mary Brady. Quality antique auction gallery that concentrates on market trends in all areas including Art Deco, Arts and Crafts, Americana, and more.

Skinner, Inc., of Boston and Bolton, Massachusetts, 2 Newbury Street, Boston, MA 02116, (617) 236-1700, and 357 Main Street, Bolton, MA 01740, (508) 779-5144. Skinner, Inc. was established in 1962 and is currently the fifth largest auction gallery in the nation. With locations in Boston and Bolton, Massachusetts, Skinner, Inc. is the foremost auction gallery in New England.

Treadway Gallery, 2128 Madison Road, Cincinnati, OH 45208, (513) 321-6742, fax: (513) 771-1472, Don Treadway, Jerri Durham, and Thierry Corthioir. American Arts and Crafts, period furniture and decorative arts, Modern furniture and decorative items, American art pottery.

Wolf's Fine Arts Auctioneers, 1239 West 6th Street, Cleveland, OH 44113, (216) 575-9653, Bridget McWilliams, director of fine arts. Specializing in gallery auctions and on-site sales, and offering appraisal services for estate, tax, and insurance purposes, and complete restoration services for antique furniture.

DEALERS
(Alphabetically by state)

CALIFORNIA

Always & Forever, 3789 24th Street, San Francisco, CA 94114, George Esparza. Specializing in retail vintage clothing, from 1940s to 1950s, for men and women; suits, tuxedos, dinner jackets, hats, jewelry, ties, Hawaiian and gabardine shirts, evening dresses, beaded sweaters, and 1940s women's suits.

Another Time, 1586 Market Street, San Francisco, CA 94102, (415) 553-8900, Pam Groot or Floyd Wyrick. Specializing in Art Deco furniture and accessories through the 1950s; Heywood Wakefield, Roseville Pottery, and Chase Chrome. Warehouse and showroom located at 911 Alhambra Avenue, Martinez, CA 94553.

As Time Goes By, 865 Market #106, San Francisco, CA 94105, (415) 543-9970, fax: (415) 957-0411, Richard Fishman, owner. Specializing in Art Deco, vintage watches, Bakelite, marcasite, cocktail accessories, European pottery, Longwy, and an extensive book collection on decorative arts.

Boomerang, 3795 Park Boulevard, San Diego, CA 92103, (619) 295-1953, David Skelley and Jeff Spense. High-quality Modern design, 1939–1969. Furniture, lighting, and decorative objects.

Centrium Furnishings, 2166 Market Street, San Francisco, CA 94114, (415) 863-4195. Specializing in furniture, lighting, decorative arts, dinnerware, industrial design, and clocks. Emphasis on designs by Eames, Nelson, Bertoia, Knoll, Russel Wright, and Walter von Nessen, from the 1920s to the 1950s.

Decorum, 1632 Market Street, San Francisco, CA 94102, (415) 864-3326, Jack Beeler, owner. One of the largest and best collections on the West Coast, specializing in French and American Art Deco lighting: ceiling and wall fixtures, floor and table lamps, all expertly restored.

Genuine Antiques & Artifacts, 2149 Union Street, San Francisco, CA 94123, (415) 921-3427, Alain Thillois, owner. French antiques directly purchased and shipped by owner from France, including Art Deco clocks, glass, ceramics, lighting, and furniture.

Golden Telecom, 5751-F Palmer Way, Carlsbad, CA 92008, (619) 929-9099 or (619) 744-9393, Dan Golden, historian. Antique telephone enthusiast with emphasis on restoring to original specifications by using original parts. An authority on current values as well as historical information. By appointment only.

Harris Gallery, 3032 Claremont Avenue, Berkeley, CA 94705, (800) 458-6609, fax: (510) 658-4851, Stephen Harris and Sarah Stocking, owners. A very broad selection of vintage posters from the Art Nouveau and Art Deco eras.

Jet Age, 250 Oak Street, San Francisco, CA 94102, (415) 864-1950, Bill Clarke, owner. Jet Age is a gallery specializing in classic modern furnishings from 1930 to 1960. Also featuring a line of custom pieces as well as complete interior design services.

Peter Keresztury Designs, 1217 Waterview Drive, Mill Valley, CA 94941, (415) 383-3008, Peter Keresztury, owner. Art Deco to 1950s furniture, accessories, art, Heywood Wakefield furniture, and interior design. By appointment only.

Frances Klein Antique & Estate Jewelry, 310 North Rodeo Drive, Beverly Hills, CA 90210, (310) 273-0155 or (800) 759-6676 (in USA), fax: (310) 273-5279, Leeann Karidis. One of the largest and finest collections of Art Deco and estate jewels in the world.

Lottie Ballou Classic Clothing, 130 West F Street, Benica, CA 94510, (707) 747-9433, Margo Adams, owner. Simply the finest in vintage clothing: elegant evening attire, delightful daywear, and exquisite accessories. Restoration, beadwork, and alterations available.

Mixed Produce, 3789½ Park Boulevard, San Diego, CA 92103, (619) 692-9927, fax: (619) 298-7932, Michael A. Reams and Arnold R. Agular. Since 1979, dealers of Streamline Deco objects and furnishings, as well as vintage clothing, jewelry, buttons, and dress patterns. Also great selection of men's cufflinks.

Paris 1925, 1954 Union Street, San Francisco, CA 94123, (415) 567-1925, fax: (415) 567-1726, Christopher Grubaugh, manager. Specializes in vintage wristwatches, such as Rolex and Patek Phillippe, and fine estate jewelry plus estate and estate-style wedding rings.

The Perfect Purse, 15466 Los Gatos Boulevard, Los Gatos, CA 95032, (408) 559-4172, Suzi Mounts. Repairs beaded bags, linings, fringe, and reframing. Also buys pre-1900 to 1920 beaded bags, chatelaine bags, children's and dolls' purses. By appointment only.

Rosebud Gallery, 1857 Soland Avenue, Berkeley, CA 94707, (510) 525-6454, Ed Forcum. Offers: 20th-century decorative arts including Georg Jensen, 1950s Italian art glass, William Spratling, Antonio Pineda, Hector Aguilar, Hagenauer, and American Indian designs.

Spell Bound, 1670 Haight Street, San Francisco, CA 94117, (415) 863-4930, Janet Spinosa, owner. The very best in style and good repair in clothing and jewelry from the Deco period. Restorations and repair.

20th Century Furnishings, 1612 Market Street, San Francisco, CA 94102, (415) 626-0542, David Dutra, owner. Specializing in American design furniture, lighting, and accessories from 1925 to 1960.

Vintage Modern, 182 Gough Street, San Francisco, CA 94102, (415) 861-8162, Thomas Lennon. Offering a good selection of Deco to mid-century furniture, lighting, jewelry, glassware, metalware, and other decorative art.

Vintage Silhouettes, 1420 Pomona Street, Crockett, CA 94525, (510) 787-7274, Janene Fawcett, owner. Specializing in men's, women's and children's vintage clothing and accessories from 1850 to 1950.

COLORADO

Omnibus Gallery, 533 East Cooper Avenue, Aspen, CO 81611, (303) 925-5567, fax: (303) 925-7805, George Sells, director. Extensive collection of original posters and prints including the works of A. M. Cassandre, Colin, Loupot, Carlu, Baumberger, Cappiello, Hohlwein, Magritte, and others, as well as earlier masters from the Belle Epoque and Art Nouveau periods.

CONNECTICUT

Linda Cheverton Art & Antiques, Box 53, Colebrook, CT 06021, (203) 379-5345, Linda Cheverton, owner. Specializing in a variety of areas including the ceramics of Susie Cooper. By appointment only.

Radioart, P.O. Box 102, Centerbrook, CT 06409, (203) 873-3360, Jim Meehan, owner. Buys and sells Catalin radios, colored plastic, tabletop radios of the 1930s and 1940s. By appointment only.

Remember When, 66 Main Street, Torrington, CT 06790, (203) 489-1566, Karen M. O'Donnell, owner. Specializing in the unique and unusual; furniture, lighting, glass, pottery, and jewelry from the 1920s, 1930s, and 1940s.

FLORIDA

A & J Unique Antiques, 191 N.E. 40th Street, Miami, FL 33137-1911, (305) 398-2194, Adam Silverstein. Art Deco furniture and accessories. Offers 4,000 square feet of bedroom furniture, tables and chairs, buffets, couch sets, and much more.

B. & S. Antique Collection, 800 N.W. 12th Terrace #4, Pompano Beach, FL 33069, (407) 274-4634, Mindy and Beverly Hersher, owners. Importers of European furniture and accessories of the decorative arts, 1890–1930. By appointment only.

California Dream, Town & Country Mall, 8306 Mills Drive, Route #184, Miami, FL 33183, (305) 274-9642, fax: (305) 598-4743, Rose Hart, owner. Antique crate label art dating from the early 1900s through World War II. True Americana. This art form has been displayed in museums throughout the world. Many Art Deco designs. By appointment only.

Decollectable, 233 14th Street, Miami Beach, FL 33139, (305) 674-0899, Paul Adrian, manager. Something for everyone from the 1700s to the 1970s; furniture, glass, pottery, jewelry, collectibles, and curios.

The Florida Picker, Box 210, Webster, FL 33597, (904) 793-1363, Michael Turbeville. Old Florida and Florida Moderne; paintings and objects of art; advertising; tropical fantasy; furniture, accessories and lighting; and a general line of antiques. By appointment only.

Madeleine France Antiques, P.O. Box 15555, Plantation, FL 33318, (305) 584-0009, fax: (305) 584-0014, Madeleine France. Specializing in René Lalique, Baccarat, and all types of art glass, with an emphasis on perfume bottles and boudoir items. By appointment only.

Modernism Gallery, 1622 Ponce de Leon Boulevard, Coral Gables, FL 33134, (305) 442-8743, fax: (305) 443-3074, Ric Emmett, owner. Specializing in American designer furniture, lighting, clocks, radios, glass, pottery, prints, sculpture, and paintings, 1925–1965.

Les Temps Passes, 6222 Alton Road, Miami Beach, FL 33140, (305) 866-4434, Nicole Sultan. French Art Deco period furniture and accessories. By appointment only.

ILLINOIS

Kelmscott Gallery, 4611 North Lincoln Avenue, Chicago, IL 60625, (312) 784-2559, fax: (616) 925-6574, Scott Elliott, president. Gallery of Modernism specializing in Frank Lloyd Wright, Prairie School, Chicago School of Architecture, Arts and Crafts, related decorative and fine arts, and an emphasis on photography.

Stephen Maras Antiques, 423 Central Avenue, Wilmette, IL 60091-1943, (708) 256-3991, fax: (708) 256-4059, Stephen Maras. Twenty-one years in business. Buying and selling Art Nouveau, Art Deco, and Vienna Secessionist items to collectors and dealers across the country.

Jacob Marley, 3334 North Clark Street, Chicago, IL 60657, Tom Neniskis. Chrome, Bakelite, steel objects, and jewelry, 1910–1940. American and European pieces chosen on the basis of style and visual impact.

Modern Times, 1538 North Milwaukee, Chicago, IL 60622, (312) 772-8871, Tom Clark and Martha Torno. One of Chicago's largest 20th-century stores, featuring furniture, lighting, decorative accessories, art, silver and costume jewelry, and vintage clothing from Deco to disco—designer to kitsch.

Salvage One, 1524 South Sangamon Street, Chicago, IL 60608, (312) 733-0098, fax: (312) 733-6829, Anne McGahan, marketing director. Salvage One maintains one of the nation's largest selections of American and European artifacts from the 18th through 20th centuries, including Art Deco mantels, doors, light fixtures, bars, ironwork, glass, and much more.

Steve Starr Studios, 2654 North Clark Street, Chicago, IL 60614, (312) 525-6530, Steve Starr. Celebrating its twenty-fifth anniversary in 1992. Art Deco furnishings.

Steve Starr is author of *Picture Perfect—Art Deco Photo Frames 1926–1946* (Rizzoli, 1991), or available from Steve Starr Studios, $33 postage paid.

Zig Zag, 3419 North Lincoln Avenue, Chicago, IL 60657, (312) 525-1060, Marsha Evaskus, owner. Offers 20th-century design, specializing in 1930s Streamline furnishings and objects, Bakelite and costume jewelry, vintage radios, and plastic purses.

MAINE

Howard & Mullen, Route 1 Ogunquit (Box 1997), Ogunquit, ME 03907, (207) 361-2774 or (207) 646-4098, Joseph Mullen. Ten years in the business, shop open seven days a week, May 1–November 1, and by appointment other times. Specialty is Chase Chrome, but deals in other items.

Albert Meadow Antiques, 10 Albert Meadow, Bar Harbor, ME 04609, (207) 288-9456, David Doherty, owner. Entire shop dedicated to Art Deco and Art Nouveau periods. Featuring large selection of jewelry, diamonds to Bakelite; pottery art glass; lamps; sterling; and Maxfield Parrish prints.

Nelson Rarities, Inc., 1 City Center, Eighth Floor, Portland, ME 04112, (207) 775-3150, Andrew Nelson or Malcolm Logan. Worldwide buyers and sellers of fine Art Deco jewelry and silver.

Orphan Annie's, 96 Court Street, Auburn, ME 04210, (207) 782-0638, Dan Poulin, owner. Specializing in Art Deco lighting, French and American glassware, pottery, jewelry, vintage clothing, Bakelite, furnishings, and any of the various items found with Art Deco styling.

MARYLAND

Carole A. Berk, Ltd., 8020 Norfolk Avenue, Bethesda, MD 20814, (301) 656-0355, Carole Berk. Specializing in 20th-century decorative art: Clarice Cliff, Keith Murray, Charlotte Rhead, Minton, Vienna Secession, Czech glass, Dorothy Thorpe, Bugatti, vintage costume jewelry, Mexican jewelry, and decorative art.

Greg and Ann Golden, P.O. Box 57379, Washington, DC 20037, (301) 946-0214 (located in Wheaton, Maryland). Specializing in Depression glass, dinnerware, Bakelite, chrome, art pottery, Czechoslovakian, and other affordable Depression-era and Moderne items. Antiques shows and by appointment.

Montage, Maryland, (301) 838-7440, Pat Boyer. Decorative arts of the 20th century. Specializing in commercial perfume bottles, art glass, art pottery, art metal to include Lalique, Tiffany, Roseville, Rookwood, Jensen, WMF, Kayserzinn. By appointment only.

Sabina & Daughter/Merchants to the Melancholy, 1637 Eastern Avenue, Baltimore, MD, (410) 276-6366, Sabina and Samantha Waldman. Located in the chapel of a 1922 convent and specializing in Art Deco furniture, lamps, telephones, and accessories. Voted "Baltimore's Best Art Deco" by *Baltimore Magazine*.

The Trinity Collection, P.O. Box 602, Easton, MD 21601, (410) 822-3907, fax: (410) 822-8731, E. Townsend Wright, Jr. Specializing in vintage wrist and pocket watches 1930s–1940s, offering moderately priced watches to high-grade timepieces; also Art Deco clocks and fountain pens. By appointment only.

MASSACHUSETTS

Morton Abromson Decorative Arts, Brookline, Massachusetts, (617) 277-1925, Morton Abromson, owner. Specializing in Art Deco and Arts and Crafts pottery and Art Deco glass, especially Boch Frères/Keramis, Longwy, Le Verre Français, and Pickington. By appointment only.

American Decorative Arts, 3 Olive Street, Northampton, MA 01060, (413) 584-6804, Chris Kennedy. 20th-century Modern design furniture and accessories. Specializing in architect/designer furniture and objects as well as Heywood Wakefield, Knoll, and Herman Miller.

Antique Arts, P.O. Box 105, Lincoln, MA 01773, (617) 259-0807, Rick Lee. 1860–1960 graphics, folk art, and lighting. By appointment only.

Antiquers III, 171A Harvard Street, Brookline, MA 02146, (617) 738-5555, fax: (617) 731-9069, Mark Feldman and Corey Warn. Dealing in fine Art Deco and Modernism with a specialization in Schneider glass, Louis Icart etchings, "Nymphette" Frankart lamps, and European art pottery.

Thomas G. Boss Fine Books, 355 Boylston Street, Boston, MA 02116, (617) 421-1880, Thomas G. Boss, owner. Illustrated books including *pochoir*; fine printing and bindings, graphics and posters, original drawings by artists such as Barbier, and books on Art Deco design.

Annella Brown, 23 Commonwealth Avenue, Boston, MA 02116, (617) 267-8049/Miami Beach (305) 864-8800, Annella Brown, owner. Specializing in fine 20th-century jewelry with an additional emphasis on Art Deco ceramics and American sculpture. By appointment only.

Deco Echoes, Box 2321, Mashpee, MA 02649, (508) 428-2324, Scott Cheverie. Mail-order catalogue dealership specializing in 1930s–1960s vintage and recreated classics. Also publisher of *The Echoes Report*, a quarterly newsletter specializing in 1930s–1960s. Subscription, $10 annually.

Divine Decadence, 542 Columbus Avenue, Boston, MA 02118, (617) 266-1477, Richard Penachio, owner. An eclectic array of 20th-century interior furnishings with focus on the Art Deco and mid-century periods, as well as selected contemporary pieces, including neon art.

Elizabeth's 20th Century, 41 State Street, Newburyport, MA 01950, (508) 465-2983, Elizabeth Baratelli, owner. Specializing in jewelry and furnishings of the Art Deco period through the great design of 1950s, including Chase, Frankart, Knoll, Herman Miller, Bakelite, Schiaparelli, Haskell, and others.

Fusco & Four, Associates, 1 Murdock Terrace, Brighton, MA 02135, (617) 787-2637, Tony Fusco and Robert Four, owners. Specializing in 1900–1950 original fine prints and other works on paper, emphasizing 1920s–1930s, artists such as Rockwell Kent, Lovet-Lorski, Lynd Ward, and many others. Appraisal services in Art Deco, posters, and fine prints. By appointment only.

Bernice Jackson Fine Art, P.O. Box 1188, Concord, MA 01742, (508) 369-9088, fax: (508) 369-1718. Specializing in posters and graphics of Italy, Switzerland, and Holland, reflecting different design periods and movements: Art Deco, De Stijl, Dada, Symbolism, as well as the impact of political movements such as fascism. By appointment only.

The Nostalgia Factory, 336 Newbury Street, Boston, MA 02115, (617) 236-8754, Rudy Franchi. Specializing in Art Deco graphics (ads, fashion plates), Deco posters (travel, ocean liner) and Deco ephemera (brochures, labels, postcards, menus, and more).

Peacock Alley Antiques, 35 Route 28, P.O. Box 964, Orleans, MA 02653, (508) 240-1804, Jerry Kibbe, owner. A 750-square-foot shop specializing in Art Deco, 1950s Modern, decorative arts. Eames, Bertoia, Herman Miller, Chase, Maxfield Parrish, others.

Pearl Washington's, 892 Bedford Street, Whitman, MA 02382, (617) 447-4454, fax: (508) 586-4281, Kathy Schneider, proprietor. Offers 20th-century decorative to practical, electric, cookie jars, kitchen items, occasional furniture, funky, glass, china, eclectic. By appointment only.

Remembrances of Things Past, 376 Commercial Street, Provincetown, MA 02657, (508) 487-9443, Helene Lyons, owner. Enchanting, zany blast from the past with particular emphasis on the 1920s and 1930s. Neon, jewelry, Art Deco, vintage phones—nostalgia from the 1900s to the 1990s.

Restoration Resources Inc., 311 Needham Street, Newton, MA 02164, (617) 964-2036, Bill Raymer, president. Architectural antique warehouse store. Architectural, antique, and reproduction items, 1880–1950.

Sparkle Plenty, 18 Nottingham Street, Newton, MA 02159, (617) 969-1193, Elizabeth Chadis, owner. Offers 20th-century vintage costume jewelry. By appointment only.

Threshold Antiques, Massachusetts Antiques Cooperative, 100 Felton Street, Waltham, MA 02154, (617) 893-8893, fax: (617) 244-8605, Lois Morog, owner. Emphasizing 20th century, including Arts and Crafts movement and Art Deco, small furniture, decorative accessories, and collector items.

MICHIGAN

Deco Doug, 106 West 4th, Royal Oak, MI 48067, (313) 547-3330, Doug Ramsey, owner. Fine Art Deco, 1920s through 1960s lamps, radios, collectibles, Chase, fountain pens, vintage watches, and accessories for the collector.

Duke Gallery, 120 Peabody, Birmingham, MI 48009, (313) 258-6848, Ann and Ned Duke, owners. Specializing in 20th-century decorative arts including Art Nouveau, Art Deco, and American Arts and Crafts, American and European glass and pottery, furniture, and lighting.

First 1/2, 12150 East Outer Drive, Detroit, MI 48224, (313) 886-3443, Jacques-Pierre Caussin, owner. Specializing in 20th-century decorative arts, with an emphasis on 1930s American design. Also sells reprints of catalogues: 1940 Herman Miller catalogue; 1952 Herman Miller catalogue with designs by Eames, Nelson, Noguchi; and 1934 Russel Wright catalogue. By appointment only.

Rage of the Age, 220 South 4th Avenue, Ann Arbor, MI 48104, (313) 662-0777, Paul Shore, owner. Decorative arts from the 1930s through the 1960s including furniture, jewelry, clothing and accessories, mainly designer items from the 1940s and 1950s.

20th Century Designs, 31505 Scone, Livonia, MI 48154, (313) 425-3788, Chuck and Kim Zuccarini, owners. Dealing in items from the late 19th century through the present. Specializing in American and European Art Deco glass, pottery, chrome, and furniture.

MISSOURI

Antique Books, P.O. Box 6395, Annapolis, MO 21401, David and Kathleen Way. Specializing in new and out-of-print books about antiques and collectibles, including Art Deco, art pottery and glass. By appointment only.

Sambeau's Ltd., 4724 McPherson Avenue, St. Louis, MO 63108, (314) 361-4636, fax: (314) 361-2216, Sam Bass, director. From signed pieces to mid-range furniture, smalls, decorative accessories, and art.

NEW JERSEY

Cookie's Collectibles, P.O. Box 627, Phuckemin, NJ 07978, (908) 722-6886, Cookie Katz, owner. Always stocking Fiesta, Harlequin, Riviera, Hall China, Russel Wright, Jadite and Bakelite, in addition to a variety of items from the 1920s to the 1950s. By appointment only.

Of Rare Vintage, 718 Cookman Avenue, Asbury Park, NJ 07712, (908) 988-9459, Bill Meisch, owner. Specializing in Deco furniture, vintage fabrics, vintage appliances, Bakelite, and rattan.

Ken Shultz, Box M 753, Hoboken, NJ 07030, (201) 656-0966, Ken Schultz, owner. Specializing in ocean liner memorabilia; models, paintings, posters, ephemera—anything to do with passenger ship travel in the 1920s and 1930s. World's Fairs, 1933 and 1939. By appointment only.

Yesterday's World, P.O. Box 235, 202 Main Street, White House Station, NJ 08889, (908) 534-5515, Herbert Rolfes, owner. Specializing in World's Fair memorabilia. Also co-author of *The World of Tomorrow: The 1939 New York World's Fair* (Harper & Row, 1989). By appointment only.

NEW YORK

Abemayor Galleries, Inc., 125 East 57th Street, New York, NY 10022, (212) 371-4789, fax: (212) 371-4789, Ernest Cohen. Large selection of fine 19th- and 20th-century sculpture, specializing in the French animalier school.

L'art de Vivre Inc., 978 Lexington Avenue, New York, NY 10021, (212) 734-3510, Patricia Fuller, president. Specializing in early 20th-century fine European antiques, French Art Deco, Bauhaus, Modernist furniture, lighting, bronzes, and objets d'art with emphasis on quality and design.

Bizarre Bazaar, Ltd., 125 East 57th Street, #24, New York, NY 10022, (212) 688-1830, fax: (212) 245-5218, Nora Knight, manager. Early 20th-century objects, transportation models, toys, art glass, jewelry, perfumes. Specializing in the unusual and surreal, always in finest condition. Always looking to purchase one piece or entire collections.

Brown Company, 89 Leonard Street, New York, NY 10013, (212) 941-4753, Nicholas and Shaunna Brown, owners. Offers 20th-century American design, vintage and modern photography, specializing in the designs of Warren McArthur Corporation, manufacturers of anodized aluminum furniture. By appointment only.

Chisholm/Bailly, 43 Greenwich Avenue, New York, NY 10012, (212) 243-8834, Nicholas Bailly or Gail Chisholm. Specializing in original lithographic posters and graphics from 1880 to the present. Artists include Cassandre, Kauffer, a strong selection of travel posters, and earlier artists such as Toulouse-Lautrec, Chéret, and Cappiello.

Chisholm Parts Gallery, 145 Eighth Avenue, New York, NY 10011, (212) 741-1703, fax: (212) 727-2778, Robert Chisholm, owner. A broad selection of fine original posters, including Art Deco travel, shipping, and product advertising from America and Europe.

Club of American Collectors of Fine Arts, Inc., 1 Lincoln Plaza, 20 West 64th Street, Suite 21K, New York, NY 10023, (212) 769-1860, fax: (212) 873-1853, Jacques P. Athias, president. One of the largest sources of museum quality pieces by Cassandre, Carlu, Lepape, Barbier, and Domergue. By appointment only.

Nicholas M. Dawes, 67 East 11th Street, New York, NY 10003, (212) 473-5111, fax: (212) 353-3845. Specialist in Lalique. Author of *Lalique Glass* (Crown, 1986). Named "the most prominent Lalique dealer in the U.S." by *Forbes* magazine, 1991. By appointment only.

Depression Modern, 150 Sullivan, New York, NY 10012, (212) 982-5699, Scott Scrymgeour, gallery director. Specializes in 1930s Streamline American furniture and accessories.

The Discerning Eye, 115 Betsy Brown Road, Port Chester, NY 10573, (914) 934-0311, Ken and Jessica Berkowitz. In twelfth year. Specializing in Art Deco, 20th-century decorative arts, American industrial design, geometric, streamlined and skyscraper-styled items, 1939 New York World's Fair. Always buying and selling. By appointment only.

Dualities Gallery, 2056 Boston Post Road, Larchmont, NY 10538, (914) 834-2773, Peter Boehm. A wide variety of antiques and decorative objects, paintings, sculpture, glass, metal, porcelain, and pottery from the 20th century.

Paula Ellman, Rego Park, New York, (718) 672-6641, Paula Ellman. Specializing in jewelry and wristwatches, Cartier, vintage art glass, Tiffany, Steuben, and others. By appointment only.

Fifty/50, 793 Broadway, New York, NY 10003, (212) 777-3208. Specializing in important 20th-century architectural and decorative arts. Featuring pieces by Paul T. Frankl, Donald Deskey, Russel Wright, Gilbert Rohde, Frank Lloyd Wright, Charles Eames, George Nelson, and others.

Historical Design Collection, Inc., New York, New York (212) 593-4528, fax: (212) 486-3188, Daniel Morris, director. Specializing in decorative arts of all the design movements in Europe and America, 1860–1960. By appointment only.

Judith Jack, Inc., 392 Fifth Avenue, New York, NY 10018, (212) 695-4004 or (800) 431-0017, fax: (212) 695-4094, Judith Rosenberg. Specializing in antique estate buyable platinum, gold, and gemstones. Active, extensive inventory. Also interested in buying jewelry. By appointment only.

Kurland—Zabar, 19 East 71st Street, New York, NY 10021, (212) 517-8576, Catherine Kurland and Lori Zabar, owners. British and American decorative arts from 1840 to 1940, specializing in the Gothic, Renaissance, and Egyptian Revivals, the Aesthetic movement, and Art Deco.

Arlene Lederman Antiques, 150 Main Street, Nyack, NY 10960, (914) 358-8616, Arlene Lederman, owner. Buys and sells vintage cocktail shakers, 18th- to 20th-century antiques, American, European, furniture, glass, decorative accessories, collectibles. Stage rentals, dealers and decorators welcome.

Maison Gerard, 36 East 10th Street, New York, NY 10003, (212) 674-7611, fax: (212) 475-6314, Gerard Widdershoven. Fine Art Deco furniture, carpets, lighting and objets d'art. Wholesale/retail, rentals and sales.

Metropolis, 44 Central Avenue, Albany, NY 12206, (518) 427-2971. Art Deco objects, furnishings, and furniture; lighting; vintage clothing and textiles; extensive collection of antique jewelry and vintage costume jewelry.

Metropolitan Art Associates, 346 New York Avenue, Huntington, NY 11743, (516) 549-8300, fax: (516) 549-6833, Stephanie Reale, wholesale manager. Specializing in limited graphics and bronze sculptures, Erté, Max, Vasarely, Neiman, McKnight, others. Also specializing in secondary market.

Mood Indigo, 181 Prince Street, New York, NY 10012, (212) 254-1176, fax: (212) 334-2341, Diane Petipas, owner. Specializing in "Fiesta" ware, Russel Wright, and other dinnerware of the 1930s, 1940s and 1950s, as well as Chase Chrome, Bakelite jewelry, 1939 New York World's Fair, novelty salt and pepper shakers.

Gerald Newman, Elmsford, New York, (914) 592-3739. Specializing in antique advertising items and World's Fair. By appointment only.

Park South Gallery at Carnegie Hall, 885 Seventh Avenue, New York, NY 10019, (212) 246-5900, fax: (212) 541-5716, Laura Gold, president. Original antique Art Nouveau and Art Deco lithographic posters.

Piacente, 38 Main Street, Tarrytown, NY 10591, (914) 631-4231, Florence Geller, owner. Specializing in alligator and leather luggage, handbags, and accessories, a very large selection. Great Hawaiian shirts, vintage clothing, textiles, furniture, and decorative items.

Poster America, 138 West 18th Street, New York, NY 10011, (212) 206-0499, fax: (212) 727-2495, Jack Banning. Graphic design of the 20th century: posters, books, ephemera, and photographs, largely from the 1920s and 1930s.

Primavera Gallery Inc., 808 Madison Avenue, New York, NY 10021, (212) 288-1569, fax: (212) 288-2102, Audrey Friedman, president. Fine examples of 20th-century decorative arts, primarily French, including Lalique, Mayodon, Daum Nancy, Pierre Chareau. Also fine and important period jewelry.

Reinhold-Brown Gallery, 26 East 78th Street, New York, NY 10021, (212) 734-7999, Susan Reinhold and Robert Brown, directors. Specializing in fine rare graphic design: original posters and works on paper from early 20th-century avant-garde movements (Bauhaus, Art Deco, Russian Constructivism, Vienna Secession), as well as work by Fluxus and Pop-Art artists and important contemporary designers.

Renee Antiques, Inc., 8 East 12th Street, New York, NY 10003, (212) 929-6870, Renee Starfield, president. One of the oldest antique dealers in New York, specializing in 19th-century Art Nouveau and Art Deco furnishings, lighting, lamps, paintings, art glass, bronzes, and furniture.

Retro Modern Studio, 88 East 10th Street, New York, NY 10003, (212) 674-0530, Arthur and Bronnie Hindin. French and American designer Art Deco: furniture, lighting, rugs, and objects.

Sapho Gallery, Inc., 1037 Second Avenue, New York, NY 10022, (212) 308-0880, fax: (212) 750-4797, Shelley Cohen, secretary/treasurer. Fine selection of authentic European Art Deco lighting, furniture, sculpture, and decorations. A large display of hand-hammered period ironwork as well as emphasis on Wiener Werkstätte.

John Sideli Art & Antiques, Box 67, Malden Bridge, NY 12115, (518) 766-3547. Specializing in Catalin radios. Author of *Classic Plastic Radios of the 1930s and 1940s* (E. P. Dutton, 1990). Available by mail order for $19.95, plus $3 shipping and sales tax where applicable.

Fred Silberman Company, 83 Wooster Street, New York, NY 10012, (212) 925-9470, Fred Silberman, partner. Specializing in Italian period furniture, lighting, pottery, glass; Hagenauer sculpture, Edward Winters enamels.

Nancy Steinbock Posters and Prints, 197 Holms Dale, Albany, NY 12208, (800) 438-1577, Nancy Steinbock, owner. Original posters published in the 1920s, 1930s and 1940s, featuring geometric design as well as products and fashion of the period. By appointment only.

20th Century Antiques Ltd., 878 Madison Avenue, New York, NY 10021, (212) 988-5181, fax: (212) 861-8119, Carol Haley. The source for Louis Icart etchings— more than 150 titles in stock at all times.

Wooster Gallery, 20th Century Furniture & Furnishings, 86 Wooster Street, New York, NY 10012, (212) 219-2190, fax: (212) 941-6678, Beatrice and Carolyn Holmes, owners. Specializing in fine French Art Deco furniture, lighting, and decorations.

OHIO

A Look Back, 449½ West Market Street, Akron, OH 44303, (216) 535-3326, Nance Darrow, owner. Features 20th-century decorative arts.

Treadway Gallery, 2128 Madison Road, Cincinnati, OH 45208, (513) 321-6742, fax: (513) 771-1472, Don Treadway, Jerri Durham, and Thierry Corthioir. American Arts and Crafts, period furniture and decorative arts, Modern furniture and decorative items, American art pottery.

PENNSYLVANIA

As Time Goes By, P.O. Box 178, Fountainville, PA 18923, (215) 345-6793, Howard Auerback and Ken Maffia, owners. Specializing in decorative, fine, and applied arts, 1920–1960, with a focus on industrial design, Venetian art glass, American Modernist jewelry, and Modern paintings and prints. By appointment only.

Calderwood Gallery, 221 South 17th Street, Philadelphia, PA 19103, (215) 732-9444, fax: (215) 732-0922, Gary and Janet Calderwood, owners. Fine-quality European furniture and accessories from the first half of the 20th century. Specialists in Art Nouveau, Art Deco, 1940s. Also specializes in Chinese Deco carpets.

Katy Kane Antique Clothing and Linens, 34 West Ferry Street, New Hope, PA 18938, (215) 862-5873, Katy Kane, president. Specializing in ladies' antique clothing and accessories, bed and table linens, with an emphasis on 20th-century couture clothing.

Moderne, 111 North 3rd Street, Philadelphia, PA 19106, (215) 923-8536, fax: (215) 635-6962, Robert Aibel, owner. Three floors filled with quality French Art Deco furniture, lighting, paintings, glass, ceramics, and other objects. Also a limited selection of quality American Art Deco and 1950s items.

South Pointe Antiques, Route 272 and Denver Road, Adamstown, PA 19501, (215) 484-1026, Ron and Marilyn Kowaleski, owners. One hundred dealers showcasing quality antiques with a good variety of Deco items. Located at Exit 21 off Pennsylvania Turnpike, one block south on Route 272. Open Friday to Monday.

Walkers Collectibles, Pittsburgh Antique Mall, Pittsburgh, PA and Canonsburg Antique Mall II, Canonsburg, PA, phone calls only: (412) 922-0862, Carol Walker, owner. Pre-1950 vintage fashion hats, jewelry, the old and unusual, World's Fair.

The Warehouse, 120 Gordon Street, Allentown, PA 18102, (215) 821-9187 or (215) 432-6565, Paul Fuhrman, owner. Specializing in Americana only: late 19th century–1960s with emphasis on sofas, chairs, chaises, and other seating. Lighting and carpets available in multiples. By appointment only.

RHODE ISLAND

The Cat's Pajamas, 227 Wickenden Street, Providence, RI 02903, (401) 751-8440, Cheri Light, owner/Michael Sivik, manager. Offers 20th-century artifacts: Russel Wright, hammered aluminum, art, children's books, copper, Mexican silver, gold jewelry, fans, lamps, clocks, folk art, small furniture, textiles.

VERMONT

Glad Rags Fine Vintage Clothing and Antiques, 6 State Street, Montpelier, VT 05602, (802) 223-1451, Ruth Smiler. Specializing in high-style 1900–1940 to wear, collect, or decorate; fine and costume jewelry, clothing for men, women, and children, fashion accessories, metal, glass, china, lamps, dresser sets, bedspreads, linens, and lace.

VIRGINIA

Dennis Boyd, Unlimited, 211 South Mulberry Street, Richmond, VA 23220, (804) 359-0518, Dennis Boyd, owner. Booths at Antique Station, Dumfries, VA, (703) 221-7534, and Antiquers Mall, Charlottesville, VA, (804) 973-3478. Specializing in Art Deco and 1950s furnishings, art glass, art pottery, and dinnerware.

Ken Forster Decorative Arts, 5501 Seminary Road, Suite 1311 South, Falls Church, VA 22041, (703) 379-1142, Ken Forster, proprietor. Eclectic section of the unusual and the rare in American and European decorative arts of the late 19th and early 20th centuries; Georg Jensen silver; American Modernism. By appointment only.

Lolly's, 115A Middlesex Drive, Charlottesville, VA 22901, (804) 979-8077, Lolly Commanday. Antiques and vintage jewelry, predominantly sterling. Considerable selection in Art Deco from Taxco, Denmark, and USA. Art Moderne sterling silver costume jewelry; Art Nouveau and Victorian. All price ranges.

Montage, Virginia, (703) 250-5426, Gloria Dunetz. Decorative arts of the 20th century. Specializing in commercial perfume bottles, art glass, art pottery, art metal, including Lalique, Tiffany, Roseville, Rookwood, Jensen, WMF, and Kayserzinn. By appointment only.

Past Pleasures Antiques, 6305 Willowood Lane, Alexandria, VA 22310, (703) 719-0896, Donald J. Selkirk. Specializing in lighting, glassware, Chase Chrome, chrome furniture, chairs, tables, Bakelite items—1920s, 1930s, 1940s, and 1950s. Also restoration of most Deco items. By appointment only.

WISCONSIN

Phoneco, Inc., P.O. Box 70, 207 East Mill Road, Galesville, WI 54630, (608) 582-4124, Ron and Mary Knappen, owners. Twenty years in business, and thirty-five employees who take great pride in their work. Restoration of telephones of all types. A large supply of Bakelite telephones from the 1930s and 1940s. By appointment only.

SHOW MANAGEMENT

(See also the listings for Art Deco Societies, many of which hold annual shows and sales of Art Deco.)

Caskey Lees & Olney, P.O. Box 1637, Topanga, CA 90290, (310) 455-2886, Bill Caskey. Producers of "The L.A. Modernism Show," held over Memorial Day weekend each year at the Santa Monica Civic Auditorium.

Indianapolis Art Deco and Vintage Clothing Show, 637 North Keystone, Indianapolis, IN 46201, (317) 261-1405 or (317) 637-1592, Carol Rettig. This show, which many nickname "The Indy Deco Show," is held every June and October. Now fifteen years old, it is considered by many as the best in the Midwest.

Peter and Deborah Keresztury, 1217 Waterview Drive, San Francisco, CA 94941, (415) 383-3008. Producers of "Art Deco-1950's Sale," held the second week of June every year, in conjunction with the Art Deco Society of California's "Art Deco Weekend by the Bay" since 1984. Perhaps the West's largest Art Deco–1950s show.

Modern Productions, 3339 Lansmere Road, Shaker Heights, OH 44122, (216) 751-5922, Cynthia Barta. Produces and promotes Art Deco and 20th-century shows. Also specializes in 20th-century events including fashion and car shows, music, decorations.

Modern Times, 1325 Abbot Kinney, Venice, CA 90291, (310) 392-6676, Tauni Brustin, promoter. The "Modern Times" show specializes in Art Deco, Modern, and 1950s and is held every October and April at the Glendale Civic Auditorium in greater Los Angeles. Each show features seventy-five exhibitors from across the country.

Sanford L. Smith & Associates, 68 East 7th Street, New York, NY 10003, (212) 777-5218, fax: (212) 477-6490, Sanford Smith. Sanford Smith's "Modernism—A Century of Style and Design," is held each November at the Park Avenue Armory in

New York City. It brings together over seventy of the finest dealers in Art Deco, Art Nouveau, Bauhaus, Arts and Crafts, and other major design movements of the past hundred years.

Stella Show Management Company, 163 Terrace Street, Haworth, NJ 07641, (201) 384-0010, Irene Stella, president. Show producers and managers in New York and New Jersey. Events include shows with fine antiques to collectibles events. At the twice-yearly "Manhattan Antiques and Collectibles Triple Pier Show & Sale" in New York City, Pier 88 has become well-known as a place to shop for Art Deco.

Winnetka Modernism Show, 620 Lincoln Avenue, Winnetka, IL 60093, (708) 446-0537, Julie Stracks, co-dealer chairman. Each November, "The Winnetka Modernism Show" offers top-quality furniture and decorative arts from 1890 to 1960 for sale by forty-five dealers from across the country.

ART DECO SOCIETIES AND PRESERVATION ORGANIZATIONS

IN THE UNITED STATES

Art Deco Society of Louisiana, P.O. Box 1326, Baton Rouge, LA 70821-1320, (504) 275-6367, Richard J. Speciale, president. Call for membership information and schedule of activities.

Art Deco Society of Boston, 1 Murdock Terrace, Brighton, MA 02135, (617) 787-2637, Tony Fusco, president. Founded in 1989, ADSB promotes the understanding, appreciation, and preservation of Art Deco and related design styles. Events include lectures, field trips, and an annual "Membership Mixer." Membership: $15 student/senior; $30 individual; $50 dual. ADSB quarterly newsletter *Motif* is available by subscription for $12 outside New England.

Art Deco Society of South Carolina, Charleston Chapter, 856-A Liriope Lane, Mount Pleasant, SC 29464, (803) 849-9289, Edward A. Browder, chairman. Founded in 1992. A statewide society that fosters preservation through education and embraces a holistic appreciation for the era and its unique treasures. Membership: $15, includes newsletter and notices of activities.

Chicago Art Deco Society, 400 Skokie #270, Northbrook, IL 60062, (708) 480-1211, Chuck Kaplan, president. CADS promotes an understanding and appreciation of the Art Deco era through newsletters and lectures. Topics related to architecture, decorative arts, and design are presented. Membership: $15 individual. *CADS Newsletter* is available by subscription for $12 annually outside Illinois.

Art Deco Society of Northern Ohio, 3439 West Brainard Road #260, Woodmere, OH 44122, Alex Kertesz, director. Founded in 1992, ADSNO promotes Art Deco in the Cleveland area, educates the public, and holds special events. Write for membership information.

Art Deco Society of Cleveland, 3300 Green Road, Beachwood, OH 44122, (216) 621-5255, Sally Weinberg, president. Membership: $25 individual. Call for schedule of activities.

Friends of Fair Park, P.O. Box 150248, Dallas, TX 75315, (214) 426-3400, fax: (214) 426-0737, Craig Holcomb, executive director. Fair Park is the largest collection of Art Deco exposition buildings in the world. Friends of Fair Park is committed to preserving these buildings and the public art of this National Historic Landmark. Membership: $40.

Detroit Area Art Deco Society, P.O. Box 1393, Royal Oak, MI 48068-1393, (313) 866-3443, Jacques Caussin and Kim Zuccharini, co-presidents. Focuses on education to increase public awareness of the style and period; documentation, including surveys, photography, and research; design to assist with information on restoration and style preservation; and entertainment, to communicate the sense of fun that characterizes the period through parties and events. Membership: $10 student; $15 individual; $25 dual. DAADS newsletter *The Modern* is available by subscription for $10 annually outside Michigan.

Art Deco Society of Los Angeles, P.O. Box 972, Hollywood, CA 90078, (310) 659-DECO, Mitzi Mogul, president. ADSLA is dedicated to the appreciation of Art Deco and Streamline Moderne and is involved in the preservation of the cultural heritage that is prominent throughout Southern California. Membership: $25 individual; $45 dual. ADSLA newsletter *The Exposition* is available by subscription for $15 annually outside California.

Miami Design Preservation League, P.O. Bin L, Miami Beach, FL 33119, (305) 672-2014, fax: (305) 672-4319, George T. Neary, director. MDPL is a nonprofit organization devoted to preserving, protecting, and promoting the cultural, social, economic, environmental, and architectural integrity of the Miami Beach Architectural District. It was organized in 1976 and is the oldest Art Deco society in the world. MDPL hosts an annual "Art Deco Weekend" each January which includes a street festival/Art Deco show and sale. Membership: $25 individual; $50 family. Members receive the MDPL newsletter *Impressions*.

Art Deco Society of New York, 385 Fifth Avenue, Suite 501, New York, NY 10016, (212) 679-DECO, William T. Weber, president. ADSNY, founded in 1980, is a nonprofit organization which encourages public awareness of all aspects of Art Deco. Membership: $20 student; $35 individual; $50 dual. ADSNY newsletter *The Modernist* comes out four times a year, is included in all memberships, and is available by subscription for $25 annually outside New York.

Art Deco Society of the Palm Beaches, 820 Lavers Circle, G-203, Delray Beach, FL 33444, (407) 276-9925, Sharon Koskoff, president and founder. The ADSPB is dedicated to preservation, education, and awareness of Art Deco architecture and 20th-century design in Palm Beach County. Expert art and design services available. Membership: $20 individual; $30 family. Members receive the ADSPB newsletter *Streamline*.

Sacramento Art Deco Society, P.O. Box 162836, Sacramento, CA 95816-2836, (916) 736-1929, Richard Unger, president. SADS is a nonprofit organization dedicated to the preservation of all aspects of the Art Deco period encompassing the years 1925–1945. Membership: $15 individual; $25 dual. The SADS newsletter *Moderne Times* is available outside California for $12 annually.

Art Deco Society of California, 100 Bush Street, Suite #511, San Francisco, CA 94104, (415) 982-DECO, Jim Sweeney, president. ADSC, a nonprofit organization founded in 1982, is dedicated to the preservation of all aspects of Art Deco in American culture between the two World Wars (1919–1942). ADSC hosts an annual "Art Deco Weekend by the Bay" in June, which includes an "Art Deco–50's Show and Sale." Membership: $25 student/senior; $35 individual; $50 dual. Members receive the ADSC newsletter *The Sophisticate*.

Art Deco Society of Washington, P.O. Box 11090, Washington, DC 20036, (202) 298-1100, Lauren Adkins, president. Since its founding in the fall of 1982, the ADSW has led the effort to save from the wrecker's ball many important Washington-area examples of Deco architecture. ADSW sponsors regular programs on a variety of Deco topics and special events, and hosts an "Annual Exposition of the Decorative Arts" show and sale each June, and an annual Art Deco ball. Membership: $25 individual; $30 family. ADSW newsletter *Translux* is available by subscription outside D.C., Virginia, and Maryland for $10 annually.

OUTSIDE THE UNITED STATES

Art Deco Society of New South Wales Inc., P.O. Box 752, Willoughby, NSW 2068, Australia, (02) 419-4259, Mary Nilsson, president. (New South Wales's capital city is Sydney.) The society aims to provide a millieu for interested people, and to build public awareness and appreciation for all aspects of the Art Deco period, thus helping to ensure the preservation of the city's Art Deco architectural heritage. ADSNSW hosts an annual "Art Deco Weekend" in October. Membership: $25–$75 (depending on category). Publications: discovery walk booklets, $2–$5 (depending on size).

Art Deco Society of Western Australia, 182 Broome Street, Cottesloe 6011, Western Australia, (09) 383-1627, Vyonne Geneve, president. (Western Australia's capital city is Perth.) ADSWA hosts the "Second World Congress on Art Deco" in October 1993, the time of its annual "Art Deco Weekend." ADSWA has been a leading voice for the preservation of Art Deco in Australia, and hosts numerous programs and activities. Call or write for membership information.

Society Art Deco Victoria, P.O. Box 1324, Collingwood, Victoria 3066, Australia, (03) 419-8741, fax: (03) 419-9293, Susie Lloyd, president; Rod Charles, vice president. (Victoria's capital city is Melbourne.) SADV was founded in 1992, with the goals of tracing the history of Art Deco in Victoria; preserving its architectural heritage; promoting dialogue to protect public and private buildings; and presenting social gatherings, lectures, walks and film screenings. Write for membership information.

Canadian Art Deco Society, c/o #101–1080 Barclay Street, Vancouver, B.C., Canada, V6E 1G7, (604) 662-7623, fax: (604) 662-7633, Donald Luxton, president. The Canadian Art Deco Society was formed in 1983 to promote awareness of the Art Deco styles and time period. Activities include building preservation lobbying; members receive a quarterly newsletter. Membership: $20.

The Twentieth Century Society (formerly The Thirties Society), 58 Crescent Lane, London SW4 9PU, England, 44-071-738-8480, Alan Powers, honorable secretary. The national amenity society for Great Britain concerned with buildings after 1914. Advises national and local government on conservation issues and campaigns for listing of buildings. Events, visits, lectures, and publications for members. Back issues of journal available. Write for additional information. Membership: £15.

Art Deco Trust, P.O. Box 133, Napier, New Zealand, Phone: 64-6-835-0022, fax: 64-6-835-3984, Robert McGregor, executive director. Founded in 1985, the Trust works for the preservation, enhancement, and promotion of the 1930s architecture of Napier. Destroyed by earthquake and fire in 1931, the entire city was rebuilt in an Art Deco style, resulting in one of the largest collections of Art Deco architecture in the world. The Trust also organizes programs for tourists, and hosts an annual "Art Deco Weekend" in February. (See also the listing under "Museums" for the Hawke's Bay Museum in Napier.) Write for information about programs and publications. Membership: $10 individual; $15 dual.

MUSEUMS

Art Institute of Chicago, Michigan Avenue at Adams Street, Chicago, IL 60603, (312) 443-3600. The new Rice Building houses the European Decorative Arts and Sculpture Department, among others. The collection of some sixteen thousand objects includes decorative arts in all media—furniture, ceramics, metalwork, glass, enamels, ivory—and sculpture from 1100 to the present. Hours: Mon., Wed., Thurs., Fri., 10:30–4:30; Sat., 10:00–5:00; Tues., 10:30–8:00; Sun. and holidays, 12 noon–5:00. Admission: Tues., free; all other times, suggested fee of $6.

The Brooklyn Museum, 200 Eastern Parkway, Brooklyn, NY 11238, (718) 638-5000, fax: (718) 638-3731. The Department of Decorative Arts, one of the museum's six collections, includes exhibitions of furniture, ceramics, glass, silver, and metalwork from the 17th century to the present, with a focus on American material. In addition, a series of twenty-eight American period rooms are installed in the fourth floor galleries. Among those represented are Gorham and Tiffany, Frank Lloyd Wright, Marcel Breuer, Emile-Jacques Ruhlmann, Maurice Marinot, Edgar Brandt, Pierre Legrain, and Jean Dunand, as well as a large collection of American Machine Age objects. Also on view is the first 20th-century period room displayed in an American museum, the Worgelt Library, a New York Art Deco room from 1928–1930. Hours: Wed.–Sun., 10:00–5:00; closed Thanksgiving, Christmas, and New Year's Day. Admission: suggested contribution, $4; students with valid I.D., $2; older adults, $1.50; free to museum members and children under twelve accompanied by an adult. Group tours or visits can be arranged through the Education Division, ext. 221.

Cooper-Hewitt Museum, 2 East 91st Street, New York, NY 10128, (212) 860-6868, fax: (212) 860-6909. The Smithsonian Institution's National Museum of Design has a collection that includes more than three hundred thousand objects spanning three thousand years of design history from cultures around the world. Hours: Tues., 10:00–9:00; Wed.–Sat., 10:00–5:00; Sun., 12 noon–5:00; closed Mondays and major holidays. Admission: general admission, $3; senior citizens and students over twelve, $1.50; free admission Tuesday nights, 5:00–9:00; Cooper-Hewitt and Smithsonian members free.

The Corning Museum of Glass, 1 Museum Way, Corning, NY 14830-2253, (607) 937-5371. The most comprehensive museum in the world illustrating the art and history of glass; more than twenty-four thousand objects present a visual and social history of glass over the past thirty-five hundred years. The collection includes Marinot,

Lalique, Steuben, and numerous other notable Art Deco designers. Hours: open daily 9:00–5:00; closed Thanksgiving, December 24 and 25, and New Year's Day. Admission: adults, $6; senior citizens and students with I.D., $5; children ages six to seventeen, $4; families (two adults and children), $14; children under six, free.

Cowan Pottery Museum (of Rocky River Public Library), 1600 Hampton Road, Rocky River, OH 44107, (216) 333-7610, fax: (216) 333-4184. A library-owned collection of art pottery made by R. Guy Cowan and Associates between 1912 and 1932 in Lake Wood and Rocky River, Ohio, numbering over six hundred items of artist-designed limited editions and production pieces in rotating displays. Cowan artists include Waylande Gregory, Viktor Schreckengost, A. Drexel Jacobson, Thelma Frazier, Margaret Postgate, and others. Hours: Mon.–Thurs., 9:00–9:00; Fri.–Sat., 9:00–6:00; Sun. during the school year, 1:00–5:00. Admission: free. Illustrated booklet on Cowan Pottery: $3.

Cranbrook Academy of Art Museum, 500 Lone Pine Road, P.O. Box 801, Broomfield Hills, MI 48303-0801, (313) 645-3312, Gregory Wittkopp, curator of collections. The Cranbrook Collection, newly installed in the museum's main gallery, highlights the achievements of Cranbrook's faculty and students since the school's inception in the 1920s. The academy attracted artists such as Carl Milles, Harry Bertoia, Eero Saarinen, Maija Grotell, Marianne Strengell, and Marshall Fredericks. The selections from the collection on display feature sculpture, paintings, furniture, ceramics, textiles, and metalwork by these and other artists. Hours: Wed.–Sun., 1:00–5:00. Admission: adults, $3; students and senior citizens, $2; children under seven, handicapped, and museum members, free.

Everson Museum of Art, 401 Harrison Street, Syracuse, New York, 13202, (315) 475-6064, fax: (315) 474-6943, Linda M. Herbert, public information officer. Included in the holdings is the most significant collection of 20th-century ceramics, including works from the 1930s by Cowan Pottery, Waylande Gregory, Carl Waters, Viktor Schreckengost, Russell Aitken, Walter Sinz, Carlton Atherton, Russel Wright, Adelaide Alsop Robineau, Edris Eckhardt, Maija Grotell, Thelma Frazier Winter, Glen Lukins, Gertrude and Otto Natzler, among many others. Hours: Tues.–Fri., 12 noon–5:00; Sat., 10:00–5:00; Sun., 12 noon–5:00. Admission: free.

Hawke's Bay Museum, 9 Herschell Street (P.O. Box 248), Napier, New Zealand, 64-6-835-7781, fax: 64-6-835-3984, Robert McGregor, deputy director. The Hawke's Bay Museum emphasizes Art Deco in its collecting policy to reflect the 1930s character of the city of Napier. Displays interpret the city's architecture and the earthquake which destroyed the city in 1931. Hours: daily, 10:00–5:00. Admission: $2.

The Jersey City Museum, 472 Jersey Avenue, Jersey City, NJ 07302, (201) 547-4514, fax: (201) 547-4584. Permanent collection with continuous exhibitions of contemporary art and regional history; extensive education programs for children and adults. Hours: Tues.–Sat., 10:30–5:00; Wed., 10:30–8:00; closed Sun.–Mon. Admission: free; membership dues, $5–$100; publications $1–$20 per publication.

The Jones Museum of Glass and Ceramics, Sebago, Maine. Mailing address: Douglas Hill, ME 04024, (207) 787-3370. Collects, preserves, and interprets the full range of the art of glass, ceramics, and porcelain. The permanent collection contains six thousand pieces from all time periods and geographic areas, over fifty firms represented from the Art Deco period. Included are designers and artists from America, Great Britain, Germany,

Austria, Bohemia, France, and Belgium, as well as Japanese, Russian, and Scandinavian examples. Active workshop and seminar program. Excellent resource library. Open May to November 14. Hours: Mon.–Sat., 10:00–5:00; Sun., 1:00–5:00. Admission: adults, $3.50; students, $2; children under twelve, 75 cents; museum members, free.

Lake County Museum, Curt Teich Postcard Archives, Lakewood Forest Preserve, 27277 Forest Preserve Road, Wauconda, IL 60084, (708) 526-0024. The Curt Teich Postcard Archives collection dates from 1898 through 1975 and includes 360,000 computer cross-referenced view and advertising postcard listings. In addition to printed postcards, the collection also includes photographs and drawings. Rich collection of images of Deco-styled structures, objects, and graphic art. Hours: Mon.–Fri., 9:00–4:30; exhibition hours daily (including weekends) 11:00–4:30. Admission: adults, $1; membership dues, $20; publication: *Image File*, $20 individual, $30 institution.

Museum of the City of New York, Fifth Avenue at 103rd Street, New York, NY 10029, (212) 534-1672, fax: (212) 534-5974. Dedicated to documenting the history of New York City. Included in the six curatorial departments is the Costume Collection, a great treasure of clothing and accessories designed or worn by New Yorkers, containing over twenty-five thousand pieces from the mid-18th century to the present. Among the designers represented from the 1900s to the 1930s are Coco Chanel, Caillot Soeurs, Madeleine Vionnet, and a broad range of New York City dressmakers. Also included is the famous Stettheimer Dollhouse, made in the 1920s and furnished entirely in Art Deco with actual sculptures and paintings by famous artists. Hours: Wed.–Sat., 10:00–5:00; Sun., 1:00–5:00. Admission: adults, $5; children, seniors, and students, $3; families, $8.

Norwest Corporation, Norwest Center, Sixth and Marquette, Minneapolis, MN 55479-1025, (612) 667-5136, fax: (612) 667-0674, David Ryan, director, Arts Program. Norwest Corporation has a core collection comprising 350 works devoted to Modernism, including many fine examples of Art Deco. Rotating exhibitions are open to the public year-round. Hours: Mon.–Fri., 8:00–5:00. Admission: free; brochures on various aspects of the collection are available.

Phoenix Art Museum, 1625 North Central, Phoenix, AZ 85004, (602) 257-1222. The Southwest's largest art museum houses outstanding collections of art from the American West to the Far East. Galleries also showcase contemporary and European art, clothing design, the famous Thorne Miniature Rooms, plus special traveling exhibitions. Hours: Tues.–Sat., 10:00–5:00; Wed., 10:00–9:00; and Sunday, 12 noon–5:00; closed Mon. Admission: adults, $4; seniors, $3; students and children six and over, $1.50; children under six, free.

Santa Barbara Museum of Art, 1130 State Street, Santa Barbara, CA 93101, (805) 963-4364, fax: (805) 966-6840, Robert Henning Jr., head curator. Outstanding regional museum with fine examples of American, Asian, and 19th-century French art, classical antiquities, prints and drawings, photography and 20th-century art. Hours: Tues.–Sat., 11:00–5:00; Thurs., 11:00–9:00; and Sun., 12:00–5:00. Admission: adults, $3; seniors, $2.50; children six to sixteen, $1.50; and children under six, free.

Virginia Museum of Fine Arts, 2800 Grove Avenue, Richmond, VA 23221-2466, (804) 367-0844, fax: (804) 367-9393. The west wing houses the Sydney and Frances Lewis Collection, consisting of 19th- and 20th-century decorative arts and contemporary paintings and sculpture. Artists and designers in this significant collection include Emile Gallé, Louis Tiffany, Frank Lloyd Wright, Emile-Jacques Ruhlmann, and many more. Hours: Tues.–Sat., 11:00–5:00; Sun., 1:00–5:00; and Thurs. evening to 8:00. Voluntary admission: adults, $4; children five and older and students, $2.

Walter Gropius House, a property of the Society for the Preservation of New England Antiques (SPNEA), 68 Baker Bridge Road, Lincoln, MA 01773, (617) 259-8843 (Gropius House) or (617) 227-3956 (SPNEA). A nonprofit organization dedicated to preserving New England's heritage, SPNEA owns and operates twenty-three house museums and eleven study properties in five New England states. The Walter Gropius House, family home of the architect Walter Gropius and the first building designed after his arrival in the United States in 1937, is a good representation of Bauhaus philosophy in a New England setting. It contains original Bauhaus furnishings, many designed by Marcel Breuer. Hours: June 1–October 15, Fri.–Sun., 12 noon–5:00; November 1–May 30, Sat. and Sun. on the first full weekend of the month. Admission: general admission, $5.

Whitney Museum of American Art, 945 Madison Avenue at 75th Street, New York, NY 10021, (212) 570-3676, fax: (212) 570-3600. Exhibitions of paintings, sculpture, prints, drawings, photography, film, and video by America's leading 20th-century artists. Hours: Wed., 11:00–6:00; Thurs., 1:00–8:00; Fri.–Sun., 11:00–6:00. Admission: general admission, $6; senior citizens and students, $4. Admission and hours subject to change.

BIBLIOGRAPHY

EXHIBITION CATALOGUES OR ACCOMPANYING BOOKS

1925. *Encyclopedie des Arts Industriels et Modernes au XXème Siecle.* Imprimeries Nationale. Twelve volumes covering the groundbreaking 1925 Paris Exposition in detail. Reprinted in French. New York: Garland Publishers, 1977.

1929. *The Architect and the Industrial Arts.* New York: Metropolitan Museum of Art.

1934. *Machine Art.* New York: Museum of Modern Art.

1966. *Les Années 1925.* Catalogue by Yvonne Brunhammer. Two volumes. Paris: Musée des Arts Decoratifs. The first major retrospective exhibition in France focusing on the 1925 Exposition, which spurred the revival of interest in Art Deco.

1970. *Art Deco.* Catalogue by Judith Applegate. New York: Finch College Museum of Art. The first retrospective in the United States.

1971. *The World of Art Deco.* Catalogue by Bevis Hillier. Minneapolis Institute of Arts. New York: E. P. Dutton. The first major retrospective exhibition in the United States, which incorporated the Finch College exhibition.

1979. *Thirties.* Catalogue by the Arts Council of Great Britain. London: Hayward Gallery, Victoria and Albert Museum. The first major retrospective exhibition in England focusing on all aspects of the 1930s.

1981. *Schneider France: Glas des Art Deco.* Catalogue by Helmut Riche. Exhibition at the Kunstmuseum, Dusseldorf. Dusseldorf: Kunst & Antiquitäten.

1981. *Lalique Glass: The Complete Illustrated Catalogue for 1932.* Introduction by John H. Martin. New York: Corning Museum of Glass in association with Dover Publications.

1983. *At Home in Manhattan: Modern Decorative Arts, 1925 to the Depression.* Catalogue by Karen Davies. New Haven, CT: Yale University Art Gallery.

1983. *Design in America: The Cranbrook Vision 1925–1950.* New York: Harry N. Abrams, in association with the Detroit Institute of Arts and the Metropolitan Museum of Art. An exhibition that focused on the important design influence of the Cranbrook Academy.

394

1984. *The 20th-Century Poster—Design of the Avant Garde.* Catalogue by Dawn Ades. New York: Walker Art Center, in association with Abbeville Press.

1985. *High Styles: Twentieth Century Design.* New York: Whitney Museum of American Art in association with Summit Books.

1986. *Vienna 1900.* Catalogue by Kirk Varnedoe. New York: Museum of Modern Art. A groundbreaking exhibition that focused new emphasis on the Vienna Secession as an early Modern design movement.

1986. *The Machine Age in America.* Book by Richard Guy Wilson, Diane H. Pilgrim, and Dickran Tashjian. New York: Brooklyn Museum in association with Harry N. Abrams. A major exhibition focusing on American industrial design.

1987. *The Art That Is Life: The Arts and Crafts Movement in America, 1875–1920.* Book by Wendy Kaplan. Boston: Little, Brown and Company, for the Museum of Fine Arts. A major retrospective on the Arts and Crafts movement documenting its impact on Modern design.

1987. *American Art Deco.* Book by Alastair Duncan. New York: Renwick Gallery, Smithsonian Institute, Washington, D.C., in association with Harry N. Abrams. The first major exhibition to focus entirely on American Art Deco design.

1988. *The Modern Poster.* Book by Stuart Wrede. Boston: Museum of Modern Art, New York, in association with Little, Brown and Company.

1989. *Art Deco en Europe.* Catalogue edited by the Société des Expositions. Brussels, Belgium: Palais des Beaux-Arts. An important retrospective on European Art Deco.

1989. *Lalique: A Century of Glass for a Modern World.* Catalogue edited by Nicholas Dawes, curator. New York: Fashion Institute of Technology. The first comprehensive survey/exhibition since 1933.

1990. *High & Low: Modern Art/Popular Culture.* Book by Kurt Varnedoe and Adam Gropnik. New York: Museum of Modern Art. Not specifically Art Deco, but an important exhibition for its focus on "low" culture: comics, advertising, graffiti, and more.

1991. *The 1920s: Age of the Metropolis.* Edited by Jean Clair. Montreal: Montreal Museum of Fine Arts. An important retrospective on the 1920s in fine and decorative arts.

1991. *Design 1935–1965: What Modern Was.* IBM Gallery, New York City, from the collection of the Montreal Museum of Decorative Arts. Book edited by Martin Eidelberg. New York: Harry N. Abrams. An important exhibition and sourcebook on modern design from the end of the Art Deco period through the mid-1960s.

1992. *The Elegant Auto: Fashion and Design in the 1930s.* Portland, ME: Portland Museum of Art. With essays by Gerald Silk, Bates Lowry and Jane Lane; Duncan Smith, exhibition developer.

HISTORIC PERIODICALS

Many of the original designs and theories of the great designers of the Art Deco era are to be found in the pages of annuals, periodicals, trade journals, and magazines published during their lifetimes. It is to these documents that auction houses and dealers as well as scholars turn for more information and for original documentation. Below are some of the more frequently mentioned magazines of the era.

The Studio, English, 1893–1950s. The Studio, Ltd., also published a number of other books and periodicals on design.

Pan, German, founded in 1885 in Berlin.

Innen-Dekoration (*Interior Decoration*), from the publishers of *Deutsche Kunst und Dekoration* (*German Art and Decoration*), German, 1890–1979.

Art et Décoration, French, Editions C. Massin, 1897–1938.

L'Art Décoratif, French, started in 1897.

Deutsche Kunst und Dekoration (*German Art and Decoration*) and *Dekorative Kunst* (*Decorative Art*), German, both founded in 1897.

Ver Sacrum (*Sacred Spring*), Austrian, started in 1898, the publication of the Vienna Secession, with numerous original designs and tipped-in plates.

Das Plakat (*The Poster*), German, 1909–1921.

Wendingen, Dutch, 1918–1931. Published by H. Th. Wydeveld, the publication for the modern architecture and the De Stijl movement in Holland.

Mobilier et Décoration (*Furniture and Decoration*), French, Editions Ed. Honore, 1920–1974.

Art and Industry, London and New York: The Studio, Ltd., 1920s–1940s.

Gebrausgraphik (*Advertising Art*), German, 1925–1944.

Vendre (*To Sell*), French, 1925–1930.

Modern Publicity: Commercial Art Annual, published by The Studio, Ltd., London, 1924–present. (Originally from 1924 as *Posters and Their Designers*; from 1925 as *Art and Publicity*; and from 1926 to 1930 as *Posters and Publicity*.)

Arts et Métiers Graphiques (*Graphic Arts and Crafts*), French, quarterly, 1927–1939. For printers and graphic designers, with numerous tipped-in plates.

Fortune Magazine, 1930–present.

Good Furniture and Decoration, American, 1920s–1930s.

Advertising and Selling, American, twenty-six issues annually, including six bimonthly *Advertising Arts* supplements, late 1920s–1930s. The *Advertising Arts* supplement, spiral-bound from the mid-1930s, carried articles on all aspects of photography, advertising design, package design, industrial design, typography, printing, and the like.

Other American publications of the 1920s–1930s which often featured new designs, either in articles or in advertising, were *The American Architect, American Home, Design, Harper's Bazaar, House and Garden, House Beautiful, Vanity Fair, Vogue, Women's Wear Daily*, and many others.

HISTORIC THEORETICAL/DESIGN REFERENCES

Bel Geddes, Norman. *Horizons: A Glimpse Into the Not Far Distant Future.* Boston: Little, Brown and Company, 1932.

Cheney, Sheldon, and Cheney, Martha. *Art and the Machine.* New York: McGraw-Hill, 1936.

Frankl, Paul. *Form and Re-Form.* New York: Harper and Brothers, 1930.

_____. *New Dimensions: The Decorative Arts of Today in Words and Pictures.* New York: Payson & Clarke, 1928.

Le Corbusier. *L'Art Décoratif d'Audjourd'hui.* Paris: Les Editions G. Cres et Companie, 1926.

BOOKS
Overviews on Art Deco

Arwas, Victor. *Art Deco.* London: Academy Editions, 1975. Revised edition, New York: Harry N. Abrams, 1992.

Battersby, Martin. *The Decorative Thirties.* New York: Walker & Company, 1969.

_____. *The Decorative Twenties.* New York: Walker & Company, 1969.

Bouillon, Jean-Paul. *Art Deco: 1903–1940.* New York: Rizzoli International, 1989.

Brandt, Frederick. *Late 19th and Early 20th Century Decorative Arts.* Sydney and Frances Lewis Collection. Richmond, VA: Virginia Museum of Fine Arts and University of Washington Press, 1985.

Brunhammer, Yvonne. *The Art Deco Style.* New York: St. Martin's Press, 1983.

_____. *The Nineteen Twenties Style.* Milan: Fratelli Fabbri Editor, 1966. London: Hamlyn Publishing Group, Ltd., 1969.

Brunhammer, Yvonne, and Tise, Suzanne. *The Decorative Arts of France: La Société des Artistes Décorateurs 1900–1942.* New York: Rizzoli International, 1990.

Bush, Donald J. *The Streamlined Decade.* New York: George Braziller, 1975.

Curtis, Tony, with Elisabeth Taylor. *20th Century Antiques.* New Jersey: Chartwell Books, 1989.

Duncan, Alastair. *American Art Deco.* New York: Smithsonian Institute, in association with Harry N. Abrams, 1987.

_____, ed. *The Encyclopedia of Art Deco.* New York: E. P. Dutton, 1988.

Eidelberg, Martin, ed. *Design 1935–1965: What Modern Was.* New York: Harry N. Abrams, 1991.

Fusco, Tony. *The Official Identification and Price Guide to Art Deco*, 1st edition. New York: House of Collectibles, 1988.

Gaston, Mary Frank. *Collector's Guide to Art Deco.* Kentucky: Collectors Books, 1989.

Gilman, John, and Heide, Robert. *Popular Art Deco: Depression Era Style and Design.* New York: Abbeville Press, 1991.

Greif, Martin. *Depression Modern, The Thirties Style in America.* New York: Universe Books, 1975.

Haslam, Malcolm. *Collector's Style Guide: Art Deco.* New York: Ballantine, 1987.

Hillier, Bevis. *Art Deco.* London: Herbert Press, 1968, and New York: Schocken Books, 1985.

_____. *The Decorative Arts of the Forties and Fifties Austerity Binge.* New York: Clarkson N. Potter, 1975.

Klein, Dan; McClelland, Nancy A.; and Haslam, Malcolm. *In the Deco Style.* New York: Rizzoli International, 1986.

Lesieutre, Alain. *The Spirit and Splendour of Art Deco.* London: Paddington Press, 1974.

McClinton, Katherine Morrison. *Art Deco, A Guide for Collectors.* New York: Clarkson N. Potter, 1986.

McConnell, Kevin. *Collecting Art Deco.* West Chester, PA: Schiffer Publishing, 1990.

McFadden, David R. *Scandinavian Modern Design 1880–1980.* New York: Cooper-Hewitt Museum, in association with Harry N. Abrams, 1982.

Menten, Theodore. *The Art Deco Style.* New York: Dover Publications, 1982.

Miller, Craig R. *Modern Design in the Metropolitan Museum of Art, 1890 to 1990.* New York: Harry N. Abrams, 1990.

Morgan, Sarah. *Art Deco, The European Style.* New York: Gallery Books, 1990.

Ostergard, Derek E. *Art Deco Masterpieces.* New York: Hugh Lauter Levin, 1991.

Pevsner, Nicolaus. *Pioneers of Modern Design.* New York: Penguin Books, 1986.

Scarlett, Frank, and Townley, Marjorie. *Arts Décoratifs 1925, A Personal Recollection of the Paris Exhibition.* London: Academy Editions, 1975, and New York: St. Martin's Press, 1975.

Weber, Eva. *Art Deco in America.* New York: Bookthrift, 1985.

Overviews of Related Design Movements

Borsi, Franco, and Godoli, Ezio. *Vienna 1900: Architecture and Design.* New York: Rizzoli International, 1986.

Neuwirth, Waltraud. *Wiener Werkstätte: Avant Garde, Art Deco, Industrial Design.* Vienna: Author, 1984.

Rowland, Anna. *Bauhaus Source Book: Bauhaus Style and Its Worldwide Influences.* New York: Van Nostrand Reinhold, 1990.

Schweiger, Werner J. *Wiener Werkstätte.* New York: Abbeville Press, 1984.

Tolstoy, Vladimir. *Russian Decorative Arts 1917–1937.* New York: Rizzoli International, 1990.

Waissenberg, Robert. *Vienna 1890–1920*. New York: Rizzoli International, 1984.

_____. *Vienna Secession*. New York: Rizzoli International, 1977.

Architecture and Preservation

Baeder, John. *Diners*. New York: Harry N. Abrams, 1978.

Bayer, Patricia. *Art Deco Architecture: Design, Decoration and Detail From the Twenties and Thirties*. New York: Harry N. Abrams, 1992.

Blake, Peter. *The Master Builders: Le Corbusier, Mies van der Rohe, Frank Lloyd Wright*. New York: W. W. Norton, 1976.

Breeze, Carla. *L.A. Deco*. New York: Rizzoli International, 1991.

Capitman, Barbara Baer. *Deco Delights: Preserving the Beauty and Joy of Miami Beach Architecture*. New York: E. P. Dutton, 1988.

Cerwinske, Laura, with photos by David Kaminski. *Tropical Deco*. New York: Rizzoli International, 1981.

Cohen, Judith Singer. *Cowtown Modern: Art Deco Architecture of Forth Worth, Texas*. College Station, TX: Texas A&M University Press, 1988.

De Witt, Dennis and Elizabeth R. *Modern Architecture in Europe, A Guide to Buildings Since the Industrial Revolution*. New York: E. P. Dutton, 1987.

Gebhard, David, and Winter, Robert. *Architecture in Los Angeles: A Complete Guide*. Salt Lake City: Peregrine Smith, 1985.

Gutman, Richard J. S., and Kaufman, Elliott, with Slovic, David. *American Diner*. New York: Harper & Row, 1979.

Hatton, Hap. *Tropical Splendor: An Architectural History of Florida*. New York: Alfred A. Knopf, 1987.

Huxtable, Ada Louise. *The Tall Building Artistically Considered: The Search for a Skyscraper Style*. New York: Pantheon, 1985.

Johnson, Carol Newton. *Tulsa Art Deco: An Architectural Era, 1925–1941*. Tulsa, OK: Junior League of Tulsa Publications, 1980.

Kinerk, Michael, and Wilhelm, Dennis. *Rediscovering Art Deco U.S.A.* New York: E. P. Dutton, 1993.

Liebs, Chester H. *Main Street to Miracle Mile: American Roadside Architecture*. New York: Little, Brown and Company, 1985.

Robinson, Cervin, and Bletter, Rosemarie Haag. *Skyscraper Style*. New York: Oxford University Press, 1975.

Stone, Susannah Harris. *The Oakland Paramount*. Berkeley, CA: Lancaster-Miller Publishers, 1981.

Striner, Richard, and Smith, Katherine Hamilton. *Mostly Moderne: A Book of Authentic Postcards From the Curt Teich Postcard Archives at the Lake County Museum.* Washington, DC: Preservation Press, 1989.

Striner, Richard, and Wirz, Hans. *Washington Art Deco: Art Deco in the Nation's Capitol.* Washington, DC: Smithsonian Institution Press, 1984.

Vlack, Don. *Art Deco Architecture in New York 1920–1940.* New York: Harper & Row, 1974.

Whiffen, Marcus, and Breeze, Carla. *Pueblo Deco: The Art Deco Architecture of the Southwest.* Albuquerque: University of New Mexico Press, 1984.

Furnishings and Interiors

Adam, Peter. *Eileen Gray: Architect/Designer: A Biography.* New York: Harry N. Abrams, 1987.

Bayer, Patricia. *Art Deco Interiors.* Boston: Bulfinch Press, Little, Brown and Company, 1990.

Camard, Florence. *Ruhlmann: Master of Art Deco.* New York: Harry N. Abrams, 1984.

Dufrène, Maurice. *Authentic Interiors From the 1925 Paris Exposition.* Paris: Charles Moreau, 1926. Republished with an introduction by Alastair Duncan, Woodbridge, Suffolk, England: Antique Collectors' Club, 1989.

Duncan, Alastair. *Art Deco Furniture.* New York: Holt, Rinehart and Winston, 1984.

_____. *Art Nouveau and Art Deco Lighting.* New York: Simon and Schuster, 1978.

Fry, Charles Rahn. *Art Deco Interiors in Color.* New York: Dover, 1977.

Garner, Phillipe. *Twentieth Century Furniture.* New York: Van Nostrand Reinhold Company, 1979.

Gresleri, Giuliano. *Josef Hoffmann.* New York: Rizzoli International, 1985.

Hanks, David. *The Decorative Designs of Frank Lloyd Wright.* New York: E. P. Dutton, 1979.

_____. *Innovative Furniture in America, 1800 to the Present.* New York: Horizon Press, 1981.

Hanks, David A., with Toher, Jennifer. *Donald Deskey: Decorative Designs and Interiors.* New York: E. P. Dutton, 1987.

Hennessey, William J. *Russel Wright: American Designer.* Cambridge: MIT Press, 1985.

Lyall, Sutherland. *Hille: 75 Years of British Furniture.* London: Elron Press, in association with the Victoria and Albert Museum, 1981.

Marcilhac, Felix. *Jean Dunand, His Life and Works.* Foreword by Bernard Dunand. New York: Harry N. Abrams, 1991.

Meadmore, Clement. *The Modern Chair.* New York: Van Nostrand Reinhold, 1979.

Ostergard, Derek E. *Bent Wood and Metal Furniture: 1850–1946.* New York: American Federation of the Arts, 1987.

Page, Marion. *Furniture Designed by Architects.* London: Architectural Press, 1983.

Russell, Frank, ed. *A Century of Chair Design.* New York: Rizzoli International, 1980.

Sculpture and Statues

Arwas, Victor. *Art Deco Sculpture: Chryselephantine Statuettes of the Twenties and Thirties.* London: Academy Editions, 1975, and New York: St. Martin's Press, 1975.

Catley, Brian. *Art Deco and Other Figures.* London: Chancery House Publishing Company, 1978.

Conner, Janis, and Rosenkranz, Joel. *Rediscoveries in American Sculpture Studio Works, 1893–1939.* Austin, TX: University of Texas Press, 1989.

MacKay, James. *Dictionary of Western Sculptors in Bronze.* Suffolk, England: James MacKay, Publisher, 1977.

Glass

Arwas, Victor. *Glass: Art Nouveau to Art Deco.* London: Academy Editions, 1977, and New York: Rizzoli International, 1977. Republished, expanded edition, New York: Harry N. Abrams, 1987.

Bayer, Patricia, and Waller, Mark. *The Art of René Lalique.* London: Quintet Publishing, 1988.

Blount, Bernice and Henry. *French Cameo Glass.* Des Moines: Author, 1986.

Charleston, Robert J. *Masterpieces of Glass: A World History From the Corning Museum of Glass.* New York: Harry N. Abrams, 1990.

Dawes, Nicholas M. *Lalique Glass.* New York: Crown Publishers, 1986.

Gardner, Paul V. *The Glass of Frederick Carder.* (Steuben.) New York: Crown Publishers, 1971.

Klein, Dan. *Glass Between the Wars: The History of Modern Glass.* London: Orbis Publishing, 1984.

Lalique, Marc and Marie-Claude. *Lalique par Lalique.* Lausanne, France: Edipop, 1977.

Madigan, Mary Jean Smith. *Steuben Glass.* New York: Harry N. Abrams, 1982.

McClinton, Katherine Morrison. *Introduction to Lalique Glass.* Des Moines, IA: Wallace-Homestead Book Company, 1978.

_____. *Lalique for Collectors.* New York: Charles Scribners' Sons, 1975.

Olivie, Jean-Luc, and Petrova, Sylva, eds. *Bohemian Glass.* New York: Harry N. Abrams, 1990.

Utt, Mary Lou and Glenn. *Lalique Perfume Bottles.* New York: Crown Publishers, 1990.

Wilson, Jack D. *Phoenix and Consolidated Art Glass 1926–1980*. Marietta, OH: Antique Publications, 1989.

Ceramics

Berkow, Nancy. *Fiesta*. Radner, PA: Wallace-Homestead, 1978.

Cameron, Elizabeth. *Encyclopedia of Pottery and Porcelain: The Nineteenth and Twentieth Centuries*. London: Faber and Faber, 1986.

Chipman, Jack. *Collector's Encyclopedia of California Pottery*. Paducah, KY: Collectors Books, 1991.

Clark, Garth. *A Century of Ceramics in the United States 1878–1978*. New York: E. P. Dutton, 1979.

Darling, Sharon S. *Chicago Ceramics and Glass*. Chicago: Chicago Historical Society, 1979.

Duke, Harvey. *Hall China, A Guide for Collectors*. Brooklyn: Elo Books, 1977.

Evans, Paul. *Art Pottery of the United States: An Encyclopedia of Producers and Their Marks*. Hanover, PA: Everybody's Press, 1974.

Griffin, Leonard, Meisel, Louis, and Meisel, Susan. *A Bizzare Affair: The Life and Work of Clarice Cliff*. New York: Harry N. Abrams, 1988.

Huxford, Sharon and Bob. *The Collectors Encyclopedia of Roseville Pottery*, 1st series. Paducah, KY: Collectors Books, 1976.

_____. *The Collectors Encyclopedia of Roseville Pottery*, 2nd series. Paducah, KY: Collectors Books, 1980.

_____. *The Collectors Encyclopedia of Weller Pottery*. Paducah, KY: Collectors Books, 1989.

Spours, Judy. *Art Deco Tableware*. New York: Rizzoli International, 1988.

Whitmyer, Margaret and Kenn. *The Collector's Guide to Hall China*. Paducah, KY: Collectors Books, 1986.

Woodhouse, Adrian. *Susie Cooper*. Matlock, Derbyshire, England: Trilby Books, 1992.

Silver

Hughes, Graham. *Modern Silver Throughout the World, 1880–1967*. London: Studio Vista, 1967.

Hughes, Graham. *Modern Silver*. New York: Crown Publishers, 1967.

Krekel-Aalberse, Annelies. *Art Nouveau, Art Deco Silver*. London: Thames and Hudson, 1989.

Lasen, Erik. *Georg Jensen Silversmith, 77 Artists 75 Years*. Washington, DC: Smithsonian Institution Press, 1980.

Jewelry

Becker, Ingeborg; von Hase-Schmundt, Ulrike; and Weber, Christianne. Translated by Edward Force. *Theodor Fahrner Jewelry: Between Avant-Garde and Tradition*. West Chester, PA: Schiffer Publishing, 1991.

Cartlidge, Barbara. *Twentieth Century Jewelry*. New York: Harry N. Abrams, 1985.

Ettinger, Roseann. *Popular Jewelry 1840–1940*. West Chester, PA: Schiffer Publishing, 1990.

Raulet, Sylvie. *Art Deco Jewelry*. New York: Rizzoli International, 1985.

_____. *Jewelry of the 1940s and 1950s*. New York: Rizzoli International, 1990.

Fashion

Bowman, Sara, and Molinaire, Michel. *A Fashion for Extravagance: Art Deco Fabrics and Fashions*. New York: E. P. Dutton, 1985.

Defert, Theirry, and Lepape, Claude. *From the Ballets Russes to Vogue: The Art of Georges Lepape*. New York: Vendome Press, 1984.

Etherington-Smith, Meredith. *Patou*. New York: St. Martin's/Marek, 1983.

Robinson, Julian. *The Golden Age of Style*. New York: Gallery Books, 1976.

Art Deco on Paper

Ades, Dawn. *Twentieth Century Poster—Design of the Avant Garde*. New York: Abbeville Press, 1984.

Arwas, Victor. *Belle Epoque Posters and Graphics*. New York: Rizzoli International, 1978.

Bartha, Georges de, and Duncan, Alastair. *Art Nouveau and Art Deco Bookbinding*. New York: Harry N. Abrams, 1989.

Belvès, Pierre. *Cent Ans d'Affiches de Chemin de Fer*. Paris: Editions La Vie du Rail, 1981.

Chwast, Seymour, and Heller, Steven. *Graphic Style: From Victorian to Post Modern*. New York: Harry N. Abrams, 1988.

Copley, Frederick S. *Art Deco Alphabets*. Pittstown, NJ: Main Street Press, 1985.

Delhaye, Jean. *Art Deco Posters and Graphics*. London: Academy Editions, 1977, and London and New York: St. Martin's Press, 1984.

DeNoon, Christopher. *Posters of the WPA*. Los Angeles: Wheatley Press, 1988.

Ercoli, Giuliano. *Art Deco Prints*. New York: Rizzoli International, 1989.

Fusco, Tony. *The Official Identification and Price Guide to Posters*, 1st edition. New York: House of Collectibles, 1990.

Hillier, Bevis. *Posters*. New York: Stein and Day, 1969.

_____. *Travel Posters*. New York: E. P. Dutton, 1976.

Holland, William, et al. *Louis Icart: The Complete Etchings*. West Chester, PA: Schiffer Publishing, 1990.

Kery, Patricia Frantz. *Art Deco Graphics*. New York: Harry N. Abrams, 1986.

_____. *Great Magazine Covers of the World*. New York: Abbeville Press, 1982.

Koschatsky, Walter, and Kossatz, Horst-Herbert. *Ornamental Posters of the Vienna Secession*. London: Academy Editions, 1974, and New York: St. Martin's Press, 1974.

Menten, Theodore. *Advertising Art in the Art Deco Style*. New York: Dover Publications, 1975.

Mouron, Henri. *A. M. Cassandre*. New York: Rizzoli International, 1985.

Packer, William. *The Art of Vogue Covers*. New York: Harmony Books, 1980.

Prokopoff, Stephen, and Franciscono, Marcel, eds. *The Modern Dutch Poster*. Urbana, IL: Krannert Art Museum, 1987, and Cambridge and London: MIT Press, 1987.

Rademacher, Hellmut. Translated by Anthony Rhodes. *Masters of German Poster Art*. New York: Citadel Press, 1966.

Rennert, Jack. *100 Posters of Paul Colin*. New York: Images Graphiques, 1979.

Schnessel, S. Michael. *Icart*. New York: Clarkson N. Potter, 1976.

Spencer, Charles. *Erté*. New York: Clarkson N. Potter, 1970.

Modern Living

OCEAN LINERS

Ardman, Harvey. *Normandie: Her Life and Times*. New York: Franklin Watts, 1985.

Fourcart, Offrey, Robichon, and Villers. *Normandie, Queen of the Seas*. New York: Vendome Press, 1985.

Gregory, Alexis. *The Golden Age of Travel: 1880–1939*. New York: Rizzoli International, 1991.

WORLD'S FAIRS

Applebaum, Stanley. *The New York World's Fair: 1939/1940*. New York: Dover, 1977.

Carpenter, Patricia F., and Totah, Paul. *The San Francisco Fair: Treasure Island, 1939–1940*. San Francisco: Scottwall Association, Publishers, 1989.

Chwast, Seymour; Cohen, Barbara; and Heller, Steven. *Trylon and Perisphere: The 1939 New York World's Fair*. New York: Harry N. Abrams, 1989.

Dickstein, Morris; Harrison, Helen; and Miller, Marc. *Remembering the Future: The New York World's Fair From 1939–1964*. New York: Rizzoli International, 1989.

Lerner, Mel; Rolfes, Herbert; and Zim, Larry. *The World of Tomorrow: The 1939 New York World's Fair*. New York: Harper & Row, 1989.

PHOTO FRAMES

Starr, Steve. *Picture Perfect—Deco Photo Frames 1926–1946.* New York: Rizzoli International, 1991.

HOLLYWOOD DECO

Albrecht, Donald. *Designing Dreams: Modern Architecture in the Movies.* New York: Harper & Row, 1986.

Alleman, Robert. *The Movie Lover's Guide to Hollywood.* New York: Harper & Row, 1985.

Mandelbaum, Howard. *Screen Deco, A Celebration of High Style in Hollywood.* New York: St. Martin's Press, 1985.

INDUSTRIAL DESIGN

Bayley, Stephen. *In Good Shape: Style in Industrial Products, 1900–1960.* New York: Van Nostrand Reinhold, 1979.

Meikle, Jeffrey L. *Twentieth-Century Limited: Industrial Design in America 1925–1939.* Philadelphia: Temple University Press, 1979.

Wilson, Richard Guy; Pilgrim, Diane H.; and Tashjian, Dickran. *The Machine Age in America.* New York: Brooklyn Museum, in association with Harry N. Abrams, 1986.

PLASTIC AND PLASTIC RADIOS

DiNoto, Andrea. *Art Plastic: Designed for Life.* New York: Abbeville Press, 1984.

Sideli, John. *Classic Plastic Radios of the 1930s and 1940s.* New York: E. P. Dutton, 1990.

CHROME

Kilbride, Richard J. *Art Deco Chrome: The Chase Era.* Stamford, CT: Jo-D Books, 1988.

_____. *Art Deco Chrome, Book 2: The Chase Continues.* Stamford, CT: Jo-D Books, 1992.

Koch, Robert, ed. *Chase Chrome: The Chase Catalogue for 1936–37.* Stamford, CT: Gladys Koch Antiques, 1978.

Sferrazza, Julie. *Krome Kraft.* Ohio: Antique Publications, 1988.

DICTIONARIES

Fleming, John, and Honour, Hugo. *Dictionary of the Decorative Arts.* New York: Harper & Row, 1977.

Garner, Philippe, ed. *The Encyclopedia of Decorative Arts 1890–1940.* New York: Van Nostrand and Reinhold, 1978.

Osborne, Harold, ed. *The Oxford Companion to the Decorative Arts.* Oxford University Press, 1985.

Jervis, Simon. *Penguin Dictionary of Design and Designers.* New York: Penguin Books, 1984.

INDEX

The CONFIDENT COLLECTOR™

KNOWS THE FACTS
Each volume packed with valuable information that no collector can afford to be without

**THE OVERSTREET COMIC BOOK
PRICE GUIDE, 22nd Edition**
by Robert M. Overstreet   76912-3/$15.00 US/$17.50 Can

**THE OVERSTREET COMIC BOOK
GRADING GUIDE, 1st Edition**
by Robert M. Overstreet and Gary M. Carter   76910-7/$12.00 US/$15.00 Can

**THE OVERSTREET COMIC BOOK
PRICE GUIDE COMPANION, 6th Edition**
by Robert M. Overstreet   76911-5/$6.00 US/$8.00 Can

•   •   •

FINE ART
Identification and Price Guide, 2nd Edition
by Susan Theran   76924-7/$20.00 US/$24.00 Can

QUILTS
Identification and Price Guide, 1st Edition
by Liz Greenbacker and Kathleen Barach   76930-1/$14.00 US/$17.00 Can

ORIGINAL COMIC ART
Identification and Price Guide, 1st Edition
by Jerry Weist   76965-4/$15.00 US/$18.00 Can

Coming Soon
BASEBALL CARD PRICE GUIDE 1994
by Allan Kaye and Michael McKeever   77235-3/$6.00 US/$7.00 Can